Lecture Notes in Information Systems and Organisation

Volume 1

Series Editors

For further volumes:
http://www.springer.com/series/11237

Richard Baskerville · Marco De Marco
Paolo Spagnoletti
Editors

Designing Organizational Systems

An Interdisciplinary Discourse

Springer

Editors
Richard Baskerville
Department of Computer
Information Systems
Georgia State University
Atlanta, GA
USA

Paolo Spagnoletti
CeRSI, LUISS Guido Carli
Rome
Italy

Marco De Marco
Guglielmo Marconi University
Rome
Italy

ISBN 978-3-642-33370-5 ISBN 978-3-642-33371-2 (eBook)
DOI 10.1007/978-3-642-33371-2
Springer Heidelberg New York Dordrecht London

Library of Congress Control Number: 2012947860

Printed on acid-free paper

Springer is part of Springer Science+Business Media (www.springer.com)

Program Committee

Richard Baskerville	Georgia State University
Marco De Marco	Guglielmo Marconi University
Ole Hanseth	University of Oslo
Giovan Francesco Lanzara	University of Bologna
Kalle Lyytinen	Case Western Reserve University
Marcello Martinez	Second University of Naples
Nancy Pouloudi	University of Athens
Frantz Rowe	University of Nantes
Paolo Spagnoletti	LUISS Guido Carli University
Jan Vom Brocke	University of Liechtenstein
Robert Winter	University of St. Gallen
Jing Zhao China	University of Geosciences Wuhan

Foreword

This book is dedicated to the memory of Sandro D'Atri, friend, colleague, and driving force, who left us too soon, in 2011, at the age of 60. Sandro made a major contribution to Organization Studies. He brought his experience of Information Systems and fused it organically with the other business studies disciplines, further expanding and completing the academic horizon of business organization. But Sandro was more than a scholar. Among other things, he was an enthusiastic advocate and promoter of IS initiatives with an inspiring ability to motivate the young, and a driving force in consolidating the management schools IS community in Italy, raising its visibility and spurring it to participate in the wider international community of IS scholars. Indeed, rarely do I attend an international IS conference today without bumping into one of his students. This book is intended to be a tribute to Sandro from the people who loved and treasured him, both as a person and a professional, in the belief that an academic contribution to the studies that he himself encouraged, nurtured, and enriched is what would have delighted him the most.

Thank you Sandro.

Marco De Marco

Contents

Contributors

Antonia Albani Institute of Information Management, University of St. Gallen, Müller-Friedberg-Strasse 8, 9000 St. Gallen, Switzerland, e-mail: antonia.albani@unisg.ch

Valentina Albano Faculty of Economics, University of Rome III, "Federico Caffè", Rome, Italy, e-mail: valentina.albano@uniroma3.it

Stefano Basaglia Bergamo University, Bergamo, Italy, e-mail: stefano.basaglia@unibg.it

Richard Baskerville Georgia State University, Atlanta, GA, USA, e-mail: baskerville@acm.org

Carlo Batini Department of Informatics, Systems and Communication (DISCo), University of Milano-Bicocca, Viale Sarca 336-U14-20126, Milan, Italy, e-mail: batini@disco.unimib.it

Ilia Bider Department of Computer and Systems Sciences (DSV), Stockholm University, Stockholm, Sweden, e-mail: ilia@dsv.su.se

Alessio Maria Braccini Dipartimento di Economia e Impresa, Università degli Studi della Tuscia, Viterbo, Italy, e-mail: abraccini@unitus.it

Francesca Cabiddu University of Cagliari, Cagliari, Italy

Leonardo Caporarello Bocconi University, Milan, Italy, e-mail: leonardo.caporarello@unibocconi.it

Nunzio Casalino Dipartimento di Strategie di Impresa e Innovazione Tecnologica, Università degli Studi Guglielmo Marconi, Via Plinio 44, 00193 Rome, Italy, e-mail: n.casalino@unimarconi.it

Marco Castelli Department of Informatics, Systems and Communication (DISCo), University of Milano-Bicocca, Viale Sarca 336-U14-20126, Milan, Italy, e-mail: castelli@disco.unimib.it

Manuel Castriotta University of Cagliari, Cagliari, Italy

Luigi De Bernardis CeRSI-LUISS Guido Carli University, Rome, Italy, e-mail: ldebernardis@luiss.it

Maurizio Decastri Faculty of Economics, University of Rome "Tor Vergata", Via Columbia 2, 00133 Rome, Italy

Paolo Depaoli CeRSI-LUISS Guido Carli University, Rome, Italy, e-mail: pdepaoli@luiss.it

Marco De Marco Guglielmo Marconi University, Rome, Italy, e-mail: m.demarco@unimarconi.it

Maria Chiara Di Guardo University of Cagliari, Cagliari, Italy

Tommaso Federici Dipartimento di Economia e Impresa, Università degli Studi della Tuscia, Viterbo, Italy, e-mail: tfederici@unitus.it

Paola Floreddu University of Cagliari, Cagliari, Italy

Mario Pezzillo Iacono Department of Economics, Second University of Naples, Capua, Italy, e-mail: mario.pezzilloiacono@unina2.it

Paul Johannesson Department of Computer and Systems Sciences (DSV), Stockholm University, Stockholm, Sweden, e-mail: pajo@dsv.su.se

Massimo Magni Bocconi University, Milan, Italy, e-mail: massimo.magni@unibocconi.it

Riccardo Maiolini LUISS Guido Carli University, Rome, Italy, e-mail: rmaiolini@luiss.it

Marcello Martinez Department of Economics, Second University of Naples, Capua, Italy, e-mail: marcello.martinez@unina2.it

Chengzhi Peng School of Architecture, University of Sheffield, London, UK, e-mail: c.peng@sheffield.ac.uk

Ferdinando Pennarola Bocconi University, Milan, Italy, e-mail: ferdinando.pennarola@unibocconi.it

Erik Perjons Department of Computer and Systems Sciences (DSV), Stockholm University, Stockholm, Sweden, e-mail: perjons@dsv.su.se

Andrea Resca CeRSI-LUISS Guido Carli University, Rome, Italy, e-mail: aresca@luiss.it

Francesca Ricciardi Università Cattolica, Milan, Italy, e-mail: francesca.ricciardi@unicatt.it

Stefano Scravaglieri Faculty of Economics, University of Rome "Tor Vergata", Via Columbia 2, 00133 Rome, Italy, e-mail: stefano.scravaglieri@uniroma2.it

Paolo Spagnoletti CeRSI-LUISS Guido Carli University, Rome, Italy, e-mail: pspagnoletti@luiss.it

Laura Tarantino University of L'Aquila, L'Aquila, Italy, e-mail: laura.tarantino@univaq.it

Debora Tomasi Faculty of Economics, University of Rome "Tor Vergata", Via Columbia 2, 00133 Rome, Italy, e-mail: debora.tomasi@uniroma2.it

Maria Laura Tozzi CeRSI-LUISS Guido Carli University, Rome, Italy, e-mail: 618071@luiss.it

Gianluigi Viscusi Department of Informatics, Systems and Communication (DISCo), University of Milano-Bicocca, Viale Sarca 336-U14-20126, Milan, Italy, e-mail: viscusi@disco.unimib.it

Robert Winter Institute of Information Management, University of St. Gallen, Müller-Friedberg-Strasse 8, 9000 St. Gallen, Switzerland, e-mail: robert.winter@unisg.ch

Stefano Za CeRSI, LUISS Guido Carli, Rome, Italy

Editors Biography

Richard Baskerville is a Board of Advisors Professor of Information Systems (IS) at Georgia State University. His research regards security of IS, methods of IS design and development, and the interaction of IS and organizations. He is a Chartered Engineer and holds a Ph.D. from The London School of Economics, University of London. He is the outgoing Editor-in-Chief of European Journal of Information Systems and member of the Editor panel.

Marco De Marco after having served 30 years at the Catholic University of Milan up to the top of the academic career—today is full Professor of Organization and Information Systems at the Guglielmo Marconi University in Rome. Marco De Marco is the author of five books that discuss the development of information systems, the computer industry, and the impact of technology on organizations, as well as the writer of several articles and essays. He is also a member of the editorial board of a number of journals. His major interests are systems development, e-government, programme evaluation, banking information systems, IT and Organizations. For his contribution to the discipline he received in 2010 the award of AIS Fellow.

Paolo Spagnoletti is Assistant Professor of Business Information Systems at LUISS Guido Carli University in Rome, Italy. He coordinates the Research Center on Information Systems of LUISS and serves as Vice President of the Italian chapter of AIS. He holds a Ph.D. from LUISS University, a Master degree in Business Engineering from Tor Vergata University and a M.Sc. degree in Engineering from La Sapienza University. He has been visiting fellow at the London School of Economics (UK), Georgia State University (USA) and INRIA-Loria (FR). His current research interests are interaction of IT and organizations, IS design of community oriented systems, and security of IS.

The Contributions of Alessandro D'Atri to Organization and Information Systems Studies

Paolo Spagnoletti, Richard Baskerville and Marco De Marco

Many authors have contributed to defining the distinct subject matter of the Information Systems (IS) field, and to clarify its relationships with other interrelated disciplines [1]. In the view of Avison and Fitzgerald, the IS field concerns "the effective design, delivery, use, and impact of information technology in organizations and society" [2]. Gregor contrasts Webster and Watson's view of IS being just another management field like organizational behavior [3] by observing that a characteristic that distinguishes IS from these fields is that it concerns the use of artifacts in human-machine systems, so that "we have a discipline that is at the intersection of knowledge of the properties of physical objects (machines) and knowledge of human behaviour" [4]. As Allen Lee describes it, "research in the information systems field examines more than just the technological system, or just the social system, or even the two side by side; in addition, it investigates the phenomena that emerge when the two interact" [5].

As to the relationships between IS and other disciplines, the initial view of the IS community is well represented by Keen, who in 1980 argued that IS, as an "applied" discipline, has to borrow theories, methods and research best practices from more mature "reference disciplines" upon which the field was drawn [6]. The initial list of reference disciplines was quite restricted (including engineering, computer science, mathematics, management science, cybernetic systems theory

P. Spagnoletti (✉)
LUISS Guido Carli University, Rome, Italy
e-mail: pspagnoletti@luiss.it

R. Baskerville
Georgia State University, Atlanta, GA, USA
e-mail: baskerville@acm.org

M. De Marco
Guglielmo Marconi University, Rome, Italy
e-mail: m.demarco@unimarconi.it

R. Baskerville et al. (eds.), *Designing Organizational Systems*,
Lecture Notes in Information Systems and Organisation 1,
DOI: 10.1007/978-3-642-33371-2_1,

and behavioral decision theory). With the growth of the field the list expanded considerably, with, e.g., political science, psychology, sociology, accounting, and finance included in the classification proposed by Culnan [7]. Gregor observes that IS shows commonalities with architecture as well, which also concern people and artifacts, or with applied disciplines such as medicine, where the products of scientific knowledge (e.g., drugs, treatments) are used by people [4].

Notwithstanding this great bunch of relationships, the conventional view in the 80's and 90's was to see IS as being near the end of an intellectual food chain, consuming theories and discovery from other disciplines, with a flow of knowledge and information entirely one way. Scholars then changed their position and started to recognize that the IS discipline had fully emerged as a discipline in its own right. In 2000 Gorden Davis, in an analysis of bodies of concepts, theories, processes, and application systems unique (or somewhat unique) to IS, identified five bodies of knowledge that had developed in the IS tradition [8]. In 2001 Allen Lee observed that the field's reference disciplines "are actually poor models for our own field. They focus on the behavioral or the technological, but not on the emergent socio-technological phenomena that set our field apart" and for this reason suggests to refer to these disciplines as "contributing disciplines" [5]. This shift in perspective is then extended by Baskerville and Myers who suggested a new scenario in which not only did the IS field pose itself as independent from traditional reference disciplines (there is clear evidence that IS research can serve as a foundation for further IS research), but it could also issue a challenge to become itself a reference discipline for others, even for those fields that previously served as reference disciplines for IS [9]. This opportunity arises because, given the growing impact of information technology in business and society as a whole, almost every other human discipline is now a potential consumer of IS research discoveries. In this new model, the flow of knowledge and information among inter-related fields become multidirectional, and IS scholars, instead of just importing knowledge, should consider the possibility to cooperate with scholars in other fields to the benefit of those other fields. IS ceases to be the end of the chain and becomes "one of the many reference disciplines exchanging ideas in an intellectual discourse" [9].

This interdisciplinary approach, along with a focus on design science, characterizes this book, which is dedicated to the memory of Professor Alessandro (Sandro) D'Atri, who passed away on April 22, 2011. Professor D'Atri started his career as a brilliant scholar interested in theoretical computer science, databases, and more generally, information processing systems. These interests became a journey through various applications, such as human–computer interaction, human-factors, ultimately arriving at business information systems and business organization. Among his many accomplishments, Sandro founded in 1998 the Research Centre for Information Systems (CeRSI) at LUISS University in Rome,[1] and he framed all of the research activities within the context of projects in applied

[1] www.cersi.it

research founded by national and international institutions. In 2003, together with his friends and colleagues Marco De Marco and Claudio Ciborra [10], he founded ItAIS,[2] the Italian Chapter of the International Association for Information Systems. Through CeRSI and ItAIS, he pursued the development of an interdisciplinary culture that integrated social sciences, systems design, and human sciences. In 2011 D'Atri was honored posthumously as a Distinguished Member of the Association for Information Systems, an honor accorded to such luminaries as Gerardine DeSanctis, Heinz Klein, Claudio Ciborra, and Charles Kreibel.

Rather than memorializing D'Atri in a retrospective work, this book aims to advance in the directions he was pursuing. It seeks to stimulate a debate about the new potential of design research in the field of information systems and organization studies as an interdisciplinary approach. Each chapter assumes a different position in the continuum between IT systems design on one extreme and organization design on the other. A great variety of theories grounded in multiple disciplines inform novel design directions.

1 Alessandro D'Atri's Legacy

The work and career of Alessandro D'Atri epitomizes the evolution of the IS field. His progressive shift in perspective on the kind of mutual relationships between "companion disciplines" is a defining characteristic of this evolution.

D'Atri scholarly career began with his appointment as lecturer of Programming Techniques at the Faculty of Engineering of the University of Calabria (1977–1980). He later served as Associate Professor of Databases at the Faculty of Engineering of the University "La Sapienza" of Rome (1983–1987) and Professor of Computer Engineering (1987–1997) and Dean of the School of Electronics (1993–1997) at the Faculty of Engineering of the University of L'Aquila. He was appointed as Professor of Business Organization and of Information Systems at the LUISS Guido Carli University in 1997.

We might be tempted to formally divide D'Atri's career in two distinct "eras": the early era focused on Computer Science (1977–1997) and the late era focused on Organization Science (1998–2011). But a deeper analysis within the two periods reveals that what may look like a sharp change of focus and direction (from technology-oriented to organization-oriented research) is actually just a step in a continuous and smooth shift of interest. It is a steady progression from more abstract disciplines towards more applied human-oriented and organization-oriented studies. The focus shifts steadily from technical systems to wider socio-technical systems involving behavioral and institutional aspects. These evolutionary paths are rather more of an unceasing enrichment of knowledge and methods than a discrete series of distinct research lines or projects; throughout their deployment, they gave rise to worthwhile bilateral contaminations among related disciplines,

[2] www.itais.org

and contributed to the creation of diverse networks of cooperation. Sandro's quest for contaminations is also reflected in his teaching activities that, after 1997, included delivery of technology-oriented courses in business-oriented schools on the one side, and delivery of organization-oriented courses in technology-oriented schools on the other side. He helped his students understand and appreciate the increasingly multidisciplinary nature of IS.

1.1 Contributions to Computer Science

In 1977 D'Atri began working on computational complexity theory, a branch of the theory of computation in theoretical computer science and mathematics that focuses on classifying computational problems according to their inherent difficulty, and relating those classes to each other (i.e. [11–13]). Computational complexity is a foundation discipline for the more applied studies in graph theory. Sandro shifted his focus in the beginning of the 80s to research on graph and hypergraph properties that were both at the level of abstract structures (i.e. [14–16]). He also used the context of graphs and hypergraphs as foundational structures in database theory (i.e. [17–20]). In these years Sandro was actually working also on database theory problems, which both stimulated his research in graph theory and also led him to new foundations for database theory research (i.e. [21, 22]).

In the second half of the 80s, D'Atri's work is characterized by a new shift toward more *applied* research problems at the intersection between database systems and Human–Computer Interaction (or man–machine interfaces, as HCI was termed at the time). His results became more and more oriented to the end-users rather than the designers (i.e. [23–25]). The shift towards human–machine systems brought a new research model that constitutes the common traits of all subsequent Sandro's work: the creation of knowledge from the design, the implementation, and the evaluation of new IT artifacts in the context of innovative projects. The genre of these projects reflects Sandro's growing interest in organizational issues. There are early techno-centric projects, focused on general database and knowledge base systems initially (i.e. [26, 27]). Later there are more specific geographical information systems (i.e. [28]). Later still are more organization-centered and multidisciplinary projects in medical informatics in the 90s (i.e. [29]). Medical informatics is an excellent example of his engagement in a multidisciplinary field, relying, among others, on data and knowledge base systems, human–computer interaction, computer-based medical records, clinical decision support systems, strategic information systems, etc. Sandro's approach did not just "import knowledge" from these fields to implement new systems, but included projects' activities that gained results to enrich the referring disciplines.

Medical informatics and e-health will remain among D'Atri's areas of interest also after his move to the LUISS Guido Carli University in 1997. Papers in these areas serve as a lens on his gradual shift of focus from technology issues (i.e. [30]) to organizational (i.e. [31–33]) and strategic issues (i.e. [34]).

1.2 Contributions to Organization Science

The second half of the 90s is characterized by D'Atri touching down in the information system area. His vision with respect to the research on information systems can be summarized with a claim taken from an email message exchanged with his team in 2010: "we finalize the research to the design of an IT artifact or a social or organizational system, and we evaluate its possible organizational impacts". He envisioned a way of working in which research addresses relevant problems, engaged in national and international cooperation with other universities and research institutions, and gained insights from the construction, intervention, and evaluation phases of innovative IT projects. In Sandro's view, the expected outcomes of the research activities were embedded in the overall project plans. These outcomes mainly related to the generalized characteristics of the artifacts, to the methodological aspects of system design and implementation, and to the organizational effects that can be captured during the pilot evaluation.

Another important aspect that characterizes this second "era" of D'Atri's career is the influence and stimulus that Claudio Ciborra's work exerted on Sandro's approach to IS research. As Sandro claims in the EJIS special issue in memory of Claudio Ciborra "I found his metaphors, such as bricolage, improvisation, tinkering, hospitality and care illuminating when I was investigating the conceptual relationship of ICT and human activity in phenomena such as the development process of an Information System or new forms of cooperation among organisations" [35]. It is quite surprising the extent to which these concepts are reflected in almost all the activities carried out by Sandro in the last 10 years of his work.

In 1998 D'Atri founded the research center on information systems (CeRSI, www.cersi.it), which he directed until his death in 2011. Under his leadership, the center became one of the leading research centers on information systems in Italy, and gained a distinctive international reputation (in 2010 CeRSI joined the ERCIS network [www.ercis.org] as its Italian representative). Under Sandro's leadership, the center conducted its research within the framework of more than 30 research projects funded by the European Commission and/or by Italian institutions and private companies. Such a conspicuous portfolio of projects has matured into a wide array of areas such as e-government, e-business, e-care, e-learning, enterprise interoperability, besides the already mentioned e-health. A selection of these projects is provided in Table 1.

Two main aspects emerge from an overview of these projects. First, the temporal link between project initiatives in the same area shows how D'Atri's new projects either evolve from a local to a national and European scale or evolve by exploiting the outcomes of previous EU projects to solve local field problems. Second, the project areas (the field problem space) are not independent; activities in one area trigger new initiatives in different areas. This interdependence applies to the solution space in which the nature of the IT artifact can be the same for different areas. For instance, a former e-health initiative at EU level (TACIT) triggers a new e-health projects at a local level (C4BIOT) and then subsequently a

Table 1 CeRSI's selected projects

Project area	Project name	Funding agency
e-government	OK-eG: Organizing knowledge in e-government (2003–2005)	Italian Ministry of research
	LD-CAST: Local development cooperation actions enabled by semantic technology (2006–2008)	EU commission, VI framework programme
e-care	HOPES: Help and social interaction for elderly On a multimedia platform with E-social best practices (2010–2013)	EU commission, AAL joint programme
e-learning	AUTOMATIC: Development of curricula and innovative training tools for industrial automation systems for people employed in SMEs (2009–2011)	EU commission—LdV programme
	EARNFILE: Evaluation and recognition of non-formal and informal learning (2009–2011)	
	OTIS: On-line training for investment on securities (2005–2008)	
	VIRTUOSE Virtual Online System for Education on Quality (2004–2007)	
	LiVES: Learning in virtual extended spaces (2010–2012)	Lazio region
Enterprise interoperability	MID-BLUE: Multimedia information distribution using bluetooth (2010–2012)	Lazio region
	INTEROP-NoE: Interoperability research for networked enterprise applications and software (2005–2007)	EU commission, VI framework programme
e-health	C4BIOIT: Campus for bioinformation technology (2006–2008)	Lazio region
	TACIT: Technologies augmenting clinical insight (2004–2006)	EU commission, VI framework programme
e-business	FAIRWIS: Trade fair web-based information services (2002–2004)	EU commission, V framework Programme

new project in the e-care area (HOPES). Moreover the same technological artifact can be applied to solve field problems in different domains. This knowledge reuse is exemplified by the development of semantic technologies in an e-government project (LD-CAST) and its subsequent re-application in e-care areas (HOPES).

A systemic view of CeRSI activities shows how these projects materialize as intertwined subsystems with many interactions at different levels. D'Atri masterfully orchestrated these interactions by guiding the evolution of this complex system, taking into account the dynamics of both inner capabilities and external environmental opportunities. In this context the research center has never espoused a single theoretical approach to ground the design and evaluation processes. Quite the contrary, it has always privileged the adoption of multiple perspectives, methods and techniques in order to be actually context- and problem-driven instead of being technology-driven. This same variety of perspectives is reflected in the way the project team members identified an impressive number of topics and adopted diverse research approaches yet always remained within the frame of Sandro's initiatives. A few examples are: virtual enterprises and supply chain management in the e-business area [36, 37], business models, trust and information security in the e-government and in the enterprise interoperability areas [38–40], studies on e-learning [41], project and innovation management [42, 43] and as previously mentioned, e-health [31].

The research dissemination activities have seen CeRSI and its members constantly active in major national and international conferences (just to name a few, ECIS, MCIS and ALPIS in the area of information systems, and WOA, Egos, EURAM, Academy of Management, and AIDEA for the areas of management and organization studies). In the 2001–2011 period, CeRSI group members published more than 200 research papers in conference proceedings, book chapters, and international journals. Such works yield a dense publication co-authoring network (illustrated in Fig. 1) that manifests the role of Alessandro D'Atri in catalyzing cooperation with other scholars.

2 Content of the Volume

The evolutionary progression of D'Atri's research suggests that design science is the next ground for advancing both Sandro's systemic view of technical and social phenomena and his continuous search for innovative solutions for managing the complexity of emergent problems. Although Sandro had not contributed directly to the discourse on design science research, the design orientation of his work emerges from almost all of his research contributions. In keeping with the aim of the book to continue Sandro's advances, and recognizing Sandro was headed this way, so go we there also. Design science is often grounded in the H.A. Simon book *The Sciences of the Artificial* in which a distinction is made between the natural sciences and the sciences related to the making of human artifacts [44]. These artifacts are necessarily material and can consist of many forms of designed

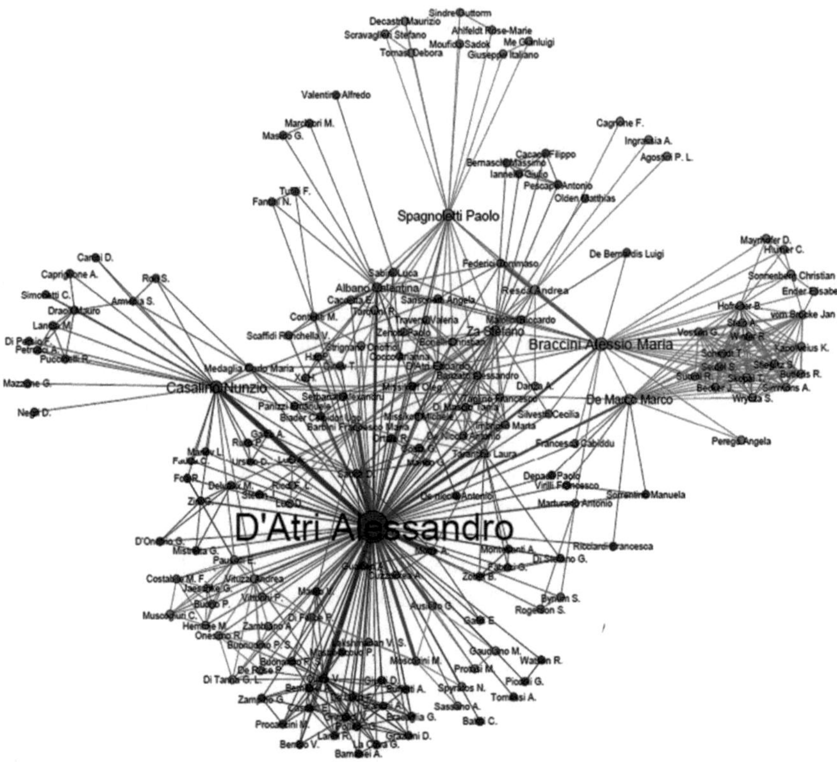

Fig. 1 Publications co-authoring network

interventions (e.g. actions, structures, processes, systems) to address field problems. The key characteristic of natural sciences is that they are descriptive and deductive in nature, being engaged in the quest for truth. On the other hand, design sciences, like architecture, engineering, and law, are prescriptive and abductive in nature. Debate about the role of these design sciences has engaged scholars in the fields of management and organization studies, and design research is now in the foreground of many conferences and top journals, especially in the IS field. Indeed in this field a particularly relevant problem involves the explicit prescription for the design and development of theoretical classes of IT systems.

The call for chapters of this book attracted many contributions that span across a variety of field problems, research goals, methods and outcomes. Sixteen chapters have been selected following a blind review process and are distributed into four parts addressing different classes of problems. For each part we provide a brief introduction below that explains how the following chapters offer advances on the themes and works of Alessandro D'Atri.

2.1 Part I: Design Science Research Principles and Methods

In the first part, four meta-level contributions open the book by providing insights into key epistemological, ontological, and methodological issues of design science research. The four chapters presented in this part have been selected because they provide the reader with a set of conceptual models and theoretical assumptions that allow a better understanding and context for the content of the parts that follow. The underpinning assumptions shared among all these chapters are the system theory foundations at the basis of design science research [44], and that these are made richer by concepts and ideas grounded in the social studies of IT [45].

The first chapter, "Design and Normative Claims in Organization Studies: a Methodological Proposal", by Francesca Ricciardi from Catholic University of Milan, provides a conceptual analysis for investigating the role of design claims and normative claims in organization studies, from both an epistemological and a methodological perspective. By referring to medicine as a discipline in which the relationship between descriptive, design, value judgment, and normative claims is well established, the chapter illustrates the genesis of a normative claim in the medical field. The story of research on puerperal fever in the nineteen century serves as an example to show the path of scientific knowledge discovery. The work is valuable because it encourages a stronger presence of design claims in both qualitative and quantitative organization studies research.

Next, researchers Ilia Bider, Paul Johannesson and Erik Perjons from Stockholm University propose a conceptualization and formalization of design science research that show the possible ways in which a design science project can be carried out. Our second chapter, "Design Science Research as Movement between Individual and Generic Situation-Problem-Solution Spaces", presents a map helping the researchers to plan their actions within design science research. The map is based on two three-dimensional spaces, one named the individual situation-problem-solution space and the other the generic situation-problem-solution space. Additionally, the authors provide two examples by using the map in order to show how design science research may differ in its types. This work is particularly notable because it astutely positions design science research as a project that must be managed in concert with research methodology.

The third chapter, "Restructuring the Design Science Research Knowledge Base: A One-Cycle View of Design Science Research and its Consequences for Understanding Organizational Design Problems", provides a meta-level discussion on how design science research can contribute to solve Organizational Design and Engineering (ODE) problems. With this aim, authors Robert Winter and Antonia Albani from the University of St. Gallen propose a framework that allows for a systematic classification and retrieval of artifacts and relates solution artifacts to problem characteristics. This framework is composed of an iterative process model and a supporting knowledge base of reusable design artifacts and organizational problems. The process model is inspired by the well known Spiral Model of software development in which design and evaluation activities alternate in an iterative way. The knowledge base structure concerns the artifact type, generality, application domain and coverage. The applicability of the proposed framework is demonstrated with an expository instantiation in the domain of change projects in organizations. This chapter is remarkable because the research draws out the continuous character of design science research programs in which the beginnings and ends of distinct cycles may be recognized in some cases as epistemological description decisions rather than ontological events.

In the fourth chapter, "Dealing with Critical IS Research: Artifacts, Drifts, Electronic Panopticon and Illusions of Empowerment", Marcello Martinez and Mario Pezzillo Iacono from the Second University of Naples, explore the IS and organizational control design problems from a critical perspective. By developing on the philosophical roots of post-structuralism and on the Foucauldian conceptualization of control, they show how the overlapping between "electronic panopticon" and "commitment practices" used by management when designing IS becomes a powerful tool for exerting influence and control in the sense of self-discipline and self-regulation. A case study of the call centre outsourcing industry is presented to support the discussion. The chapter provides insights on the role of "power of control" in the analysis and design of IT and organizational artifacts. In particular it shows how and why IT artefacts enable and constrain human behaviours and how the managerial discourses frame organizational reality by impacting on drift, beliefs, and perceptions. It is an outstanding conclusion to our first part by raising our awareness of that the act of designing a technological artefact is inherently an act of managerial control in organizations.

2.2 Part II: Design and Evaluation of IT Artifacts

The four chapters in the second part are related to the design and evaluation of IT artifacts that satisfy specific requirements (such as being user-centered, managing knowledge in a dynamic environment, enabling crowdsourcing, and e-participation). These works extend previous contributions by D'Atri in the Human Computer Interaction [25] and knowledge management [29] domains by taking into account the role of IT in contributing to the openness of organizational systems and in enabling new cooperative models and new feedbacks mechanisms. These contributions recall Sandro's revelation that, "in the context of cooperative systems the unpredictable behavior of actors involved and the openness of technology made me investigate new roles of technology and new forms of cooperation based on trust mechanisms instead of hierarchical structures" [35]. For instance this is the case for design principles and models emerging in the e-care, crowdsourcing, and e-participation domains.

This part opens with, "User Centered Systems Design: the Bridging Role of Justificatory Knowledge" by Paolo Spagnoletti from LUISS University and Laura Tarantino from University of L'Aquila. This fifth chapter addresses the field problem of developing successful user centered systems when IT artifacts are expected to fit with the dynamics of complex socio-technical systems such as organizations. A synthetic view on the evolution of the main paradigms in Human Computer Interaction (HCI) is provided and current methods for the design of user centered systems are critically analyzed through the lens of a conceptual framework based on "The Anatomy of a Design Theory". The discussion is also supported by an expository instantiation in the context of an e-care project. As a result of this analysis the authors maintain that HCI, which is pragmatic in nature, can benefit from a structured contamination with concepts grounded in the IS design research stream. The contribution is important because it illustrates the usefulness of introducing research into practice.

In "A Design Theory for Dynamic Competencies Mapping Systems", Luigi De Bernardis and Riccardo Maiolini from LUISS Guido Carli University, address the field problem of dynamically mapping competencies with IT. They use the IS design theory constructs for deriving a set of meta-requirements from kernel theories grounded in the knowledge management tradition. These meta-requirements are then linked with a set of prescriptions for the design of an IT system supporting the dynamic mapping of competences within organizations. This sixth chapter also introduces a possible plan, based on the adoption of text mining software, for evaluating the effectiveness of the proposed solution. This work is important because it advances to both managerial research and practice by providing a new and sustainable way for updating skill inventories and job descriptions.

In the seventh chapter, "Open Innovation and Crowdsourcing: a Cross Case Analysis", Francesca Cabiddu, Manuel Castriotta, Maria Chiara Di Guardo and Paola Floreddu from the University of Cagliari address the field problem of designing IT platforms that effectively support crowdsourcing activities. The paper provides a cross-case analysis of two initiatives for generating innovation through the contribution of communities of customers. In order to frame the analysis, authors adopt a theoretical framework grounded on the concept of design theory and on previous literature on crowdsourcing and open innovation. Crowd integration, efficiency of creative process, community structure, and open culture are adopted as dimensions for understanding the link between requirements and design components of two crowdsourcing platforms that are analyzed through a netnography approach. The main contribution is an evaluation framework for supporting the design of IT artifacts that foster creativity among online communities. From a D'Atri perspective, however, we find importance in the work's observations about how people can productively cooperate in creative design with minimal organizational control structures and managerial intervention.

This part of the book culminates in "New Internet-based Relationships Between Citizens and Public Administrations: Challenges for Platforms Design". Alessio Maria Braccini and Tommaso Federici from the University of Tuscia (Italy), address the design of web 2.0 tools for enabling e-participation. In this eighth chapter, we see design as a bottom up process promoted and performed by citizens for increasing the transparency of governments' actions and improving their policies. They analyze four cases in which original or official data about the activity of governments and public administrations are distributed through the Internet by private subjects. They see the characteristics of the IT artifacts in terms of spirit, technology, data, audience, language, and user interaction. The value of this work is particularly important because it proposes an explanatory design theory linking general requirements to general components by referring to three kernel theories, namely Social Capital, Absorptive Capacity, and Agency Theories.

2.3 Part III: Design and Evaluation of Organizational Practices

The third part collects four chapters focused on the design of organizational artifacts such as team composition, learning processes and spaces, and performance management systems. The two central chapters of this part are well connected with D'Atri's research activities in the e-learning domain [32, 41] and his interest in the role of IT for supporting learning processes. While less directly anchored to Sandro's work, the first and the last chapters of this part contribute a more complete view of the different levels involved when design is applied to organizational systems. In fact these contributions provide insights on the team composition decisions and on the design of organizational control systems respectively.

In the ninth chapter, "Designing Teams for Enhancing Individual Added-Value Use of Technology: The Role of Competition and Dynamics among Team Members", Stefano Basaglia from University of Bergamo and Leonardo Caporarello, Massimo Magni and Ferdinando Pennarola from Bocconi University, address the organizational problem of underutilization of implemented technologies. They focus on a mix of team-level conditions and individual characteristics for predicting employees' intention to explore new technology. According with their results, managers may consider creating competitive team structures that emphasize a tight integration of technology use into employee work practices. Moreover team composition should be based upon a balance in individual attributes for facilitating the emergence of technology "creative explorers" within each team. This chapter is powerful in its operating assumption that success and failure is not a binary characteristic, and while the assumption is itself not new, the work advances novel techniques for managing the utilization phenomena on the continuum rather than the contradiction.

Next, Nunzio Casalino from Marconi University addresses the field problem of finding the designability edge at which organizational systems designers can effectively operate to enable learning to occur. Our tenth chapter, "Design Principles at the Edge of the Designable: Non-Formal and Informal Learning in SMEs", achieves this goal by exploring and describing in depth the organizational concept of informal learning at the workplace. The conceptual analysis lies on the results of European project aimed at investigating the complex dynamics of non-formal and informal learning processes in Small and Medium Enterprises.

The initial results provide insight into the designable aspects of for promoting such learning and elements that capture the results from such learning. In such a way, the designers design the before-edge and the after-edge of the informal processes. We found this work particularly important for its pragmatic theory: Because human behavior cannot be designed effectively, we can still design effectively at the edges of this behavior.

At the intersection of architecture, information systems, and organizations, we find our eleventh chapter, "Designing Innovative Learning Spaces in Higher Education at a Turning Point: Institutional Identities, Pervasive Smart Technologies and Organizational Learning". In this chapter, Chengzhi Peng from the University of Sheffield reports and reflects on the findings of an ICT-based design experiment in a higher education institution. The focus is the design of a large scale Web-based 3D virtual university campus modelling system aimed at supporting the design of learning spaces in a real institutional context. The core argument is that such digital modelling platform can be a useful tool in fostering organizational learning and improving institutional performance. Aside from the conspicuous richness of the intersection, this work is important because the merger yields an abstract design space: the "learning landscape". This architectural goal is an abstract place defined both by physical space and human behavior; still, this research shows how it is one that can be represented holistically and manipulated prescriptively by information technologies.

The twelfth and concluding chapter in this part is, "Performance Management Systems as Driver of Public Administration Improvement: a Dream?" Debora Tomasi, Stefano Scravaglieri and Maurizio Decastri from Tor Vergata University address the field problem of implementing Performance Management Systems (PMS) in public administrations (PAs). They present the results of an action design research project for the implementation of a PMS in an Italian PA. A set of prescriptive rules for the successful application of PMS principles to PAs are derived from the generalization of the empirical findings. The contribution is expressed in the form of testable propositions related to the meta-design and to the design method for future artifact design. The importance of a design research case such as this one, in terms of D'Atri's directions, cannot be understated. Decisions about how to manage human performance are not only loaded with the future of sanctions and rewards, but will also shape how people will behave, what they will do, and what the organization can accomplish. Such a "loaded" application means design decisions are conspicuous to stakeholders, and perhaps the most ideal setting for the transparency that is available from design science research.

2.4 Part IV: Design and Evaluation of Managerial Strategies

In the concluding part of the book, we find four chapters that are related to the design and evaluation of managerial strategies such as IT strategic planning in the e-business, e-government, and e-health domains. D'Atri developed interests in such topics in the last part of his career by enlarging the scope of the organizational systems under control (and of the artifacts for controlling them) to the level of cooperative systems [36–38] and nationwide governance models (such as in the context of e-government and e-health [34]).

We open with, "Design on a Societal Scale: The Case of E-Government Strategic Planning", by Carlo Batini, Gianluigi Viscusi and Marco Castelli from University of Milano-Bicocca. This chapter regards the implementation of a comprehensive method for the design and planning of service-oriented information systems with special emphasis on e-government initiatives. They test the appropriateness of this method in the context of an information integration initiative in the Tunisian Ministry of Agriculture and Hydraulic Resources. In this case, the authors evaluate the adequacy of the method and examine whether the method provides a contribution to some of the challenging issues mentioned by Simon for the design of artifact on a societal scale, namely the problem representation and the organizations in social design. The results are important because the issues and directions are scaled to *societal* design, a much more ambitious direction than technological or organizational design.

Next, Stefano Za and Paolo Depaoli from CeRSI-LUISS Guido Carli University propose a stage model of organizational learning built on existing literature and on the needs of the most innovative kinds of SMEs. This is our fourteenth chapter, "Towards The Redesign of E-Business Maturity Models for SMEs". Two sets of considerations support the proposal of an updated conceptual stage model. The first one concerns the heterogeneous world of SMEs, and the second set of considerations concerns the role of information technology and systems. The paper combines relevant areas to pursue the research aims. For example, *Business needs* (derived from the relevant environment as a combination of people, organization, and technology) and *Applicable knowledge*. The interplay of technology and organization is considered according to Orlikowski's principle of 'entanglement in organizational practice' of technology. This work is important because it provides outcomes with practical guidance both for entrepreneurs and policy makers.

In the fifteenth chapter, "Offline and Online Communities: Great Differences and Some Similarities", Andrea Resca and Maria Laura Tozzi from LUISS Guido Carli University investigate the concept of community by comparing characteristics of online and offline communities. The discussion is articulated along two perspectives. The first is derived from online and virtual communities, widely explored in studies related to ICT and Computer Mediated Communication. The second perspective is derived from the offline community, a classical object of analysis of sociological studies. A particular focus is given to the analysis of the organizational forms that characterize both offline and online communities. The comparison of market, bureaucracy, and clan with organizational forms that characterize the cyberspace according to the current literature leads to the rather timely conclusion that many online communities are not communities in the offline sense. This finding is important because it recognizes the label *community* may have a fundamentally different meaning online.

Our concluding sixteenth chapter is by Valentina Albano from Roma Tre University. In "The Role of Network Governance Models in the Design of Local ehealth Policies", Albano addresses the field problem of successful eHealth implementation by focusing on the mechanisms of coordination and control of network-level activities as a driver for the design of successful eHealth interventions. She adopts the concept of policy network as analytical tool for investigating the influence of the structural relationship between political institutions and the design of successful policy arrangements related to the diffusion of eHealth. Three cases of eHealth policy networks are comparatively analyzed in order to show how these models of network governance operate and influence the design of eHealth strategies. This paper is remarkable because several design activities become intertwined: design of policies, design of a network to help design the policies, and design of strategies related to these policies. The presence of this nested design problem in the eHealth domain makes the relevance to D'Atri's research directions all the more salient.

Our goal in this book was to actively energize Sandro's research directions by formulating and offering the next advances. As a prominent scholar, the research he completed should rightfully serve as a launchpad for better research, new ideas, and further studies. As such, even this volume should *not* be regarded as a final tribute to Sandro. It is rather the next, first steps taken in his absence. We are confident that the sixteen chapters that follow, embodied in the work of 35 authors and 12 editors, will further launch other works by other authors who will thus be able to stand on the shoulders of Professor Alessandro D'Atri.

Acknowledgments We acknowledge Laura Tarantino, former student, colleague and friend of Sandro, for helping us in tracing the path of his scholar contribution. We also offer our sincere appreciation to the members of the editorial board for this book both for promoting the initial submissions and for their countless hours spent in reviewing and improving the chapters.

Appendix

Alessandro D'Atri's selected publications

Disciplinary area	Co-author
Computational complexity	Ausiello et al. (1977)
	Ausiello et al. (1980)
	Ausiello et al. (1981)
Graph theory	Ausiello et al. (1985)
	Ausiello et al. (1986)
	Ausiello et al. (1986)
	Moscarini (1988)
Graph theory and database theory	Ausiello et al. (1983)
	Batini (1980)
	Moscarini (1986)
	Ausiello et al. (1986)

(continued)

(continued)

Disciplinary area	Co-author
Databases	Moscarini et al. (1983)
	Saccà (1984)
	Ricci (1988)
	Di Felice et al. (1989)
Databases and human–computer interaction	Tarantino (1989)
	Laenens et al. (1991)
	Clementini (1991)
	Motro (1999)
Telemedicine and e-health	Tarantino et al. (1993)
	Di Stefano et al. (1995)
	Currò et al. (2000)
	Casalino et al. (2005)
	Currò et al. (2007)
	Spagnoletti et al. (2011)

References

1. Grover, V., Ayyagari, R., Gokhale, R., & Lim, J. (2006). A citation analysis of the evolution and state of information systems within a constellation of reference disciplines. *Journal of AIS, 7*, 270–325.
2. Avison, D., & Fitzgerald, G. (1995). *Information systems development: Methodologies*. London: Techniques and Tools.
3. Webster, J., & Watson, R. T. (2002). Analyzing the past to prepare for the future: writing a literature review. *MIS Quarterly, 26*, 13–23.
4. Gregor, S. (2006). The nature of theory in information systems. *MIS Quarterly, 30*, 611.
5. Lee, A. S. (2001). Editor's comments: MIS quarterly's editorial policies and practices. *MIS Quarterly, 25*, iii–vii.
6. Keen, P. G. W. (1980). MIS research: Reference disciplines and a cumulative tradition. In E. R. McLean (Ed.), *Proceedings of the first international conference on information systems* (pp. 9–18). Philadelphia: ACM Press.
7. Culnan, B. M. J. (1987). Mapping the intellectual structure of MIS, 1980–1985: A co-citation analysis. *MIS Quarterly, 3*(11), 341–353.
8. Davis, G. (2000). Information systems conceptual foundations: Looking backward and forward. In R. Baskerville, J. Stage & J. DeGross (Eds.), *Organizational and social perspectives on information technology* (pp. 61–82). Boston: Kluwer Academic Publishers.
9. Baskerville, R., & Myers, D. (2002). Information systems as a reference discipline. *MIS Quarterly, 26*, 1–14.
10. D'Atri, A. (2005). ItAIS (the Italian chapter of AIS) remembers. *European Journal of Information Systems, 14*(5), 454–455.
11. D'Atri, A., Ausiello, G., Gaudiano, M., & Protasi, M. (1977). Classes of structurally isomorphic NPOptimization problems. *Lecture Notes in Computer Science, 53*, 222–230.
12. D'Atri, A., Ausiello, G., & Protasi, M. (1980). Structure preserving reductions among convex optimization problems. *Journal of Computer and System Sciences, 21*(1), 136–153.
13. D'Atri, A., Ausiello, G., & Protasi, M. (1981). Lattice theoretic ordering properties for NP-complete optimization problems. *Annales Societatis Mathematicae Polonae Series IV, 4*(1), 83–94.
14. D'Atri, A., Ausiello, G., & Saccà, D. (1985). Strongly equivalent directed hypergraphs. *Annals of Discrete Mathematics, 25*, 1–26.

15. D'Atri, A., Ausiello, G., & Saccà, D. (1986). Minimal representations of directed hypergraphs. *SIAM Journal on Computing, 15*(2), 418–432.
16. D'Atri, A., & Moscarini, M. (1988). On hypergraph acyclicity and graph chordality. *Information Processing Letters, 29*(5), 271–274.
17. Batini, C., & D'Atri, A. (1980). Schema hypergraphs: A formalism to investigate logical database design. In H. Noltemeier (Ed.), *Lecture notes in computer science 100, Graph-theoretic concepts in computer science* (pp. 177–194). Berlin: Springer Verlag.
18. Ausiello, G., D'Atri, A., & Saccà, D. (1983). Graph algorithms for functional dependency manipulation. *Journal of the Association for Computing Machinery, 30*, 752–766.
19. D'Atri, A., & Moscarini, M. (1986). Recognition algorithms and design methodologies for acyclic database schemes. *Advances in Computing Research, 3*, 43–67.
20. Ausiello, G., D'Atri, A., & Moscarini, M. (1986). Chordality properties on graphs and minimal conceptual connections in semantic data models. *Journal of Computer and System Sciences, 33*, 179–202.
21. D'Atri, A., Moscarini, M., & Spyratos, N. (1983). Answering queries in relational databases. *Sigmod Record, 13*(4), 173–177.
22. D'Atri, A., & Saccà, D. (1984). Equivalence and mapping of database schemes. In U. Dayal, G. Schlageter & L. H. Seng (Eds.), *Proceedings of 10th international conference on very large data bases* (pp. 187–195). Singapore: Morgan Kaufmann Publishers.
23. D'Atri, A., & Ricci, F. L. (1988). Interpretation of statistical queries to relational databases. *Lecture Notes in Computer Science, 339*, 246–258.
24. D'Atri, A., Di Felice, P., & Moscarini, M. (1989). Dynamic query interpretation in relational databases. *Information Systems, 14*(3), 195–204.
25. D'Atri, A., & Tarantino, L. (1989). From browsing to querying. *Data Engineering, 12*(2), 45–55.
26. D'Atri, A., Laenens, E., Paoluzzi, A., Tarantino, L., & Vermeir, D. (1991). A graphical browser to object-oriented knowledge bases. *Database Technology, 4*, 45–55.
27. D'Atri, A., Motro, A., & Tarantino, L. (1999). ViewFinder: An object browser. *Information and Software Technology, 41*, 211–234.
28. D'Atri, A., Di Felice, P., & Clementini, E. (1991) *A spatial data model underlying human interaction with object-oriented spatial databases. 15th Annual International Computer Software and Applications Conference, COMPSAC'91* (pp. 110–117). Tokyo, Japan: IEEE Computer Society Press.
29. D'Atri, A., Tarantino, L., & Di Stefano, G. (1994). On the representation and management of medical records in a knowledge based system. *Expert Systems with Applications, 6*(4), 469–482.
30. D'Atri, A., Fabrizi, G., Montesanti, A., Tarantino, L., & Zobel, B. (1995). MILORD: Multimedia interaction with large object-oriented radiological and clinical databases. *Studies in Health Technology and Informatics, 24*, 167–173.
31. D'Atri, A., Currò, V., Mauro, V., Buonanno, P. S., Mastroiacovo, P., & Bernabei, A. (2000). Accessing information on medical/health websites by Italian families: A pilot study. *Clinical Pediatrics, 39*(2), 68–69.
32. Casalino, N., D'Atri, A., & Fadda, C. (2005) *Organisational impact and exploitation of the results of an Italian research project for ehealth and medical training. ECIS 2005—European Conference on Information Systems.*
33. Currò, V., Zambiano, A., Onesimo, R., D'Atri, A., Buonuomo, P. S., & Vituzzi, A. (2007). The influence of quality criteria on parents' evaluation of medical web-pages: An Italian randomized trial. *Technology and Health Care, 15*, 399–406.
34. Albano, V., Spagnoletti, P., Caccetta, E., D'Atri, A., & Tarquini, R. (2011) *Supporting policy definition in the e-health domain: A QCA based method, HEALTHINF. Refereed Conference Proceedings.*
35. D'Atri, A. (2005) Bricolage in system design and trust in cooperation. *European Journal of Information Systems, 14*(5), 452–453.

36. D'Atri, A., & Motro, A. (2008). VirtuE: A formal model of virtual enterprises for information markets. *Journal of Intelligent Information Systems, 30*, 33–53.
37. D'Atri, A., Spagnoletti, P., Banzato, A., Bonelli, C., D'Atri, E., Traversi, V., & Zenobi, P. (2009). *From supply chains to supply networks: the beer game evolution. Proceedings of INCOM 2009, 13th IFAC Symposium on Information Control Problems in Manufacturing.*
38. Braccini, A. M., Spagnoletti, P., & D'Atri, A. (2008). Analysing business models for cross border E-services provided by the chambers of commerce. *In: Proceedings of 16th European Conference on Information Systems, Galway, 9–11 June 2008.* http://aisel.aisnet.org/ecis2008/230Paper230.
39. Spagnoletti, P., Za, S., & D'Atri, A. (2007). *Institutional trust and security, new boundaries for Virtual Enterprises. Proceedings of 2nd International Workshop on Interoperability Solutions to Trust, Security, Policies and QoS for Enhanced Enterprise Systems.* Helsinki University Printing House, HELSINKI—FIN.
40. Spagnoletti, P., & D'Atri, A. (2006). *Information Systems security design: A case study based approach. WWW/Internet 2006, Proceedings of the IADIS International Conference* (pp. 435–443).
41. Braccini, A. M., Za, S., & D'Atri, A. (2010). Investigating end users' satisfaction of the usage of an E-learning platform: A statistical analysis. *Elearning, 2*, 21–34.
42. Sansonetti, A., & D'Atri, A. (2009). *The exploitation of outcomes within european research projects: The spin-off strategy. IRNOP IX Research Conference on "Organizing by Projects".*
43. Sansonetti, A., & D'Atri, A. (2009) *IT spin-offs into the European research framework: An innovative configuration. AMCIS 2009, 15th Americas Conference on Information Systems.*
44. Simon, H. A. (1996) The sciences of the artificial. Cambridge: MIT Press.
45. Ciborra, C. (2000) From control to drift: The dynamics of corporate information infrastructures. In C. U. Cibbora, K. Braa, A. Cordella, B. Dahlbom, A. Failla, O. Hanseth, V. Hepsø, J. Ljungberg, E. Monteiro & K. A.Simon (Eds.), *From control to drift the dynamics of corporate information infrastructure* (p. 246). Oxford: Oxford University Press.

Part I
Design Science Research Principles and Methods

Design and Normative Claims in Organization Studies: A Methodological Proposal

Francesca Ricciardi

Abstract This paper focuses on the pivotal role of Design Claims in scientific research. In fact, Design Claims link the adoption and/or use of a specific artifact (for example, a procedure, or a belief) to measurable and relevant effects. By doing so, Design Claims continuously spot gaps in theory, and then force to scientific advancements. This paper suggests that the dramatic lack of Design Claims (and consequently of Normative Claims) in Organization Studies not only results in lack of relevance, but also deprives our discipline of the beneficial epistemological interplay that should take place between design, normative and descriptive statements. This epistemological teamwork, where present, results in a "mirroring effect" that makes other fields of studies, such as Medicine, viable and relevant. Models and frameworks developed in Organization Studies, on the contrary, often result in epistemological dead ends: once emanated, their specific influence in the real world is rarely object of further specific interest. It is just as if Medicine scholars, after developing a theory on a certain health issue, were not interested in measuring how the adoption of that specific theory in the world of practice performed. Some methodological suggestions are then provided, to encourage a stronger presence of Design Claims in both qualitative and quantitative Organization Studies research.

Keywords Design claims · Normative claims · Artifact adoption · Epistemological status of organization studies

---

F. Ricciardi (✉)
Università Cattolica del S. Cuore, Milan, Italy
e-mail: francesca.ricciardi@unicatt.it

R. Baskerville et al. (eds.), *Designing Organizational Systems*,
Lecture Notes in Information Systems and Organisation 1,
DOI: 10.1007/978-3-642-33371-2_2,

1 Introduction

Let us compare the two following statements:

1. People should quit smoking.
2. Cancer risks rapidly decrease after quitting smoking.

The first statement is aimed at suggesting how the world ought to be, and the second is aimed at describing how the world is. In epistemological reflections [1], statements of the first type are often referred to as normative or prescriptive, and statements of the second type are referred to as descriptive.

Although a clear distinction between normative and descriptive claims is very important for scientific rigor, they are often two faces of the same cognitive medal. Common knowledge, in fact, easily unifies statements number 1 and 2 into the following: "Cancer risks rapidly decrease after quitting smoking, *then* people should quit smoking".

After this simple example, we can say that even the more classical descriptive cause-effect claims, by their very nature, implicitly generate normative claims if:

- *The cause is buildable* (it is perceived as subject to choice or avoidance, to creation or destruction. For example: it is possible to quit smoking);
- *The effect is not neutral in comparison to the cause* (it is perceived as good or bad by a value judgement. For example: cancer prevention is good, even in comparison to the difficulties of quitting smoking).

Why does the scientific tradition keep normative and descriptive claims separated? Because, from a scientific point of view, nothing can be considered obvious, not even the goodness of cancer prevention. Thus, in the vast building of science, normative and descriptive claims are linked by claims that investigate the *goodness*, on the one side, and the *buildability*, on the other side, of the described situations. Value judgment research, in order to investigate goodness, and design oriented research, in order to investigate buildability, play a pivotal role in this framework (see Fig. 1). Ethical (but also aesthetic or ecological) claims, on the one side, and design claims, on the other side, can "fill the gaps" between descriptive and normative claims.

The example presented above, then, becomes:

1. Cancer risks rapidly decrease after quitting smoking (descriptive statement): *so, since*
2. people taking medicine A/following method B more probably succeed in quitting smoking, with costs and risks A'/B' (design statement) *and*
3. diminishing cancer risks is more important than avoiding the unpleasant aspects of medicine A/method B (value judgment statement), *then*
4. people should quit smoking [by taking medicine A/by following method B] (normative statement).

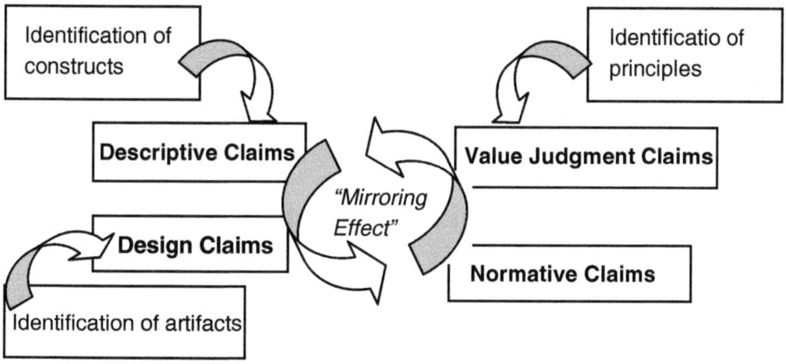

Fig. 1 The pivotal role of value judgment claims and of design claims between normative and descriptive claims

From an epistemological point of view, then, the distinction between normative and descriptive claims or statements is sound and clear. Attempts have been made to introduce a similar distinction between disciplines: according to this approach, there are descriptive disciplines or sciences, such as, for example, Physics or Biology, and normative disciplines or sciences, such as, for example, Architecture or Medicine. In this view, only normative disciplines are concerned with design (and value judgments). But, although authors supporting this idea are often very influential [2], I think that this view is epistemologically weak.

In fact, also the so-called "normative" disciplines develop descriptive claims, and also "descriptive" disciplines are engaged in design challenges: for example, an important stream of studies in Architecture is focused on the descriptive study of ancient construction patterns, whilst an important stream of studies in Physics is focused on the development of new-generation electric power stations.

Thus, I will not enter the debate about the "descriptive—versus—normative nature" of Organization Studies. I assume that our discipline, like all sciences, can host claims spanning from the former to the latter type. Moreover, as I will seek to demonstrate in the paragraphs below, I suggest that a more dynamic interaction between normative, design, value judgment and descriptive claims would be an important factor for scientific viability also for our discipline. Organization Studies, in fact, have been providing almost only descriptive claims so far [3].

In this theoretical paper, I will then concentrate on the possible role of Design Claims and Normative Claims in organization studies, from both an epistemological and a methodological point of view. I will refer to Medicine as a yardstick, since in this discipline the relationship between descriptive, design, value judgment and normative claims is well established, and rooted in a viable interaction between research and practice.

Research Questions:

(a) *Could the disciplinary tradition of Medicine inspire Organization Studies as for the interplay between Design Claims and Descriptive Claims?*

(b) *What are the main consequences of the lack of Design Claims in Organization Studies?*
(c) *What innovations in research methods are needed to enhance the contribution of Design Claims in Organization Studies?*

2 Artifacts and Design Claims: Definitions

In Design Claims, the key subject is the *artifact.*

The definition of artifact adopted here is borrowed from ecological and evolutionary studies: artifacts are prostheses of human knowledge [4], i.e., they are tangible or intangible human creations thanks to which human knowledge travels and evolves outside the individual human body [5]. For example, a hammer treasures a great amount of competences on materials and on ergonomic issues; an oral poem, like the Iliad, treasures oceans of knowledge on human psychology. This definition includes both the cultural, intangible artifacts that social and psychological studies usually focus on, and the tangible, technological artifacts that are usually at the core of design oriented approaches.

Human life develops within complex networks of people, artifacts and natural elements. *Artificial systems* are identifiable clusters in such networks: for example, a village is an artificial system including citizens, norms, buildings, a local language, a river, a climate, etc. [6].

Organizations are artificial systems where people create and use many artifacts. A great deal of organizational knowledge is included or embedded in them [7]. Important artifacts for organizational life include, for example, archives, procedures, norms, best practice models, process management frameworks, myths, rituals, beliefs, reward mechanisms, hierarchical structures, contracts, communication protocols, or IT tools.

Artifacts are never the "perfect" outcomes of dedicated, rational design processes: since they are subject to selective pressure and to continuous, opportunistic, extemporary exploitations and modifications, they result from evolutionary dynamics as well. In other words, an artifact is a child of its designer, on the one side, and of the endless chain of its artificial ancestors, on the other side. Once born and separated from its designer, it will go on its own path, being modified, directly or indirectly, by users and by the interactions with the environment.

In-depth understanding of artifacts, then, is a challenging issue: classical, "mechanical" processes of classification and description are often not sufficient to effectively identify a specific "Artifact of type A". A longitudinal, evolutionary understanding of the interactions between the ancestor artifacts, their designers and the (chain of) challenges they were confronted with throughout time is often necessary to understand the key features, the potentialities, the internal constraints of a class of artifacts.

Once identified, a class of artifacts can become the main character of those fruitful scientific claims, which were defined above as "Design Claims".

Typical structures of Design Claims are the following:

i. Under conditions Z, the adoption/use of artifact A is associated with the occurrence of phenomenon X, which in turn is associated with the occurrence of phenomenon Y.
ii. Under conditions Z, the adoption/use of artifact A influences the relationship between phenomenon X and phenomenon Y.
iii. Under conditions Z, phenomenon K influences the adoption/use of artifact A.

Adopting the well-known language of quantitative studies [8], we could say that:

- In case (i), phenomenon X mediates the relationship between the use of Artifact A and the outcome Y. An example of this kind of claim could be: "in a sample of US firms with more than 100 employees, the use of Artifact A (=a High Performance Work Practice model for HR) was found associated to diminished employee turnover and increased productivity, and then to increased financial performances" (elaborated from [9]).
- In case (ii), the use of Artifact A moderates the relationship between the predictor X and the outcome Y. An example of this kind of claim could be: "in a sample of manufacturing firms, the presence of Artifact A (=a strong organizational safety climate) was found associated to an attenuated relationship between job insecurity and accidents" (elaborated from [10]).
- In case (iii), the adoption/use of Artifact A is seen as the outcome of previous phenomena. An example of this kind of claim could be: "in companies adopting Artifact A (= Enterprise Resource Planning—ERP systems), mimetic pressures were found to have positively affected top management participation in Artifact A assimilation process, and top management participation, in turn, positively affected Artifact A usage within such companies" (elaborated from [11]).

3 The Pivotal Role of Design Claims in the Evolution of Scientific Research

The growing debate on Design Research, in which Information Systems studies play a pioneering role, stresses utility as the main goal of Design Research outcomes [12].

This insistence on utility probably stems from a reaction to the lack of relevance of many traditional Organization Studies outcomes, that our discipline must frankly admit [13]. Nevertheless, in this paragraph I will seek to demonstrate that not only are Design Claims potentially very useful for the world of practice, but they may also be powerful catalysts of innovative and non-trivial descriptive (and value judgment) research.

To do so, I will use a famous story, borrowed from the first book (originating from his doctoral thesis) of Louis-Ferdinand Céline [14].

3.1 *Doctor Semmelweis and the Outrageous Wash-Your-Hands Procedure*

In the first 1840s, there were two Obstetrical Clinics in the Vienna General Hospital. The two clinics admitted at alternate days, but the First Clinic had a bad reputation and women begged on their knees to be admitted to the Second Clinic. Many women even preferred to give birth in the streets if their delivery occurred in a day in which only the First Clinic admitted patients. A young Hungarian physician who worked at the First Clinic, Ignaz Semmelweis, focused on this problem. In the language of today's Organization Studies research, we could describe his first researches in the following way:

Puerperal fever researches: step 1
Research Outcome: Identification of a Normative Claim developed by users.
Research Method: Qualitative (interviews, participant observation).
"Women feel that it is better to give birth in the streets than in the First Clinic. They are really scared by the doctors of the First Clinic. They think that there is something wrong with the First Clinic: women die there."

Semmelweis studied the records and he found that those women were tragically right.

Puerperal fever researches: step 2
Research Outcome: Identification of a Descriptive Claim. Research Method: Quantitative (statistical analysis).
"Puerperal fever mortality rates are 150 % higher in the First Clinic than in the Second Clinic. Mortality rates of the First Clinic are remarkably higher than those of street deliveries, too."

Semmelweis was obsessed by the dilemma: what was wrong with the First Clinic? Some months after, a physician and friend of Semmelweis died few days after being accidentally injured by an autopsy tool during a post-mortem examination at the First Clinic. Semmelweis found that his friend's corpse displayed pathological features similar to those of puerperal fever. He then hypothesized that some "cadaverous particles" had caused both his friend's death, and the high mortality rates in the First Clinic. In fact, in the First Clinic, doctors used to perform obstetrical visits after performing autopsies, whilst in the Second Clinic women were visited and helped only by midwives, who were not engaged in autopsies. Sommelweis hypothesized that the invisible "cadaverous particles" could be removed by washing the doctors' hands with a chlorine solution, since this solution seemed capable to remove the "cadaverous smell".

Puerperal fever researches: step 3
Research Outcome: Identification of a Design Claim, type (i). Research Method: Quantitative (experiment).
"The adoption of the experimental procedure (all doctors of the First Clinic now wash their hands with chlorine solution before obstetrical visits), made the hygienic conditions of the First Clinic similar to those of the Second Clinic, and consequently the First Clinic mortality rates immediately dropped to levels similar to those of the Second Clinic."

A further statement obviously followed:

Puerperal fever researches: step 4
Research Outcome: Identification of a Value Judgment Claim. Research Method: Logical Deduction from Ethical Principles.
"Protecting women from the risks of puerperal fever is more important than avoiding the bother and the costs of washing hands with chlorine solution."

And then:

Puerperal fever researches: step 5
Research Outcome: Identification of a Normative Claim. Research Method: Deduction from previous claims.
"In obstetrical clinics, doctors who perform autopsies should wash their hands with chlorine solution before obstetrical visits."

But there was no theoretical explanation at that time for the hypothesis that doctors carried an invisible infection on their very skin or under their nails. So, since the idea that doctors were responsible for so many deaths was not pleasant, it was rejected. Semmelweis was dismissed from the Vienna hospital; after him, the procedure of washing hands was abandoned, and the mortality rates returned to tragic levels. He left Vienna and worked in two other hospitals, in Pest, where he instituted again chlorine washings, and obtained again impressive results. But the scientific community continued to reject his doctrine, which was weakened by the lack of an explanatory theoretical framework supporting it. Semmelweis started suffering from severe depression and died in a mental hospital, in 1865. The year after, Pasteur published the first of his major works: the germ theory of disease finally offered an in-depth explanatory description of the process against which Semmelweis had already found an effective solution.

Puerperal fever researches: step 6
Research Outcome: Identification of a Descriptive Claim. Research Method: Experiments.
"Living germs, invisible to the naked eye, cause infections if they are given the possibility to pass from infected to healthy bodies."

Puerperal fever researches: step 7
Research Outcome: Identification of a Normative Claim. Research Method: deduction from previous experiments, surveys, and ethical judgments.
"All medical personnel should wash carefully their hands with solutions and methods that are proven effective in destroying germs, before each and every visit."

3.2 Scientific Research as a Team Play

Doctor Semmelweis's story exemplarily illustrates how Design Claims and Descriptive Claims desperately need each other.

Semmelweis's Design Claim synthesized above in Step 3, although rejected by most Positivist members of the academic community of his times, raised fervent discussions on the basic concept of "contagion", put the bases for abandoning some then-mainstream theories (whose application caused epidemics of puerperal fever), and created strong motivations to find a sound explanation to the "outrageous effectiveness" of chlorine washings. When Pasteur and Koch eventually published their theories, synthesized above in Step 6, they found a world that was eager to listen to them, also thanks to Sommelweis's work. Many hospitals, thus, adopted the prescription synthesized in Step 7, and it was then possible to conduct precise large-scale surveys to soundly confirm the germ theory of disease.

I then suggest that the sole descriptive claims may be sufficient to keep a research stream viable only if they do not consider phenomena subject to value judgments (like, for example, in studies on the Big Bang).

In all the other cases, I suggest that science should be a team play, where Descriptive Claims, Design Claims, Value Judgement Claims and Normative Claims are players cooperating for the same final goal: they should all take to the field, they should all be given the possibility to play; they should keep themselves continuously aware of the position of their team-mates in the play field, and they should be willing to "pass the ball" of the research state-of-the-art from each other.

I also suggest that, in this team, Design Claims play a pivotal role. In fact, Design Claims are disrespectful mirrors that may suddenly force theories to know their own limits.

Here are some examples of how Design Claims can "pass the ball" to Descriptive research:

- How do you explain that I *can* build phenomenon Y by using an artifact A, even if this should be impossible according to your theory?
- How do you explain that I *cannot* build phenomenon Y, even if I used an artifact A under conditions Z, consistently with your theory?
- Look, I used artifact A (e.g., a normative claim, "wash your hands"), which is soundly consistent with your theory, and I could build phenomenon Y as predicted: your theory is corroborated.

The key point is *that scientific claims themselves are artifacts.*

So, it is possible to test their validity (their capability to "tell the truth") by longitudinally studying the successes and failures of the subjects (e.g., organizations) purposefully adopting them. For example, if a company adopts procedures (normative statements) and/or beliefs (descriptive statements) which are consistent with a certain theory, and then the company experiences changes in its performances, it is possible to study this dynamic phenomenon as a quasi-experiment that corroborates/falsifies the involved theory. In a similar way, if an organization adopts an artifact that is not directly a scientific claim, but can be considered an expression or a consequence of it (for example, the company adopts a certain specific Information System consistent with a certain theory of Supply Chain Management), studies on the consequences of this adoption may result in interesting theoretical advancements.

Thus, this paper asserts that Design Claims are important not only for enhancing the relevance of the discipline to the world of practice, but also in order to enhance the rigor, viability and dynamism of its descriptive outcomes.

4 "Artifact Blindness" and Loss of the "Mirroring Effect": Aspects of the Lack of Design Claims in Organization Studies

Many organizational changes are triggered by artifacts, when e.g., new models, or new rules, or new IT tools, or new communication styles are adopted. Nevertheless, the consequences of the adoption of a specific organizational artifact are rarely at the core of Organization Studies claims. Moreover, our discipline tends to dedicate different levels of attention to intangible organizational artifacts, on the one side, and to tangible organizational artifacts, on the other side.

4.1 "Tangible" Organizational Artifacts in Organization Studies

Organizational scholars often come from economics/social sciences backgrounds, and tend to be scarcely interested in the numerous tangible artifacts that shape organizational life, such as, for example, buildings, IT tools, or technological infrastructures. Artifacts of this type are often perceived as technological "givens", out of the focus of social studies, and consequently they are almost never specifically described in Organization Studies.

For example, around the year 2000 many scholars were concerned by the fact that it seemed hard to establish a clear correlation between a generic construct "IT adoption" and organizational performances [15]. The specific characteristics of the IT artifacts in which investment had been made were not considered worth of description [16]. If we looked at these research efforts with the eyes of Semmelweis, maybe we would feel uneasy.

Semmelweis would not be really interested in claiming "there is a relationship between the hospital's hygiene and mortality rates performances". *What* hygiene? The claim must be more specific. Doctors must wash their hands (which is more important, say, than washing the hospital's floors), before every visit (and not, say, every evening) with chlorine solution and careful nail brushing (and not, say, with scented soap). In other words: *the artifact matters*. What specific artifact is adopted by an organization, under certain conditions, can make the difference. How can we investigate, for example, the relationship between IT adoption and organizational performance if we don't understand "what specific IT" we are talking about? [16]

This "blindness" towards tangible artifacts in Organization Studies may be partially explained by the fear of losing disciplinary identity. In fact, the reasons why a certain tangible artifact works (or not) are often understandable with the help of another discipline only. For example, it is Computer Science that may explain some of the reasons why a certain IT artifact gives a competitive advantage. As a consequence, many Organization Science scholars prefer to protect their disciplinary identity and to avoid the inter-disciplinary contamination implied in artifact analysis. When a discipline is young and still not completely self-confident, such fears may influence the researchers' choices.

We suggest that this "artifact blindness" hinders the healthy development of Design Claims, and then makes the "scientific team play" between different types of claims more difficult in our discipline. As a consequence, also the incisiveness and dynamism of Descriptive Claims is negatively affected.

4.2 "Intangible" Organizational Artifacts in Organization Studies

Intangible organizational artifacts, such as procedures, norms, beliefs, customs, policies, managerial models, institutional traditions etc., are of course more familiar to Organization Studies scholars [17] than the tangible/technological artifacts described in the paragraph above.

As a consequence, in this case there are not those inter-disciplinary difficulties that may hinder the creation of specific Design Claims when the artifact is tangible.

Nevertheless, proper Design Claims of the types described in Paragraph 1 (structure types i, ii and iii) are, again, quite rare. Even intangible artifacts tend to be considered as "givens", and actively linking them to performances does not seem to be at the core of organizational scholars' interests.

As a consequence, Descriptive Claims are much, much more frequent than Design Claims in our discipline. The typical statement in our discipline is, for example, *"inter-organizational trust influences negotiation processes and exchange performances"* (synthesized from [18]). Statements capable to complement such a descriptive general statement with a more specific, artifact-focused claim, like "under conditions Z, the adoption of artifact A (e.g., a certain type of belief, a certain type of communication tool, a certain type of reward/punishment norm) can enhance inter-organizational trust, which in turn influences negotiation processes and exchange performances" are almost absent. It is just as if Semmelweis stopped at Step 2, just stating that being admitted at the First Clinic made the probabilities of deadly infections higher!

The negative consequences of this scarcity of Design Claims not only include the perceived relevance of the outcomes of our discipline, but also its scientific vivacity.

In fact, many intangible organizational artifacts, such as e.g., models, procedures, or beliefs, may be built or fine-tuned or made famous by scholarly research: if the scholarly community renounces to assess the performances resulting from the adoption of such models, procedures or beliefs, an important possibility of scientific advancement gets lost.

So far, few Organization Studies publications have been studying how the adoption of a theory-rooted belief, or model, or procedure influences organizational phenomena. Models and frameworks developed in Organization Studies often result in epistemological dead ends: once emanated, their specific influence in the real world is not object of further interest. It is just as if Medicine scholars, after developing a theory on a certain health issue, were not interested in measuring how the adoption of that specific theory and consequent health care protocol in the world of practice performed.

I then suggest that the lack of such "mirroring effect" provided by the interplay between Design and Descriptive Claims severely narrows our discipline's potentialities.

5 Some Methodological Proposals for Design Claim Oriented Research in Organization Studies

5.1 Some Proposals for Quantitative Researches

Cross-sectional surveys (based on regression analysis) on samples of similar organizations are the most consolidated research method in Organization Studies.

But this kind of investigation may not be the ideal one to understand the effects of artifact adoption, and then it may be difficult to yield good Design Claims on the basis of this methodological approach. In fact, the process of artifact adoption and use develops throughout time along co-evolutionary paths, where previous constraints and context conditions play a key role. The "horizontal cut" provided by cross-sectional surveys may be scarcely effective in highlighting the vertical dimension of such a process. For example, in a famous paper Rafaeli and Sutton [19] focused on the consequences of the adoption of a new artifact in a chain of stores. The new artifact was a procedural norm for shop assistants: "always smile

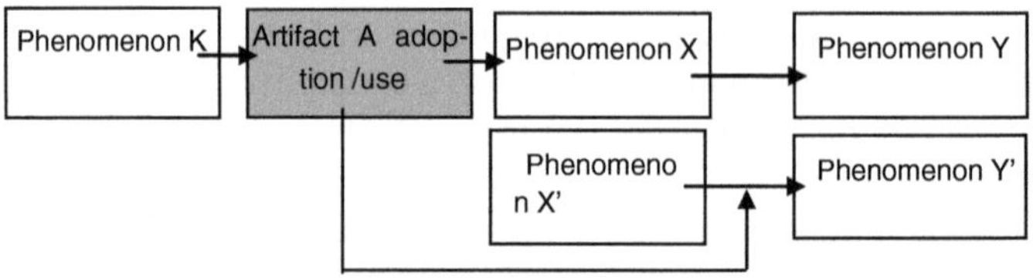

Fig. 2 Artifact adoption and use can be fruitfully considered as a mediator, as a moderator, as a predictor and as an outcome in quantitative hypotheses

and kindly answer to the customers' questions". Rafaeli and Sutton measured the level of compliance to this norm in several stores, and then compared the performances of stores where the compliance was higher (shop assistants smiled a lot) with the economic performances of stores where the compliance was lower. They where surprised to find that the performance was higher in shops where shop assistants smiled less. They concluded that the adoption of the "smile policy" negatively affected the performances.

But this conclusion appears weak to a design-claim educated eye. In fact, Rafaeli and Sutton just compared the "horizontal" performances of the different shops. They collected their measurements only once, and only after the adoption of the "smile policy". Should a shop have displayed an impressive improvement in its individual performances after the adoption of the policy, Rafaeli and Sutton could not have noticed it: data on previous years' performances were not even included in the list of Control Variables.

In a nutshell: *scholars adopting quantitative approaches and interested in Design Claims should take into consideration also alternative methods, different from traditional surveys. Longitudinal quasi-experiments, conducted by keeping under strict control the context conditions and the evolutionary development of artifact adoption and use, are probably a good option. The tradition of crossover studies for example, which has been soundly developed in Psychology and Medicine, could be a useful reference point.*

The framework synthetically representing the rich quantitative research fields opened by Design Claim Testing is provided in Fig. 2.

5.2 Some Proposals for Qualitative Researches

An important contribution to the building and fine-tuning of Design Claims (and consequently of Normative Claims) may come from Qualitative Research tradition, too. Qualitative studies, in fact, are already used to long-term, in-depth longitudinal studies; moreover, qualitative researchers' refined capabilities in extracting concepts from users and practitioners may provide the discipline with valuable tools to overcome the "artifact blindness" that affects our scholarly community. In other words, most key steps to identify the constructs effectively describing organizational artifacts may come from qualitative studies.

On the other side, qualitative researchers usually come from a psycho-sociological background, and then they tend to be scarcely interested in artifacts, especially the tangible ones. Such scholars usually consider artifacts as "givens" and concentrate on nuances of social negotiations and emotional interactions. This scarce interest towards artifacts is very frequent even among researchers who are strongly oriented to participate in organizational innovation processes, such as Action Research oriented scholars [13]. Nevertheless, there is a growing awareness on the role of artifacts in social interactions: for example, the physical characteristics of the workplace, or the triggering effects of some specific Internet tools, are raising growing interest, so complementing the traditional customs of behaviorist social science [20].

In a nutshell: scholars adopting qualitative approaches should use the potentialities of their methods to concentrate also on understanding organizational artifacts as evolving human "prostheses", which play a key role in organizational social interactions. A valuable contribution on the part of qualitative research would be, for example, the identification of the key artifact features perceived by artifact creators and/or users: this may allow to understand how organizational artifacts are granularly classified and defined by those who interact with them.

6 Conclusions, Limitations and Further Research

Design Claims were defined in this paper as scientific statements focusing on the antecedents and consequences of the adoption/use of specific artifacts. Artifacts were understood as prostheses of human knowledge, subject to evolution and to social dynamics within complex systems, such as organizations or competitive markets. Organizational artifacts may be both tangible (e.g., IT tools or TLC infrastructures) and intangible (e.g., procedures, norms, models, traditions). This paper took Medicine as a disciplinary yardstick and sought to demonstrate that a major presence of Design Claims in Organization Studies would enhance not only the relevance of our discipline to the world of practice, but also its scientific vivacity and rigor, thanks to the "mirroring effect" resulting from the interplay between Descriptive, Design and Normative Claims.

This paper also briefly focused on the fact that Design Claims put out novel methodological challenges both to qualitative and quantitative research traditions. In particular, cross-sectional surveys, which are the favourite research method of quantitative scholars, may be not optimal for investigating the longitudinal process of artifact adoption, that may rather require, for example, crossover approaches. The qualitative tradition of Action Research, on the other side, given its strong rooting in social sciences traditions, has been scarcely used to focus on artifacts so far. As a consequence, an enhanced role of Design Claims in our discipline calls for methodological innovations in Organization Studies.

References

1. Adler, M. (1985). *Ten philosophical mistakes*. New York: MacMillan.
2. Simon, H. (1969). *The sciences of the artificial* (1st ed.). Cambridge, Mass: MIT Press.
3. Richard, L., Daft, R. L., Arie, Y., & Lewin, A. Y. (1990). Can organization studies begin to break out of the normal science straitjacket? An editorial essay. *Organization Science, 1*(1), 1–9.
4. De Marco, M., Fiocca, R., & Ricciardi, F. (2010). The ecology of learning-by-building: Bridging design science and natural history of knowledge. In R. Winter, J. L. Zhao, S. Aier (Eds.), *Global perspectives on design science research. 5th international conference, DESRIST 2010*, St. Gallen, Switzerland.
5. Lorenz, K. (1973). *Behind the mirror. A search for a natural history of human knowledge*. New York: Harcourt Brace.
6. Jackson, M. C. (2000). *Systems approaches to management*. London: Springer.
7. Bateson, G. (1979). *Mind and nature: A necessary unity*. New York: Ballantine.
8. Baron, R. M., & Kenny, D. A. (1986). The moderator–mediator variable distinction in social psychological research: Conceptual, strategic, and statistical considerations. *Journal of Personality and Social Psychology, 51*(6), 1173–1182.
9. Huselid, M. A. (1995). The impact of human resources management practices on turnover, productivity and corporate financial performances. *Academy of Management Journal, 38*(3), 365–872.
10. Probst, T. M. (2004). Safety and insecurity: Exploring the moderating effect of organizational safety climate. *Journal of Occupational Health Psychology, 9*(1), 3–10.
11. Liang, H., Saraf, N., Hu, O., & Xue Y. (2007). Assimilation of enterprise systems: the effect of institutional pressures and the mediating role of top management. *MIS Quarterly, 31*(1), 59–87.
12. Österle, H. et al. (2010). Memorandum on design-oriented information systems research. *European Journal of Information Systems, 20*(1), 7–10.
13. Baskerville, R. L. (1999). Investigating Information Systems with action research. *Communications of the AIS Archive, 2*(3es).
14. Céline, L. F. (1937). The life and work of semmelweis, tr. by Robert Allerton Parker. Boston: Little, Brown and Company.
15. Ray, G., Muhanna, W. A., & Barney, J. B. (2005). Information technology and the performance of the customer service process: A resource-based analysis. *MIS Quarterly, 29*(4), 625–652.
16. Orlikowski, W., & Iacono, C. (2001). Desperately seeking the "IT" in IT research—a call to theorizing the IT artifact. *Information Systems Research, 12*(2), 121–134.
17. Schein, E. H. (1990). Organizational culture. *American Psychologist, 45*(2), 109–119.
18. Zaheer, A., McEvily, B., & Perrone, V. (1998). Does trust matter? Exploring the effects of interorganizational and interpersonal trust on performance. *Organization Science*, 9(2), 141–159.
19. Rafaeli, A., & Sutton, R. I. (1987). Expression of emotion as part of the work role. *The Academy of Management Review, 12*(1), 23–37.
20. Gagliardi, P. (Ed.). (1990). *Symbols and artifacts: Views of the corporate landscape*. Berlin: De Gruyter.

Design Science Research as Movement Between Individual and Generic Situation-Problem–Solution Spaces

Ilia Bider, Paul Johannesson and Erik Perjons

Abstract Design science is an emerging research paradigm in the Information Systems area. A design science project typically includes the activities of problem analysis, requirements definition, artifact development, and evaluation. These activities are not to be seen as sequential but can be carried out in any order. The purpose of this paper is to propose a conceptualization and formalization of design science research that show the possible ways in which a design science project can be carried out. The proposal is based on the state oriented view on business processes and suggests that design science research can be viewed as movements in a space of situations, problems and solutions.

Keywords Design science · Information systems · Business process

1 Introduction

1.1 Motivation

Design science is an emerging research paradigm in the Information Systems (IS) area. To make design science more widely accessible, there is a need for clear

I. Bider · P. Johannesson (✉) · E. Perjons
Department of Computer and Systems Sciences (DSV), Stockholm University, Stockholm, Sweden
e-mail: pajo@dsv.su.se

I. Bider
e-mail: ilia@dsv.su.se

E. Perjons
e-mail: perjons@dsv.su.se

R. Baskerville et al. (eds.), *Designing Organizational Systems*,
Lecture Notes in Information Systems and Organisation 1,
DOI: 10.1007/978-3-642-33371-2_3,

guidelines on how to use it, which are targeted at students and young researchers as well as experienced researchers accustomed to other ways of conducting research. One of the main issues that research students need to understand is that a research process can be conducted in many alternative ways while still staying within the design science paradigm.

The main way of presenting results of research of the design science type is starting from a situation, presenting the identified problem, setting the requirements, describing the solution, presenting the results of tests whether the solution solves the problem in the given situation, or/and a set of similar situations [1]. If the test shows that the solution does not solve the problem, it is redesigned, and tested again. Even when it is not explicitly stated that this sequence was the actual order in which the research was conducted, this kind of presentation may create an impression that this is how the research actually was done in real-life, which is often far from the case.

One problem to be solved when creating guidelines for conducting design science research is how to determine where in the process the researcher is at a given moment, and what are the alternatives to proceed. The goal of this chapter is to propose a solution to this problem. More exactly, we propose a kind of a map which helps the researcher to identify his/her position in the design science process, and explicitly shows the possible ways that are open for the researcher to continue. This "map" is aimed to serve as a foundation for creating practical guidelines on design science research in the future.

1.2 Design Science in Information Systems Research

Design science research [1–3] is related to finding new solutions for problems known or unknown [4]. To count as related to research, a solution should be of a generic nature, i.e., applicable not only to one unique situation, but to a class of similar situations. A generic solution for real-life problems cannot be proven in a formal way, but requires testing via implementation of the solution in one or more situations and investigation whether it solves the intended problem or not. The solidness of the verification, of course, depends on the number of implementations, and the diversity of situations in which the solution has been tested. However, the first step always is to implement and verify a generic solution in at least one situation. In the literature, this is called demonstration [1].

There is a substantial difference between design science on one hand and wide spread qualitative and quantitative empirical methods [5] on the other. The latter are aimed to investigate real life situations as is, or as they were at some point in the past, and find commonalities between them which can give rise to a theory that explains the current or past state of affairs. Focusing on the present and past also allows employing statistical methods as there is a possibility to gather information on many similar real-life situations, insuring that the size of a sample is sufficiently large for relying on statistical methods.

Focusing on the present and past in such a dynamic area as IS has a major drawback. Such a focus means that research follows the industry/practice and explains its successes and failures rather than showing new ways to proceed. Design science research with its focus on generic problem solving tries to overcome this drawback. This kind of research can be considered as an activity aimed at generating and testing hypotheses about future solutions. Therefore, demonstration is a critical part of design science, as it shows whether a hypothesis is worth adoption or needs to be discarded or improved.

Design science research, on its own, cannot provide sufficient evidence in favor of a hypothesis. It can only demonstrate that it could work in one or several specific situations. The real proof comes when and if the industry/practice adopts the solution, which generates sufficiently many examples of its usage in real life, so that standard empirical methods can be employed to prove or disprove the hypothesis generated by design science. Therefore, design science research cannot be placed in the same category as standard empirical methods, but should be regarded as complimentary to them.

Summarizing the above deliberations, we agree with [2] that design science represents a distinct research paradigm—generating hypotheses on how the future could look like and making initial filtering of them in order to remove hypotheses not worth of pursuing. IS is not the only field within the social sciences where design science research is applicable. Marxist theory, when it first emerged, can be said to have followed the design science approach by proposing a solution for all the evils of capitalism, though it failed to produce even one demonstration where this solution would work. The difference of IS from other fields in the social sciences is the greater dynamics of the IS industry/practice, where new solutions are introduced and tested all the time. This gives a greater opportunity for design science research to take a leading position in this field.

1.3 Artifacts in IS Design Science Research

As was mentioned in the previous subsection, design science concerns generic solutions, not the individual ones. A generic solution is always a template that can be adjusted to a specific situation to which the solution is to be applied. This template can be defined in different ways, e.g., as a model, or as a method that shows how to transform the original situation to a new and better one. In design science literature such a template is often referred to as to an (scientific) artifact. We call this artifact a primary artifact.

In addition to the primary artifacts, design science research in IS may include secondary artifacts inherent to the field of Information Systems. In essence, IS investigates technology enabled human organizations and practices, to which nowadays belong any private company, public administration, interest organization, or a bunch of youngsters playing an interactive game with each other. Thus, IS is tightly connected to the technological artifacts (e.g., an ERP system or an e-service) used to tie together technologically enabled organizations and practices. IS deals with both development and use of such technological artifacts. A generic solution in IS is often built around some technological artifact, e.g., the solution includes the development and/or introduction in organizational practice of some type of an IT-system. We refer to such technological artifacts as secondary artifacts.

In this paper, we do not investigate various types of primary and secondary artifacts. Instead, the discussion is conducted in terms of individual and generic solutions, while artifacts are referred to only in the explanatory examples. An individual solution concerns a specific situation which disappears as soon as an attempt to solve it has been made, and, normally, cannot be restored. A generic solution can be applied to many real-life situations, and thus can be tested more than once.

1.4 Moving Between the Two Worlds

As explained in Sect. 1.2 , design science research aims at generating and testing generic solutions for various problems. To do that, a researcher needs to move in and between two worlds: the world of real situations and real solutions, and the world of generic (abstract) situations and solutions. The movements in these two worlds cannot be totally independent of each other; movement in one world needs to be coordinated with movement in the other world.

There is no fixed way in which the movement inside and between the two worlds should be accomplished. One can start with designing a new solution for a known problem and then design a generic solution based on it, using the individual solution as an example. One can also start from the opposite pole—design a generic solution for the problem unknown and search for a situation where such generic solution can be applied to transform this situation to a better one.

The goal of this paper is not to prescribe the way to conduct research, but define a "map" that includes both worlds. The map is aimed at helping the researcher to plan his/her movements inside and between the worlds, and find a way out when a kind of dead end is reached. For example, if a generic solution does not work very well in a situation where it should, the researcher does not need to rush to discard the solution, or try to modify it. He/she can instead try to find some other type of situations, or other problems where the solution fits better.

The rest of the paper is structured in the following way. In Sect. 2, we introduce a number of quasi-formal notions, with the help of which we can define the meaning of design science research and the ways it could be conducted. In Sect. 3, we discuss in which circumstances individual problem solving gives opportunities for design science research. In Sect. 4, we discuss examples of a research that aims at finding a generic solution from the beginning. Section 4.1 discusses a case where a researcher moves to the world of generic situation/solutions in order to find a solution for a problem in a particular real-life situation. The individual

Fig. 1 Individual SPS-space

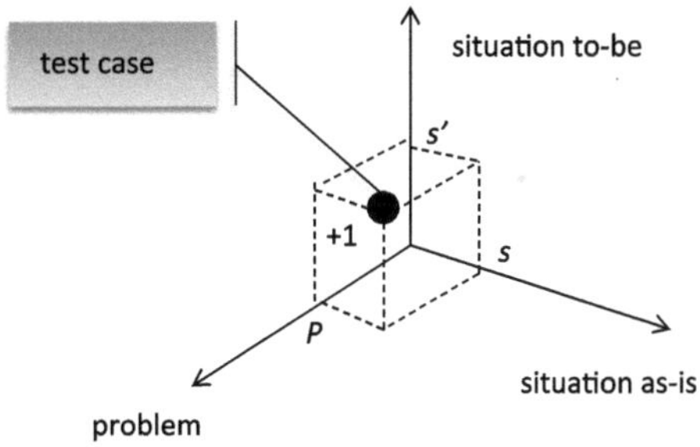

solution is then obtained by instantiation of the newly designed generic solution. In Sect. 4.2, we discuss a case where research starts from finding a generic solution and proceeds to finding a situation where it could be applied. Section 5 reviews related works. Section 6 is devoted to the discussion of the material presented. Section 7 presents plans for future work.

2 Formalizing Design Science Research

In this section we present a set of notions that leads to a quasi-formal definition of design science research. These notions will be used in the next sections to explain the ways of how design science research could be conducted. The formalization is done along the following lines. As the first step, we introduce a space for individual (specific) problem solving as consisting of three dimensions: *situation as-is*, *situation to-be*, and *problem*, see Fig. 1. A point $< s, s', P >$ in this space is called a test case. A weight of $\pm$ 1 is assigned to a test case according to the following rule:

- +1 is assigned if transforming situation s into s' solves problem P. In this case s' is said to be a solution for problem P in situation s.
- -1 is assigned otherwise.

As the next step, we introduce a space for generic problem solving as consisting of three dimensions: *generic situation as-is*, *generic situation to-be*, and *generic problem*, see Fig. 2. We consider that a generic situation (as-is or to-be) is represented by some kind of a template (t or t') that defines a set of similar situations, the template serving as an extension of this set. A point $< t, t', GP >$ in this space is called a hypothesis.

As the third step we establish correspondence between the two spaces based on the following rule test case $< s, s', P >$ serves as representation (or instantiation) of hypothesis $< t, t', GP >$ if situation as-is s belongs to the generic situation as-is defined by template t, situation to-be s' belongs to the generic situation to-be defined by template t', and problem P belongs to the generic problem GP, see Fig. 3.

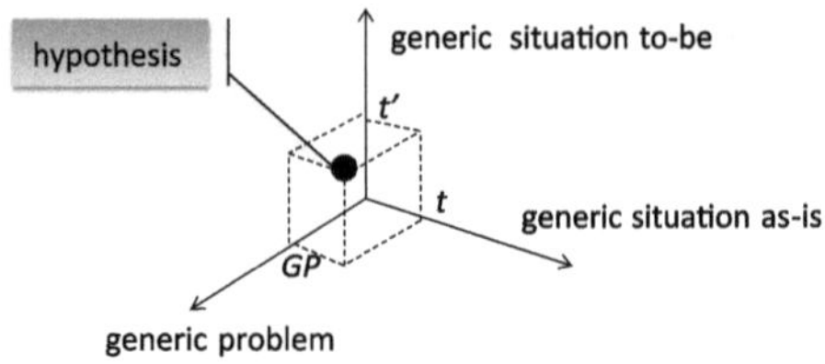

Fig. 2 Generic SPS-space

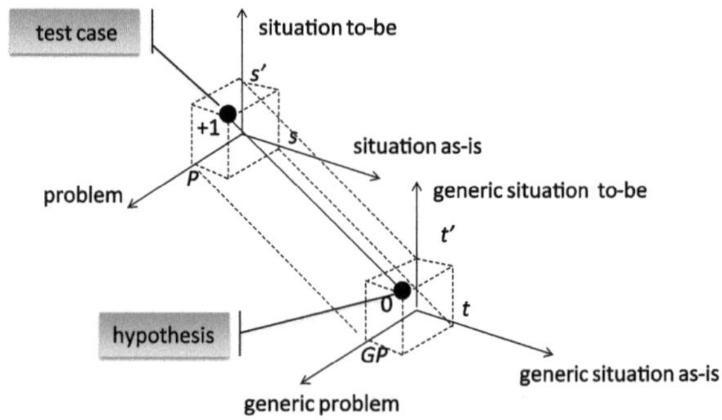

Fig. 3 Correspondence between the spaces

Based on the correspondence between the two spaces, we can assign a weight to a hypothesis according to the following rule:

- -1, if there is a test case $< s, s', P >$ with weight -1 that represents the given hypothesis $< t, t', GP >$. In this case, we say that t' cannot serve as a generic solution for generic problem *GP* in generic situation *t*.
- 0 if there is one or few test cases $< s, s', P >$ with weight +1 that represent the given hypothesis $< t, t', GP >$. In this case, we call t' a potential generic solution for generic problem *GP* in generic situation *t*.
- +1 if there are many test cases $< s, s', P >$ with weight +1 that represent the given hypothesis $< t, t', GP >$. In this case, we call t' a verified solution for generic problem *GP* in generic situation *t*.

In the following Sects. 2.1–2.3, we will explain the three steps above in more details.

2.1 Individual Problem Solving Space

We define a *situation* as a "state of affairs or combination of circumstances" in a particular part of the world. A situation has some structure, but we are not interested in details of it in this paper. As an example of a situation consider the following:

"activities at the sales office of SoftMotors in Stockholm", where SoftMotors is an imaginary company.

Denote the set of all possible situations s as S. S includes all situations that are in effect now, the ones that happened in the past, and the ones that could be imagined in the future.

Transformation of situation s (situation as-is) into situation s' (situation to-be) is called *implementation* of s' in s, and is denoted $s' \leftarrow s$.

As soon as the transformation happens, the original situation becomes part of the past, and the new one changes the status of being imaginary (possible) to becoming part of the present. We consider that this transformation is, normally, not reversible, i.e., the old situation cannot be restored, and thus no other transformation can be applied to it. For example, if SoftMotors fires all their sales staff and hire engineers to conduct sales activities instead, we consider the old situation as not reachable. Even if the old staff is rehired, probably, their trust in SoftMotors management will not remain the same.

Completing implementation is associated with *costs* in effort and time. The closer situation s' is to s, the smaller is the cost of transformation. It is impossible to define the concept of closeness in strict terms for a general case. In this paper, we just consider that the more s and s' share the same elements and internal structure, the closer they are, which potentially leads to lower costs of implementing s' in s. For example, the result of introducing a CRM (Customer Relationship Management) system at the sales office of SoftMotors (without changing its staff) can be considered as relatively close to the original situation in which there was no CRM system in place.

We also consider that there is some limitation on the "length" of a possible transformation). For example, we may consider that a situation in which SoftMotors sales office changes their sales people to engineers as reachable, but the sales office becoming the engineering department as unreachable. Note, that a situation not reachable in one transformation may be reachable is several consecutive transformations over time. Denote the set of situations reachable from s as $R(\mathrm{s})$.

A *problem* P is a set of situations ($P \subset S$) considered to be undesirable from some point of view. As an example, suppose that in the sales office of SoftMotors, each sales person works on his/her own and never coordinates his/her work with the colleagues. Management considers this situation as a problem, as prospects could be lost when a sales person pursuing it becomes temporarily (sick) or permanently (leaves the company) unavailable. Formally, this problem can be defined as a set of situations in which

the progress of pursuing a prospect in the sales office of SoftMotors in Stockholm is visible only to one sales person.

Let P be a problem, then for each situation s that belongs to P ($s \in P$) we say that situation s has problem P, or there is a problem P in situation s.[1] Denote the set of all possible problems P as Π.[2]

A *solution* for a problem P in situation s ($s \in P$) is a situation s' such that s' does not have problem P, i.e. $s' \notin P$. An example of a solution to the problem above is a situation in which:

> all activities related to pursuing a prospect in the sales office of SoftMotors in Stockholm are registered in CRM system *Oracle on demands* and are made visible to all members of the staff

We call a solution s' *justifiable* if the cost of the implementation is reasonable with respect to the seriousness of the problem P in s that the solution is aimed to solve.[3]

We call a solution s' *acceptable* if it does not contain any other major problem that is not present in s. For example, the CRM system to be implemented is so difficult to use that all current sales staff will not be able to handle it, and everybody leaves.

Testing s' as an acceptable solution for a problem P in s means implementing s' in s and verifying that:

- s' is justifiable for P in s,
- s' is really a solution for s, i.e., $s' \notin P$, and
- s' is acceptable, i.e., does not include other major problems.

A space with dimensions S (situation-as-is), S (situation-to-be), Π (problem) of the kind in Fig. 1 is called a Situation-Problem–Solution space, or *SPS-space* for short. A point $< s, s', P >$ in the SPS-space is called a *test case*. Testing s' as a solution for problem P in situation s is considered as assigning a weight to the test case $< s, s', P >$ in the SPS-space according to the following rule:

- Weight +1 is assigned in the case s' showed to be *justifiable* and *acceptable* solution for problem P in situation s,
- Weight −1 is assigned otherwise.

---

[1] The problem can be defined in very broad terms, however, for all practical purposes only the intersection between the problem P and a set of situations reachable from s, $R(s)$ is important for any given situation s.

[2] $\Pi \subset P(S)$, where $P(S)$ is the set of all subsets of set S.

[3] Obviously, the first sign of "justifiable" is being "reachable", i.e. $s' \in R(s)$.

2.2 Generic Problem Solving Space

A set of situations with similar internal structure is called a *generic situation* or *g-situation* for short, and is denoted as *GS*. As an example of g-situation, consider "Activities at sales offices of all companies in Stockholm", or "Activities at sales offices of all companies all over the world". The set of all possible g-situations is denoted as Σ.

As a criterion of similarity for situations in a g-situation, we consider existence of a *pattern/template t* that can be found in the internal structure of each situation that belongs to the given g-situation. Denote all possible templates as T. We consider a pattern/template to be a sentence in some formal language that includes variables and constants. Continuing the example from Sect. 2.1, we can create several templates of situations:

1. Activities at sales office of company x located at Stockholm
2. Activities at sales office of company x located at y
3. Activities at sales office of company x located at y such that the progress of pursuing a prospect is visible only to one sales person
4. Activities at sales office of company x located at y not using any CRM system
5. Activities at sales office of company x located at y using *CRM on demand* from Oracle to make the progress of pursuing a prospect visible to all members of staff
6. Activities at sales office of company x located at y using CRM system from Salesforce to make the progress of pursuing a prospect visible to all members of staff
7. Activities at sales office of company x located at y using CRM system c to make the progress of pursuing a prospect visible to all members of staff

We consider that all templates are constructed from a universal set of variables V. For example, in template (1–8) above, variable x stays for a company.[4]

Assigning each variable $v \in V$ a value is called a mapping. Denote a set of all possible mappings as M. Let $m \in M$ be a mapping and $t \in T$ a template, then situation s obtained from t by substituting variables in t with values according to m is called instantiation of t via m, and is denoted as $s = t(m)$.

The example considered in Sect. 2.1 is an instantiation of template (2) above, where map $m = \{x = SoftMotors, y = Stockholm\}$.

A class of situations defined by template t is denoted as $GS(t)$, $GS(t) = \{s = t(m) \mid m \in M\}$; in other words, $GS(t)$ includes all possible instantiations of template t.

A pair of templates t', t defines a class of transformation $\{s' \leftarrow s \mid s' = t'(m), s = t(m), m \in M\}$. We will call such class a generic transformation, or

[4] Existence of a template presumes existence of an algorithm that generates all situations that belong to a given template t by assigning values to the variables of the template.

g-transformation for short, and denote it as $t' \leftarrow t$. A g-transformation $t' \leftarrow t$ defines a transformation for each situation s from $GS(t)$ into a situation s' from $GS(t')$.

Using templates (1–7) above, we can define the following generic transformations:

(5) ← (4), (6) ← (4), (7) ← (4), (6) ← (5).

The first three transformations, (5) ← (4), (6) ← (4), (7) ← (4), refer to introducing a CRM system where it did not exist, the last one, (6) ← (5), refers to changing the existing CRM system from Oracle to Salesforce.

A problem that exists in all instances of some generic situation is called a generic problem and is denoted as GP. Formally, we can define a generic problem as follows: let $GS(t) \in \Sigma$ be a g-situation and $GP \in \Pi$ be a problem such that $GS(t) \subseteq GP$, then we say that g-situation $GS(t)$ has (generic) problem GP, or there is a (generic) problem GP in g-situation $GS(t)$.[5]

A *generic solution* or *g-solution* for short for a (generic) problem GP in g-situation $GS(t)$ ($GS(t) \subset GP$) defined by template t is a template t', such that $GS(t') \cap GP = \varnothing$. In other words, all situations that belong to $GS(t')$ do not have problem GP.

For example, templates (5), (6), (7) represent generic solutions for the generic problem defined by template (3) in situation (4).

A g-solution $GS(t')$ is called *justifiable* for $GS(t)$ if for each $m \in M$, $t'(m)$ is justifiable for situation $t(m)$. In the same way, a g-solution $GS(t')$ is called *acceptable* if for each $m \in M$, $t'(m)$ is acceptable solution for problem GP in situation $t(m)$.[6]

A space with dimensions T (template for g-situation as-is), T (template for g-situation to-be), Π (generic problem) of the kind in Fig. 2 is called a generic Situation-Problem–Solution space, or generic *SPS-space* for short. A point $< t, t', GP >$ in the generic SPS-space is called a *hypothesis*.

We say that test case $< s, s', P >$ corresponds to the hypothesis $< t, t', GP >$ if there exists a mapping $m \in M$ such that $s = t(\mathrm{m})$ and $s' = t'(\mathrm{m})$ and $R(s) \cap P = R(s) \cap GP$, which is illustrated in Fig. 3. We also say that test case $< s, s', P >$ represents hypothesis $< t, t', GP >$, or hypothesis $< t, t', GP >$ generalizes test case $< s, s', P >$, and denote this fact as $< s, s', P > \Leftrightarrow < t, t', GP >$.

Let $< s, s', P >$ be a test case that represents hypothesis $< t, t', GP >$, i.e., $< s, s', P > \Leftrightarrow < t, t', GP >$, to which weight +1 has been assigned. Then we call $< s, s', P >$ a *demonstration* for template t' to be an acceptable g-solution for generic problem GP in g-situation $GS(t)$.

Let $< t, t', GP >$ be a hypothesis, and r be a representative sets of corresponding test cases such that $r = \{< s, s', P > \mid < s, s', P > \Leftrightarrow < t, t', GP >$, and

---

[5] Using templates, $GS(t)$ has a problem GP if for each $m \in M$, $t(m) \in GP$.

[6] Note that our notion of solution template roughly corresponds to the idea of artifact widely used in the design science literature [2, 3].

for each pair $< s_1, s'_1, p_1 >, < s_2, s'_2, p_2 > \in r, s_1 \neq s_2\}$ and to each test case $< s, s', P > \in r$ weight +1 has been assigned. Then we call r a *verification* for t' being an acceptable g-solution for generic problem GP in g-situation $GS(t)$. We will not try to clarify the meaning of *representative* set, just assuming that the larger is the set the more solid is verification.[7]

Now, we can assign weights to the hypothesis $< t, t', GP >$ from the generic SPS-space. This is done according to the following rule:

- Positive weight of +1 is assigned if there is a *verification* for template t' to be an acceptable g-solution for problem GP in g-situation $GS(t)$.
- Negative weight of -1 is assigned if there is a corresponding test case in the individual SPS-space $< s, s', P > \Leftrightarrow < t, t', GP >$ with the weight -1 assigned to it. As was defined in Sect. 2.1, negative weight means that solution s' has been tried for P in s and showed to be no solution at all, or an unacceptable solution.
- Weight 0 is assigned if there is at least one demonstration for $< t, t', GP >$ (and no negative examples have been found so far).

2.3 *Definition of Design Science Research*

In terms of the previous subsections *design science research* can be defined as a set of activities aimed at choosing a hypothesis in the generic SPS-space and assigning a weight to it, if it has not been assigned yet, or changing the weight already assigned to it. In other words, design science research deals with finding, demonstrating and verifying generic solutions. Assignments can be:

- From *nothing* to 0—demonstrating that a new g-solution can work,
- From 0 to +1—proving that g-solution should work for all situations described by the *as-is* template,
- From nothing, 0, or +1 to -1—finding that the generic solution does not work for some situations described by *as-is* template.

As we see from the list, demonstration and verification are essential parts of the design science research, which means that the research activities are not concentrated only in the generic SPS-space, but researchers also needs to move between generic and individual SPS-spaces. Here, we need to add one reservation. As was already mentioned in Sect. 2.3, it is not feasible for a design science

---

[7] Note that we can consider any individual situations s as a generic one GS, where set GS consists of one element only, $GS = \{s\}$. In this case, the template for GS would not contain any variables. Such interpretation could reduce the number of SPS-spaces to consider from 2 to 1. Though this solution could be preferable from the pure mathematical point of view, we will not pursue it in this paper, as we consider the two spaces construction as being easier to explain and visualized.

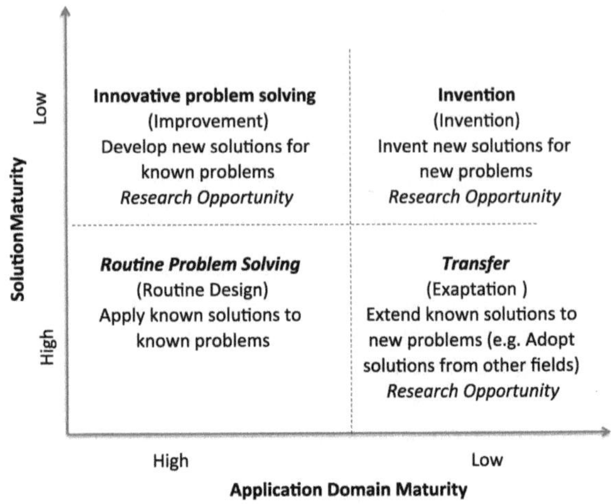

Fig. 4 The application domain maturity/solution maturity matrix adopted from [4]

researcher to test a generic solution in a number of cases sufficient to verify it. To provide conditions for sufficient verification, industry/practice should adopt the solution, so that there will be many cases available for investigation. Investigating these cases, carried out without the involvement of the original design science researchers, falls into the scope of empirical research (using qualitative and quantitative methods). It is this kind of research that can provide final verification of a generic solution.

3 Starting from Individual Problem Solving

Though not equal to individual problem solving, design science research can be initiated by finding a solution for a specific problem in a specific situation. Cases of problem solving that offers opportunities for research are discussed in [4], and are visualized in the Application Domain Maturity/Solution Maturity matrix. Below, we formalize the findings from [4] by introducing four different types of individual problem solving. The matrix, adapted to our terminology, is presented in Fig. 4. The main difference between our matrix and the original one from [4] is the names of the quadrants, the original names from [4] are presented in parenthesis in Fig. 4.

1. *Routine problem solving* (see Fig. 5)—finding a solution to a problem P in situation s via finding a corresponding hypothesis $< t, t', GP >$ in the generic SPS-space with weight +1 (verified generic solution) assigned to it and using this hypothesis for designing a solution for situation s.

   Example: if we consider that introducing a CRM system is a verified generic solution for the problem of non-cooperation between sales staff, then introducing

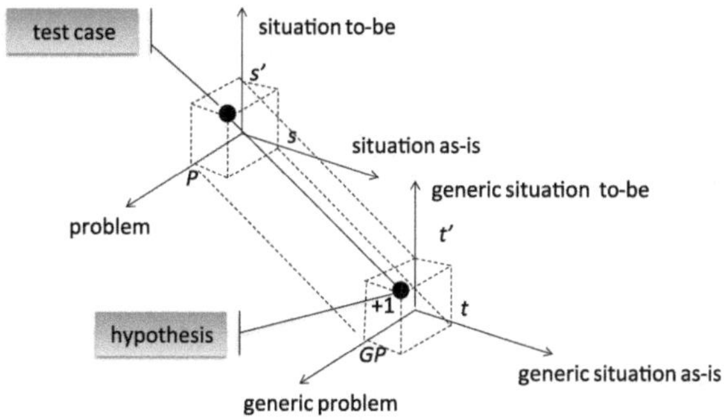

Fig. 5 Routine problem solving

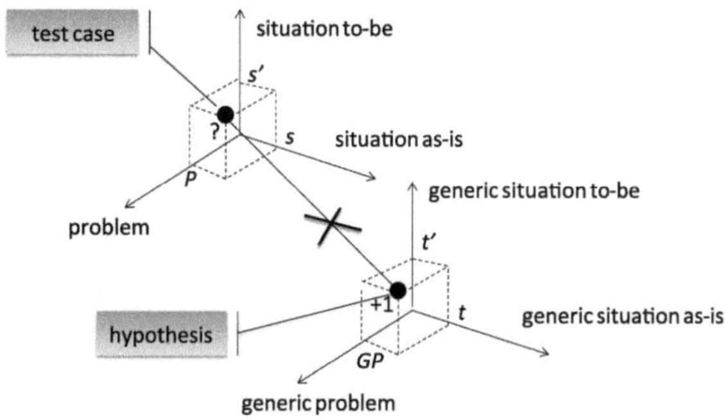

Fig. 6 Innovative problem solving

such a system in the sales office of SoftMotors in Stockholm belongs to the routine problem solving.

Formally, routine problem solving means finding $< t,\ t',\ GP >$ with weight +1 such that $R(s) \cap P = R(s) \cap GP$ and there is a mapping $m \in M$ for which $s = t(m)$, and using $t'(m)$ as a solution for problem P in s.

Routine problem solving in its pure form offers no opportunity for design science research.

2. *Innovative problem solving* (see Fig. 6)—finding a solution s' for a problem P in situation s that cannot be derived from an already known g-solution. Innovative problem solving concerns finding a new (or the first) solution for a known problem.

Example: Designing and introducing a system to support sales activities at SoftMotors in Stockholm that is not similar to any known sales support systems constitutes innovative problem solving. Here, we assume that the system is aimed to solve the known problem: "the progress of pursuing a prospect is visible only to one sales person".

Formally, innovative problem solving can be defined as finding a solution such that test case $< s,\ s',\ P >$ does not correspond to any known hypothesis $< t,\ t',\ GP >$ in generic SPS-space to which a weight of 0 or +1 has been assigned.

Innovative problem solving presents an opportunity for researchers to find a hypothesis $< t, t', GP >$ for which $< s, s', P >$ is a representation. If found, $< t, t', GP >$ gets the weight of 0, test case $< s, s', P >$ being regarded as a demonstration for it.

3. *Transfer*—testing a generic solution designed for another problem or the same problem in different class of situations, or both.

Example: Successful introduction of some Wiki software, developed to solve other problems, to support sales activities at SoftMotors in Stockholm, could be considered as an example of transfer.

Formally, transfer means applying hypothesis $< t, t', GP >$ (with weight of +1) to a test case $< s, s', P >$ such that $GP \cap R(s) \neq P \cap R(s)$ (different problem in relation to the current situation), or $s \notin GS(t)$ (different original situation) or both.

Problem solving of type transfer presents an opportunity for researchers to find a new hypothesis $< t_1, t', GP_1 >$ for which $< s, s', P >$ is a representation. If found, $< t_1, t', GP_1 >$ gets the weight of 0, test case $< s, s', P >$ being regarded as a demonstration for it.

4. *Invention*—testing a transformation to a new situation s' without clearly defined problem in original situation s to solve. This is a process of discovering new opportunities. After transformation has been completed one can discover which problem P has been solved by comparing situations s and s'.

Example: We can use the same example as for *Innovative problem solving* above, but assume that the sales office of SoftMotors in Stockholm functions very well, and there are no particular problems to solve. In this case, designing and introducing a system to support sales activities that is not similar to any known sales support systems constitutes an invention. The difference between the two cases is as follows. Innovative problem solving will require validating that the problem has been solved, while invention will require investigation of which previously unidentified problems have been solved.

Invention presents an opportunity for researchers to find a new hypothesis $< t, t', GP >$ in the generic SPS-space for which $< s, s', P >$ is a representation. If found, $< t, t', GP >$ gets the weight of 0, test case $< s, s', P >$ in the individual SPS-space being regarded as a demonstration.

Classifying problem solving in four types, as above, constitutes some idealization of reality. In practice, some mixture of these types is more probable than a pure adherence to one of them. For example, while following the route of routine problem solving, one can slightly change the recommended solution making it a bit innovative. Another example, after introducing a routine solution, one can discover that besides the original problem, this solution has solved another problem, therefore making the process a bit of invention.

4 Generic Problem Solving

Any of the of individual problem solving types presented in the previous section, except the routine one, can serve as a starting point for initiating design science research via generalizing a newfound solution and finding a point in the generic SPS-space that this solution represents. However, starting from the individual problem solving is not the only way of conducting design science research. The movement between individual and generic SPS-spaces can be done in many different ways. In this section, we present examples of generic problem solving from our practice. Note that these examples do not cover all alternatives of generic problem solving. Section 4.1 discusses a case where a researcher moves to the world of generic situation/solutions in order to find a solution for a problem in a particular real-life situation. The individual solution is then obtained by instantiation of the newly designed generic solution. In Sect. 4.2, we discuss a case where research starts from finding a generic solution and proceeds to finding a situation where it could be applied.

4.1 Innovative Generic Problem Solving

Term "innovative generic problem solving", or IG problem solving for short, is built in association with innovative (individual) problem solving introduced in the previous section. As the name implies, IG problem solving is aimed at finding an innovative generic solution for a known generic problem. A generic problem can be discovered in two ways, either:

1. An individual problem has been discovered in a real-life situation and has been generalized before an attempt to solve it has been undertaken.
2. Previous research has established the fact of a problem existence via employing qualitative or/and quantitative empirical methods.

It can also be both, first a researcher identifies a specific problem in a specific situation and then discovers that the generic problem related to it is already known.

Figure 7 illustrates steps in innovative generic problem solving. If research is initiated by *discovering an individual problem* (case 1 in the list above), the following seven steps could be applied:

1. Establish (refine) the problem P for the given situation s (arrow 1 in Fig. 7)
2. Generalize the situation by creating a template t for which s is instantiation (arrow 2a), and defining a generic problem GP that includes P (arrow 2b)
3. Design a solution template t' (arrow 3)
4. Instantiate a solution to a situation to-be s' (arrow 4)
5. Implement s' in s
6. Evaluate the result and assign a weight to test case $< s, s', P >$ in the individual SPS-space

Fig. 7 Generic innovation

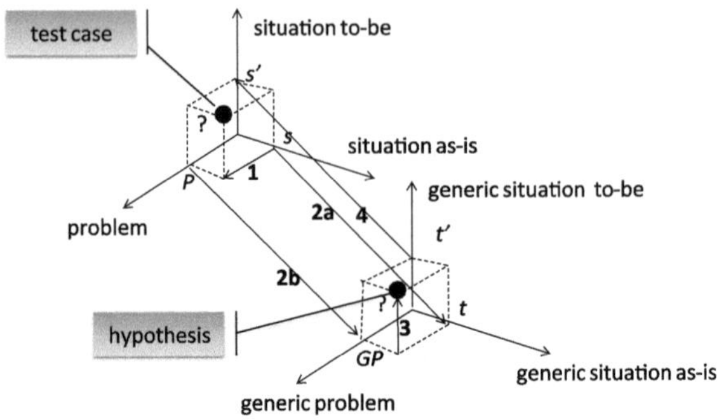

7. Promote the result to the hypothesis $< t, t', GP >$ in the generic SPS-space. If $< s, s', P >$ is assigned weight +1 then $< t, t', GP >$ gets weight 0 (see Fig. 3), otherwise -1.

If research start with a *known generic problem* (case 2 in the list presented in the beginning of this subsection), the process starts with step 3 (see Fig. 7), and will require additional step between steps 3 and 4 of finding a situation *s* to which a solution can be applied. This new step may also be required in a case when, due to some practical reasons, the generic solution cannot be tested in the original situation from which the search for a solution has been initiated. For example, the situation may no longer exist by the time a generic solution has been found.

To illustrate IG problem solving, we will shortly overview a case from our own practice. In 2003–2006, we were engaged in a research project, called INKA [6] aimed at investigating effects from the introduction of an integrated business process support and knowledge management system into operational practice of a non-profit interest organization. Soon after the first version of the system had been developed and put into operation, we discovered that very few used it, which made it impossible to investigate any effects. An investigation was conducted on the causes of the failure, which resulted in critique of the usability of the system, i.e., the system design was not sufficiently intuitive and user-friendly.

After this discovery, the user interface of the system was totally redesigned [7] and the users were once more invited to use the system. The result was negative this time as well, i.e., very few used the system. However, nobody was criticizing the system design any longer. The situation was plainly explained by a statement from one of the supposed users: "I am sure that the system is very good, but I do not know what I should use it for". As nobody was "blaming" the system, the attention of our research group was moved to search for the reasons of failure elsewhere.

As the research focus in the project was not in the introduction process itself, we tried to apply routine problem solving first. However, our search for a generic solution in the literature gave no result. Solutions recommended for conducting an organizational change where related to planning it in the right way from the very beginning. This was not the case in our project. We were in the middle of not so

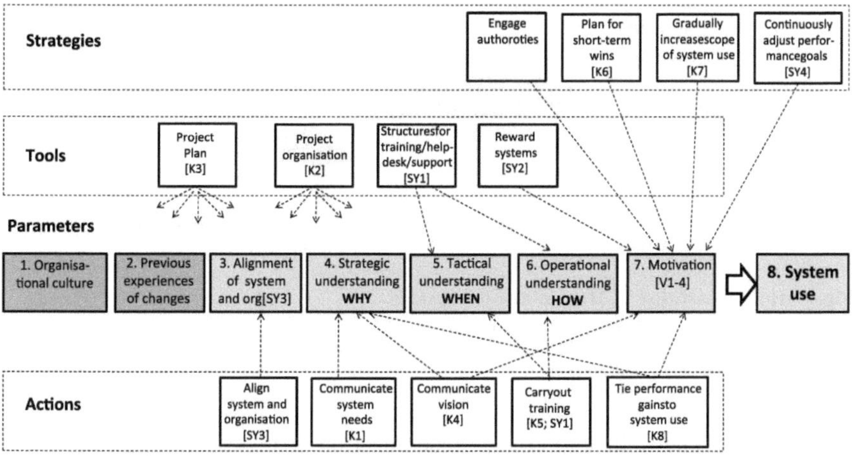

Fig. 8 Element of A^3

successful system introduction that we could not "rewind". The only way to proceed for us was to invent a solution ourselves.

A solution was designed as a general methodology for conducting a system introduction process that was possible to apply even in the middle of unsuccessful introduction [8] (In Swedish). The methodology was called A^3—Assess-Adjust-Apply. The main idea behind A^3 is a number of measurable parameters that can be assessed at any point of introduction process, and a number of means of control that can be employed for influencing the values of these parameters, see Fig. 8. The means are grouped into three categories: actions, tools and strategies. The process is driven by periodic assessment of parameters and choosing means of controls to proceed based on the values of these parameters.

A^3 was tested in the original situation with some success. We were able to higher the usage of the system to some degree. However, due to the reason outside our control, i.e. changes in the management of the interest organization with which we worked, we could not fully complete our testing.

Summarizing the above, we started with a situation with a problem—introduction process that "stammered". We generalized the problem and devised a generic solution for it—a way of conducting the introduction process that drives the system usage up. We (partly) applied this generic solution to the original situation. Right now, we are still looking for new situations where A^3 can be applied to subject our generic solution to additional tests.

Fig. 9 Human-assisting vs Human-assisted systems

4.2 Generic Invention

We consider generic invention as a generalization of invention in the individual SPS-space described in Sect. 3, which amounts to testing a new solution in a given situation without having any specific problem to solve. Accordingly, generic invention means finding a generic solution for an unknown generic problem. What is more, generic invention can start without full understanding of in which situations the solution is to be applied, which should be found at a later stage. To give an example of a generic invention, we overview a case from our own practice described in details in [9].

In the middle of 1980th one of the authors with a number of collaborators was engaged in a research project, called CHAOS, aimed at developing a theoretical framework for designing of what we then called "human-assisted systems". The idea was explained with two pictures presented in Fig. 9, one representing traditional at the time human-assisting systems (left part of Fig. 9), the other one a new paradigm of "human-assisted systems (right part of Fig. 9). The project acronym CHAOS stood for Concurrent Human-Assisted Object Systems.

In a human-assisting system, a computer helps a human being to perform certain tasks, e.g., to write a letter, print an invoice, complete a transaction, etc. The relations between these tasks, and the aim of the whole process, are beyond the understanding of the computer, but are a prerogative of the human participant. In a human-assisted system, the roles are somewhat reversed, the computer has some knowledge about the process and keeps it running as long as it can. When the system cannot perform a task on its own or figure out what to do next, it will ask the human participant for assistance. The human-assisted system frees human beings from tedious, routing work, like searching for information, bookkeeping, reporting, allowing them to concentrate on things at which they are best, i.e. decision making.

The main idea of human-assisted systems was that the users and the system should work in a symbiosis. The symbiosis should be flexible which means such cooperation between the system and its users where the distribution of responsibilities between them may change in time. It means that the points of interaction between the system and its users may change, thus we need to have a model in which such changes do not require substantial modifications. The latter requires having a model in which both human and system actions are represented uniformly on equal footing.

The project was of theoretical nature. We had one example in mind though, creating a computer programmer's secretary, a system that would help a programmer to managed his/her job, i.e., to ensure that the programmer does not forget to compile and test after making changes in the source code. The "secretary" should considerably extend the capability of the tools like make/build that existed at the time. The project continued for 2 years, from 1984 to 1986, and produced a model that consisted of the following components:

- A set of atoms,
- A set of objects
- A code of laws and
- A set of connectors, each connector hanging on a group of objects that must obey a certain law.

Objects have complex structure expressed by including in their "bodies" a set of connectors that hang on other objects making the latter sub-objects to the former. An object's body can also include a connector hanging on the object itself. The dynamics of the objects-connectors model can be defined by a machine in which a connector is regarded as a processing unit that monitors its operands. A connector:

- Awakes when one of its operands has been changed,
- Checks whether the law still holds by reading the condition,
- Restores it when it has been broken,
- Falls asleep.

A law can be fully deterministic, or not. Non-determinism can concern the condition of awakening, or rules of restoring the low, or both. A connector with a non-deterministic law is called a boundary connector. A boundary connector cannot do its job alone. Some help is needed, and here is where human being are introduced in the model. Humans are parts of boundary connectors to help when to awake, or/and how to restore the state of the objects entrusted to this connector.

As we mentioned above, a connector can both be included in the body of an object, and "hang" on this object. This allows an object to reconfigure itself based on changes in other objects. Such reconfiguration can include adding new connecters or removing the existing ones, including the one that completes the reconfiguration itself. The model itself was published later as a theoretical platform [10, 11].

It took several years to figure out in which situations the objects-connectors model could be applied. At that time the author who had participated in the CHAOS project worked for a small Swedish IT-consulting company. The company had developed a system to assist salespersons in the pharmaceutical industry, and the author's task was to support and further develop this system.

A salesperson in this industry was driving around the country, meeting doctors at various hospitals and leaving them samples of new drugs. The system was intended to keep order in his/her business, e.g., plan the trips, have a track of which samples where left in which hospital, and when it is time to follow up the previously made contact. It also helped to gather statistics and analyze sales potential. The business, hence the system, was built around such concepts as, activity, plan activity, report execution of activity, plan follow-up activities, like a phone call.

While working with the system, the author built a model of the sales business in the pharmaceutical domain in terms of objects-connectors model. In this model, a sales lead on which a sales-person is working is represented as an object. As sub-objects, the model includes a hospital, and a doctor to whom this particular lead is related. A planned activity is represented by a boundary connector that wakes up at the deadline point and asks the salesperson to complete it. While executing the activity, the sales person writes a report and plans further activities. In terms of the model, the boundary connector that represents a planned activity removes itself from the body of the lead-object adding at the same time some other connectors (i.e., new planned activities) to it. Part of these activities are calculated based on the fixed rules, others are added manually by the sales person behind the "steering wheel" of the boundary connector that represent an activity under execution.

Creating a model as above gave an idea of one generic situation for which the objects-connectors model could be applied. It could be used for building IT-systems that support business processes. This was tested in several areas with some successes and failures, details of which are reported in [9].

The case above represents a generic invention that consisted of creating a high-level model without having a well-formulated individual or generic situation in mind. An application area for this model was discovered later and more or less by chance. Note, however, that it was not actually a pure chance, as the authors were looking for a generic situation where the model could fit.

5 Related Research

Design science has been proposed as a distinct paradigm in information systems research. In [2], the design science paradigm is contrasted to the behavioral science paradigm. Behavioral science aims at creating theories that explain and predict human and organizational phenomena in the context of information systems. Design science, on the other hand, is the scientific study of artifacts within practices as they are developed and used by people with the goal of solving practical problems. Historically, design science originates from the engineering disciplines and the sciences of the artificial [2]. Its study object is the creation and use of artifacts that can advance individual as well as organizational and societal flourishing. A main tenet of design science is that knowledge and understanding of a practical problem and its solution can be acquired through the creation and use of an artifact, e.g., an IT system, a model or a method.

In design science, the artifact represents a general solution to a class of problems [3]. In this chapter we have introduced the concept of generic problem, generic solution as well as generic situation. We interpret design science research as a movement between two worlds: the world of real (individual) situations and real solutions, and the world of generic (abstract) situations and solutions. This movement between these two worlds is also described in the work of Lee and others [12], but the two worlds in this work are called the instance domain and the abstract domain. In [12], moving from an instance problem and an instance solution to an abstract problem and an abstract solution is called abstraction, and is seen as a way of theorizing in Design Science. Moving from an abstract problem and an abstract solution to an instance problem and an instance solution is called de-abstraction.

In comparison with our approach, [12] does not use the concept of situation. We believe that adding this concept extends the options for a researcher to proceed when a particular test case shows negative results. Besides an option to modify the proposed solution/artifact, the researcher can search for a different, in some respect, situation where the solution/artifact may work.

Designing artifacts can be viewed as a search process through a solution space, [13]. According to this view, the designer starts with setting up a solution space consisting of possible solutions to a given problem. The designer then makes a first design decision, thereby pruning away parts of the solution space. He/she continues and makes further design decisions, which further narrow the space. The process goes on and can be viewed as a systematic exploration of the solution space. At each step, the designer is guided in her decision making by some criteria and requirements on the artifact. This guidance can sometimes take the form of a goodness or utility function, which can be used to determine which design decisions to make. The author of [13] has even argued that the search process can be more or less automated using AI techniques. Though this has not proved feasible, the view of design as a search process is useful in supporting communication, planning and structuring of design work. Our work is akin to that of [13] but differs in that we introduce a space that is spanned by the dimensions of solutions as well as problems and situations.

In the work of Anderson and others [4], four cases of problem solving that give opportunity for research are presented. These four cases have been formalized in Section 3 according to our basic concepts. The chapter also introduces other types of movement between individual and generic SPS-spaces, such as innovative generic problem solving, see Sect. 4.1. The work by Sein and others in [14] points out that IT artifact are typically developed and shaped by their interaction with an organizational context. Therefore, design science research needs to interleave concurrently the activities of creating an artifact, introducing it into an organization, and evaluating it. The basic assumptions of this approach are reflected in our notions of moving between the individual and generic SPS-spaces.

Fischer and Gregor [15] argue for a more thorough investigation of reasoning logic of models for carrying out design science research. They present an idealized model of the hypothetico-deductive method, including the contexts of discovery and justification, and forms of reasoning. Our chapter can be interpreted as a attempt to investigate the reasoning logic in design science.

6 Discussion

In this section, we discuss how the notions introduced in this paper could be used for explaining and conducting design science research. We do not intend to analyze all aspects of design science research process, the aim being just to demonstrate how the proposed apparatus could be used in various stages of the process.

6.1 Tracking the Progress of Design Science Research

As it has been discussed in the introduction, design science research in IS is aimed at generating and testing hypothesis related to the future use of technology in organizations. In our conceptual quasi-formal model of Sect. 2:

- Generating a hypothesis equals to finding a new point $< t, t', GP >$ in the generic SPS-space that has not been investigated at all, or only partly investigated in the past.
- Testing the hypothesis equals to:

- Finding a test case $< s, s', P >$ in the individual SPS-space such that it represents hypothesis $< t, t', GP >$, i.e.: $< s, s', P > \Leftrightarrow < t, t', GP>$
- Implementing s' in s
- Evaluating whether s' is an acceptable solution for problem p in situation s.

As was discussed in Sects. 3 and 4, the order in which the steps above are completed can differ from case to case. For example, in one case, hypothesis generation can precede testing (Sect. 4), and in the next case, it could be vice versa (Sect. 3).

With the help of our notions, the final state of the design science research process could be represented as an octo-tuple $< t, t', GP, s, s', P, i, w >$, where i is a boolean variable that shows whether the solution s' has been implemented in s, w is the weight (i.e., +1, 0 or -1) assigned to $< s, s', P >$. If we allow any component of the octo-tuple to be undefined, (denote this fact as "?"), then the octo-tuple can be used to represent an intermediate state of the research process. Below, we present two examples of intermediate states along with descriptions of steps they warrant for continuing the research process:

- $< ?, ?, ?, s, s', P, true, +1 >$—research that starts from the individual problem solving, e.g., invention, and requires generalization as its next step
- $<?, t', ?, ?, ?, ?, ?, ?, ? >$ –research that starts with discovering a generic solution for a problem unknown. This state warrants discovering a generic situation where the solution could be applied. This is the case with generic invention as described in Sect. 4.2.

Finding a way for representing the state of the design science research process allows us to consider this process as any other business process, at least from the state-oriented point of view [16]. The main concept of the state-oriented view on business processes is a state of the process instance. The state is defined as a position in some state space. A state space is considered multidimensional, where each dimension represents some important parameter (and its possible values) of the business process. Each point in the state space represents a possible result of the execution of a process instance. If we add the time axis to the state space, then a trajectory (curve) in the space–time will represent a possible execution of a process instance in time. A process type is defined as a subset of allowed trajectories in space–time. The goal of a process instance is defined as reaching a certain area (surface) in the state space called the set of final states. When a process instance is not in a final state, action should be planned aimed at moving nearer to the nearest final state.

The octo-tuple $< t, t', GP, s, s', P, i, w >$ introduced above can be used to represent a position of a research process instance in the process state space. The goal of an instance then can be defined as eliminating all question marks "?" from the tuple.

6.2 In Search for Solutions: Requirements

When design science research comes to a state where the original situation (specific or generic) has been specified, and the problem (specific or generic) has been identified, the next logical step is looking for a solution. In the terms of octo-tuples introduced in the previous section, this can be identified as:

- $< ?, ?, ?, s, ?, P, ?, ? >$—individual problem solving
- $< t, ?, GP, s, ?, P, ?, ? >$—generic problem solving that starts with an individual situation and problem, see Sect. 3
- $< t, ?, GP, ?, ?, ?, ?, ? >$—generic problem solving that starts with a generic situation and generic problem, see Sect. 3.

Search for a solution is a creative process that is impossible to fully predict and/or regulate. However, some general steps in this process can be recommended, one of them being related to specifying requirements in terms of [17] or objectives in terms of [1]. In the terms of this paper, requirements can be considered as a way of reducing the set of situations, or templates of situations among which the solution can be found. Such reduction can be achieved based on two considerations:

- *Reachability of solution*—taking into consideration whether it is possible to implement a solution in a given situation as-is. For example, moving the SoftMotors office from Stockholm to the Moon could be considered as not reachable, while moving it to India could be considered as reachable.
- *Unintended consequences*—taking into consideration other known problem that a solution might bring about. For, example, all sales staff may leave the office if a cumbersome CRM system is introduced to support sales activities.

Determining requirements of the first type, reachability of solution, could be facilitated by formalizing the idea of distance between situations. Though the concept of distance is practically impossible to define in general terms, it might be done in a specific domain to which the given problem belongs.

Determining requirements of the second type, unintended consequences, could be facilitated by constructing a generic situations-problems space in which all problematic points are marked.

Both types of requirements help to narrow down the search in the solution space in terms of [13].

6.3 Implementing Solution

When a design science research process has reached one of the following states:

- $< t, t', GP, s, s', P, ?, ? >$,
- $< ?, ?, ?, s, s', P, ?, ? >$,
- $< ?, ?, ?, s, s', ?, ?, ? >$,
- $< t, t', ?, s, s', ?, ?, ? >$,

it is time for implementing s' (solution) in s (original situation). Dependent on the distance between s and s', this could be a simple, or quite a complicated process. There can be a known method for implementation, or the method needs to be devised before the solution could be implemented. An example of situation where it needed to be devised is presented in Sect. 4.1. The designing of the implementation method described in Sect. 4.1 has been completed according to the design science approach. Here, we have an example of recursive decomposition where implementation of a solution creates a new problem to solve.

6.4 Evaluating Solutions

When a design science research process has reached one of the following states:

- $< t, t', GP, s, s', P, true, ? >$,
- $< ?, ?, ?, s, s', P, true, ? >$,
- $< ?, ?, ?, s, s', ?, true, ? >$,
- $< t, t', ?, s, s', ?, true, ?>$

it is time for evaluating the results [2]. With a well define problem, this step can be a relatively simple one. When the problem is loosely defined or unknown (marked by "?"), the evaluation could be quite a complicated process on its own, which can bring about a new problem to solve. An example of such a case is presented in [18], which discusses the research on measuring effects from introduction of business process support systems.

For evaluating purpose, one might need to apply empirical research methods as discussed in [2, 17].

6.5 Generalizing

When a design science research process has reached one of the following states:

- $< ?, ?, ?, s, s', P, true, +1>$,
- $< ?, ?, ?, s, s', P, true, ? >$,
- $< ?, ?, ?, s, s', P, ?, ? >$,
- $< ?, ?, ?, s, s', P, ?, ?>$

it could be time for generalizing the result going from a solution for a particular problem in an individual situation to solving a generic problem in a generic situation. This step is called abstraction in design science literature [12].

To complete generalization, one needs to find out whether the problem exists in other situations. The latter could be done via literature search, as we have done in the case described in Sect. 4.1. If the literature search produces no results, the question should be solved via field studies according to the methods of empirical research. The latter case constitutes another example (from the one discussed in Sect. 6.4) of usage of other methods in design science research as discussed in [2, 17].

6.6 Finding a Way Out

When a design science research process has reached state $< t, t', GP, s, s', P, true, -1 >$, the researcher needs to decide how to proceed. As we are dealing with research, not with problem solving as such, the choice is not limited to trying to find another generic solution t'' for the original generic problem GP. For example, the researcher can investigate whether the solution will be satisfactory for another set of original situations by changing template t to some other template t_1. Alternatively, or at the same time, the researcher can search for other problems that the suggested solution can solve.

7 Conclusion: Plans for the Future

The authors had two personal motivations/goals for initiating research reported in this paper:

- Firstly, as we actively use design science approach in our own research, we were interested in a better understanding of it.
- Secondly, our university department encourages bachelor, master and PhD students to conduct their research and write their theses in accordance to design science. To do this effectively, they need guidelines that give them clear view on all alternatives that the design science paradigm offers.

While we feel that with this work we have achieved some success in pursuing the first goal, achieving the second goal needs additional work. We plan to continue our work in the direction of creating readable (not formal) guidelines for conducting design science research based on the ideas and quasi-formal notions presented in this paper. This can be considered as a test for the model of the design science research process presented in this paper.

References

1. Peffers, K., Tuunanen, T., Rothenberger, M.A., & Chatterjee, S. (2007). A design science research methodology for information systems research. *Journal of Management Information Systems, 24*(3), 45–78.
2. Hevner, A.R., March, S.T., & Park, J. (2004). Design science in information systems research. *MIS Quarterly, 28*(1), 75–105.
3. Baskerville, R.L., Pries-Heje, J., & Venable, J. (2009). Soft design science methodology. DESRIST 2009, New York, NY: ACM, pp. 1–11.
4. Anderson, J., Donnellan, B., & Hevner, A. (2011). Exploring the relationship between design science research and innovation: a case study of innovation at Chevron. Communications in Computer and Information Science. New York, NY: Springer.
5. Neuman, W. L. (2006). Social research methods. Qualitative and quantitative approaches. Boston: Pearson.
6. Andersson, B., Bider, I., & Perjons, E. (2004). *Integration of business process support with knowledge management—a practical perspective. Practical aspects of knowledge management (PAKM, 2004), LNCS 3336*, New York, NY: Springer, pp. 227–238.
7. Andersson, T., Bider, I., & Svensson, R. (2005) *Aligning people to business processes. Experience report.* Software Process Improvement and Practice (SPIP), Vol. 10, No 4, pp. 403–413.

8. Bider, I., & Perjons, E. (2006). Accessing an ongoing introduction of an IT system in operational practice (In Swedish), Inka project report, available at (2012-07-01): http://www.ibissoft.se/projects/inka/INKA_rapport_II.pdf.
9. Bider, I. (2011). *In search for a good theory: commuting between research and practice in business process domain. LNBIP*, Vol. 81, New York, NY: Springer, pp. 16–30.
10. Bider, I., Khomyakov, M., & Pushchinsky, E. (2000). Logic of change: semantics of object systems with active relations. *Automated Software Engineering (ASE), 7*(1), 9–37.
11. Bider, I., & Khomyakov, M. (2003). New technology—great opportunities. How to exploit them. In: Filipe, J. (ed.), *Enterprise information systems IV*, Kluver, pp. 11–20.
12. Lee, J. S., Pries-Heje, J.,& Baserville, R. (2011). *Theorizing in Design Science Research. DESRIST 2011, LNCS 6629*, New York, NY: Springer, pp. 1–16.
13. Simon, H. (1969). The sciences of the artificial. MIT Press, Cambridge, Mass.
14. Sein, M. K., Henfridsson, O., Purao, S., Rossi, M., & Lindgren, R. (2011). Action design research. *MIS Quarterly, 35*(1), 37–56.
15. Fischer, C., & Gregor, S. (2011). *Forms of reasoning in the design science process. DESRIST 2011, LNCS 6629*, pp. 17–31.
16. Khomyakov, M., & Bider, I. (2000). *Achieving workflow flexibility through taming the chaos. OOIS 2000—6th international conference on object oriented information systems*, New York, NY: Springer, pp. 85–92.
17. Wieringa, R. J. (2009). Design science as nested problem solving. In: *Proceedings of the 4th international conference on design science research in information systems and technology*, Philadelphia: ACM, pp. 1–12.
18. Bider, I., & Perjons, E. (2007). Effects from introduction of business process support systems and how they can be measured. In B. Pernici & J. A. Gulla (Eds.), *CAiSE'07 workshop proceedings* (pp. 369–377). Trondheim, Norway: Tapir Academic Press.

Restructuring the Design Science Research Knowledge Base

A One-Cycle View of Design Science Research and its Consequences for Understanding Organizational Design Problems

Robert Winter and Antonia Albani

Abstract The contribution of this paper is twofold. We revisit the three-cycle procedural view of Design Science Research (DSR) as introduced by Hevner, and we propose a structuring mechanism for the DSR Knowledge Base (KB) and the problem/context specification that supports our revisited DSR procedure. Regarding the first contribution, we argue that each design cycle has rigor related as well as relevance related aspects. We therefore introduce a *one-cycle view* of DSR, comprised of alternating core activities *design* and *evaluation*. With every iteration, the understanding of the environment and the problem to be solved are enhanced. Additionally, every design iteration allows for revisiting the Knowledge Base in order to improve the problem solution. Concerning the second contribution, we propose to structure the DSR KB by means of two *two-dimensional maps* to support an efficient search for existing, reusable solution artifacts. One map concerns the *application scope*; the other one concerns the *artifact character*. Solution artifacts are then organized with regard to their type, generality, application domain and coverage. We demonstrate the applicability of the proposed DSR KB structure using the domain of change projects in organizations as an exemplar.

Keywords Procedural Views of Design Science Research · Design Science Research Knowledge Base · Artifact Reuse · Design Problem Specification

R. Winter (✉) · A. Albani
Institute of Information Management, University of St. Gallen, Müller-Friedberg-Strasse 8, 9000 St. Gallen, Switzerland
e-mail: robert.winter@unisg.ch

A. Albani
e-mail: antonia.albani@unisg.ch

R. Baskerville et al. (eds.), *Designing Organizational Systems*,
Lecture Notes in Information Systems and Organisation 1,
DOI: 10.1007/978-3-642-33371-2_4,

1 Introduction

Organizational Design and Engineering (ODE) (sometimes also addressed as Enterprise Engineering) is a discipline that studies organizations from an engineering perspective [1]. This means that organizations are considered to be purposefully designed and implemented systems. Such systems can be re-designed and re-implemented if there is a need for change. The problems that need to be solved in such a context while addressing the organization in a holistic way are of complex nature and multifaceted. Since most organizational solutions will include not only task and people components, but also information technology (IT) components like software systems and IT infrastructure components, ODE and information systems (IS) design and engineering have a different focus, but many commonalities. IS solutions, i.e., IT solutions embedded in a task and people context, need to be adaptable to changing conditions and goals, so that IS design and engineering needs to put special emphasis not only on ensuring the alignment of business structures and supporting software systems, but also on supporting the adaptability of IS. The solutions of such complex organizational problems need to be constructed in a systematic way.

Since ODE considers organizations as designed and engineered complex systems, and because there are many similarities with IS design and engineering, the Design Science Research (DSR) approach for IS can also provide a basis to solve organizational design problems. Several DSR approaches are available and have been applied in practice to aid ODE. Examples of such approaches, among many others, are the Business Engineering Approach [2], Design and Engineering Methodology for Organizations (DEMO) [3], Zachman framework [4], ArchiMate method [The Open 5], Business Process (Re)Engineering Approach [6, 7], or ARIS framework [8]. Such approaches successfully address certain aspects of organizational problems, e.g., identifying essential business transactions in order to decide about splitting or allying of organizations (by applying the DEMO method), identifying business processes (by applying the Business Process (Re)Engineering Approach), or integrating business aspects as well as IT aspects (by applying the Business Engineering Approach). They aim at building and testing various kinds of designed artifacts (e.g., software systems, procedures/ project plans, but also reference models or reusable methods) as solutions to certain ODE design problems or even better to classes of similar ODE design problems. Due to the complex and holistic nature of organizational design and engineering problems often one approach alone does not give full support to reach a desired end. Real-world ODE often requires several approaches to be combined because multiple aspects have to be covered and/or the problem combines characteristics of several domains; E.g., applying both the DEMO and Business Engineering approaches in order to provide an inter-organizational business-to-IT solution for the essential transactions that are outsourced by an organization. In order to be able to select and combine these approaches, (1) the existing and successful applied DSR approaches need to be recognized regarding their core contribution to the field, and (2) the problem with its goals and contexts need to be under-stood in order to be able to define possible solutions to the given problem. A DSR framework would provide guidance in solving such complex ODE problems in a systematic way. However, to our knowledge no such framework exists so far. We therefore aim at the development of a DSR framework that

1. allows for a systematic classification and retrieval of DSR artifacts and
2. relates solution artifacts to problem characteristics.

The Knowledge Base (KB) in DSR as introduced by Hevner [9] provides a simple structure of applicable DSR approaches. Hevner differentiates practical knowledge and research knowledge. He explains that DSR problem solving processes follow three cycles in order to derive at rigorous solutions to relevant, important design problems. First we find a differentiation of the KB into problem knowledge and solution knowledge more adequate in order to better understand the relationship between the right means to achieve the desired end. Second, in the process of deriving at the desired ends, we do not see DSR as a three-cycle approach, but rather as a one-cycle approach. In Sect. 2 we therefore propose to restructure the DSR KB and to redefine the DSR process. In Sects. 3 and 4 we then detail the new structure of the DSR KB regarding solution components and solution requirements, respectively. In Sect. 5 we illustrate the applicability of our proposal by using the ODE domain "organizational change" as an exemplar. Section 6 concludes the chapter and outlines future work.

2 Challenges of the One-Cycle View of Design Science Research

Since different DSR proposals often widely vary with regard to foundations, goals, and processes, Hevner [9] has introduced a generic DSR framework comprising three cycles—relevance, design and rigor cycles—, which should be present and clearly identifiable in every piece of DSR. This 'three-cycle view of DSR' is illustrated in Fig. 1.

In the *relevance cycle* the requirements of the application domain are defined and introduced into the design process. Additionally, the resulting research artifacts are established in the environment (e.g. by field-testing) in order to demonstrate their problem solving utility. In the *rigor cycle* domain experience and expertise as well as existing generic design products and processes are introduced into the design process in addition to scientific theories and methods. Additionally, new generalizable knowledge derived from the design process is added to the knowledge base (KB) for reuse. The *design cycle*, which is essentially a solution search procedure, iterates between the core activities of building and evaluating design artifacts. "[…] multiple iterations of the design cycle […] [are necessary] before contributions are output into the relevance cycle and the rigor cycle." [9].

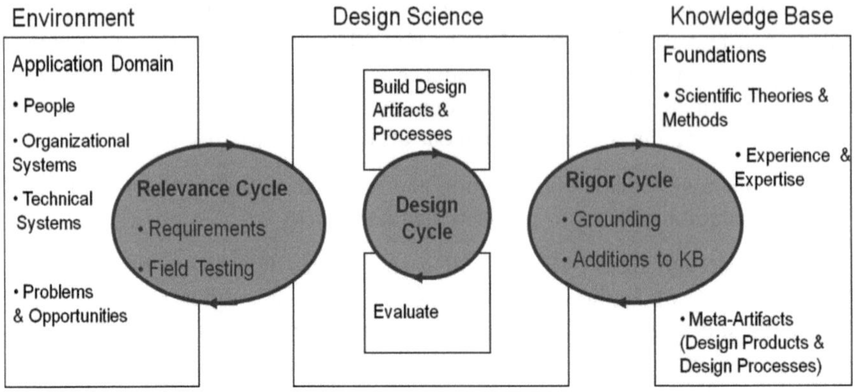

Fig. 1 Three-cycle view of DSR [9]

Since Hevner's framework is generally applicable for any constructional problem and result type in DSR, it might be a starting point to frame specific DSR proposals. However, it has some drawbacks. First, it does not fully support the recognition that "[…] artifacts emerge in interaction with the organizational elements." [10]. This conclusion results from Hevner's proposal of having three cycles in DSR, where the design cycle has dependencies on the relevance and the rigor cycles but at the same time is independent during the actual execution of the research [9]. Second, it does not give guidance neither for organizing the knowledge base in order to be able to find the right means (e.g., existing solution components or methods) to reach the desired ends, nor for organizing the understanding of the design problem in order to define the desired ends.

Regarding the first drawback a DSR method has been proposed recently, called Action Design Research (ADR) that "[…] conceptualizes the research process as containing the inseparable and interwoven activities of building the IT artifact, intervening in the organization, and evaluating it concurrently" [10]. The aim of ADR is to provide a method that has build-in relevance and rigor cycles providing explicit guidance for designing innovative IT artifacts in combining building, intervention and evaluation activities. It combines Action Research (AR) (see e.g., [11]) with DSR where AR has organizational intervention at its very heart.

In line with the guiding ideas of ADR and inspired by the Spiral Model in software development [12] we revisit Hevner's three cycle view and argue that the design cycle of Hevner has *rigor related and/or relevance related characteristics within each single iteration*. We therefore propose a *one-cycle view of DSR*, which is comprised of alternating core activities *design* and *evaluation* within one and the same cycle. Every iteration of the cycle allows revisiting the DSR KB (shown in the right cylinder of Fig. 2) in order to improve the problem solution, and developing a better understanding of the environment and the problem to be solved (shown in the left cylinder of Fig. 2). The cycle iterates until a sufficiently useful solution has been developed. When the iteration exits, a problem solving means has been developed and novel artifact components together with their related

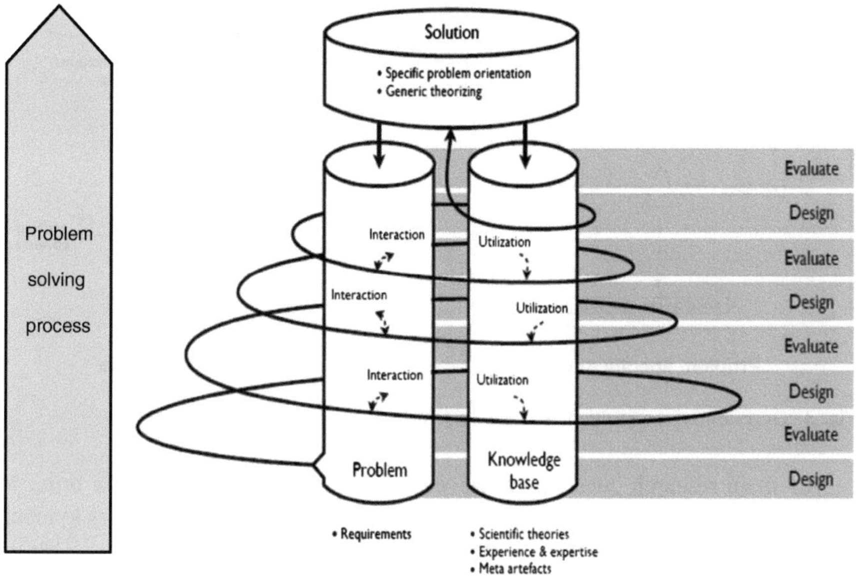

Fig. 2 One-cycle view of DSR (adapted from [13])

problem characteristics are added to the DSR KB. Our one-cycle view of DSR is illustrated in Fig. 2.

Regarding the second drawback mentioned above, we go even further and propose to restructure the DSR KB in order to better support design artifact reuse. As introduced by Hevner [9], the DSR KB differentiates practical knowledge and research knowledge and explains that this knowledge is applied in the rigor cycle in order to derive at the desired solution. We find a structure of the DSR KB in problem knowledge (*Problem cylinder* left in Fig. 2) and solution knowledge (*Knowledge base cylinder* right in Fig. 2) more adequate in order to better understand the relationship between the right means to achieve the desired ends.

The idea of a one cycle view on a problem solving process is not new and has been successfully applied e.g., in the Spiral Model of software development and enhancement [12]. We have been inspired by this model in several aspects; First, the determination of objectives, alternatives and constraints have had an impact on the structuring of the problem knowledge by means of understanding the different solution alternatives based on different design goals and contexts (explained later in this section). Second, having the development and verification of the artifact not as a separate cycle in the Spiral Model underlined our conviction that the design, relevance and rigor cycles belong together and should not be separated. Further, having different types of artifacts that may be designed and evaluated in different cycles (in the spiral model these are the different portions of the product and the different levels of abstraction) satisfied our need to restructure the DSR KB in order to better find the right means for each artifact type to derive at the desired ends.

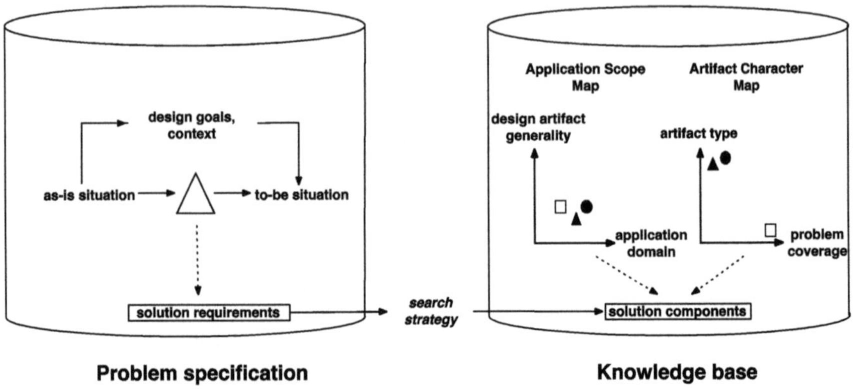

Fig. 3 Overview of the problem and KB structure

The main research questions however, which need to be answered in order to support the application of the proposed one-cycle problem solving process to reach organizational improvements concern are:

1. How to structure the DSR KB, in order to better understand which solution components and foundational guidelines have been successfully applied for which kinds of organizational problems
2. How to structure the problem base in order to systematically manage solution requirements, design goals, and the organizational context.

An overview of the proposed approach on how to structure the problem base as well as the DSR KB and how the two bases are related one to another is shown in Fig. 3.

Based on specified *solution requirements* the corresponding *solution components* need to be found by means of an adequate *search strategy*. The solution requirements result from comparing the *as-is situation* to the *to-be situation*, which implies a transition path. Each to-be situation however is related to defined *design goals*, and both the to-be situation and the as-is situation are related to a design problem *context* [14]. Once the solution requirements have been specified, an adequate search strategy is required to identify artifacts that contribute to the problem solution, i.e. that constitute components of the to-be solution and/or that support the transformation. This search strategy is strongly dependent on the organization and the structure of the DSR KB. For the structuring of the DSR KB we propose two two-dimensional maps. One map concerns the *application scope*; the other one concerns the *artifact character*. The search for applicable existing design artifacts can be organized efficiently if these artifacts are organized with regard to their type, their generality, their application domain and their coverage.

In the following sections we will propose a structuring approach for both the DSR KB and the problem specification. We will then show how the proposed structure enables an effective search for solution components based on specified solution requirements.

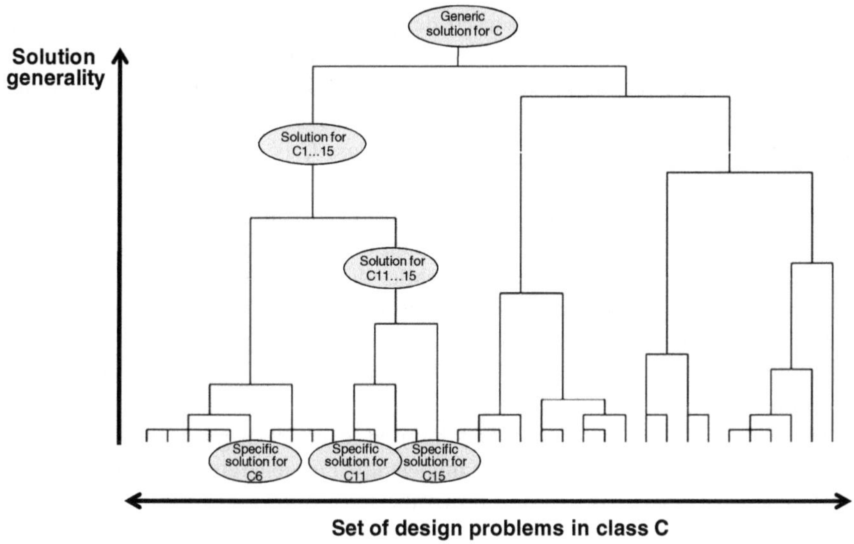

Fig. 4 Visualization of ultrametric distances between design solutions within a design problem class [15]

3 Structuring the DSR Knowledge Base for Reuse

We propose to differentiate *application scope* and *artifact character*. Both can be specified using *two-dimensional maps*.

The *application scope* map is based on Winter's [15, 16] approach to identify design factors and represent as-is design solutions in DSR. The approach starts with an as-is analysis step in order to explore domain specific contingencies. For that purpose, it needs to be tested, (a) which potential contingencies (that have been identified by literature analysis) in fact have influence on the observed design solutions and (b) which relevant contingencies load on the same design factor, i.e. which influences are closely related. For that purpose, a large number of observed practices in the regarded domain need to be specified by as many as potential (dependent) items, and the status of every potential contingency for every case needs to be specified as potential (independent) item. Then a principal component analysis is carried out to explore which independent items load how much on which component that explains the variance of the dependent items. The components can be understood as design factors, i.e. as aggregate levers that explain a large portion of the variance of the observed design solutions. The design dimensions define a multi-dimensional space in which every observed solution can be interpreted as a point. In order to reduce the variety of the observed design solutions, an agglomerative cluster analysis is carried out. This second as-is analysis step yields a manageable number of clusters whose cluster centers can be interpreted as 'representative' as-is solutions. The observed cases and their ultrametric distances can be visualized using a dendrogram-like tree diagram (see Fig. 4).

The (dis)similarity of two observed design solutions corresponds to the generality level of their link. If two solutions are very similar, their link is represented on a low level of generality—and vice versa. Based on the solution (dis)similarities visualized by the tree diagram, a reasonable clustering level needs to be determined. The broader the design problem class C is defined, the more design solutions can be covered in the tree diagram.

We base one component of our design artifact 'mapping' approach on such tree diagrams. In the application scope map, one dimension represents the level of generality of the design artifact, while the other is used to differentiate application domains and sub-domains. Design artifacts on higher levels of generality are applicable to a broader scope of design problems, while artifacts with lower generality are better suited to be useful for more specific design problems.

The search strategy in order to find the right level of design artifact abstraction is as follows: The search starts on the highest level of generality by identifying the most generic artifacts. By moving down the tree following the path to the final node where the domain of the problem to be solved is defined (see Fig. 4), more specific design artifacts are added to the existing set of generic design artifacts. This continues until the final node in the tree has been reached. If the found design artifacts along the path do not sufficiently cover the requirements, they need further to be developed.

The *artifact character map* is based on Albani and Winter's conceptual framework for design and engineering in information systems [17] as shown in Fig. 5.

The necessity for the conceptual framework arose from the fact that several classifications of DSR artifacts exist, but the relationship between the existing artifacts is missing. Each artifact type contributes to understand specific aspects of the approaches, but without the defined relationships a complete understanding of the means-end relationships is not possible. The contribution of the work of Albani and Winter [17] is that they put the existing artifacts in relationship. The result of their work is the conceptual framework as introduced in Fig. 5, which allows for a systematic analysis and comparison and eased combination of approaches. Since existing approaches need not only to be of practical relevance, but also theoretically sound, the framework provides the necessary artifacts to examine also the theoretical grounding of the approaches.

We base the second component of our KB structuring proposal, the artifact character map, on the constructional framework of Albani and Winter [17] and define the following two dimensions: One dimension results from the constructional framework introduced in Fig. 5 and differentiates the following artifact types: (a) underlying concepts and constructs, (b) foundational explanatory and/or predictive theories, (c) general components provided, (d) conditions or capabilities needed or possessed, (e) applied methods and resulting models, and (f) concrete design solutions. The other dimension denotes the problem coverage of the artifact, i.e. it specifies to what extent a design problem is addressed through artifacts of the respective type.

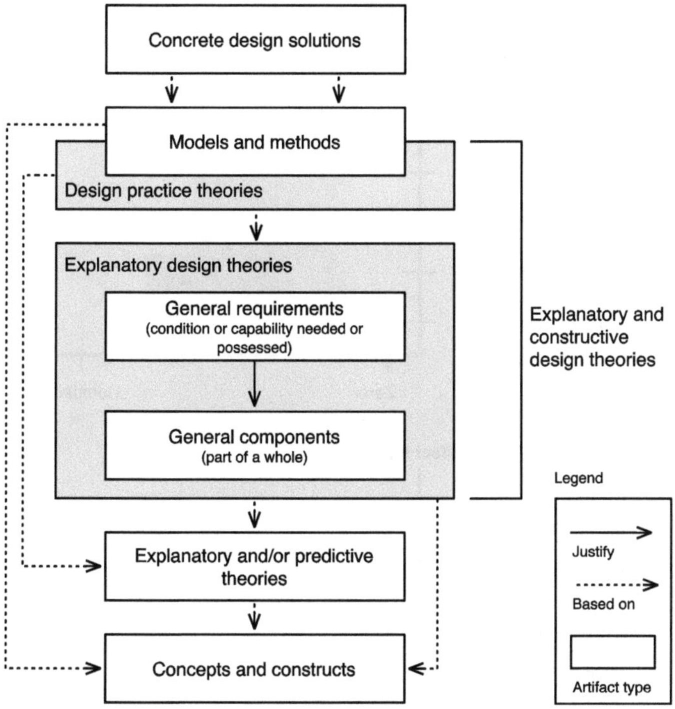

Fig. 5 Conceptual framework for design and engineering in information systems [17]

For a DSR approach, the artifact character map then represents which proposed artifact types address a design problem to what extent. E.g., does the approach provide clearly defined methods, constructs and concepts, which need to be used to design the solution, or does an existing approach already provide some concrete design solutions, which may be used directly as solutions to the identified problem. In Fig. 6 two exemplary artifact character maps are illustrated:

- The upper artifact character map represents an approach, which is strongly based on theory and clearly defines concepts/constructs to be used in order to derive at the required solution for a given problem. However, the map also indicates that this approach does not provide a large array of concrete design solutions, which could be used directly as a result for certain design problems. An example for this type of DSR approach is the Design and Engineering Methodology for Organizations (DEMO) [3].
- The lower artifact character map differs clearly from the upper in the sense that concepts and constructs are provided and have been used to design already a wide range of concrete solutions. However, the represented DSR approach has no clearly defined theoretical base. Nevertheless the approach provides a collection of concrete design solutions, which can be used directly to meet a particular need. An example for this type of DSR approach is ARIS [8].

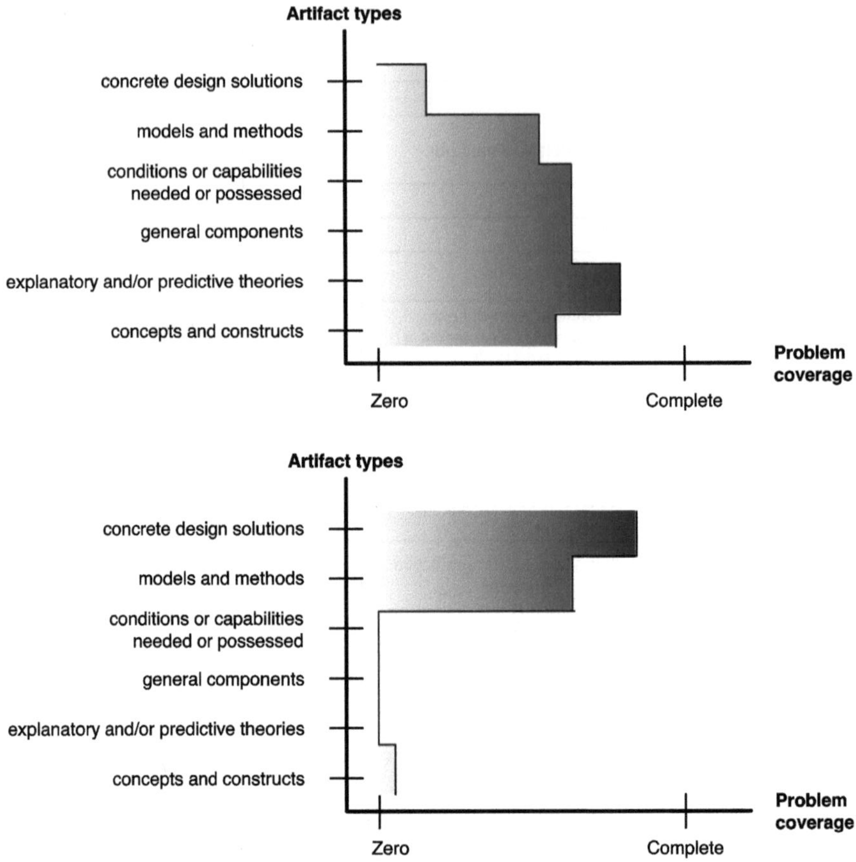

Fig. 6 Exemplary artifact character maps (adapted from [17])

In [17] the usefulness of the artifact character map is demonstrated by characterizing two very different ODE approaches: enterprise engineering and situational process-oriented information logistics. While both approaches aim at contributing to the same problem class, namely supporting the management of organizational change by means of generic artifacts, they are quite different regarding artifact types and design problem coverage.

The artifact character map helps to understand how approaches differ, and to identify an appropriate approach for certain artifact type and problem coverage. The search strategy for identifying the suitable solution for a design problem is implied by the structure of the artifact character map. By knowing in which application domain the problem is situated and therefore having identified the possible artifact types through searching the application scope map, the artifact character map further helps to identify the approach, or a combination of different approaches, to solve the given problem. The search in the artifact character map starts from the very specific solutions, namely the fit of a concrete design solution to the defined problem (see Fig. 5). If no concrete design solution is found one dives deeper in the artifact character map trying to instantiate reference models or methods in order to be able to adapt them for solving the given design problem. If this is not applicable the need for using design theories or finding explanations for relevant aspects in the identified problem domain is given. If none of those steps supports the problem solving there is a need to look for, or to define appropriate concepts and constructs. These concepts and constructs then build the basis to define the other artifact types in the artifact character map in order to develop the appropriate approach for solving the very specific design problem.

While the application scope maps allows to understand re-use potentials of existing design solutions with regard to their generality and domain, the artifact character map allows to understand which type of contribution an existing design approach can make. If existing DSR solutions are represented in both maps, a wide array of their relevant properties is made available for search so that the DSR process can locate potentially applicable solution artifacts for a given design problem efficiently.

4 Solution Requirements, Goals, and Context

The left part of Fig. 3 illustrates the main components of the problem specification: The *as-is situation*, *to-be situation*, as well as the *design goals* and the *design problem* context need to be understood in order to define the *solution requirements*. The solution requirements result from comparing the as-is situation to possible to-be situations. Such a comparison implies the definition of a path that transforms the as-is situation into the desired to-be situation.

While the as-is analysis aims at understanding the existing solution and therefore is based on observed data, to-be design might be more innovative and creative [16]. Depending on how much certainty exists about the 'right' solution approach, there are different ways to specify the to-be situation. If e.g., success factors for the respective domain have been researched that explain solution performance in sufficient detail and generality, to-be solutions might be derived in a very straightforward way. If 'best' (or at least successful) practices and their relation to relevant contingencies are commonly accepted in the respective domain, to-be solutions might also be specified directly. The more immature a domain is, however, the less well defined is the step of designing to-be solutions. Winter [16] presents three alternatives that use different performance valuations and are applicable in different stages of maturity:

- *Goal-oriented transition* assumes that as-is solution clusters (as shown in Fig. 4) can be generally valuated with regard to a certain goal vector. Using its individual goal vector, a company can evaluate whether the as-is solution is good enough or which other solution cluster (that has been realized by other companies) it wants to realize. Since all solution clusters are defined with regard to the same set of design factors, all possible transitions can be completely specified.

- *To-be solution survey* assumes that there is sufficient empirical knowledge available on to-be solutions in the respective domain. To-be solution clusters then can be specified in exactly the same way as as-is solution clusters have been discovered, i.e., by researching potential contingencies, collecting field study data and applying principal component analysis and agglomerative cluster analysis. If as-is and to-be data are collected within the same survey, transitions within the respective domain can be directly observed for every case. Neither a goal vector needs then to be defined, nor have situations to be evaluated using that goal vector. As-is and to be solution clusters might however reference different design factors so that the specifications of observed transitions is not as straightforward as for goal-oriented transition.
- If available for the respective domain, other applicable techniques for to-be solution design include *maturity models* or application of *design theories.* Basically every design/creativity technique is applicable. The more the applied technique deviates from the design factors and as-is solution specifications, however, the more difficult it gets to systematically specify transitions.

Transitions to to-be solutions define solution requirements which constitute the main input source for the searching of the appropriate solution components as introduced in Sect. 3.

5 Demonstration

We illustrate the applicability of the suggested approach by using the domain of "organizational change" as an exemplar. Even if there are many approaches around for organizational change, it still remains a major challenge for companies. Baumöl [18, 19] elaborated on this topic and tried to answer one major question, namely: "[…] how can the uniqueness of each change project be taken into consideration and yet a procedure of method construction be used which allows for making use of best practices, experiences and existing methods or, at least, parts of methods" [19]. While Baumöl's focus was on the creation of situational methods to support the change processes in organizations, we use some of her outputs to show how to search for adequate solution artifacts, which support organizational change, having the DSR KB structured as proposed in our approach. Baumöl conducted an analysis on 89 cases consisting of interviews, published cases studies and methodologies, covering the major topics to be addressed in the change process, namely strategy, leadership, sustainability, performance measurement and IT. In addition she applied cluster analysis to gain knowledge about reference contexts of change, which resulted in the following five clearly distinguishable clusters [19]:

1. Change projects having a focus on comprehensive strategy adaptation.
2. Change projects having a focus on redesigning the communication and interaction with customers and the business network.
3. Change projects dealing with growth strategies and cultural aspects placed in a technological context.
4. Change projects having a focus on process engineering or process redesign.
5. Change projects dealing with the improvement of agility of the organization.

A subset of these clusters is shown in Fig. 7. The observed and analyzed actual company solutions are represented as numbers (1-52). We adapted these results by adding a selection of exemplary design artifacts on different levels of generality.

While the reusable design artifacts on higher level of generality (e.g., the DEMO method [3], the Zachman framework [4] or the ArchiMate method [5]) are applicable to a wide range of organizational change projects, those on lower levels (e.g., Situational Management Method for Process Oriented Information Logistics (SMM for POIL) [20, 21]) deal with a concrete type of organizational change in a more specific way.

As explained in Sect. 3, the search strategy for identifying artifacts that can help to solve the required organizational problem, starts on the highest level of abstraction. While diving deeper in the tree, additional design artifacts are added as possible means to contribute to the desired ends.

As an example, we look at the case of redesigning the information logistics processes. In traversing the tree from the top to the bottom (to a specific solution, which is the closest solution to the problem that needs to be solved) the following design artifacts are added to the set of possible means: DEMO method [3], Zachman framework [4], ArchiMate method [5], Unified Modelling Language (UML) [22], ARIS framework [8], Business Process Modeling Notation (BPMN) [23], Reference Modeling [24], and SMM for POIL method [20, 21]). After quite a diverse set of potentially useful design artifacts has been identified by the search procedure, the next step is to better understand the specifics of the approaches in order to select the most relevant ones. Building on related DSR work, Albani and Winter [17] suggest an IS design and engineering approach for that purpose. The application of the conceptual framework to the different approaches allows for a better classification of approaches contributing to a better selection of an appropriate approach and, if necessary, a suitable and feasible composition of different approaches in order to reach the desired end. For the DEMO and the SMM for POIL approaches, Albani and Winter [17] demonstrate a concrete amalgamation whose results are shown in Figs. 8, 9.

DEMO is based on different kernel theories (*explanatory and/or predictive theories*) with clearly defined *concepts* and *constructs*. The basic concepts of DEMO, summarized by Dietz in the *Performance in Social Interaction (PSI) theory* [3 pp 81-125], constitute the *explanatory design theory*. The models and the modeling method together constitute the *design practice theory* of the *conceptual framework* (see Fig. 8). The design practice theory and the explanatory design

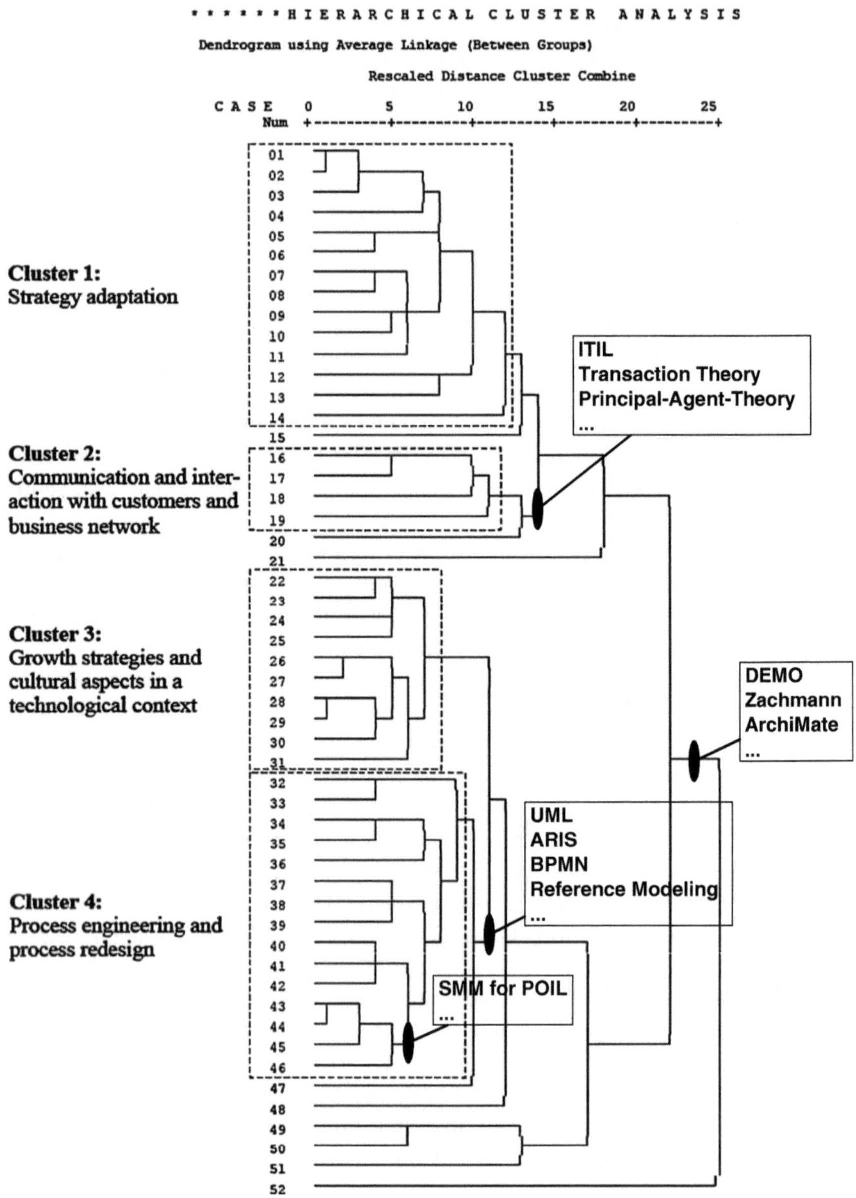

Fig. 7 Application scope map for organizational change (adapted from [19])

theory together compose the *explanatory and constructive design theory*, which is the DEMO methodology.

Regarding SMM for POIL, 21 reusable method fragments can be considered as *general design solution components*, which can be composed in order to derive at a

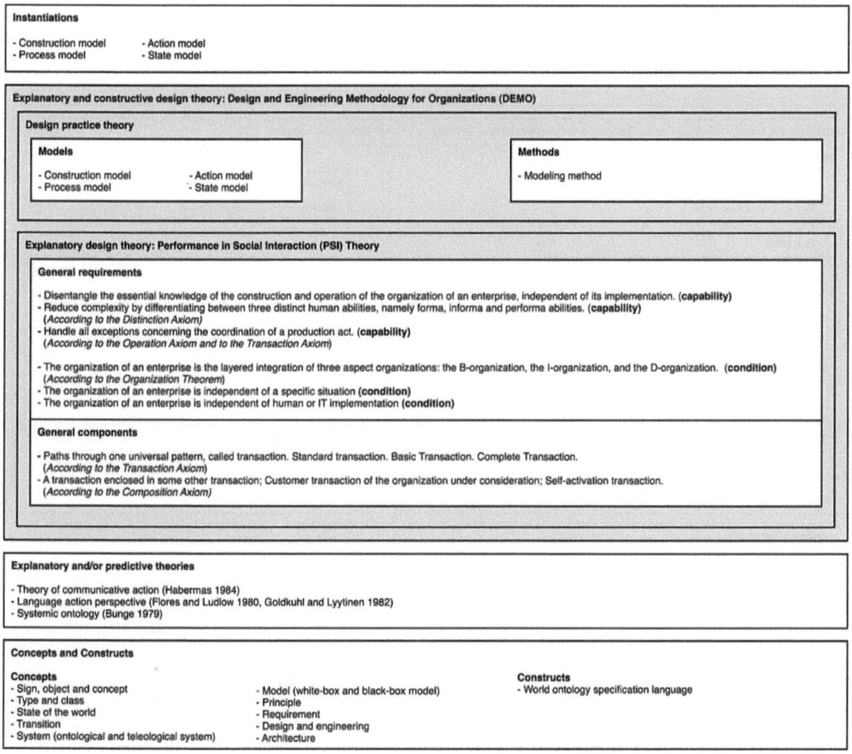

Fig. 8 Application of the conceptual framework to DEMO [17]

situated POIL method. To derive at a concrete solution, which is described by means of *instantiations* of *process models*, *information models* and *role models*, the following sequential design steps need to be performed: design problem analysis, classification of design problem (project type), situated method configuration, and situated method adaptation. Being sufficiently generic for the addressed problem class, the method steps together with the resulting models constitute a *design practice theory*. The whole approach is based on an *explanatory/predictive theory*, namely contingency theory, which explains why the performance of certain POIL solutions depends on design project goals and the design problem context.

The resulting artifact character map e.g., for DEMO is shown on top of Fig. 6. It visualizes the results of the analysis in applying the conceptual framework in a graphical manner. For each of the artifact types, as introduced in Fig. 7, such an analysis is recommended in order to gather a complete understanding of the approaches available for supporting the change process in organizations. A summary of the main contributions of the analysis of all approaches introduced in in Fig. 7 is illustrated in Fig. 10.

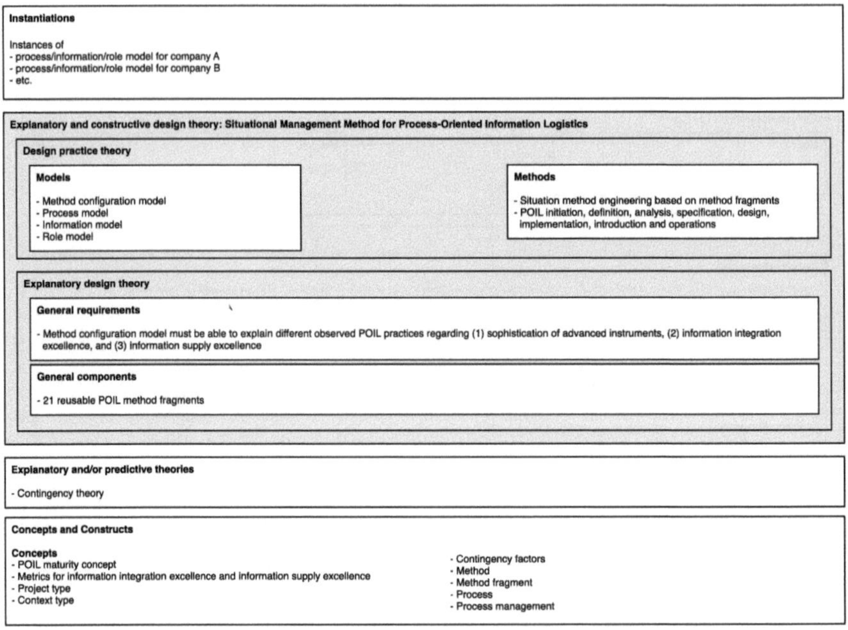

Fig. 9 Application of the conceptual framework to SMM for POIL [17]

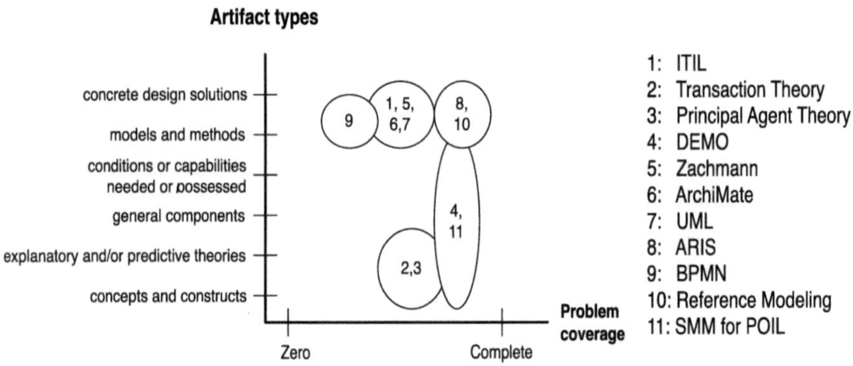

Fig. 10 Artifact character map for organizational change

In such a highly aggregated map, as visualized in Fig. 10, only the main focus (strengths) of reusable design artifacts can be visualized. For a detailed representation, the use of an artifact character map for each single approach is recommended (as shown in Fig. 6).

Using solution requirements and the two two-dimensional maps—the domain scope and the artifact character map—it is possible to identify solution components in a systematic way. As already mentioned above, real-world design problems often require several solution components (i.e. reusable design artifacts) to be combined because multiple aspects have to be covered and/or the problem combines characteristics of several domains.

Taking the example of redesigning the information logistics processes as shown above, Albani and Winter [17] demonstrate how a combination of DEMO and SMM for POIL leads to improved solution designs. The fact that both approaches aim at contributing to the same problem class, namely the support of management of organizational change by means of artifacts, which can be implemented or adapted to specific situations at hand, results from searching the application scope map (shown in Fig. 7). By consulting the artifact character map, which is based on the analysis of the two approaches by means of the conceptual framework for IS design and engineering, it becomes apparent that the result types of the two approaches differ completely. While DEMO focuses on designing the essence of an organization, SMM for POIL aims at the development of generic IS management methods that are adaptable to various design problem contexts and design goals.

The analysis and comparison of the two approaches enables the creation of a composed approach, i.e. one that combines situational solution support with modeling the essence of an organization, in order to construct more complete and improved solutions.

6 Conclusions and Future Work

Design problems in organizations require a systematic solution process that needs to be supported by efficiently organizing reusable solution knowledge. In our opinion, the differentiation of three cycles in DSR is artificial, and therefore the differentiation of a rigor related, a relevance related and a problem-solving related KB as a consequence should be avoided. We rather understand that every design cycle has rigor related as well as relevance related activities. Every design iteration involves learning more about the design problem and identifying additional elements of the KB components that might contribute to the solution. As a consequence, the KB of reusable design artifacts and the problem specification base should be organized in a way that supports this one-cycle DSR view.

We propose to annotate every potentially reusable design solution by information on artifact type, artifact generality, application domain and problem coverage. These four reference dimensions can be used to differentiate two two-dimensional maps that support a structured access and systematic identification of potentially relevant design artifacts: application scope map and artifact character map.

Building on a concrete design artifact amalgamation exemplar from the IS design and engineering field, we extended the demonstration example to the domain of organizational change. If we do not only know the design artifact type and its generality, but can also relate it to an application domain and define its problem coverage, then a systematic search can be defined that identifies potentially relevant reusable solution artifacts in an efficient way, thereby supporting the solution search process significantly.

The example of Baumöl [18, 19] is just one possible example for showing the applicability of our approach. However, it is a very good example since it already provides a first structuring of the knowledge base for organizational change problems. Baumöl [18, 19] has not only identified and validated problem domains and sub-domains of organizational change, but also used a large empirical base to identify successful patterns of instrument usage in organizational change projects. This knowledge will provide further opportunities to specify and validate application scope maps and artifact character maps that are not focused as much on IS design and engineering, as the example used in this paper was (DEMO and SMM for POIL). Due to the tight mutual links between organizational designs and IS designs, we are convinced that our design search procedure and design knowledge organization approach is not restricted to complex, situational IS design problems, but is useful for all kinds of organizational design and engineering where solutions need to amalgamate different reusable design artifacts and the understanding of the design problem is enhanced (and new potentially reusable existing solution components become apparent) in every cycle.

Acknowledgments This project is supported by the Swiss National Science Foundation (SNSF).

References

1. Albani, A., Jan L.G. Dietz, & Verelst, J. (2011) Preface. In A. Albani, J. L. G. Dietz, & J. Verelst (Eds.), *Advances in Enterprise Engineering V*. Berlin: Springer.
2. Österle, H. & Winter, R. (2003) Business engineering. In H. Österle & R. Winter, (Eds.)*Business engineering - Auf dem Weg zum Unternehmen des Informationszeitalters*. (pp. 3–19). Springer: Berlin etc.
3. Dietz, J.L.G. (2006) *Enterprise ontology: Theory and methodology*. Berlin: Springer.
4. Zachman, J. A. (1987). A Framework for information systems architecture. *IBM Systems Journal, 26*(3), 276–292.
5. Group, T.O. (2012) *ArchiMate 2.0 specification*. The open group series: Van Haren Publishing.
6. Hammer, M.& Champy, J. (1993) *Reengineering the corporation: A manifesto for business revolution*. New York: HarperCollins Publishers.
7. Davenport, T. H., & Short, J. E. (1990). *The new industrial engineering: Information technology and business process redesign. Sloan Management Review, 31*(4), 11–27.
8. Scheer, A.W., & Schneider, K, (2005) ARIS: Architecture of Integrated Information Systems. In P. Bernus, K. Mertins, & G. Schmidt (Eds.) *Handbook on architectures of information systems* (pp. 605–623). Berlin:Springer.
9. Hevner, A. R. (2007). A three cycle view of design science research. *Scandinavian Journal of Information Systems, 19*(2), 87–92.
10. Sein, M., et al. (2011). Action design research. *MIS Quarterly, 35*(1), 37–56.
11. Baskerville, R.L. (1998) Diversity in information systems action research methods. *European Journal of Information Systems, 7*(No. 2, June), 90–107.
12. Boehm, B. (1986). A spiral model of software development and enhancement. *SIGSOFT Software Engineering Notes, 11*(4), 14–24.

13. Efeoglu, A., et al. (2012) *Design science research in enterprise information systems. In Proceedings of the CONFENIS 2011 workshop, forthcoming*
14. Bucher, T., et al. (2007) *Situational method engineering: on the differentiation of "Context" and "Project Type"*. In *Situational method engineering: fundamentals and experiences*. Boston: Springer.
15. Winter, R. (2011) Problem analysis for situational artefact construction in information systems. In A. Carugati & C. Rossignoli, (Eds.), *Emerging themes in information systems and organization studies*, Physica: Heidelberg.
16. Winter, R. (2012) Construction of situational information systems management methods. *International Journal of Information System Modeling and Design (forthcoming).*
17. Albani, A., & Winter, R. (2012) *A conceptual framework for Design and engineering in information systems*. St. Gallen: University of St. Gallen.
18. Baumöl, U. (2005) *Situative methodenkonstruktion für die organisationale Veränderung*. St. Gallen: Universität St. Gallen.
19. Baumöl, U. (2005) *Strategic agility through situational method construction*. In *Proceedings of the European academy of management annual conference 2005.*
20. Bucher, T. (2009) *Ausrichtung der informationslogistik auf operative Prozesse: Entwicklung und evaluation einer situativen methode*. Verlag: Hamburg.
21. Bucher, T., & Dinter, B. (2012). Situational method engineering to support process-oriented information logistics: identification of development situations. *Journal of Database Management, 23*(1), 31–48.
22. Fowler, M., & Kendall, S. (2000) *UML Distilled: a brief guide to the standard object modeling language* (2nd ed.) Object technology series. Wesley: Longman Inc.
23. OMG (2006) *Business Process Modeling Notation (BPMN) Specification*. OMG.
24. Fettke, P., & Loos, P. (2003). Classification of reference models - a methodology and its applications. *Information Systems and e-Business Management, 1*(1), 35–53.

Dealing with Critical IS Research: Artifacts, Drifts, Electronic Panopticon and Illusions of Empowerment

Marcello Martinez and Mario Pezzillo Iacono

Abstract The chapter explores the diversity of topics, views and perspectives focused on the relationship between information systems (IS) and control, from a critical perspective. The work reflects upon the framework of Critical IS Research and its relation to Foucaultian approach and IS practice, informing the discussion on the ways IS and managerial Discourses framing the organizational reality. For this purpose, a case study of call centre outsourced industry is presented. We have explained how the overlapping between "electronic panopticon" and "commitment practices" used by management becomes a powerful tool for exerting influence and control in the sense of self-discipline and self-regulation. From this point of view, these tools are merely illusions of empowerment, representing only an apparent departure from traditional form of control, reiterating the idea of technological Discourse as a means of manipulation.

Keywords Artifacts · Drifts · Control · Electronic panopticon · Critical · Call centre

1 Introduction

Control in organizations has long been a topic of interest for researchers and practitioners, who generally recognize that control in some form is inescapable. In the managerial debate, the concept of control is normally used in broad,

M. Martinez (✉) · M. P. Iacono
Department of Economics, Second University of Naples, Capua, Italy
e-mail: marcello.martinez@unina2.it

M. P. Iacono
e-mail: mario.pezzilloiacono@unina2.it

R. Baskerville et al. (eds.), *Designing Organizational Systems*,
Lecture Notes in Information Systems and Organisation 1,
DOI: 10.1007/978-3-642-33371-2_5,

non-discriminating way to identify diverse ideologies and practices that have been developed to organize productive activity [1]. It is definitively evident that without the right typologies of control mechanisms it becomes impossible to be sure that worker will decide to submit to the logic of the firm, in order to get the maximum commitment at the lowest cost [2]. Managerial interest in control mechanisms stems from their use as a means of securing the objectives attributed to organizations by their most influential stakeholders usually, owners, managers and administrators [3].

Information Systems (IS) are often described as a disciplinary technology intended to regulate the actions of workers and produce information to improve the ability of managers for surveillance of the outcomes of those activities [4]. In particular, Critical IS Research (CISR) aims at revealing, criticizing and explaining how the development and use of IS in organizations and society in the pursuit of efficiency and rationalization increase social and organizational control, with potential detrimental consequences for some stakeholders and society as a whole [5].

The chapter explores the diversity of topics, views and perspectives focused on the relationship between IS and control, from a critical perspective. More specifically this work reflects upon the framework of Critical IS Research (CISR) and its relation to post-structuralism, IS practice, as well as other critical social studies [6]. In doing so it hopes to inform the discussion on the ways IS might control the way we work, live and think through, for example, framing the organizational reality. In this literature, interpretations of power and control are influenced by Foucaultian/post-structuralist approach [7]. So, our analysis will develop according this view.

The chapter will be organized in the following manner. A preliminary review will be made of the state of critical thinking in the fields of IS and organization, focusing on the conceptualization of CISR, the wide range of theoretical perspectives related to critical analysis of IS and the main topics questioned. Then we will review the CIRS literature on organizational control, discovering interpretations of the following concepts: electronic panopticon, emancipation, "socially shaped" drifts and technological discourses. After describing the methodology used for the empirical analysis a case study is described and examined. It focuses on the work practices of call centre outsourced industry. Finally, our conclusions will be explained and discussed.

2 Critical IS Research: Conceptualizations and Perspectives

The meaning of the concept "critical" related to IS is not self-evident. Under this respect, the main goal of this paragraph is to make clear this conceptualization, analyzing its various interpretations. It is not our intention here to present an exhaustive and comprehensive set of criteria for what constitutes CISR, but rather to illustrate a comprehensive summary of the different views regarding this subject.

First of all, it's good to point out that CIRS is included in the broader branch of Critical Management Studies (CMS). During the late twentieth century, a number of schools of thought have questioned power relations and organizational control implied by management. These included labour process theory [8], critical versions of postmodernism [9] and feminist organization studies [10]. As Spicer et al. [11] state, these attempts to question management are now brought together under the umbrella of CMS. The widespread use of CMS label to identify alternatives to established conceptions of management followed the publication of Alvesson and Willmott's [12] edited collection "Critical Management Studies" [13]. Thenceforth CMS has emerged as a movement that questions the authority, legitimating and relevance of mainstream thinking and practices. It reject the mainstream view that organizations are adequately represented as rational instruments for achieving shared goals and/or as media for satisfying people's need through producing good or service [14]. From the standpoint of CMS, the dominant paradigms of management are informed by a technical rationalist perspective, which sees management practices and tools as neutral, objective, impartial, scientific techniques designed to enable the effective achievement of goal. Rather a CMS view identifies management actions and rhetoric as a social practices derived from historical and cultural relation of power. In other words, all management knowledge is "socially situated" [15]. Adopting an inclusive view, Howcroft [16] encompasses critical research on IS as the branch of IS studies in opposition to technological determinism, which assumes that technological development is autonomous and that societal development is determined by the technology. On the contrary, critical approach seeks to challenge (rather than justify) technological imperatives as natural and inescapable, interpreting the adoption of IS by recourse to a wider social, political, historical, economic and ideological context. CISR typically emphasizes the effects of ICT on people (e.g. on their thinking, working conditions and identities [17]), organizations and societies (e.g. highlighting the fetish of statistics and preoccupation with targets which ICT facilitate and feed).

The basic assumption of this view is that technology (interpreted as both a body of artifacts and practices and as a specific artifact/object) is not neutral, but it is "socially shaped". In other words, it has embedded beliefs, values, culture and perceptions of both the designers and the consumers. These groups will have different view about the most appropriate design of the artifact, or even whether it is a desirable technology at all. In this context, technological artifacts can be viewed as culturally constructed and interpreted, not only in how technology is thought of but in its design and implementation [18].

In the Orlikowski and Baroudi's [19] well-known taxonomy, CISR is interpreted as an alternative to the more consolidated approaches of positivism and interpretivism. On one hand CISRs accuse positivist of defending the status quo, reinforcing power structures and strengthening managerial control over organizations and people's work. On the other hand, they also blame interpretive researcher for accepting the status quo and being too relativist and passive. In the opinion of Cecez-Kecmanovic [20], the main aim of CISR is to transform the social/organizational systems in terms of actors, IS, organizations (including their dynamic and relationships), by revealing and explaining how an information system, supposedly implemented with the purpose to increase efficiency and effectiveness, increased control and decreased autonomy and human agency.

CISR embraces a range of theoretical perspectives and social movements from various forms of Marxism, through Frankfurt School to post-structuralism. In particular, Brockelsby and Cummings [21] make a distinction between two principal branches of social critique, one ending in Habermas and the other in Foucault.

The Habermas lineage, largely related to distortion in communication [22], is typically interested in elaborating a systemic theory that can be applied "to collectively emancipate others from a worse to a better state" ([21], p. 741). The focus of Frankfurt School was the desire not only to expose inadequacies in society but also to encourage reflection upon and emancipation from such inadequacies as were identified [23].[1]

The second lineage referring to Foucauldian post-structuralist approach theorization. Our analysis, as said, develops according this view. In a recent analysis representing a sort of manifesto of critical thought, after having identified the philosophical roots of post-structuralism in the contributions of the sixties and seventies by the French philosophers Derrida (cf. concept of deconstructionism), Deleuze (subjectivity and relation), and especially Foucault (power and panopticism), Jones [24] illustrates its interpretative framework, focusing on three key issues:

- the role of communication and language as basic elements in processes that build meaning, as a text and form of representation for organizational relations, and consequently as an interpretative key for organizational analysis;
- the reconstruction of the concept of subjectivity, intended as a sense of self, through a discovery of its internal dynamic, revealing influences exercised by society, conflicts of power, and the structures of cultural discourses;
- the need to interpret organizations in a logic based on anti-essentialism: i.e. a tendency to criticize or, in any case, go beyond socially legitimized assumptions, acquiring an awareness of the influence of the position of the observer/

[1] Emancipation was a central thrust of the early Frankfurt School, partly explainable by its Marxist lineage. The concept of emancipation developed by Alvesson and Wilmott [28] describes the process through which "individuals and groups become freed from repressive social and ideological conditions, in particular those that place socially unnecessary restrictions upon the development and articulation of human consciousness" (p. 432). In Habermas view, emancipation requires what he calls "communicative action". One of the key themes in his writings is the need for mutual understanding through undistorted communication/language. In relation to IS the concept of emancipation leads to "emancipator IS development" and to "participatory design", including the organizational use of IS. The concern is how the development and use of IS entrench social structures that oppress organizational actors. From this point of view, IS should be designed, not just for organizational effectiveness, but also to emancipate people from undesirable social and physical constraints.

researcher in studying social phenomena; in other words, a perspective that takes into consideration reflexivity [25].

This approach, influenced by Foucault's concepts of power/knowledge, has focused on the methods with which managerial actions, interpreted in terms of discourse, contribute towards influencing and shaping self-control and self-regulation [26] and, at the same time, on how employees implement processes of resistance and reaction towards management action (emancipation) [27, 28].

The basic concepts in Foucault's work are: (i) Discourse (with a capital D); (ii) archeology of knowledge; (iii) genealogy of knowledge; (iv) and the panopticon metaphor.

Firstly, power/knowledge is exercised through discursive and non-discursive practices carried out as part of the Discourse, understood as that particular way of thinking, *forma mentis*, or cultural and institutional framework [29] that defines the partial perspective of a group of people. In other words, "Discourse" represents the broader social and/or organizational cultural systems with own values, language, symbols and rules: the "talked" and "textual" nature of everyday interaction in organization [30]. Under this respect, Foucault [31] encourages a view of Discourse as the medium through which power relations create speaking subjects. The second "Foucauldian concept", as we said, is archeology of knowledge. It can be seen as directly related to the clarification of the history of the rules that regulate particular discourses. The genealogical analysis aims to show how a given system of thought (a discursive formation) is the result of contingent events of history, and not the outcome of rationally inevitable trends. Finally, Foucault uses the idea of the pantopticon as a metaphor for the operation of power and surveillance in contemporary society. We deal with the Panoptical view in depth in the paragraph 3.

3 The Foucauldian Conceptualization of Control

The basic concept behind a post-structuralist approach is to be found in power of control as interpretative key to processes, analyses and organizational design. These studies typically explore shift from simple control to technical control to bureaucratic control and, most recently, to normative control.

It has generally been argued that management, in line with the features of post-Fordist organizational systems, has changed the methods of implementing organizational control, institutionalizing a concept of it that is less geared towards heteronomy (to be guided from the outside), based simply on respect for rules and the hierarchy, and more focused on self-regulation of behaviors and the creation/strengthening of a sense of commitment towards the organization [32]. Therefore, the way power of control is exercised typically constitutes the (mainstream) key to interpreting the difference between bureaucracy and post-bureaucracy. But, according to critical approach, while the rationale of post-bureaucratic organizational programming is apparently oriented towards the pursuit of flexibility, autonomy and enhancement of personal qualities, in reality it operates as an attempt to extend and render more comprehensive the capacity for standardization and control. In this sense, Barker [33] suggests that ICT is implicated in new forms of "concertive control".

The key of this perspective can be found—as we said—within the conceptualisations of Michel Foucault, a French historian and philosopher frequently quoted in organisational studies. Foucault [34] explains his interpretation of the concept of the power of control by referring, metaphorically, to the contribution made by English philosopher Jeremy Bentham and his works relating to an innovative type of prison: the Panopticon. Bentham identified the Panotpicon as a type of architectural and organisational solution to improve the efficiency of the penitentiary system. The prison is constructed as a circular structure around a central tower, topped with a watch house or observation point; the cells are laid out in a ring around the tower. Each prisoner can therefore be seen at any moment thanks to a window in the cell that faces towards the tower, but prisoners cannot come into contact with each other due to the side walls, or even see the guard due to the reciprocal positioning of the tower's observation windows and the windows in the cells.

Foucault saw power as something that is exercised rather than possessed: it is not attached to agents and interests but is incorporated in numerous practices. The Panopticon represents an instrument designed to inform the prisoners that they are being supervised, that they are being watched, although they can never be quite sure of knowing if and when they are actually being controlled: this knowledge tends to modify their behaviour [35]. The Panopticon metaphor, therefore, is important when considering the concept of post-Fordist control: visibility is not being seen, but the possibility of being seen. From this point of view, power of control is not expressed only when exercised, but in its capacity to be exercised, or in the knowledge that we may be observed. The visibility that IS provide to specific features of the organizational activity means that they are become objects around which interests are negotiated and political process enacted [36].

So, the power of control in post-Fordist models (from Total Quality Management to team-working) would not be manifested through the supervision, the formalisation and standardisation of movements, or even time and activities. Instead, control and coercion become self-control and self-constraint, and are carried out in accordance with the organisational design. In this sense, the new organisational formulas do not represent a victory over Taylorist principles, but an improvement and widening of them due to the increased efficiency of self-regulation in actions and behaviour on an operational level with respect to heterological regulation, linked, for example, to the mechanism of supervision.

Finally, we have to point out that the theme of panoptic self-surveillance and monitoring goes beyond the post-structuralist/Foucauldian approach and the authors committed to this area, reappearing, for instance, in a number of Bauman's works (e.g., [37, 38]). Zygmunt Bauman's intriguing and inspiring writings offer much for the understanding of surveillance in the twenty-first century. In his view, technologically mediated surveillance is carried on at a distance, separating in space and also in time those whose data are manipulated and the institutions engaged in their manipulation. In particular Bauman [39] sees the emergence of post-panoptic forms of power: these are mobile, nomadic forms of control that utilize coded information to monitor, predict and direct the conduct of individuals.

4 IS in the Foucauldian Perspective: Controlling Workforce, Processes and Structure

The critical literature on IS and control suggests that the design and the implementation of ICT might affect organizational control at least in two interdependent ways: controlling workforce and controlling organizational processes/structures.

In the age of the smart machine" by Zuboff [40] challenges the traditional labour view that managers use technology primarily as a means of controlling their workforce. She draws IS as the electronic panopticon, underlining as it avoids face-to-face contact between managers and employees, makes work practices visible and emphasizes the division of work. In particular, the author shows how the informating function of IS reveals the organization as the managing of "electronic text" in which Bentham's criterion of "at-a-glance" management becomes doubly instantaneous because organizational processes are represented as they actually happen [41].

It should once more be noted that Foucault's followers reject the notion of the awareness of subjects, preferring the idea of the discursive construction of control and subjectivities: the interests of human beings are neither independent nor self-aware, but represent positioning in a discourse. Organizational actions are influenced through a mechanism of self-monitoring, rather than direct control and supervision. This invokes the Zuboff's notion of electronic panopticon in which employees are enlisted in their own control because they believe that are subject to constant surveillance.

The concept of surveillance is strongly committed with the Foucault's notion of discipline. Foucault saw the panopticon as illustrating modern discipline via surveillance. From this standpoint, the training, work routines, appraisal systems and (electronic) self-surveillance are all exercising discipline in that management provide resources for normalization [42]. Understood in this way, the management practices and discourses impacts on the normalization of individuals' judgments about legitimate and non-legitimate actions. Sewell and Wilkinson [43], focusing on the just-in-time and total quality management practices in the manufacturing environment, suggest that these practices require systems of surveillance better than those offered by traditional bureaucracies. They argue that firms typically accomplish these purposes by introducing two disciplinary forces. The first is exerted by the supervision in each quality circle or group, by peers (horizontal process). The second is exerted by IS that operate as surveillance and control systems (vertical process).

To sum up, in a critical view IS development enables controlling workforce through electronic monitoring of their behavior—either directly via cameras, or through the 'electronic traces' they leave—controlling outputs or through normative control, e.g. as manifested in self-disciplining acts and concertive control and related to "fields of visibility".

According to CISR the second way in which IS affect organizational control is linked to the influence on organizational processes and/or structures, facilitating control and coordination of activities at different levels, simultaneously enabling and constraining those activities.

Firstly, in terms of control relating to organizational processes, it is worth noting Ciborra's [44] work [45]. In contrast to the prevailing view in IS literature, he suggests that IS artifacts may drift, i.e. "they deviate from their planned purposes for variety of reasons often outside anyone's influence" (p. 4) and puts forward a notion "of technology with a certain degree of autonomy and inner dynamics; of technology both as a drifting system and as a organism to be cultivated" (p. 32). In short, ICT infrastructures tend to have a life of their own: they drift as a result of their usages, design choices, organizational routine, human resource management, user resistance, and/or other unforeseeable behaviors of both systems and humans [46]. Building on this perspective, Rajao and Hayes [47] claim that this drift can be understood as a result of power relations and negotiations between diverse conceptions of controls [48]. Under this idea, the design and use of ICT artifacts tend to reflect the local dominant conceptions of control [49]. Thereby, the managerial distortions in technology discourse can significantly affect the drift processes.

Moreover, some studies have shown that IS are designed to support existing structures and that their use tends to strengthen the structures and ways of organizing which are already in place [50]. To understand where the power of control is embedded (or where it should be embedded) in a group or organisation requires first analysing the distribution of decisional power, or rather the level of centralisation/decentralisation. Evaluating a company's level of centralisation or decentralisation requires discovering where the decisions that influence its characteristic activities are made. In fact, power is not to be understood as an absolute concept, but as an element that presents itself in a relationship between the players involved. If the decisional power is delegated to a limited number of positions or organisational units, the company structure may be termed as centralised. If the power is instead distributed across a greater number of positions or organisational units, the structure is termed as decentralised. Decentralising power obviously causes issues with the control of behaviour. Decentralising decisions does not ensure that the actions taken and implemented are consistent with the objectives and the interests of the organisation.

Bloomfield and Coombs [51] suggest that centralization and decentralization might be seen not as "opposites" but as "mutually dependent", and IS as simultaneously supporting both. ICT have capacity for supporting flexible organizational structures and simultaneously constraining flexibility by making embodied routines more rigid.

The overlapping between the two dimensions illustrated (controlling workforce and controlling processes/structures) establishes a broader view of considering the relationship among IS and control in organizations: we refer to the impact of IS on sense-making [52] and organizing [53] processes at different levels of organizational life (individual, group and organizational levels). Sense-making frameworks operate to interpret the flux and make sense to equivocal inputs. Knight and Murray [54], among the others, focusing upon the political dimension of organizing, stress the role of manipulators of managerial discourse and practices, and technological tools: they account for how organizational actors make sense of and enact actions, behaviors and artifacts in their local context. In other words, ICT both create new conditions of possibility, e.g. new ways of organizing, and are implicated in different control mechanisms, e.g. they enable and constrain what we do and how we do it. They also influence the way we see things and think about them, or indeed what we perceive and think, and in doing so they frame organizational reality. Introna [55] interprets the relationship between IS and organizations not only as an electronic panopticon, but also as embedded in the "micro physics" of everyday life, power relations, discourse and knowledge. Bloomfield and Danieli [56] claim that in the "fabrication" of IS, the constitutive concepts of the dominant discourses and knowledge instituted in organizational practices have to be definite and organizational phenomena reconciled with them. Finally, Brooke [57] points out that the discursive nature of IS suggests that they are implicated in mobilizing specific representations of organizational reality.

5 Empirical Analysis

5.1 The Panopticism in the Call Centre Workplace

Call centres have become a convenient and widely used channel through which organizations communicate with their customers. They have been identified as a stressful place to work [58], due to the pervasive role played by computer information technology, in a workplace where the agent is isolated by the structured nature of their work. It has been argued that call centres represent a modern form of taylorism: they evoke the factory typically based on tayloristic principles and on assembly line that, especially in Italy, are the symbol of precariousness and little respect of workers' rights. Technology is the most obvious link between the contemporary call centre and taylorism [59]. The application of technology to monitor and electronically scrutinize performance coupled with the use of targets to focus and evaluate worker activity—from the distribution of calls in queues to the calculation and assignment of roster schedules—have all conspired to contribute to an industry reputation for a back-breaking work environment.

The combination of telecommunications and IS technologies typically allows employees to interface with customers on the phone, while simultaneously entering information into a specialized computer program. So, this technological integration facilitate managerial control over the labour process, through automatic call distribution, or predictive dialing systems. These systems distribute and set the pace of work, while monitoring employee performance through real-time statistical displays [60]. Further, call centre is made up of a mix of information technology, organizational features and new services provided, where both features from past times, such as the tayloristic principles, and new models to provide customer service live together.

Fernie and Metcalf [61] have utilized Foucault's adaptation of Panopticon to claim that electronic surveillance had rended perfect the supervisor power. They presented their findings as a validation of applicability of the electronic Panopticon perspective of the call centre. So Fernie and Metcalf invoke analogies to incarceration and omniscient scrutiny: "All that is needed, then, is to place a supervisor in a central tower and to shut up in each cell… a worker… They are like so many cages, so many small theatres, in which each actor is alone, perfectly individualized and constantly visible… Visibility is a trap… In call centres, the agents are constantly visible and the supervisor's power has indeed by "rendered perfect"—via the computer monitoring screen—and therefore its actual use unnecessary" (pp. 8–9).

5.2 Methodology

By the end of 1990s, the Italian call centre industry has growing up rapidly due to two different events: the de-regulation of telecommunications and public utilities, and the proliferation of mobile phones. Telecommunications has been the leading area in call centre development, than evidence of the growth in importance of call centre could be seen in the finance, insurance and commerce sectors as well as the public sector. In this context, Italian outsourcing industry of call centre has been an expanding market made up of many small and very small companies and few multinational ones.

In the following paragraph a case study [62] of work practices of Italian call centre outsourced industry is presented. Our interest is in call centres as socio-technical systems.

The analysis is based on a qualitative investigation conducted in terms of grounded theory. In the opinion of Jabar et al. [63], the qualitative research methodology approach is viewed as significant in IS research due to the value of capturing and explaining what is going on in real organization and "it enabled us to understand the interaction of social organization and information systems" (p. 50). In particular, the characteristics of grounded theory, inductive, contextual and processual, fit with the interpretive rather than positivist orientation of this research [64].

We analyse empirical material collected at a call centre, named Fastcall.[2] Fastcall could be labelled as "high quality call centre". With the term "high quality" call centre, we refer to a type of call centre where rather complex services are being delivered to the customer in a non-standardized mode of communication. Though there may well be standardized procedures for the agents how to handle each case in the company's information system, the agents are not supposed to communicate that to the customer at all, but rather, to treat the customer in an "individual" way in order to keep up the customer's attachment to the company.

It is an outsourced call centre operating on the behalf of about ten clients. It is a spinoff of a publishing company specialized in the publication of newspapers ads. It has been operating for about 10 years in direct marketing with particular experience in CRM and telephone services where it developed the technical and managerial know-how for the management of customer relationships. During the research period about 150 staff were employed on the site. Fastcall offers both inbound and outbound activities: the services offered range from outbound telemarketing campaigns to telesales, credit reminder, telephone surveys to support the commercial network, as well as inbound activities such as customer care services, help desk and purchase orders.

The collection of empirical data was carried out using a heterogeneous plurality of instruments. The methods include: document analysis, semi-structured interviews and participant observations. Fieldwork was carried out between April and early August 2011.

In particular, the analysis is based on a total of 26 semi-structured interviews with 2 managers, 3 team leaders and 20 call centre operators. The study is therefore based on an analysis that combines the interpretations and perceptions of middle management with the personal working experience of the more operational members. The interviews were guided by a questionnaire of wide-ranging, including questions about: the organization of the department (e.g. What is your job? How is work organized? How can you describe your life at work? How is your workplace?), HR practices (e.g. What is your human resource management policy? What about the evaluation/training system?), relationship among actors (e.g. How are the relations among colleagues and with team leaders?), physical environment (e.g. Are you satisfied with the amount of your allocated work space?; Is there adequate space between you and your nearest colleague?), technology functioning (e.g. Can you describe the specifications of the software used at the call centre?) and socio-technical interplays (e.g. How can a "certain" characteristic of the information system influence your way of working?)

During his fieldwork, the second author spent 2–3 days a week in the call centre, following the work schedule of the personnel from 8 am–2 pm or from 2–6 pm on alternate weeks.

---

[2] The name used is fictitious.

We sought to deconstruct the most frequent affirmations concerning control, ICT, effectiveness and empowerment; these represented the "text" which we tried to interpret.

5.3 Data Analysis[3]

The employees of Fastcall are able to interact with customers while at the same time working with computer-based systems which mark working time and control its quality. In the examined organization, call centre operators are organized in teams and each team has a team-leader who doesn't interact directly with customers, but is responsible to coordinate the members and to interface with the middle management. Operators must be logged on to the phone for 95 % of their working day, which includes agreed log outs for the following: a 10 min break and one-to-ones with their supervisor.

A call management system counts the number of daily incoming phone calls, which corresponds to the average number of times customers dial the toll-free number. This datum is necessary to quantify the amount of phone calls that the call centre will have to manage. The call-handling process can be summarized as follows: when the customer calls, the call is switched to the first available operator. As soon as the operator receives the call, on his personal computer monitor personal and contractual data of the customer appears. Hence ICTs implemented have allowed call centre leaders, from their desks, to track the number of calls that call centre agents take within any given time, the speed with which they answer the calls, the duration of the calls, the number of abandoned calls and the time that agents spend off the phone. In fact, team leaders are able to monitor every minute that agents spend in the office.

In addition to these quantitative measures, calls are recorded. This enables team leaders to listen the conversations in order to assess the agents tone of voice, enthusiasm and friendliness.

Roberto, one of the eight team-leaders, had this to say: "The software used by the company, called Teamviewer, measures the number of calls each operator makes or receives every half hour, and the duration of each conversation. As team leaders, we compare the "telephone" data with the data entered in the PC to analyse whether operators provide certain information, make bookings, succeed in selling products or services, etc. We can check if an operator self-excludes himself/herself from a call, and for how long. We can, at any moment, listen in on the conversations of each team member".

Fulvia, a young operator hired over 2 years ago, adds: "I'm alone in the tiny cubicle that is my work station. In fact, the white panels that subdivide the large open space we share as telephone operators don't allow us to talk, joke or simply

[3] The author of this paragraph is Alessia Berni, alessia.berni@uniparthenope.it.

see other colleagues or our team leader... our vital space measures around 55 cm^2... however, not being able to see doesn't mean we can't be observed... using their remote control, the team leaders can check what I'm typing on my keyboard or where I move my mouse at any time... at times I feel like I'm in a company broadcast of Big Brother."

The operator has to satisfy the need of the customer (efficacy) as soon as possible (effectiveness). In order to support the operators, the system includes also an intranet with a complex search engine which allows the operator to find the required information. Because all the process is mediated by the personal computer, it is manage the system in the best way. If the operator can interact effectively with the system, he will be able to concentrate the effort on the satisfaction of customer need, rather than on the use of the system.

Another operator, Elisabetta, a young university graduate who has been working barely a month, had this to say: "As soon as I have a new call in my headset, the category of the user I'm speaking to appears on my computer screen... in fact, each user is classified by the company with one of three labels: "copper", "silver" and "gold", depending on the level of spending the user is associated with. If the customer is labelled as silver or gold, I have to pass the call to other colleagues who manage bigger spending customers... as a newly hired employee, I can only take care of the copper customers... who are usually the most annoying... but I can't complain because it actually makes me feel a little freer... having to deal with the gold customers means increasing the possibility of being listened on by the team leaders... which means they're checking every word you say ... and you always have to be nice, perfectly informed on the product, etc."

So, this call centre epitomizes a modern factory where technology plays a relevant part: information technology automatically allocates work, monitors employees performance, the amount of workload, etc.

For Marco, an expert operator: "When I'm working on the in-bound, if it takes me more than four rings to answer a call at least three times over the period of an hour, the team leader immediately comes over to ask if anything's the matter. When I'm working on the out-bound, if it takes me too long between one call and the next, I get a blinking signal on my computer screen... it's a sort of reminder... if I ignore it... and don't pick up the call, the computer will automatically call...".

To sum up, a number of parameters are used as criteria to control and compare team results: the number of calls per hour, average phone calls and average on-hold times, the accomplishment of at least one task out of n useful contacts or according to average duration of each call. As far as inbound activities are concerned, the parameters to be observed can be average answer time for toll-free numbers, the percentage of agreed abandoned calls, the maximum allowed duration of a phone call, or the percentage of phone calls answered within n seconds. Moreover, as we said, a call's quality is evaluated against a mixture of technical, social and attitudinal criteria that includes: adherence to a script, call opening and closing, accuracy of information, product knowledge, helpfulness, enthusiasm, and professional tone.

Giorgia, an operator who's been working at Fastcall for over four years, had this to say: "I mostly work as an in-bound operator… The average time for a conversation deemed ideal by the company is around 3 min, and the average time any team must absolutely not exceed in a given work shift is 4 and a half minutes. I start to get very anxious every time a call is nearing 3 min. I look agonizingly at the seconds ticking by on my display. We're constantly monitored by the computerized information system … so that exceeding the time parameters considered standard will lead to a monetary penalty not just for me personally, but for the work group I belong to. In fact, a part of our pay is variable and is tied to the team's productivity… I try to be as fast and clear as possible with customers… but I can feel the clock "ticking down my back", almost as if it were a countdown on a time bomb".

The team leader manages and controls the team, coordinating the operational activities, ensuring staff turnover and the resolution of any critical issues. He propose and implements any corrective action. He has responsibility for a team of fifteen staff and they are expected to spend around 80 per cent of their time with team members, coaching, providing feedback on individual and team performance and identifying training needs. In addition to staff dedicated specifically to customer contact, team leader operates on site a number of employee carrying out support activities who control the functionality of systems, equipment and telephone lines, providing support to consultants for troubleshooting problems related to infrastructure and technology. Sometimes he helps the team to resolve complex issues, which require a greater degree of autonomy, and assigns tasks to various members of the group, encouraging job rotation, providing the right service level related to the expected workload. He are also expected to build motivation and bring some "fun" into the working environment by introducing spot prizes (at the discretion of the team leader), raffles and ad hoc bonuses.

As a Fastcall manager explained: "One month, for example, each employee on each employee on a certain team received a bonus of €100 because the abandoned call rate was less than 5 per cent. Moreover, there is a suggestion pattern, which was aimed at involving operators and encouraging them to think about ways of improving organizational processes or physical layout with raffle prizes for bright ideas".

In brief, HRM included use of continuing training, a wider use of performance-related pay and greater involvement in quality improvement teams.

It should be finally noted that in the formal document and informal communication workers are considered (by managers) key resources with higher competences and skills that are able to give customers unique solutions and to give answer to complex questions. Management stress the emphasis upon the quality of the employee-customer relationship. Whereas behind a statement concerning "empowerment as source of development, innovation, creativity and change" we can recognize a more complex and contradictory orientation pertaining to human resources management. The agents receive general guidelines only, and training how to communicate, but are supposed to do the "fine tuning" themselves. Although the management point out the calm environment and the different culture of the organization many quantitative targets apply across the call centre generally, especially statistical measurement of operators' output. In addition, other managerial practices are utilized to reinforce the centrality of target attainment: the prominence of promotion criteria, the use of charts to display team and individual performance and intra-company competition. In particular, the company encouraged team competition by publishing table grading and comparing the performance. The best performer is awarded at the end of each month.

Once of the company's managers told us that: "At the end of each month we organize a big group meeting in the conference room, where we disclose the name of the most productive team… we try to make the meeting fun, sort of like a big get-together… the team members from the winning group are awarded various types of benefits, from meal tickets to free passes at a nearby gym. The team leader, instead, gets a pay bonus of about 10 %."

5.4 Discussion

We have to emphasize the bureaucratic nature associated with standardization of processes and products where work is highly controlled and reutilized. Computer technology plays a crucial part in call centre processes as IS always remind workers that "although no manager may be physically present, every aspect of their performance may be … constantly measured" [65].

By making agents more calculable through normalizing disciplinary practices such as comparative performance measures, power becomes more anonymous and functional. Management relies most heavily on technology to pace and direct work and to monitor and evaluate the behaviors. Control institutionalized through technology is strengthened and deepened by the use of post-bureaucratic control in shaping organizational behaviors, reproducing a Panopticon structure both in terms of electronic surveillance and in terms of behavioral (self) regulation and discipline. Such dimensions are complementary rather than distinct: the overlapping between electronic and behavioral control mechanisms aims at combine (and balance) quantity goals with quality goals.

The call centre analyzed combines different management practices and discourses. On one hand computer technology, by virtue of frequency of use, and proximity to the call centre agent, has developed to such an extent that it provides a substitute for leadership in call centres. Many of the monitoring functions commonly associated with supervision are provided by the technology call centre agents employ on the job, thus reducing the need for this level of organizational hierarchy. On the other hand, the most commonly used concepts are: increase in the sense of identification with the company, value sharing, a clearer perception of the sense of participation, responsibilization and commitment at all levels of the organization. In practice reference is made to a set of elements designed to build and multiply internal consensus: the set of premises to decision-making which influence and shape the judgemental ability of the organizational actors.

The difficulty of overcoming resistance and building consensus on the basis of elements of participation tends to be camouflaged by the modification of the actors' perceptions and evaluation abilities. So, the embodies extensive forms of control, albeit reflective of the enduring influence of scientific management [66].

The overlapping between "electronic panopticon" and "commitment practices" becomes a powerful tool for exerting influence and control: a sort of concerted control in which the employees tend to internalize the dominant codes, until they emancipate themselves and become the most active controllers and regulators of themselves, their behavior and, through peer pressure, of their team colleagues [67]. In this perspective both IS and managerial rhetoric can be identified above all as providing leverages for manipulation designed to create conditions and cognitive premises which have an impact on behavior, a sophisticated mechanism of indoctrination and socialization of the existing culture, fostering standardization and efficiency. Managerial Discourses could be interpreted as a lever for standardizing values, a representation of the organizational ideology seen, in terms of Kunda [68], as an authoritarian system of meanings construed like a map by the power holder in order to decipher the reality and act accordingly. In fact the controlling mechanism tends to self-control and self-discipline rather than the traditional heterogeneous form. In short, technologically mediated surveillance becomes a tool for management to "seduce" workforce—in terms of self-regulation—and processes.

As Bauman [69] stated : "… there is no more Big Brother watching you; it is now your task to watch the swelling ranks of Big Brothers and Big Sisters, and watch them closely and avidly, in the hope of finding something useful for yourself: an example to imitate or a word of advice about how to cope with your problems, which, like their problems, need to be coped with individually and can be coped with only individually" (p. 30). Using subtle commitment techniques, the hateful effects of the traditional modern Panopticon are reduced and hidden. Even though workers are effectively controlled they perceive themselves as free individual whereas (p. 32): "individualization consists of transforming human identity from a 'given' into a 'task' and charging the actors with the responsibility for performing that task and for the consequences (also the side-effects) of their performance. In other words, it consists in the establishment of a de jure autonomy (whether or not the de facto autonomy has been established as well)".

6 Conclusions

The chapter provided an overview of views as well as some examples and illustrations to vast amount of Critical IS control practices. In particular, we have focused on the Foucauldian perspective because we believe that his notion of power of control in being productive as well constraining, positive as well as negative, distributed rather than centralized in a single location either personal or institutional, seems to resonate with contemporary organizational life [70].

Technological innovations have led to the availability of data, so that abundant information for control purposes seems to be available. The question that has been raised is to whom is the information available and for which purposes the information can be used. We have been used to see the control literature and language in which control is phrased as dominated by the passive form. Hence, the active part and the power position of that "controller" is not addressed. We rarely ask who uses the control data for which purpose.

In the light of this perspective, and in keeping with the poststructuralist paradigm, IS are viewed as a lever used by management and, more generally, by dominant groups who tend to act on the premises of organisational choices and behaviours to consolidate or increase their control over other organisational groups. We have tried to show how e why IS enable and constrain what we do and how we do it, underlying how the managerial Discourses impact on their drifts, the way we see things and think about them, or indeed what we perceive and think, and in doing so they frame organizational reality.

CISR has, at times, been criticized for its lack of engagement with empirical issues. Our case study provides an empirical example of the application of a Foucauldian perspective on power of control to an understanding of the implementation of organizational IS. The case illustrates the presence of a degree of alignment between dominant conceptions of control and IS artefacts. We have explained how the overlapping between "electronic panopticon" and "commitment practices" used by management becomes a powerful tool for exerting influence and control, in the sense of self-discipline and self-regulation. From this point of view, these tools are merely illusion of empowerment, representing only an apparent departure from traditional form of control, reiterating the idea of Discourse as a means of manipulation.

References

1. Ezzamel, M., Willmott, H., & Worthington, F. (2001). Power, control and resistance in the factory that time forgot. *Journal of Management Studies, 38*(8), 1053–1080.
2. Contu, A. (2007). Groups and teams at work. In: H. Willmott, D. Knights (Eds.), *Introducing organizational behaviour and management*. London: Thomson Learning.
3. Willmott, H. (2005). Theorizing contemporary control: Some postructuralist responses to some critical realist questions. *Organization, 12*(5), 747–780.
4. Doolin, B., & McLeod, L. (2005). Towards critical interpretivism in IS research. In: D. Howcroft, E. M. Trauth (Eds.), *Handbook of critical information systems research: Theory and application* (pp. 244–271). Cheltenham, UK: Edward Elgar.
5. Cecez-Kecmanovic, D., Klein, H. K., & Brooke, C. (2008). Exploring the critical research agenda in information systems research. *Information Systems Journal, 18*(2), 123–135.
6. Adler, P. S., Forbes, L. C., & Willmott, H. (2007). Critical management studies. *Academy of Management Annals, 1*, 119–179.
7. Avgerou, C., Mansell, R., Quah, D., & Silverstone, R. (2007). *The Oxford handbook of information and communication technologies*. Oxford: Oxford University Press.
8. Braverman, H. (1974). *Labour and monopoly capital*. New York: Monthly Review Press.

9. Alvesson, M., & Deetz, S. (2000). *Doing critical management research*. London: Sage.
10. Ashcraft, K. L. (2009). Gender and diversity: Other ways to make a difference. In M. Alvesson, T. Bridgman, & H. Willmott (Eds.), *Oxford handbook of critical management studies*. Oxford: Oxford University Press.
11. Spicer, A., Alvesson, M., & Kärreman, D. (2009). Critical performativity: The unfinished business of critical management studies. *Human Relations, 62*(4), 537–560.
12. Alvesson, M., & Willmott, H. (1992). *Critical management studies*. London: Sage.
13. Pezzillo Iacono, M., Toraldo, M. L. (2011). Handbook dei critical management studies review: Prospettive critiche agli studi manageriali. *Performance & Management, 2*, 49–54.
14. Alvesson, M., Bridgman, T., & Willmott, H. (Eds.). (2009). *Oxford handbook of critical management studies*. Oxford: Oxford University Press.
15. Pezzillo Iacono, M., Esposito, V., Mercurio, R. (2012) Controllo manageriale e regolazione dell'identità organizzativa: la prospettiva dei Critical Management Studies. *Management Control, 1*, 7–26.
16. Howcroft, D. (2009). Information System. In M. Alvesson, T. Bridgman, & H. Willmott (Eds.), *Oxford handbook of critical management studies*. Oxford: Oxford University Press.
17. Doolin, B. (2002). Enterprise discourse, professional identity and the organizational control of hospital clinicians. *Organization Studies, 23*(3), 369–390.
18. McLoughlin, I., & Harris, M. (1997). *Innovation, organizational change and technology*. London: International Thompson Business Paper.
19. Orlikowski, W. J., & Baroudi, J. J. (1991). Studying information technology in organizations: research approaches and assumptions. *Information Systems Research, 2*(1), 1–28.
20. Cecez-Kecmanovic, D. (2005). Basic assumptions of the critical research perspectives in information systems. In D. Howcroft & E. Trauth (Eds.), *Handbook of critical information systems research: Theory and application* (pp. 19–46). UK, Edward Elgar: Aldershot.
21. Brocklesby, J., & Cummings, S. (1996). Foucault plays Habermas: An alternative philosophical underpinning for critical systems thinking. *Journal of the Operational Research Society, 47*(6), 741–754.
22. Myers, M. D., & Klein, H. (2011). A set of principles for conducting critical research in information systems. *MIS Quarterly, 35*(1), 17–36.
23. Brooke, C. (2002). Critical research in information systems. *Journal of Information Technology, 17*(2), 45–47.
24. Jones, G. (2009). Poststructuralism. In M. Alvesson, T. Bridgman, & H. Willmott (Eds.), *The Oxford handbook of critical management studies*. Oxford: Oxford University Press.
25. Fournier, V., & Grey, C. (2000). At the critical moment: Conditions and prospects for critical management studies. *Human Relations, 53*(1), 7–32.
26. Sveningsson, S., & Alvesson, M. (2003). Managing managerial identities: Organizational fragmentation, discourse and Identity Struggle. *Human Relations, 56*(10), 1141–1193.
27. Alvesson, M., & Willmott, H. (2002). Identity regulation as organizational control: Producing the appropriate individual. *Journal of Management Studies, 39*, 619–644.
28. Alvesson, M., & Willmott, H. (1992). On the idea of emancipation in management and organization studies. *Academy of Management Review, 17*(3), 432–464.
29. Consiglio, S., Moschera, L., Berni, A., Cicellin, M. (2010) Institutional logics and the rise of a new organisational field, 6th New Institutionalism Workshop, Lyon.
30. Alvesson, M., & Karreman, D. (2000). Varieties of discourse: On the study of organizations through discourse analysis. *Human Relations, 53*(9), 1125–1149.
31. Foucault, M. (1977). *Discipline and punish*. New York: Vintage.
32. du Gay, P., & Salaman, G. (1992). The cult[ure] of the consumer. *Journal of Management Studies, 29*, 615–633.
33. Barker, R. J. (1993). Tightening the iron cage: Concertive control in self-managing teams. *Administrative Science Quarterly, 38*, 408–437.
34. Foucault, M. (1980). *Power/knowledge*. New York: Pantheon.
35. Franco, M., & Mariano, S. (2007). Information technology repositories and knowledge management processes: A qualitative analysis. *Vine, 37*(4), 440–451.

36. Doolin, B. (2009). Information systems and power: A Foucauldian perspective. In C. Brooke (Ed.), *Critical management perspectives on information systems* (pp. 211–230). Oxford: Butterworth Heinemann.
37. Bauman, Z. (2001). *Community: Seeking safety in an insecure world.* Cambridge: Polity Press.
38. Bauman, Z. (2002). *Society under siege*. Cambridge : Polity Press.
39. Bauman, Z. (1998). *Globalization. The human consequences.* New York: Columbia University Press.
40. Zuboff, S. (1988). *In the age of the smart machine: The future of work and power.* New York: Basic Books.
41. Cooper, R. (1991). Formal organization as representation: Remote control, displacement, abbreviation. In M. Reed & M. Hughes (Eds.), *Rethinking organization.* London: Sage.
42. Alvesson, M. (2010). Self-doubters, strugglers, storytellers, surfers and others: Images of self-identities in organization studies. *Human Relations, 63*(2), 193–217.
43. Sewell, G., & Wilkinson, B. (1992). "Someone to watch over me": Surveillance, discipline and the just-in-time labour process. *Sociology, 26*(2), 271–289.
44. Ciborra, C. U. (2000). A critical review of the literature on the management of corporate information infrastructure. In C. U. Ciborra (Ed.), *From control to drift: The dynamics of corporate information infrastructures* (pp. 15–40). Oxford: Oxford University Press.
45. Klecun, E. (2011) Information and communication technologies as control mechanisms. *Proceeding VII CMS International Conference, Naples.*
46. Ciborra, C. U. (2002). *The labyrinths of information: Challenging the wisdom of systems.* Oxford: Oxford University Press.
47. Rajao, R., & Hayes, N. (2009). Conceptions of control and IT artefacts: An institutional account of the Amazon rainforest monitoring system. *Journal of Information Technology, 24*(4), 320–331.
48. Fligstein, N. (1990). *The transformation of corporate control.* Cambridge, Mass: Harvard University Press.
49. Martinez, M. (2011). ICT, productivity and organizational complementarity. In: C. Rossignoli, A. Carugati (Eds.), *Emerging themes in information systems and organization studies* (pp. 271–281). Heidelberg: Physica-Verlag.
50. Orlikowski, W. J. (2000). Using technology and constituting structures: a practice lens for studying technology in organizations. *Organization Science, 11*(4), 404–428.
51. Bloomfield, B., & Coombs, R. (1992). Information technology, control And power: The centralization and decentralization debate revisited. *Journal of Management Studies, 29*(4), 459–470.
52. Weick, K. E., Sutcliffe, K. M., & Obstfeld, D. (2005). Organizing and the process of sensemaking. *Organizations Science, 16*(4), 409–421.
53. Orlikowski, W. J. (2002). Knowing in practices: Enacting a collective capability in distributed organizing. *Organization Science, 13*(3), 249–273.
54. Knights, D., & Murrey, F. (1994). *Managers divided: Organizational politics and IT management.* London: Wiley.
55. Introna, L. D. (1997). *Management, information and power.* London: Macmillan.
56. Bloomfield, B., & Danieli, A. (1995). The role of management consultants in the devleopment of information technology: The indissoluble nature of socio-political and technical skills. *Journal of Management Studies, 33*(1), 27–46.
57. Brooke, C. (2009). *Critical perspective on information systems.* Oxford: Elsevier.
58. Mulholland, K. (2002). Gender, emotional labour and team working in a call centre. *Team Working in a Call Centre, Personnel Review, 31*(3), 283–303.
59. Berni, A. Pezzillo Iacono, M., Martinez, M. (2012) Organizational change and dynamics of control: An analysis of Italian Call Center Workplace. *Chinese Business Review, 11*(4), 402–410.
60. Callaghan, G., & Thompson, P. (2002). (2002), "We recruit attitude": The selection and shaping of routine call centre labour. *Journal of Management Studies, 39*(2), 233–254.

61. Fernie, S., & Metcalf, D. (1998). (Not) hanging on the telephone: Payment systems in the new sweatshops. *CEP Discussion paper, 390*, 1–41.
62. Yin, R. K. (2003). *Case study research: Design and methods* (3rd ed.). Newbury Park, CA: Sage.
63. Jabar, M. A., Sidi, F., Selamat, M. H., Ghani, A. A. A., & Ibrahim, H. (2009). An Investigation into methods and concepts of qualitative research in information system research. *Computer and information Science, 2*(4), 47–54.
64. Orlikowski, W. J. (1993). CASE tools as organizational change: Investigating incremental and radical changes in systems development. *MIS Quarterly, 17*(3), 309–340.
65. Macdonald, C. L., Sirianni C. (Eds.) (1996) *Working in the service society*. Temple University Press. Philadelphia.
66. Bain, P., Taylor, P. (2000) Entrapped by the "electronic panopticon" Worker.resistance in the call centre, New Technology. *Work and Employment, 15*(1), 2–18.
67. Canonico, P., De Nito, E., Mangia, G., Mercurio, R., & Esposito, V. (2009). Interpreting projects: Bureaucratical mechanisms to enforce control or lever for change. *Organizacja I Zarzadanie, 3*(7), 5–16.
68. Kunda, G. (1992). *Engineering culture: Control and commitment in a high-tech corporation*. Philadelphia: Temple University Press.
69. Bauman, Z. (2000). *Liquid modernity*. Cambridge: Polity Press.
70. Knight, D., Willmott, H. (2011) *Organizational analysis*. Essential readings, Cengage learning EMEA.

Part II
Design and Evaluation of IT Artifacts

User Centered Systems Design: The Bridging Role of Justificatory Knowledge

Paolo Spagnoletti and Laura Tarantino

Abstract In this paper we debate on the possibility of enhancing current Human Computer Interaction (HCI) methods by proposing a structured view on current approaches to the design of IT artifacts which is grounded on the Information Systems (IS) literature. We adopt a design research approach by focusing on the design problem of "designing user centered systems" and by applying a framework based on "The anatomy of a design theory" [1], to better understand the nature of current User Centered Design methods. Our discussion brings to both a deep understanding on the design problem domain (the design of User Centered Systems) and a conceptual contribution at the meta-level of the design research debate. Interaction designers can benefit from the proposed conceptualization by following a more holistic approach in the analysis of the context of use. As a consequence IT artifacts are expected to better fit with the dynamics of socio-technical systems at different levels (i.e. individual, group, organizational, institutional, etc.). The value of our proposal lies in the approach adopted for conducting the research and in the research outcome itself (design theory).

Keywords User centered systems · Design theory · e-Care

P. Spagnoletti (✉)
CeRSI-LUISS Guido Carli University, Roma, Italy
e-mail: pspagnoletti@luiss.it

L. Tarantino
University of L'Aquila, L'Aquila, Italy
e-mail: laura.tarantino@univaq.it

R. Baskerville et al. (eds.), *Designing Organizational Systems*,
Lecture Notes in Information Systems and Organisation 1,
DOI: 10.1007/978-3-642-33371-2_6,

1 Introduction

Human–computer interaction (HCI) can be defined as "the discipline concerned with the design, evaluation and implementation of interactive computing systems for human use and with the study of major phenomena surrounding them" [2]. It is concerned, among others, with the joint performance of tasks by humans and machines, and hence it requires to study people and their tasks, computer technology and the ways these influence each others, with the aim of defining principles, guidelines and design approaches that bring to the development of usable systems. A different perspective on the interaction between people, algorithmic processes, data and technology come from the field of Information Systems (IS): as Gregor points out, a distinguished characteristic of the IS field is that it "concerns the use of artifacts in human–machine systems" [3]. More precisely, with the words of Lee, "research in the information systems field examines more than just the technological system, or just the social system, or even the two side-by-side; in addition, it investigates the phenomena that emerge when the two interact" [4].

The clear overlapping of intents (meta-goals) between the two fields suggests to investigate, both at the theoretical/methodological level and at the empirical level, possible contaminations that enrich the body of knowledge on which HCI and IS rely, and in particular to investigate whether and to which extent can the research on IS contribute to the design of interactive systems. Exploring the interstices between these two disciplines can make great intellectual progress as suggested by Baskerville and Myers who advocate a multidirectional view of the knowledge creation process among different fields of studies [5].

In the attempt to provide a unified view on theories in the IS field, Shirley Gregor has proposed a general classification based on five categories. Among these categories she introduces the "theories for design and action" that are rooted in the design science tradition and focus on "how to do something". These theories are prescriptive in nature and have different goals with respect to those aimed to analyze, explain, and predict existing phenomena which traditionally belong to the domain of natural and social sciences. Although Information Systems Design Theories (ISDT) differ from the other categories of theories, their role in design research is still at the center of the IS scholarly debate [6]. For instance in a recent work Baskerville and Pries-Heje argue that an explanatory component is embedded in each ISDT as an essential component [7]. While other contributions recognize the existence of a mutual relationship between IT artifacts and the existing knowledge base [8]. Independently from the role of ISDTs, there is a common agreement in the design research community on the existence of an evaluation system that makes a problem solution preferable with respect to others in achieving a certain goal. In other words, a system of values underpins a design research effort and is used to establish the desirable scenario to be achieved through the designed artifact, with respect to both technical properties and ethical issues.

Since the goal of designing interactive systems is at the core of any HCI research effort, a theoretical review of HCI contributions can benefit from the concepts, models and frameworks developed in the IS design research stream. This is even more true if we consider the multidisciplinary nature of the HCI field that encompasses contributions (at least from) psychology, cognitive science, ergonomics, sociology, computer science, engineering, business, graphic design. All these disciplines have to work side-by-side not only in terms of experts and consultants belonging to a design team, but, before all, in terms of a structured and organic body of theories that affect actual design processes centered on users and incorporating both cognitive models for assessing and/or predicting the usability of the product under design and analytical/empirical techniques for evaluating whether such a product meets the user's requirements [9]. In particular, over the years the human-centered product development stood out as a usability oriented iterative design process reversing the traditional technology-centered process, and recognizing the need of "designing the interface first, and then implement to the interface design" [10] ("interface" here has to be intended, in a broad sense, as the environment—its characteristics, modalities and paradigms—through which users accomplish their tasks, how they do them and how the system responds). According to current methodologies for developing User Centered Systems (UCS), the interactive system is achieved by a design cycle that iterates among the activities of defining requirements, designing, prototyping and evaluating, until satisfaction. Design, prototyping and evaluation are based on the knowledge of users, technology and tasks, that, at least for the requirements elicitation, comes in the form of analytical, explanatory or predictive rules resulting in design prescriptive rules (e.g. knowledge on the human eye and the visual perception may result in rules about where to put a visual item on the screen, or knowledge about the human memory may result in rules about the optimal length of chunks of visualized information).

The objective of this paper is to enhance current UCS design methodologies by providing a theoretical review of HCI paradigms. Concepts and principles from the ISDT literature provide the lens for analyzing trends in HCI research and to identify possible directions for future theory development. Our assumption is that a deep investigation from a design science perspective can highlight the benefits of enlarging the scope of HCI kernel theories in the realm of social sciences and humanities towards a new generation of methods and methodologies. In other words we aim at investigating on how a design science perspective can be used to combine business and humanistic values [11] and to enrich the "science" side of HCI to better assist designers in predicting the success of their choices. Nevertheless we recognize the value and the contribution of the "craft" side in the HCI craft-science tension [9].

The paper is structured as follows. We first describe the design theory framework on which we base our contribution. Then we provide a synthetic view on the evolution of the main paradigms in HCI. After that we analyze the foundations of current UCS design methods through the lens of the ISDT main constructs. We then provide an expository instantiation based on the evidences collected in the context of a European project for the development of an IT platform enabling social interaction of elderly persons with their social entourage. Finally we close the paper by discussing implications for research and practice.

2 The Design Theory Framework

The first authors who have asserted that design research provides a theoretical contribution in the form of an ISDT, are Walls, Widemeyer and El Sawy in their ISR paper on 1992 titled "Building an Information System Design Theory for Vigilant EIS" [12]. Fifteen years later, Gregor and Jones revise this work and define a set of six core components and two additional components for specifying a design theory so that it can be communicated, justified, and developed cumulatively [13]. These authors share the view of considering an ISDT as grounded on Kernel Theories (KT) and being itself the main outcome of a design research effort. A different perspective on design research in IS has been proposed by [14] and is based on the work of March and Smith [15]. These authors put the IT artifact at the center of a design research effort, maintaining that constructs, models, methods and instantiations are "the concrete prescriptions that enable IT researchers and practitioners to understand and address the problems inherent in developing and successfully implementing information systems within organizations". Finally a third position emphasizes the importance of artifact impact and utility in spite of artifact theoretical grounding. Nevertheless the contribution of external explanatory theories is still considered by these authors important for enhancing the design theory validity [16]. By referring to these three views on the input and output role of theories with respect to a design research process, a recent contribution has identified three schools of thought named "kernel theory fundamentalist", "design theory opponents", and "kernel theory pragmatist" respectively [17]. We will come back on such distinction later, for analyzing the epistemological positions of current HCI approaches.

In this paper we share the view of the kernel theory fundamentalists school and we agree on the fact that ISDTs are the natural outcome of a design research effort and provide grounding for artifact construction. Therefore we adopt the "anatomical skeleton" for IS design theories proposed by Gregor and Jones by adding some development on the relationships among these elements.

The explanatory power of a design theory as complementary to its prescriptive value has been recently conceptualized by Baskerville and Pries-Heje [7] who see the centrality in design science research of the functional or teleological explanations linking the artifact with its environment. They introduce the constructs of capabilities and conditions as characterizing the general requirements of a design solution and they describe the interaction between general requirements and general components as circular: "The definitions of general requirements and general components must be circular. Requirements specify (and explain) the reasons for components. Components are justified by requirements".

We argue that the Purpose and Scope (P&S) definition of a design theory as described by Gregor and Jones embeds the artifact mutability design components as well as the capabilities described so far. In fact, in order to describe the set of meta-requirements or goals that specify the type of artifact to which the theory applies and also defines the boundaries of the theory, both the capabilities needed

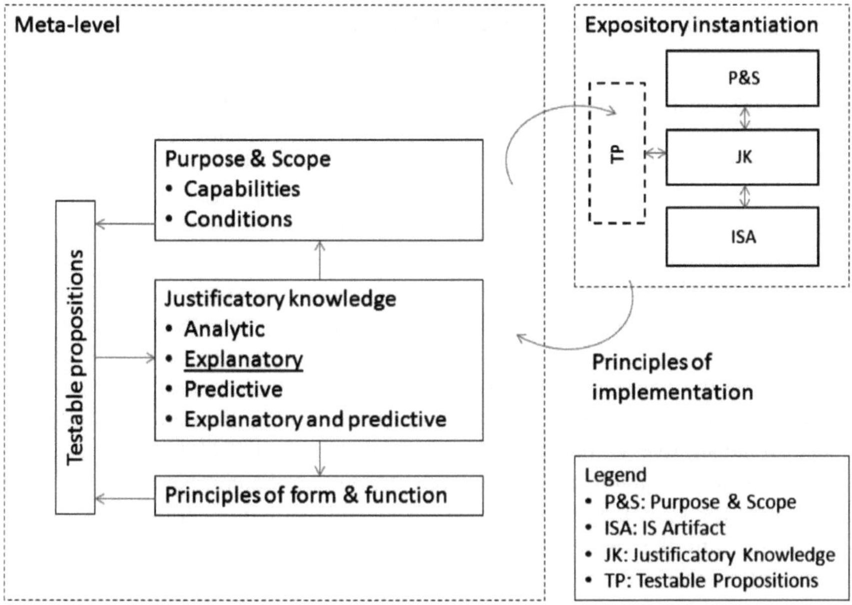

Fig. 1 Relationships among ISDT components

or possessed by the artifact must be represented. Furthermore the artifact mutability defined as "the changes in state of the artifact anticipated in the theory" is related to the presence of conditions that makes the functional explanation either perpetual or conditioned to some circumstances.

A second assumption is related to the way in which the justificatory knowledge (JK) is related to the remaining design components. We see it as the source of analytical tools, explanatory, and predictive theories informing the purpose and scope definition as well as the abstract architecture of the IS artifact (ISA). This body of knowledge receives feedback from the other components in the form of testable propositions in which capabilities and conditions are related to the principles of form and function by the means of technological rules which are truth statements about the design theory [18].

Finally, by referring to the relationship of these generalized elements with the additional components we assume that an expository instantiation can serve as an expository device and for purpose of testing. This conceptual operation is called projection and it has a fundamental role for deriving principles for implementing the theory in specific contexts [7].

Our interpretation of the relationships among all these elements is depicted in Fig. 1 where we provide a framework on which we base the following discussion.

3 A Theoretical Review of HCI Research

HCI has been a particularly dynamic field, in large part due to the continuous increase of hardware capabilities. In the last century, depending on the research focus, different communities have contributed to this field with multiple methods and theoretical traditions [19]. In his paper titled "Three faces of Human–Computer Interaction" Jonathan Grudin provides a detailed history of the development of the Human-factor and Ergonomics, HCI in Management Information Systems, and Computer–Human Interaction streams of research which focus on computer operations, information systems and management, and discretionary hands-on use respectively.

Following the works of Kuhn [20] and Agre [21], three paradigms have been identified in HCI, each of which takes a different metaphor of interaction [22]. The theory of generative metaphors has been developed in [21] for analyzing the typical questions of interest for a research stream and the corresponding methods and criteria for knowledge creation. Each metaphor of interaction bring certain phenomena into the center of investigation, while marginalizing others. Phenomena of interest, questions, methods and validation procedures are the main constructs used by [22] to characterize three paradigms in HCI literature. The first paradigm is based on the metaphor of interaction as man–machine coupling where the central goal of the design is to optimize the fit between man and machine. This human factors perspective is an a-theoretic and pragmatic approach to which engineering, programming and ergonomics disciplines provide the grounding for empirically validated objective hypotheses. The second paradigm dominates the HCI discourse and is based on the metaphor of interaction as information exchange and communication where the primary goal of HCI is optimizing the accuracy and the efficiency of information transfer among computers and their users. This objective is achieved through the definition of abstract models of interactions that enable to systematically compare alternative design solutions. Finally the third paradigm is based on the metaphor of interaction as phenomenologically situated and its main focus is on the construction of meaning and on the complexity around the system.

We agree with authors claiming that this conceptualization allows to develop an overall understanding of the nature of interaction and good practices around design and evaluation. In fact it provides a lens for the interpretation of the broadening process of HCI from its original roots in engineering research and later in cognitive science towards the more contemporary strands of research focusing for instance on the dynamic context of use, socially situated actions, indirect multiple goals, non-task oriented computing, and other approaches that do not fit well in the first two paradigms.

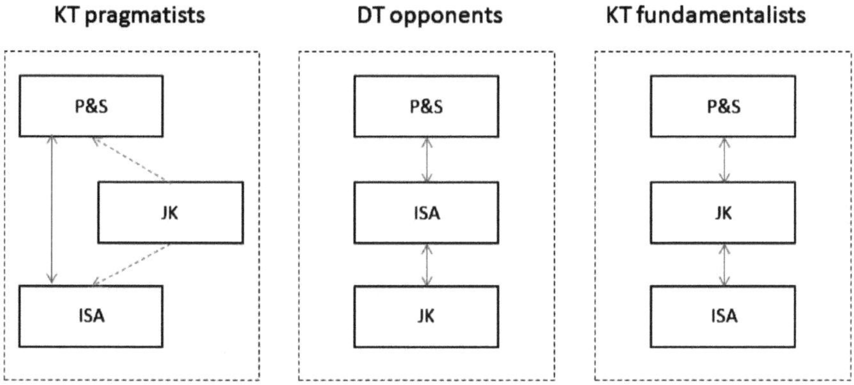

Fig. 2 Design theory schools (adapted from [17])

3.1 The Role of Theories in HCI Research

With these premises it becomes evident that the role of theories in the HCI field is somehow evolving with consequences on the epistemological positions of the different paradigms. Referring to the current debate on design research in IS, we argue that analyzing the relationships among design components within the three HCI paradigms can lead to achieve a better understanding on their epistemological position. In fact, since almost any HCI development can be seen as an instantiation of the general ISDT concept, a deep investigation on the nature of its components can set up the floor for generating new theories bridging the HCI and the IS fields.

The analysis proposed by Harrison, Tatar and Sengers represents a first step in this direction since, as the authors confirm, "recognizing a set of ideas as a paradigm is important because it allows us to perceive and discuss the organization of thought at the level of a system rather than just as component pieces". From such broad perspective is possible to sort out the problems that are interesting and likely to be solved, to suggest success criteria for finding their solutions, and to guide evaluation and acceptance of work in the field. Our goal is to move one step further, by providing a framework for systematically analyzing both the ontological and epistemological nature of HCI contributions.

Although the paradigmatic view is too general to fulfill the objectives of this paper, we find interesting to derive from this conceptualization a parallel with the three school of thought characterizing the ISDT literature (Figs. 2, 3).

In HCI contributions belonging to the Human-factor paradigm theories may (not necessarily) inform both the purpose and scope definition and the principles of form and function. This condition can be assimilated to the Kernel Theory (KT) pragmatists school in design research where the focus is on solving the problem of maximizing some utility function by the means of a technological tool with a pragmatic approach.

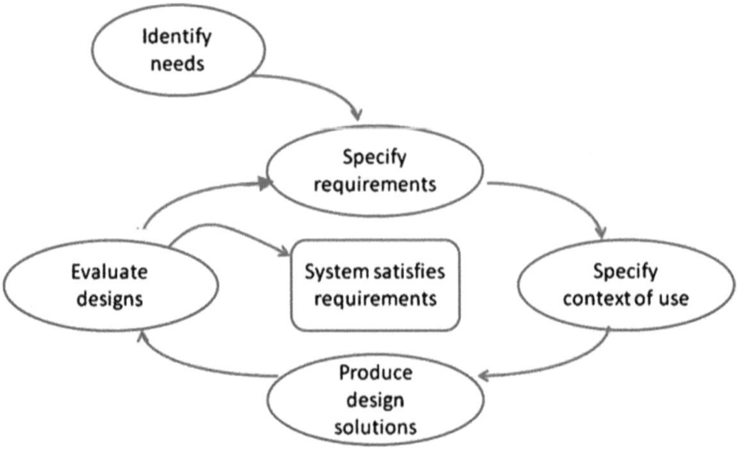

Fig. 3 The iterative user centered design process

A different epistemological position can be assigned to most of the Cognitive/ Information Processing HCI contributions. These indeed share the characters of the Design Theory (DT) opponents school, in which the knowledge base has the twofold role of providing input and receiving feedbacks in the form of scientific theories and methods, experience and expertise and previously developed design product and processes [23]. In this case the design and the evaluation of the IT artifact plays the central role and the process for creating knowledge is well represented in the three cycle view illustrated by [14]. In this view an iterative process bridges the design science activities with the contextual environment of the research project on the one side, and with the knowledge base of scientific foundations, experience, and expertise that informs the research project on the other.

The third paradigm is more difficult to conceptualize since the purpose and scope of the theory and its principles of form and function are both dependent on the context and on the construction of meaning that surrounds the situated activities in which technology is appropriated. Here the justificatory knowledge becomes a fundamental tool for providing the researcher with a palette of situated design and evaluation strategies and at the same time it is enriched by the better understanding of situated complex phenomena.

4 Towards a Design Theory for UCS

In this section we concentrate the analysis on a specific design problem belonging to the HCI domain: the design of User Centered Systems. This design problem is general enough for embracing the three HCI paradigms and provides sufficient details for drawing an illustrative example of how an HCI method can instantiate an ISDT. The further discussion will investigate the benefits of this analysis for both fields.

4.1 Purpose and Scope

The user-centered approach to design was proposed as a response to design failures arising in traditional computer-centered approaches where interface designers are consulted too late, when the software has already been designed or is nearly complete, and the option of heavy corrections is too costly [9]. It has to be observed that formal expertise of domain experts, while including knowledge of parameters and details of the problem to be solved, typically does not extend to issues related with human psychology, ergonomics, and the other fields that inform the interaction design.

A fundamental condition for an effective design is the recognition of what the product should be. As Norman points out, although this may sound obvious this is the task most often ignored and most often done too quickly, poorly, and superficially [24]. In order to elicit users' requirements and devise product functions and properties that meet these requirements, a user centered oriented repertoire of observational techniques descending from anthropology, sociology, experimental psychology and cognitive science has to be used. However, Norman observes that none of these disciplines has developed a methodology really appropriate for applied observation and testing (p. 193), which does not need the precision of the traditional scientific method and, above all, prefers speed and estimation to accuracy. Contextual design is the example of a design method based on this sort of "rapid ethnography" [25].

Defining the purpose and scope of UCS is a problematic task which requires a careful understanding of contextual elements and a deep understanding of the artifact mutability requirements. The third paradigm of HCI introduces new elements of human life as included in the Human–Computer interaction such as culture, emotion and experience. The focus is thus defined as "what the second wave is not: non-work, non-purposeful, non rational, etc." [26]. This change in the overall objectives of the interaction design effort deeply affects all the elements of the purpose and scope design component and their functional relationships with both principles of form and function and principles for implementation.

4.2 Justificatory Knowledge

The possible links between the justificatory knowledge and the remaining components of a design theory has been already described in general terms in the previous section. Here the objective is to instantiate the epistemological distinctions between the three paradigms into the realm of UCS design methods.

Knowledge about users' common traits constitutes the foundation on which HCI is grounded and may be expressed in terms of analytical, explanatory and predicting theories regarding cognitive psychology and human physiology and representing facts about, among others, users' input/output channels (vision, hearing, touch), motor control, human memory (sensory, short-term and long-term memory), thinking (reasoning and problem solving), human attention. Not surprisingly, almost every book on interaction design includes overviews on these aspects (e.g., [9, 27, 28]). These ground theories are, in turn, the basis on which theories for design and action are built. For example, principles from the Gestalt psychology school translate into general visual design principles (see, e.g., [29]); theories on visual perception translate into rules on where to put visual items on the screen and on whether or not to attach animation to them depending on whether they fall into the foveal or the peripheral vision, ruled by different types of receptors [9]; psychological studies on human attention constitute the basis on which researchers built design guidelines for ambient and alerting information systems [30].

As the field became more and more mature, the foundation has broadened its extent to include theories on the computer and on the computer mediated interaction as well. A typology of interaction devices or the typology of dialogue types (menu selection, form filling, dialog boxes, along with their specializations) presented in [27], can be, for example, regarded as analytic theories according to Gregor's framework [3]; again, in turn, they translate into design principles. At a even higher level of abstraction we may find typologies of interaction paradigms, as in [31], and explanatory and design theories built from them [32].

4.3 Principles of Form and Function

In order to illustrate the nature and the evolution of principles of form and function we refer to the work of Bødker [26] in which the author surveys the challenges for HCI theories with respect to the broadening context of use and application types. The principles that define the structure, organization, and functioning of the design product must take into account the fact that today technology spreads from the workplace to our homes and everyday lives and culture. For instance when designing UCSs aimed to support work and non-work technologies the abstract "blueprint" cannot underestimate the fact that mobile technologies make possible to work in many places and that a network-oriented shared use of documents and services across physical place is possible. Whereas the PC idea was to gather as much functionality as possible in one computer and to support groups working with a collection of applications, now the focus is on how to use pervasive technologies, ambient technology, augmented reality, small interfaces, tangible interfaces, etc. across contexts and communities, and beyond work.

New concepts such as webs-of-technology have been introduced to replace the view of single, monolithic devices or systems with technology that must be seen and used in relation to many other devices, applications and systems. "Webs-of-technology are used to describe ubiquitous interaction as a process of negotiation between the users and the technology, focusing on the availability of technology and interpretability of services".

4.4 Testable Propositions

Testable propositions provides a means to translate the theoretical outcomes of a design research effort into concise hypotheses about the system. Although a design proposition is only an approximation of what will work in different contexts, propositions are considered as useful means for communicating the generalized aspects of a design theory in a form that can be instantiated or empirically tested in other contexts.

When testable propositions refer to the prescriptive knowledge embedded in a design theory, they take the form of heuristic propositions: "If you want to achieve Y in situation Z something like action X will help" [11]. A discussion on prescriptive propositions in the UCS domain is provided by [33] who propose a method for checking their consistency and validity across multiple instantiations with an approach based on configuration theory [34]. An example of such propositions is: "When face to face requirement analysis is performed with unstructured techniques under time constraints, the outcome of the project is a scarce usefulness of the interactive system".

Although the issue of justifying ISDT findings through the empirical test of such generalized statements is still debated in the IS field, we recognize the importance of testable propositions in evidencing the focus of an ISDT. By referring to the elements of our design framework we would expect a different form for UCS issues belonging to different paradigms. A testable proposition in the form "If problem A then solution B" is more suitable for expressing the research results in the first paradigm where conditions are seen as problems and principles of form and function as optimal solutions. A testable proposition in the form "If context A and requirement B then solution C" is suitable for a Cognitive/Information Processing UCS design approach where the context determines the conditions for some needed capabilities (requirements) and the solution optimizes the interaction. Finally for UCS methods in the third paradigm, a less standardized and more open form can describe the variety and the complexity of the context. An example is provided by Hanseth and Lyytinen [35] who have summarized in five rules their design theory for dynamic complexity: design initially for usefulness, build upon existing installed base, expand installed base by persuasive tactics to gain momentum, make the design of IT capabilities as simple as possible, modularize the Information Infrastructure.

4.5 Principles of Implementation

As pointed out by Raskin, the process of designing interactive systems relies on a crucial first step that makes sure that the interface design conforms with universal psychological facts [10]. After this is achieved, differences across individuals and groups can be addressed and, finally, task specific requirements may be taken into consideration. Though in practice the design proceeds in an iterative manner (as depicted in Fig. 3), these three ideal steps from generality to specificity may come in handy in our investigation on theories in HCI. These principles are today well accepted, indeed requirements and recommendations for human-centered principles and activities throughout the life-cycle of computer-based interactive systems are also provided by ISO 9241-210:2010.

Whatever the technique used to carry on field studies (contextual inquiries, focus groups, interviews, etc.), one of the main aim of this design step is to address the second of Raskin's three ideal steps: finding differences across individuals and groups, with respect to the expected usage of the system. These differences get coded into the users' classification, which is the basis for the definition of "personas", fictional characters created to represent the different user classes that might use the product in a similar way (though there is a great debate in the HCI community on the use of "personas", empirical studies seem to show their effectiveness in the design [36]). Personas, storyboards and scenarios are design tools that help designers to formalize system's functional and non functional requirements, and to model tasks. Actually, several iterations of the general scheme in Fig. 3—each involving designing, prototyping and testing—are necessary to move from initial vague requirements to final delivery of the product. Every prototype produced during this process has to be evaluated by means of appropriate methods to assess its usability [37], i.e., its effectiveness (i.e., the extent to which the intended goals of the system can be achieved), its efficiency (i.e., the time, the money, the mental effort spent to achieve these goals), and the satisfaction (i.e., how much the users feel themselves comfortable using the system).

4.6 Expository Instantiation

Although the analysis of UCS methods through the lens of the ISDT components has the objective to instantiate more general HCI contributions, we believe that performing a further projection step of the above mentioned concept into a concrete example can provide the benefits of an expository instantiation.

With this aim we present the case of an intelligent multimedia platform providing innovative social e-services for European elderly persons and their social entourage (as carers/supporters and IT tutors when needed) that is under development in the context of a European project and in which the authors of this paper are involved as design experts [38, 39]. The ultimate goal of the project is to enhance socialization, quality of life and autonomy of elderly persons by preventing isolation and loneliness, and generating positive social experiences and behavior. In few words, the European project proposes to foster social interactions through the development of an accessible, easy-to-use and innovative IT platform to provide a forum of well aging, an exchange of "social best practices" and socialization services in a European network. The general requirements at the basis of the project proposal demand for the integration of a range of IT-based solutions for: (1) managing existing e-information by exhaustive search of available information (Web and databases crawling) and intelligent structuring (i.e. TextMining) in the system repository; (2) transforming selected information into personalized solutions; (3) providing validated solutions as "e-Social Best Practices" (SBP). All these services must be provided through a Web 2.0 approach by supporting the social interaction of end users. These characteristics make the design phase of the platform an instantiation of what we have defined as UCS so that it does not only provide usable services to some particular types of end users (i.e. elderly people, care givers, etc.) but also supports their social interaction. Furthermore, the sustainability of the online community supported by the platform represents a fundamental part of the business model. Since all the properties that have been illustrated referring to UCS apply in this case, it is a suitable candidate for instantiating an UCS design theory and representing it through the above mentioned design components.

The application of state-of-the-art principles of implementation led the team in charge of performing the requirement analysis to concentrate on the inner characteristics of users. Indeed, the knowledge base suggest that for an elderly oriented IT platform to be successful, special focus has to be put on the interaction environment, which encompasses devices, techniques and paradigms used to communicate with and through the system. This is an example of a prescriptive rule addressing the field problem of designing IT platforms for elderly people. Strategies to motivate elderly in using the implemented services must be accompanied by a careful attention on limitations deriving from physical (visual, auditory, motor) and cognitive impairments, and from scarce e-literacy [40]. As a consequence of these basic assumptions, a set of requirements have been drawn which are related to adaptation to user's impairments representing the instance of a constraint in the purpose and scope component. The principles of implementation adopted by the team of HCI experts are in line with the principles of implementation and are based on "personas" definition through users inquiries, low/high fidelity prototypes, visual design, gestalt theory, user-based assessment. Furthermore a set of theoretical proposition will be tested in the evaluation phase in order to validate the functional or teleological relationship linking the principles of form and function with capabilities such as accessibility, usability, ergonomics, cost of information access, gestures' intuitiveness, memory workload, affordance, consistency.

Although the above mentioned process represents a perfect instantiation of the traditional UCS approach, a number of additional issues are emerging during the iterative phases of requirement analysis. In fact, the platform can be regarded from multiple perspectives, different but interrelated and all aimed at the same goal: designing an interaction environment suitable for elderly people and their care networks. For instance at organizational level it can be seen as an IT systems for supporting communities (i.e. online, offline), at strategic level as an intelligent solutions for e-care service providing and at social level as a system for improving the quality of life of citizens. Each of these perspectives challenges the initial

Table 1 The design theory for UCS

	UCS based on human factors	UCS based on cognitivism/ information processing	UCS based on phenomenologically situated approach	Evidences from the empirical case
P&S	Optimizing fit between man and machine Ergonomics, no manual, usability, accessibility	Optimizing accuracy and efficiency of information transfer Characteristics of the interaction environment	Sociability Personalized contents Privacy	Adaptation to user's impairments Ubiquitous computing, ambient intelligence, community awareness, interoperability, security Sociability, personalized contents, privacy
JK	To concentrate on the inner characteristics of users and devices	UCS based on Human Factors Theories grounded in the "science" stream (i.e. biology, organization, sociology, etc.)	Situated nature of meaning and meaning creation	Specific theories on elderly people (grounded on physiology, psychology, usability engineering) Grey digital divide Online/offline communities dynamics Computer Supported Cooperative Work
PFF	GUI	Context specific interaction environment Knowledge management	Cognitive prosthesis Non task oriented computing	W3C standards Semantic functionalities Social networking
PI	Experiments	Iterative requirement elicitation Contribution of domain experts Risk assessment Compliance assessment	Narrative, ethnography, ethnomethodology, ethology, action research, practice-based research, interaction analysis	Experiments involving elderly people "personas" definition through focus groups and contextual inquiries with elderly and care givers Iterative development Low/high fidelity prototypes, visual design User-based assessment Interaction matrix and metaphores
TH	If problem A then solution B	If context A and requirement B then solution C	Build or do not build something	Sociability is enabled by a set of tools that implement the public square, the social window, and the courtyard metaphors

definition of purpose and scope in terms of capabilities, constraints, constructs, and artifact mutability. As a consequence the design of the platform requires a deeper understanding of the context in which the artifact is situated which cannot be afforded with an a priori model representing the generalized information processing system.

The relationships among UCS design principles belonging to the three paradigms and their instantiation in the case are summarized in Table 1. The richness of elements listed in the fourth column confirms the need for a more structured design theory for UCS in which the purpose and scope is enriched by contributions provided trough methods listed in the third paradigm of HCI.

Another interesting element emerging from the case is related to the vision of the team HCI experts of conceiving the interaction environment as a set of cooperative "cognitive prosthesis" that leverage and extend human intellectual capacities. By conceptualizing a "cognitive prosthesis" as a compensatory strategy for human limitations may benefit HCI design methodologies as a whole when extending the function of prosthesis from "compensatory" to "augmenting", and considering IT products as "amplifying" human capabilities while seamlessly integrating within the ambient (coherently with anthropological views of technical object as natural extensions of the human body). This additional result provides an example in the HCI domain of how the design of a new system can contribute to the development of the knowledge base through the introduction of new concepts, methods and theories emerging from the activities of the design cycle.

5 Conclusions

In this paper we assert HCI, which is pragmatic in nature, can benefit from a structured contamination with concepts grounded in the IS design research stream. Through the lens of a design research framework we perform a theoretical review on HCI with a particular focus on the aspects related to the design of User Centered Systems. Our discussion provides a deep understanding of the field problem of designing UCS and sets up the basis for the development of an holistic theory for the design of innovative UCS. This contributes to the knowledge base to which interaction designers refer when designing new IT artifacts in their context of use. In addition a contribution at a meta level is provided through the analysis of the theoretical foundations of current HCI method. The final goal of the design theory proposed is to enhance the capability of practitioners in developing IT artifacts fitting with the dynamics of socio-technical systems (communities, organizations, society, etc.). Further research will concentrate on the open issues of the UCS-ISDT justification through empirical and conceptual validation.

Acknowledgments This chapter has been drafted in the context of the HOPES project "Help and social interaction for elderly On a multimedia Platform with E-Social best practices" funded by the EU Commission under the AAL Programme.

References

1. Gregor, S., & Jones, D. (2007). The anatomy of a design theory. *Journal of the Association for Information Systems, 8*, 312–335.
2. ACM SIGCHI: Special interest group on computer-human interaction curriculum development group. Retrieved from http://old.sigchi.org/cdg/
3. Gregor, S. (2006). The nature of theory in information systems. *Management Information Systems Quarterly, 30*, 611.
4. Lee, A. S. (2001). Editorial. *Management Information Systems Quarterly. 25*(1), iii–vii.
5. Baskerville, R., & Myers, D. (2002). Information systems as a reference discipline. *Management Information Systems Quarterly, 26*, 1–14.
6. Baskerville, R., Lyytinen, K., Sambamurthy, V., & Straub, D. (2010). A response to the design-oriented information systems research memorandum. *European Journal of Information Systems, 20*, 11–15.
7. Baskerville, R., & Pries-Heje, J. (2010). Explanatory design theory. *Business & Information Systems Engineering, 2*, 271–282.
8. Hevner, A. R., March, S. T., Park, J., & Ram, S. (2004). Design science in information systems research. *Management Information Systems Quarterly, 28*, 75–105.
9. Dix, A., Finlay, J., Abowd, G. D., Beale, R. (2004). *Human-computer interaction*. New York: Prentice Hall.
10. Raskin, J. (2000). *The humane interface: New directions for designing interactive systems*. Reading: Addison-Wesley Professional.
11. Aken, J. E. V. (2004). Management research based on the paradigm of the design sciences: The quest for field-tested and grounded technological rules. *Journal of Management Studies, 41*, 219–246.
12. Walls, J., Widmeyer, G., & El Sawy, O. A. (1992). Building an information system design theory for vigilant EIS. *Information Systems Research, 3*, 36–59.
13. Gregor, S., & Jones, D. (2007). The anatomy of a design theory. *Journal of the Association for Information Systems, 8*, 312–335.
14. Hevner, A. R., March, S. T., Park, J., & Ram, S. (2004). Design science in information systems research. *Management Information Systems Quarterly, 28*, 75–105.
15. March, S. T., & Smith, G. F. (1995). Design and natural science research on information technology. *Decision Support Systems, 15*, 251–266.
16. Goldkuhl, G. (2004). Design theories in information systems-a need for multi-grounding. *Journal of Information Technology Theory and Application (JITTA)*, *6*(2), 59–72.
17. Fischer, C., Winter, R., & Wortmann, F. (2010). Design theory. *Business Information Systems Engineering, 2*, 387–390.
18. van Aken, J. E. (2004). Management Research Based on the paradigm of the design sciences: The quest for field-tested and grounded technological rules. *Journal of Management Studies, 41*, 219–246.
19. Grudin, J. (2005). Three faces of human–computer interaction. *IEEE Annals of the History of Computing, 27*, 46–62.
20. Kuhn, T. S. (1996). *The structure of scientific revolutions*. Chicago: University of Chicago Press.
21. Agre, P. E. (1997). *Computation and human experience*. Cambridge: Cambridge University Press.
22. Harrison, S., Tatar, D., Sengers, P. (2007). The three paradigms of HCI. In alt. chi. *Session at the SIGCHI.*
23. Hevner, A. R. (2007). A three cycle view of design science research. *Scandinavian Journal of Information Systems, 19*, 87–92.
24. Norman, D. A. (1998). *The invisible computer*. Cambridge: MIT Press.
25. Beyer, H., Holtzblatt, K. (1998). *Contextual design: Defining customer-centered systems*. San Francisco: Morgan Kaufmann.

26. Bødker, S. (2006). When second wave HCI meets third wave challenges. In*Proceedings of the 4th nordic conference on human-computer interaction: Changing roles*, Oslo, Norway, Oct 14–18, pp. 14–18.
27. Shneiderman, B. (1998). *Designing the user interface*. Reading: Addison-Wesley.
28. Ware, C. (1999). *Information visualization–perception for design*. London: Academic Press, Morgan Kaufmann Publishers.
29. Mullet, K., Sano, D. (1995). *Designing visual interfaces*. Mountain View: SunSoft Press.
30. Matthews, T., Dey, A. K., Mankoff, J., Carter, S., Rattenbury T. (2004). A toolkit for managing user attention in peripheral displays. In *Proceedings of the 17th annual ACM symposium on user interface software and technology UIST 04* (pp. 247–256). New York: ACM Press.
31. D'Atri, A., & Tarantino, L. (1989). From browsing to querying. *IEEE Data Engineering Bulletin, 12*, 46–53.
32. D'Atri, A., Tarantino, L. (1994) A browsing theory and its application to database navigation. In J. Paredaens & L. A. Tenenbaum (Eds.), *Advances in database systems: Implementations and applications*, CISM Courses and Lectures No. 347, Wien: Springer Verlag.
33. Di Mascio, T., Spagnoletti, P., Tarantino, L., Za, S. (2012). Successful UCD practices under IT project constraints. In *IADIS International Conference Information Systems* (pp. 433–437).
34. Spagnoletti, P. (2010). Qualitative comparative analysis for conducting multiple case study research: Concept and discussion. *Proceedings of IFIP 8.2/Organizations and Society in Information Systems (OASIS), 10*, 8–11.
35. Hanseth, O., & Lyytinen, K. (2010). Information infrastructures: The case of building internet. *Journal of Information Technology, 25*, 1–19.
36. Long, F. (2009). Real or imaginary: The effectiveness of using personas in product design. In *IES Conference 2009. Irish Ergonomics Review, Proceedings of the IES Conference 2009*, Dublin, pp. 1–10.
37. Hartson, H. R., Andre, T., & Williges, R. (2001). Criteria for evaluating usability evaluation methods. *International Journal of Human-Computer Interaction, 13*, 373–410.
38. Spagnoletti, P., & Resca, A. (2012). A design theory for IT supporting online communities. In *Proceedings of the 45th Hawaii International Conference on System Sciences*, pp. 4082–4091.
39. Spagnoletti, P., Resca, A., Russo, V., Taglino, F., Tarantino, L. (2012). Building theories from IT project design: The HOPES case. In: Te'eni D. et al. (Ed.) *Information Systems: A Crossroads for Organization, Management, Accounting and Engineering* (pp. 451–459), Physica-Verlag, Heidelberg.
40. Fisk, A. D., Rogers, W. A., Charness, N., Czaja, S. J., & Sharit, J. (2004). *Designing for older adults*. Boca Raton: CRC Press.

A Design Theory for Dynamic Competencies Mapping Systems

Luigi De Bernardis and Riccardo Maiolini

Abstract This paper describes a research in progress that addresses the design problem of dynamically mapping competencies with IT. In turbulent markets, companies face the problem of an expansive maintenance of competencies inventory. They have to choose between maintaining those systems and manage new knowledge or abandoning them and risk being less competitive. Using IS design theory [1], we'll try to identify meta requirement, products and process requirements and testable hypothesis in order to develop an IT tool able to classify old and new competencies in a dynamic way. The hypothesis will be tested comparing a real competence inventory (elaborated by ISFOL, an Italian public entity) with an inventory coming from an IT tool designed with this methodology. These activities are planned in three phases. As first step, we extract from ISFOL database a list of competencies required for financial organizational roles. The second step is to hypothesize which sources could provide these competencies in order to verify extracting competencies from the "corpus" articulated in those sources. The third steps of this process will be to compare ISFOL skills inventory for financial industry and the inventory that comes from a DCMS (Dynamic Competencies Mapping System).

Keywords Design theory · Competence · Job description

L. De Bernardis (✉)
CeRSI, LUISS Guido Carli, Rome, Italy
e-mail: ldebernardis@luiss.it

R. Maiolini
LUISS Guido Carli, Rome, Italy
e-mail: rmaiolini@luiss.it

R. Baskerville et al. (eds.), *Designing Organizational Systems*, Lecture Notes in Information Systems and Organisation 1,
DOI: 10.1007/978-3-642-33371-2_7,

1 Introduction

Traditionally, human resource management tools include job descriptions and skill inventories. More recently, the need to save costs forced companies to reduce their effort in mapping competencies and in describing job positions. In a turbulent market, that activity becomes too expansive to be sustainable. Anyway, the need is for a tool open to new competencies required by business. Nevertheless, a HR policy needs those tools in order to estimate knowledge gaps and to plan training programs. Can IT solution give a chance to create a tool easy to be update?

The concept of competency is based on a theory of performance. According to Boyatzis [2] maximum performance occurs when the person's capability is coherent with the needs of the job demands and the organizational environment. The method of competencies [2] has as its object in the suitability to the "jobs" of people and in the evolution of the organizational systems. In his analysis of "The competent manager", he tries to identify keys indicators able to predict high performance in a specific job. Mapping competencies companies can manage a more effective recruitment, carriers and organizational development. Other studies identified among best performers. Three clusters of behavioral habits as threshold abilities that are: (1) expertise and experience (2) knowledge, and (3) an assortment of basic cognitive competencies [3].

The most adopted methodologies for mapping competencies are BEI (Behavioral Event Interview) and Repertory Grid. Behavioral Event Interview (BEI), has been designed in order to identify "generic competencies" [4], articulated in operational, support, influence, managerial, cognitive, personal effectiveness and based on personal experiences. Using critical methodology [5] each people is required to describe his experiences. The interview is oriented for identifying and comparing in each situation desired and real actions. Repertory Grid is a methodology based on Kelly's studies [6] on construct psychology. Each supervisor distinguishes for each role competencies of best performers and middle performers.

These methodologies are based on interviews of employees in order to identify the distinctive competencies of best performers. Can these approaches explain competencies creation and innovation?

2 The Design Theory Framework

Theories in Information Systems have been classified as follow [7]: development of theories for analyzing, theories for explaining, theories for predicting, theories for explaining and predicting. A theory that gives explicit prescriptions on how to design and develop an artifact has been named as "IS design theory" by Walls et al. [1]. They argue that design product is composed by meta-requirements, meta-design (features), kernel theories and a set of testable design product hypothesis

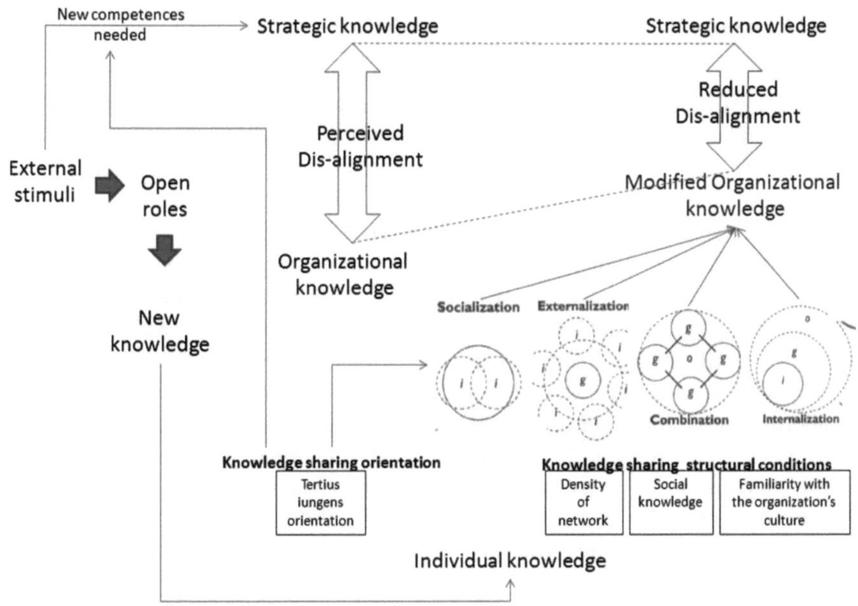

Fig. 1 Kernel theory

and design process is composed by the design method, kernel theories and a set of testable design process hypothesis.

As first step, we identify the purpose of the theory. The purpose of a design theory for building an IT system supporting dynamic competence mapping is to explain *how an organization can align its knowledge to external innovation stimuli using a dynamic competencies mapping system*. The design problem is referred to the need for specific requirements and methods of an IT system supporting the dynamic mapping of competencies.

The resulting model is shown above. It is a model that contributes in giving an answer to a "*how*" research question. Therefore, it describes a process of change instead of causal relationships among concepts.

This model describes how a company can reduce the dis-alignment between strategic knowledge and organizational knowledge using a dynamic competencies mapping system. The starting point is some external stimuli that modify at the same time strategic knowledge and individual knowledge. Individual knowledge can become organizational knowledge if supported by the four modalities of SECI (Socialization, Externalization, Combination, Internalization) model and this process can be easier if both individual and structural conditions are verified. The new organizational knowledge brings back the alignment to the starting level. In the following pages, we analyze which is the role of four constructs of this model in facilitating this process (Fig. 1).

2.1 Alignment with Strategic Knowledge

Performance of the firm is influenced by both internal and external alignments [8]. The tradeoff between market structure and strategic priorities has been studied in order to find evidences with organizational goals and individual behaviors [9]. Several contributions emerged within this field of research. We find interesting those researches that find evidences in the processes of strategic alignment that consider the role of transaction costs explanation [10] and opportunities that emerge from gaining new competencies [11]. The identification of specific mechanisms that rise transaction costs serves to understand the level of cooperation and identification of new competencies inside strategic alliances [9]. The alignment of internal and external stimuli has been conceptualized in the literature as environmental constrains [12] and it allows organization to interpret and orientate the general relationship between social and organizational structure [13] within companies. On the other hand, it is important when talk about strategic alignments to consider tradeoffs between core capabilities and core rigidities [14] that can negatively influence the relationship between performance and strategic alignment.

Other studies analyze relations between structure of the market and performance of the firm. This relation is the same of Bain's framework "structure of the market—conduct of the firm—performance" [15]. Bain paid less attention to the "conduct of the firm" and, even if other authors [16] modified his framework giving more emphasis to "conduct", two strong assumptions are still in their framework. The first assumption is the fact that organizations are "individual entities": this assumption is very often used to simplify reality. Even if the assumption that rational behavior has been replaced by bounded rationality, considering organizations as individuals is a too strong simplification. On the contrary, the alignment among strategy and people's behavior is one of the most important problem within the company life. The second assumption is that the market is an entity with clear characteristics and boundaries. Actually, the market is a competitive interaction among firms and/or can be considered interaction among customers with several priorities. The capability to understand external changes in terms of new technologies and customers' new orientation is a fundamental issue for those companies that compete in a turbulent environment [17, 18]. Consequently, after realize the necessity to align new competencies to external stimuli, the performance depends from the dynamic side of companies [19] to learn quickly and to build new strategic assets [20] or transform existing ones [21].

Evidences of dis-alignment within organizations were found by Norton in a survey. His findings were summarized as follows [22]: in 60 % of organization there is no connection between strategy and budget, in 70 % of organization there is no connection between middle management incentive and strategy, 85 % of executive board spend less than an hour per month discussing strategy, 95 % of people don't understand company strategy, 90 % of organizations fail in translating strategy into actions. They proposed the Balanced Scorecard as a tool of alignment. It consists of a strategy map composed by four perspectives: financial, customers, processes, learning and growth. In each perspective, there are some objectives. Those objectives are linked to others in different perspectives with cause-effect relationships. Therefore, objectives in learning perspective are often linked to customers' needs. Competencies maps support learning activities because they define job descriptions. We argue that a dynamic competencies mapping can support strategic alignment because learning can be focused on competencies that come from new customers' needs.

Hence, we propose:

P1 In a turbulent environment a dynamic competencies mapping supports alignment with strategic knowledge

2.2 Organizational Knowledge

The way for managing organizational knowledge and learning have been studied in terms of how to manage different typologies of knowledge and in terms of how to innovate knowledge [23].

That theory of organizational knowledge creation [24–29] have undergone two phases of development. The first phase had two dimensions [24, 26]. The "epistemological" dimension is the "social interaction" between tacit and explicit knowledge where knowledge is converted from one type to another [24, 25]. Four typology of knowledge conversion were defined: tacit to tacit (Socialization); tacit to explicit (Externalization); explicit to explicit (Combination), and explicit to tacit (Internalization). They use the metaphor of a "spiral" of knowledge creation [26] called SECI model. This dimension works at individual level. The second dimension, "ontological", works at inter-organizational level [26]. Individual's knowledge can be crystallized in the organization [24]. These epistemological and ontological dimensions have been integrated with the concept of "ba" [27, 28, 30]. "Ba" is a shared context of knowledge creation and the difference between information and knowledge can be defined as the possibility to contextualized information.

Analyzing the SECI model, the first step is defined Combination is described as "systematizing concepts into a knowledge system". Externalization converts tacit into explicit knowledge. It seems to be the traditional concept of organizational knowledge creation because it is translated from individual to collective [24]. In addition, Socialization—the exchange of tacit knowledge among people—is considered in this model a way for creating organizational knowledge. Therefore, it should be supported by companies. The final cell of Nonaka's matrix is labeled internalization ("a process of embodying explicit knowledge into tacit knowledge"). It is a definition close to "learning" or to "learning by doing" [25, 26].

How can a map of competencies help this process? Combination (systematizing concepts into a knowledge system) can be helped because a skill inventory can be part of this knowledge system. Externalization (translation of individual in collective knowledge) can be supported if competencies' map is an "open" way to share knowledge. Socialization (the exchange of tacit knowledge among people) can be a source of new knowledge if technological tools (for instance forum or blog) allow to analyze the content of interaction. Finally, Internalization ("a process of embodying explicit knowledge into tacit knowledge") can be helped if job descriptions include expected competencies for each organizational role and, therefore, people are motivated in embodying those competencies.

Hence, we propose:

P3 A formal map of competencies helps translation of individual knowledge in Organizational knowledge

2.3 Knowledge Sharing Orientation

The organizational knowledge process creation has been discussed largely in managerial literature. For instance, Adler [31] argued that Nonaka's theory is too static and inadequate for a dynamic model. In order to emphasize organizational knowledge innovation, [32] examines, at micro level, in an engineering division of an automotive manufacturer, the so-said *tertius iungens* (or "third who joins") in opposition to the *tertius gaudens* orientation emphasized in structural holes theory [33]. *Tertius iungens* promote innovation by connecting people in their social network and introducing disconnected individuals (Fig. 2).

In their model, there are three independent variables, two individual (*tertius iungens* orientation and knowledge) and one structural (density of network). Focusing on *tertius iungens* orientation, it is defined as a "predisposition to bring people together in collaboration". Therefore, the inclusion of these tertius iungens in the SECI process of knowledge creation can facilitate the effectiveness of that process.

Hence, we propose:

P2 A Tertius Iungens orientation can help knowledge innovation.

2.4 Knowledge Sharing Structural Conditions

Knowledge sharing orientation can be considered dependent on individual competencies and values or on the network structure (Fig. 1). A line of work suggests that both structure and characteristics of individuals are important in the consideration of such action. Innovative action is therefore likely to be a function not

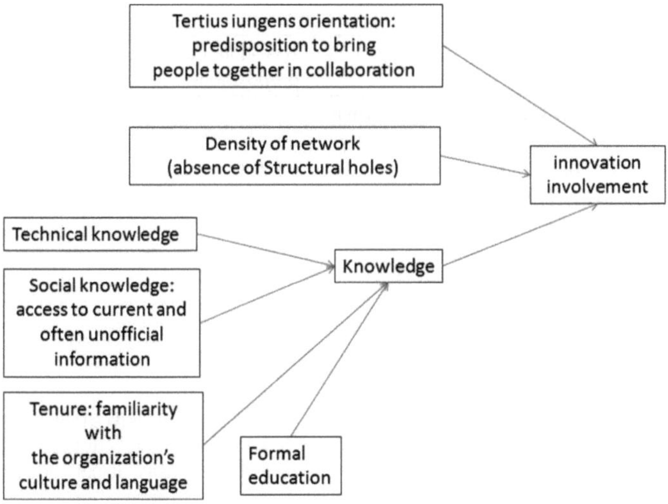

Fig. 2 Tertius Iungens theory

Table 1 Constructs and propositions

Kernel theories and key papers	Construct	Related propositions
Kaplan R. Norton D., Strategic alignment, Harvard Business School Press (2007)	Alignment with strategic knowledge	P1 In a turbulent environment a dynamic competencies mapping supports alignment with strategic knowledge
I. Nonaka, and R. Toyama, 'The knowledge-creating theory revisited: knowledge creation as a synthesizing process'. Knowledge Management (2003).	Organizational knowledge	P3 A formal map of competencies helps translation of individual knowledge in organizational knowledge
D. Obstfeld, Social networks, the Tertius Iungens orientation, and involvement in innovation (2005)	Knowledge sharing orientation	P2 A Tertius Iungens orientation can help knowledge innovation.
D. Obstfeld (2005)	Knowledge sharing structural conditions	P4 A high density of network can help knowledge innovation

only of the strategic orientation but also of the individual toward action of the network [32].

Hence, we propose:

P4 A high density of network can help knowledge innovation

The table above summarizes these propositions (Table 1).

Table 2 Meta-Requirements

Requirement	Description	Associated applied theoretical model propositions
MR1	A DCMS should support informal exchange of tacit knowledge	
MR2	A DCMS should facilitate in recognizing competencies	P3 A formal map of competencies helps translation of individual knowledge in organizational knowledge
MR3	A DCMS should facilitate in institutionalizing new competencies	
MR4	A DCMS should support links among different explicit knowledge	
MR5	A DCMS should contribute to develop roles able to create ties among people	P2 A Tertius Iungens orientation can help knowledge innovation. P4 A high density of network can help knowledge innovation
MR6	A DCMS should facilitate the updating of expected skills for each job	P1 In a turbulent environment a dynamic competencies mapping supports alignment with strategic knowledge

3 The Dynamic Competencies Mapping Design Theory

This study proposes to define Meta Design (product requirements) and/or Design Methods according to the meta-requirement identified for each knowledge creating modality of Nonaka's model and for knowledge innovation modality at micro and macro level. In the following table (Table 2), starting from propositions, meta-requirement have been identified. Then, from each mode of Nonaka's SECI knowledge creation model integrated with innovation organizational needs, have been defined meta-design product requirements and process methods. They are finally translated in testable hypotheses. Combining P1 through P5 and recasting them in a prescriptive mode yields DCMS meta-requirements MR1 through MR6 listed in Table 2.

The relationships between explanatory statements and prescriptive statements described by Goldkuhl [34] can be useful in order to identify product requirements from the theoretical propositions defined above. An explanatory statement link a cause to an effect. For instance, we argued that "A Tertius Iungens orientation can help knowledge innovation". On the contrary, a prescriptive statement is not true or false, it is more or less useful [34]. It links a prescribed action to a goal. Following our example, the prescription "A DCMS should contribute to develop roles able to create ties among people" (MR5)—that requires to include in the system features for informal description of new competencies (MD1)—has the goal to help knowledge innovation.

Table 3 From meta-requirements to meta design

Requirement description		Meta design description	
MR1	A DCMS should support informal exchange of tacit knowledge	A DCMS should contextualize knowledge in the specific organizational "BA" A DCMS should include features for informal description of new competencies (forum,...)	MD3 MD1
MR2	A DCMS should facilitate in recognizing competencies	A DCMS should create categories that make sense for people in the organization (tag, ...)	MD4
MR3	A DCMS should facilitate in institutionalizing new competencies	A DCMS should include a search engine for external searching of new competencies. The analyzed "corpus" should include external sources.	MD2
MR4	A DCMS should support links among different explicit knowledge	A DCMS should notice people about new competencies included in the inventory in order to give them the opportunity to verify if they have those competencies.	MD5
MR5	A DCMS should contribute to develop roles able to create ties among people	A DCMS should include features for informal description of new competencies (forum,...)	MD1
MR6	A DCMS should facilitate the updating of expected skills for each job	A DCMS should support a dynamic revision of job definition and description	MD6

Following this logic, Table 3 shows specific relationships among meta-requirements and meta-design components and Table 4 classifies meta design into three categories.

Table 4 lists a set of Meta Design features for a DCMS required in a definition of competence mapping as shown above. From the point of view of product design, it should provide suggestions about sources of competencies, methodologies of classifying and output in terms of organizational roles design.

Among the requirements included in Sources of competencies, MD1 states that a DCMS should include features for informal description of new competencies. The DCMS should include features like forum where people can post suggestions for mapping new competencies. In addition, MD2 states that DCMS should include a search engine for external searching of new competencies. The corpus that will be analyzed should include a web search in order to identify in studies or competitors' documentation information about new skills required. Finally, MD3 states that DCMS should contextualize knowledge in the specific organizational "BA". It is the virtual or physical place where knowledge makes sense. Therefore, a sort of validation for new competencies should be included in the update process. This plurality of sources can prevent the risk of opportunism in indicate new competencies when they are a threat for people in the organization. This is reported as one of the problems that incumbent companies found when they face a radical technological innovation. A case study about Oticon provides an example

Table 4 Meta-design

Meta-design	Description
Sources of competencies	
MD1	A DCMS should include features for informal description of new competencies (forum,...)
MD2	A DCMS should include a search engine for external searching of new competencies
MD3	A DCMS should contextualize knowledge in the specific organizational "BA"
Categorization criteria	
MD4	A DCMS should create categories that make sense for people in the organization (tag, ...)
Outputs	
MD5	A DCMS should notice people about new competencies included in the inventory
MD6	A DCMS should support a dynamic revision of job definition and description

Table 5 Testable design product hypotheses

Hypotheses	Description
PROD1	A DCMS that includes a search engine for external searching of new competencies (MD2) and contextualization of knowledge in the specific organizational "BA" (MD3) will aligned with market needs.
PROD2	A DCMS that includes informal definition of competencies (MD1) using categories that make sense for people in the organization (MD4) will improve its comprehension among people.
PROD3	A DCMS that includes informal definition of competencies (MD1) will facilitate innovation.
PROD4	A DCMS that supports a dynamic revision of job definition and description (MD6) and that notices people about new competencies included in the inventory will help a training needs mapping aligned with market requirement.

regarding the transformation of traditional acoustic device in "in the ear" electronic device [35].

Our design proposes a criterion for categorization. It is linked to the possibility for users to "tag" sentences in documents as a potential new competence (MD4). In this way, DCMS creates categories that make sense for people in the organization, because they used its own language.

From the point of view of outputs, MD5 (A DCMS should notice people about new competencies included in the inventory) requirement suggest to design an "alert" that inform people about new competencies included in the skill inventory. Moreover, MD6 (A DCMS should support a dynamic revision of job definition and description) should be translated in a full integration with job descriptions management. Those job descriptions should be modified in a dynamic way in order to lead people development toward a target aligned with strategies.

The meta-requirement and meta-design components of our design theory must be empirically tested by developing and using a specific DCMS. Table 5 lists examples of hypotheses about the theory.

Table 6 Design methods

Design method	Description
DM1	A DCMS should be developed basing categorization of competencies on sources linked to social interaction.
DM2	A DCMS should be defined on both social and documental analysis and interviews to top performers.

Table 7 Testable design process hypotheses

Hypotheses	Description
PROC1	A design for a specific DCMS based on a social cooperation will be judged by users to be superior to one designed using only interviews.

The hypothesis PROD1 a DCMS that includes a search engine for external searching of new competencies (MD2) and a contextualization of knowledge in the specific organizational "BA" (MD3) will be aligned with market needs. Our design gives this opportunity for competencies that have documental origins because the "corpus" identifies the sources to analyze but this analysis can be run continuously. Even other competencies, especially those analyzed in social forum, could be underline new competencies.

The hypothesis PROD2 stated that a DCMS that includes informal definition of competencies (MD1) using categories that make sense for people in the organization (MD4) will improve its comprehension among people. Our design tries to build a communication channel among people in the organization and the skills definition and management. The creation of forum dedicated to discussion about competencies is a non-hierarchical way to allow these flows of information.

The hypothesis PROD3 stated that a DCMS, that includes informal definition of competencies (MD1), will facilitate the innovation. The definition of organizational roles depends on how processes are defined, on how organizational chart is designed and on how work organization is managed. Nevertheless, the rise of new competencies can be a source of innovation for all organizational tools included organizational roles.

The hypothesis PROD4 stated that a DCMS that supports a dynamic revision of job definition and description (MD6) and that notices people about new competencies included in the inventory will help a training needs mapping aligned with market requirement. In a turbulent environment, organizational tools risk to be too static and to lose their mission to support effectiveness of organizations. The possibility to update competencies and roles can give back to these tools their capability to achieve their mission and in this way overcome the risk to be considered obsolete.

The design process component of our design theory is focused on the continuity and dynamicity of input and output production. We can identify two Design Methods (Table 6).

Starting from these statements it is possible to define two Testable Design Process hypotheses (Table 7).

The hypotheses PROC1 stated that a design for a specific DCMS based on a social cooperation will be judged by users to be superior to one, designed using only interviews. Our design is based on a process more inclusive and cooperative. In this way, users are more motivate to cooperate and recognize the output of DCMS as part of their effort. In addition, the language could be closer to users' one and facilitate a mindful use of skills inventory and organizational roles.

A system designed according to these prescriptions can achieve, at the same time, the result to involve people in continuous update of skill inventory, provide a higher understanding of that inventory and, as theoretical consequence, a contribution to knowledge management research.

4 A Feasible Evaluation Plan for Testing DCMS Requirements

Before developing a DCMS, in order to test the architecture designed above, we plan to verify if text-mining software can provide a result comparable with an existing skill inventory.

4.1 The Selected Existing Skill Inventory

A skill inventory is a list of competencies required in different organizational roles within the company. It is used for recruiting, training and HR development. A traditional methodology starts from interviews to top-performers for each organizational role. This approach requires to know or to define measurements of performance in order to identify top-people to be interviewed. In addition, this kind of methodology has an internal view (top performers are compared among people that within the organizational have that organizational role). Therefore, there is the risk to build a system that does not take in account competencies that is rising in the market. The output of these interviews is a list of distinctive competencies for each organizational role. Of course, some of those competencies can be replied in more than one organizational role. The aggregation of all competencies creates a skills inventory.

The skill inventory that we will use to check our results has been elaborated by an Italian Agency (ISFOL) and its use is free for Italian workers, companies and students. This system is articulated on 805 professional roles. Each has been described using 400 indicators. For each organizational role, the application provides items about main tasks, knowledge, skills and attitudes, and working styles. For instance, for the organizational role "HR employee" 33 tasks have been identified. For the same role, 30 knowledge items have been sorted according to their specific weights in terms of complexity and importance. Skills and attitudes (80 items) have been sorted in the same way. Of course, many items have a weight so low that could be ignored for that specific organizational role. Working styles (17 items) describe some behaviors need for that role (perseverance, stress resistance, self-control, ...).

As first step, we extracted from ISFOL database a list of competencies required for financial organizational roles. We include only competencies that have not been classified as "not important". The category "knowledge" is very general because of the ISFOL methodology has been designed in order to be suitable for any companies that needs it. A concrete use of ISFOL system should be customized in this category with lows, internal procedures, internal informatics applications, price lists and other sources.

The ISFOL skills inventory is articulated in five categories (knowledge, skills, attitudes, general activities and work styles). The first category is heterogeneous and it is too general (only eight competencies). Probably, a concrete application of ISFOL model would be more detailed and customized. Among those competencies, we find normative knowledge, market knowledge, specialized knowledge (financial), ICT knowledge, linguistic knowledge, technology knowledge, mathematic knowledge.

4.2 Fit of Text Mining Functionality with DCMS Requirements

In order to simulate the results of a DCMS we will use a software application for text analysis and text mining in order to understand how many requirements would be respected.

Text mining systems use methodologies both statistical and linguistic. Their analyses allow to extract information and to respect principles of data mining and text mining. The representation is supported by quantitative data related to words and, at level of context, fragments or documents [36–43]. We define "corpus" the "universe" of documents analyzed. Its size can be very large (millions of words). The automatic processing allows to identify some peculiarity for each text analyzed. Text mining applications are composed by a set of tools that allow the analysis of any type of linguistic data articulated in many texts or in a single corpus. From, the analysis you can extract information (peculiar language, language relevant, specific language). Other studies analyze how to build in a network a company profiles starting from their key documents. In this case, a search engine is used to identify the competencies needed in a given project [44].

We compared products requirements with functions available in text mining software and underlined possible integrations of sources and outputs (Fig. 3).

The table at page 137 summarizes this analysis (Table 8).

In conclusion, it seems to be possible using a text mining software application in order to test the possibility to extract competencies only for the documental analysis of a corpus of documents.

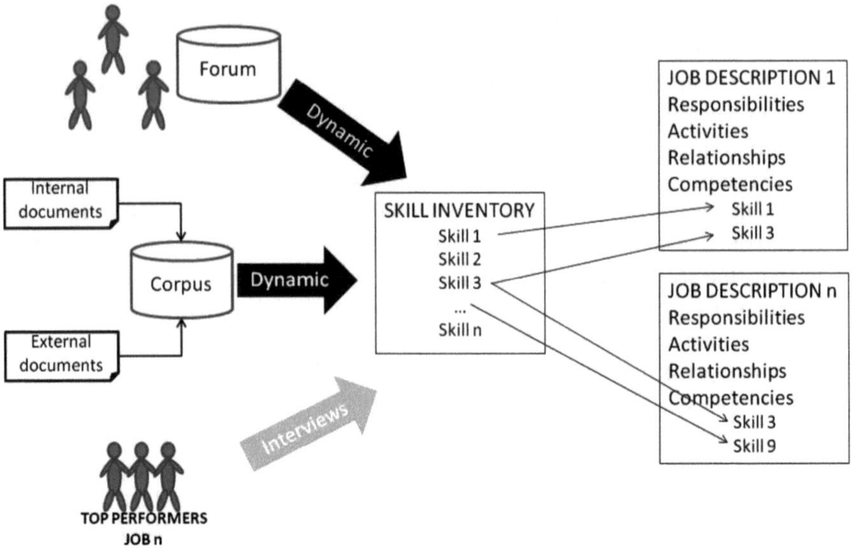

Fig. 3 Sources and outputs

Therefore, we need to define the sources of this "corpus". In order to make this task easier, it is possible to design a chart with two dimensions: update need level and tacit or explicit knowledge. This chart gives us some suggestions about how to find the sources for the DCMS. For competencies included in the area with high update need and explicit knowledge we can use laws, internal procedures, technical manuals, …, as inputs for DCMS. Technological and market knowledge could be update from both documental (internal and external) and informal sources. For competencies included in the area with low update need and explicit knowledge, we can find documental sources but they could be excluded from the competencies updated frequently. Other competencies could be included using traditional methodologies. In the area with high update need and explicit knowledge we find normative, ICT and specialized knowledge. Technological and market knowledge have high update need but they are in the middle between tacit and explicit because the sources are both documental and informal. In the area with low update need and explicit knowledge, we find linguistic and mathematic knowledge because they have both documental sources and low changing rate. In the area with low update need and tacit knowledge, we find all other competencies categories (skills, attitudes, general activities and work styles).

It is therefore possible to define the different sources for each group of competencies. In the following table, for each group of competencies have been identified the source typology, the specification of sources origin (external, internal or both) and the tool to be implemented (Table 9).

Table 8 Comparing product requirements and text mining functionalities

Meta-design	Description	Text mining functionality	Possible integration
Sources of competencies			
MD1	A DCMS should include features for informal description of new competencies (forum,…)	Informal descriptions of new knowledge could be included in the "corpus" to be analyzed	A forum where people can describe new knowledge should be created
MD2	A DCMS should include a search engine for external searching of new competencies	Extracting new competencies form the "corpus" in a continuous way, it is possible an update of needed competencies	
MD3	A DCMS should contextualize knowledge in the specific organizational "BA"		The new competencies extracted by data mining need to be reviewed in term of language and coherence with HR system
Categorization criteria			
MD4	A DCMS should create categories that make sense for people in the organization (tag, …)	Using "corpus" edited by employees and using words written by them it could be easier the use of a language understandable by people within the organization	
Outputs			
MD5	A DCMS should notice people about new competencies included in the inventory	Text mining can provide lists of new competencies	
MD6	A DCMS should support a dynamic revision of job definition and description		A tool that describe competencies for each role should be included in a DCMS

5 Conclusions

In this paper, we elaborated a design theory for IT that supports a dynamic mapping of competencies. The aim of this contribution is to address the possibility to overcome update problems through the design of an appropriate system. Starting from a kernel theory about knowledge creation and innovation, we defined a set of meta-requirements, meta-designs, design-methods, and testable hypotheses.

Table 9 Competencies, sources and tool to be implemented

Group of competencies	Source typology (Documental, informal or both)	Sources origin (external, internal or both)	Example of sources	Tool to be implemented
Normative knowledge	Documental	Both internal and external origin	T.U.F. law MiFID European Directive Internal procedures	Semantic tool for automatic categorization
ICT knowledge	Documental	Both internal and external origin	Internal application manuals External application manuals	Semantic tool for automatic categorization
Specialized knowledge	Documental	Both internal and external origin	Financial products	Semantic tool for automatic categorization
Technological knowledge	Both documental and informal	Both internal and external origin	Internal technical manuals	Semantic tool for automatic categorization and social forum analyzer
Market knowledge	Both documental and informal	Both internal and external origin	Pricing list Market statistics	Semantic tool for automatic categorization and social forum analyzer
Linguistic knowledge	Both documental and informal	External origin	Critical competencies underlined by interviewed people	Interviews with top performers
Mathematical knowledge	Both documental and informal	External origin	Critical competencies underlined by interviewed people	Interviews with top performers
Skills, attitudes, general activities and work styles	Informal	Internal origin	Critical competencies underlined by interviewed people	Interviews with top performers

The resulting designing requirements allow to underline the need to consider this kind of tool from both a product and a process point of view. The social issues underlined in this study force each user to make an effort of implementation and assimilation of the resulting tool.

Our study will contribute firstly to managerial research and practice providing a new and sustainable way for updating skill inventories and job descriptions. This methodology will be an interesting way to develop new branches of research that try to reduce the common trade-off between academic research and practical instruments. In order to understand the mechanism that allows the identification of the most important competencies, our future studies will also consider experimental models to understand the behavioral perspectives of designing competencies within companies.

On the other hand, from a theoretical perspective, our study will give a relevant contribution in order to try to understand the relationship between technological and non-technological capabilities [45] that companies try to resolve in order to exceed competencies traps [46]. These considerations push our study to another significant position inside the academic discussion, and in particular into the discussion on the relationship between turbulent contexts and the necessity to adapt competencies and capabilities [19] through the identification of instruments that allow competencies codification [47]. Finally, we hope that future studies will concentrate on the strategic perspective of Dynamic Competencies Mapping Systems as a new way to achieve competitive advantages.

References

1. Walls, J. G. et al. (1992). Building an information system design theory for vigilant EIS. *Information Systems Research, 3* (1), 36–59.
2. Boyatzis, R. E. (1982). *The competent manager*. New York: John Wiley.
3. Spencer, L. M., & Spencer, S. M. (1993). *Competence at work: Models for superior performance*. New York: John Wiley & Sons.
4. McClelland, D. C. (1973). Testing for competence rather than intelligence. *American Psychologist, 28*(1), 1–40.
5. Flanagan, J. C. (1954). The critical incident technique. *Psychological Bulletin, 51*(4), 327–358.
6. Kelly, G. A. (1955). The psychology of personal constructs (vol. 2). New York: Norton.
7. Arazy, O., Kumar, N., & Shapira, B. (2010). A theory-driven design framework for social recommender systems. *Journal of the Association for Information Systems*, *11* (9), Article 2.
8. Brown, S. L. & Eisenhardt, K. M. (1997). The art of continuous change: Linking complexity theory and time-paced evolution in relentlessly shifting organizations. *Administrative Science Quarterly*, *42*(1), 1–34.
9. Eisenhardt, K. M. & Schoonhoven, C. (1996). Resource-based view of strategic alliance formation: Strategic and social effects in entrepreneurial firms. *Organization Science*, *7*(2), 136–150.
10. Williamson, O. E. (1985). *The economic institution of capitalism*. New York: Free Press.
11. Hennart, J. F. (1991). *The nature of the transnational firm*. London: Routledge.
12. Kimberly, J. (1975). Environmental constraints and organizational structure: A comparative analysis of rehabilitation organizations. *Administrative Science Quarterly, 20*(1), 1–9.
13. Stinchcombe A. (1965). Social structure and organizations. In J. G. March (ed.), *Handbook of organizations* (pp. 153–193). Chicago: Rand McNally.
14. Barton, D. (1992). Core capabilities and core rigidities: A paradox in managing new product development. *Strategic Management Journal, Summer Special Issue, 13*, 111–126.

15. Bain, J. S. (1959). *Industrial organization*. New York: Wiley.
16. Scherer, F. M. (1980). *Industrial market structure and economic performance*. Boston: Hougthon Mifflin Company.
17. Tripsas, M., & Gavetti, G. (2000). Capabilities, cognition, and inertia. *Strategic Management Journal, 21*, 1147–1161.
18. Kaplan, S. & Henderson, R. (2005). Inertia and incentives: Bridging organizational economics and organizational theory. *Organization Science, 16*(5), 509–521. (Frontiers of Organization Science, Part 2 of 2).
19. Teece, D. J., Pisano, G., & Shuen, A. (1997). Dynamic capabilities and strategic management. *Strategic Management Journal, 18*(7), 509–553.
20. Garvin, D. A. (1988) *Managing quality: The strategic and competitive edge*. New York: Free Press.
21. Amit, R. & Shoemaker, P. (1993). Strategic assets and organizational rent. *Startegic Management Journal, 14* (1), 33–46.
22. Kaplan, R. & Norton, D. (2007). *Strategic alignment*. Boston: Harvard Business School Press.
23. March, J. (1991). Exploration and exploitation in organizational learning. *Organization Science, 2* (1) 71–87.
24. Nonaka, I. (1994). A dynamic theory of organizational knowledge creation. *Organization Science, 5*(1), 14–37.
25. Nonaka, I., Byosiere, P., Borucki, C. C., & Konno, N. (1994). Organizational knowledge creation theory: A first comprehensive test. *International Business Review, 3*(4), 337–351.
26. Nonaka, I., & Takeuchi, H. (1995). *The knowledge-creating company*. Oxford: Oxford University Press.
27. Nonaka, I., Toyama, R., & Konno, N. (2000). SECI, Ba, and leadership: A unified model of dynamic knowledge creation. *Long Range Planning, 33*, 5–34.
28. Nonaka, I., Toyama, R. & Byosière, P. (2001). A theory of organizational knowledge creation: Understanding the dynamic process of creating knowledge. In M. Dierkes, A. B. Antel, J. Child, I. Nonaka (Eds.), *Handbook of organizational learning and knowledge* (pp. 491–517). Oxford: Oxford University Press.
29. Nonaka, I., & Toyama, R. (2003). The knowledge-creating theory revisited: Knowledge creation as a synthesizing process. *Knowledge Management Research & Practice, 1*, 2–10.
30. Nonaka, I., Konno, N. & Toyama R. (2001). Emergence of Ba. A conceptual framework for the continuous and self-transcending process of knowledge creation. In I. Nonaka, & T. Nishigushi (Eds.), Knowledge emergence. *Social, technical and evolutionary dimensions of knowledge creation*. (pp. 3–29) New York: Oxford University Press.
31. Adler, P. S. (1994). Comment on managing innovation as an organizational knowledge creation process. In I. Nonaka, J. Allouche, & G. Pogorel (Eds.), *Technology management and corporate strategies: A tricontinental perspective* (pp. 110–124). Amsterdam: Elsevier.
32. Obstfeld, D. (2005). Social networks, the tertius Iungens orientation, and involvement in innovation. *Administrative Science Quarterly*, 50 (1), 100–130.
33. Burt, R. S. (1995). Structural holes: the social structure of competition, Cambridge: Harvard University Press.
34. Goldkuhl, G. (2004). Design theories in information systems—a need for Multi-grounding. *Journal of Information Technology Theory and Application, 6*(2), 59–72.
35. Foss, N. (2003). Selective intervention and internal hybrids: Interpreting and learning from the rise and decline of the oticon spaghetti organization. *Organization Science, 14*, 331–349.
36. Bolasco, S. (2008). Corpora e liste di frequenza d'uso: criteri e tecniche per l'analisi automatica dei testi, in Monica Barni, Donatella Troncarelli e Carla Bagna (Eds.) Lessico e apprendimenti. La dimensione lessicale nell'educazione linguistica (p. 352). F. Angeli, Milano.
37. Bolasco, S., Pavone, P. (2008). Multi-class categorization based on cluster analysis and TFIDF. In S. Heiden & B. Pincemin (Eds.), *JADT2008* (vol. 1, pp. 209–218), Presses Universitaires de Lyon.

38. Bolasco, S., Pavone, P. (2007). Automatic dictionary and rule-based systems for extracting information from text. In *Classification and data analysis 2007. Book of short papers CLADAG2007* (pp. 255–258). EUM—Edizioni Università di Macerata.
39. Bolasco, S. (2007). Criteri e tecniche della statistica testuale per l'analisi automatica dei testi. In A. Grassi (Ed.) Demografia e Statistica: un ricordo di Enzo Lombardo tra scienza e cultura, Dipartimento di Studi Geoeconomici Linguistici Statistici Storici per l'Analisi regionale (pp. 29–56). SAPIENZA Università di Roma.
40. Bolasco, S., D'Avino, E., Pavone, P. (2007). Analisi dei diari giornalieri con strumenti di statistica testuale e text mining, in Maria Clelia Romano (a cura di) I tempi della vita quotidiana. Un approccio multidisciplinare all'analisi dell'uso del tempo (pp. 309–340). Roma, ISTAT.
41. Bolasco, S. (2005). Statistica testuale e text mining: alcuni paradigmi applicativi. *Quaderni di Statistica, Liguori Ed., 7*, 17–53.
42. Bolasco, S. (2005). La reperibilità statistica di tendenze diacroniche nell'uso delle parole. In I. Chiari e T. DeMauro (Eds.), Parole e Numeri. Analisi quantitativa dei fatti di lingua (pp. 335–354). Aracne, Roma.
43. Bolasco, S., Bisceglia, B., Baiocchi, F. (2004). Estrazione di informazione dai testi in Mondo Digitale, III, 1, 2004, pp. 27–43.
44. Formica, A., Missikoff, M., Pourabbas, E., Taglino, F. (2010) Semantic search for enterprises competencies management.
45. Majumdar, B.A. (1982). Innovations. product developments and technology transfers: An empirical study of dynamic competitive advantage. *The case of electronic calculators*. Washington: University Press of America.
46. Teece, D. J. (1988) Technological change and the nature of the firm. In G Dosi, C Freeman, R Nelson, G Silverberg, L Soete (Eds.), *Technical Change and Economic Theory* (pp. 256–281), London: Pinter Publisher.
47. Eisenhardt, K. (1989). Making fast strategic decisions in high-velocity environment. *Academy of Management Journal, 32*(3), 543–576.

Open Innovation and Crowdsourcing Communities Design: A Cross Case Analysis

Francesca Cabiddu, Manuel Castriotta, Maria Chiara Di Guardo and Paola Floreddu

Abstract While a great amount of literature has focused on the effects of open innovation and crowdsourcing strategy on firms' competition and generation of ideas, we know little about how to design an IT artifact to manage the supporting of creativity among on line communities. Defining an interpretative framework which is based on the Design Theory concept, this paper aims to contribute to this body of knowledge by means of a cross-case study, focused on the design evaluation of two crowdsourcing-supporting IT platforms. We develop a theoretical framework for crowdsourcing communities, aimed to identify how the design characteristics shape the competition to generate new ideas, thereby influencing the crowdsourcing strategy.

Keywords Crowdsourcing · Design science · Usability · Interactivity · Functionality · Accuracy

1 Introduction

Over the last decade, following the seminal contribution of Henry Chesbrough, "Open Innovation", defined as "the use of purposive inflows and outflows of knowledge to accelerate internal innovation, and expand the markets for external use of innovation, respectively" [1], has increasingly attracted substantial attention from practitioners and academics.

The concept that to profit from a novel idea, firms should not necessarily discover and develop it themselves was already supported by the literature on customer and user integration into innovation activities [2] but the emphasis on

F. Cabiddu (✉) · M. Castriotta · M. C. Di Guardo · P. Floreddu
University of Cagliari, Italy
e-mail: fcabiddu@unica.it

R. Baskerville et al. (eds.), *Designing Organizational Systems*,
Lecture Notes in Information Systems and Organisation 1,
DOI: 10.1007/978-3-642-33371-2_8,

inflows and outflows of knowledge to decrease the cost and time for developing new ideas, core to open innovation, has generated a plethora of new and most fruitful innovation strategies [3]. Moreover, thanks to recent technologies, including many Web 2.0 applications, firms can now use effective tools for integrating customers into the early stages of the innovation process [4–6]. In this line, some researchers have explored, within the open innovation framework, the impact of a crowdsourcing strategy on the firm's inventive activities [7]. The term crowdsourcing describes a Web-based business model that harnesses the creative solutions of a distributed network of individuals through what amounts to an open call for proposals. In other words, a company posts a problem online and a vast number of individuals offer solutions to the problem.

While a great amount of literature has focused on the effects of open innovation and crowdsourcing strategy on firms' competition and generation of ideas, we give our contribution within recent studies related on how to design an IT artefact supporting on line communities [8]. In this vein we focus our attention on how to design an IT artifact to manage creativity within a crowdsourcing platform. In particular, how the design of the artifact may shape the firm's open innovation and crowdsourcing strategy has been largely un-theorized and its empirical importance has been overlooked. In fact, creating and effectively using a crowdsourcing IT artifact is extremely complicated for a firm: a well-designed system enables productivity and generation of successful ideas, a poor design is the greatest barrier to both.

Defining an interpretative framework which is based on the Design Theory concept, this paper aims to contribute to this body of knowledge by the means of a cross case study focused on the design evaluation of two IT platforms supporting crowdsourcing and open innovation strategy. This approach allows to investigate the link between the firms design choices and the behaviour of the online crowdsourcing community. We develop a theoretical framework of crowdsourcing communities, seeking to identify how the design characteristics shape the competition to generate new ideas and thereby influence the crowdsourcing strategy.

Analyzing the design of the crowdsourcing online artifacts of Mulino Bianco and Sturbucks, two important firms in the bakery & food and beverage markets, we give explicit prescriptions on how to design and support social interaction among members of a crowdsourcing community for new ideas generation.

The paper is organized as follow. Section 2 defines the design science approach and our framework. Section 3 illustrates the method used, Sect. 4 describes the data and Sect. 5 discusses the results and reports the concluding remarks.

2 The Design Theory Framework

IS design theory is concerned with how to design an artifact (design product), and the design process [9, 10]. The design product is composed of meta-requirements, meta-design principles, kernel theories and testable hypotheses. The design process is the sum of the steps and procedures taken to develop an artifact. In this

Table 1 The design theory framework of crowdsourcing communities

The design theory components	Crowd integration	Efficiency of creative process	Community structure	Open culture
Meta-requirements	Democratizing innovation High level of inclusion of end users	Brainstorming Lateral thinking dynamics Collect individual knowledge	Supporting creative user activities Support motivations of contributors	Transparency Sociability
Meta design	Multiple languages Glossary of technical terms Audio access for visually impaired Site map A to Z index Faqs Search engine	Propose an idea section Rate other people ideas section Ideas in action section Comments section	Democratizing innovation tools User profile Idea description Linking people to ideas Cash prizes No cash prizes Addressing tutors Career application Rank ideas Addressing expert Peer communication	Protocol and rules No broken links Audio/video files Customer consultation Content arranged by topic discussed Ranking of ideas proposed
Testable dimensions	Usability	Interactivity	Functionality	Accuracy

paper, we refer only to the design product, in particular we focus on the identification of the set of requirements and design characteristics that should guide the construction and management of a crowdsourcing community. By building a design theory of IT supporting crowdsourcing communities, we identify how the design characteristics shape the competition to generate new ideas and thereby influence the crowdsourcing strategy.

As summarized in Table 1, our framework is organized in a multidimensional perspective based on crowdsourcing and open innovation theories. In this case, in some sense, different kernel theories have been taken into consideration in order to build a comprehensive framework for designing IT artifacts for crowdsourcing communities. A kernel theory, which may be an academic theory or a practitioner theory in use, is useful in framing the area of applicability of the systems, as well as in evaluating the design theory and the final product.

Following Walls et al. [9, 10] meta-requirements "describes a class of artifacts hypothesized to meet the meta-requirements" [9, 10]. The final component is a set of testable dimensions that we use to verify whether the meta-design satisfies the meta-requirements [9, 10].

The first dimension is based on the observation that open communities need a strong "crowd integration" to exploit collective intelligence power [11]. The IT platform supporting "crowd integration" needs an efficient design to stimulate a democratizing innovation culture and a high level of inclusion of end users [11] (meta-requirements). To achieve these goals (meta-design) the web site should be designed in such way as to have multiple language choice; to comply with accessibility standards; a glossary of technical terms; a site map; an A to Z index; a FAQs section; and a search engine. The testable dimension that we applied to verify whether the meta-design satisfies meta-requirements is usability. Usability refers to the ease in accessing information and browsing the web portal by users [12]. Usability is "the extent to which a product can be used by specified users to achieve specified goals with effectiveness, efficiency and satisfaction in a specified context of use" (ISO 9241-11, 1998).

The second dimension that characterizes our framework is based on the observation that the principal goal of a crowd community is to foster an early ideas generation phase, and implies a strong attitude towards the efficiency of the creative process [1, 13, 14]. Meta-requirements focus on the efficiency of creative process, and can be identified as technical and theoretical creativity tools aimed to foster lateral thinking through innovative and traditional methods [13, 14]. Brainstorming activities, or the simple collection of individual knowledge, need the creation of an artifact that enables the users to propose, rate, comment and explore ideas in action, in order to stimulate new high quality services and product output (meta-design). The testable dimension that we used to verify whether the meta-design satisfies meta-requirements is interactivity. Interactivity is a measure of the degree of immediate feedback [15]. Interactivity in web communities is expected to improve the bidirectional communication between companies and customers.

The third dimension comes from the consideration that crowdsourcing relations imply a peculiar community website structure in order to support motivation among contributors [16, 17]. When designing a community structure, the goal is to support and allow creative user activities and to collect them by motivating contributors [17] (meta-requirements). IT artifacts that allow the building of a strong and an efficient crowdsourcing community structure are (meta-design): democratizing innovation tools; user profile; idea description; linking people to ideas; cash prizes; addressing tutors; career application; rank ideas; addressing experts; peer communication. Functionality is determined by the technical components of an IT platform that support user's activities within business processes and improve their productivity [16]. The criterion of functionality is divided into two parts: Technical functionalities, and Organizational functionalities. The first part refers to the technical components in an IT platform that stimulate and encourage people to participate in the community. Organizational functionalities refer to measures that enable users to engage in conversations with online experts, or some incentives like cash or non-cash prizes that encourage contributions in the community.

The last dimension is based on the idea that open culture is a key factor for collecting, connecting and developing the dynamics related to content receptivity and the need for transparency in the relationship between customers, peers and firms. Meta-requirements focus on open culture environment to promote sociability and transparency between members in order to create a developing trust in their relationships [18]. Meta-designs are: protocols and rules; no broken links; audio/video files; customers' feedback forms; content arranged by topic discussed; proposed ideas ranking. The testable dimension that we applied to verify whether the meta-design satisfies meta-requirements is accuracy. Accuracy is defined as the capability of an IT artifact to provide correct results or effects [19, 20]; in other words, it is concerned with those aspects that indicate a high degree of web site sophistication. Users need an IT artifact that contains the right data and the right level of detail [21].

3 Research Method

This research is based on an in-depth, inductive netnography cross case study of the Mulino Bianco and Starbucks web communities. Netnography approach, or online ethnography, refers to a number of related online research methods that adapt to the study of the communities and cultures created through computer-mediated social interaction [22–24]. A netnography approach for the case study is purely observational, in the sense that the researcher is a type of specialized lurker [23]. The qualitative data for our netnography analysis come from a cross case analysis of two selected online communities, the "Nel mulino che vorrei" and "MyStarbucksidea" websites. Cross case analysis enables the comparison of multiple cases against predefined categories, in search of similarities and differences, and by classifying the data according to our theoretical framework.

3.1 The Cross Case Study

Mulino Bianco is a part of the Italian Barilla S.p.a. brand portfolio, and manufactures a wide variety of bakery products. Barilla is a world leader in the pasta market. The firm has 26 factories among which there are macaroni (pasta) factories, flourmills, and bakehouses. The R&D department takes advantage of 250 researchers employed in six branches based in Italy, USA, Russia, France, Germany, and Sweden. Mulino Bianco manufactures a wide variety of bakery products, such as cookies, biscuits, snacks, sweets and cakes, bread, crackers and a wide range of smoothies and juices. Mulino Bianco is trying to adopt an open innovation approach within the typical Web 2.0 paradigm. In particular, the project "Nel mulino che vorrei" is part of an Open Innovation strategy linked to an outside-in process. The community was founded on March 8, 2009 and is an example of co-generation projects and crowdsourcing; an open workshop which enables people to get in touch with the "Mulino Bianco" world and to propose ideas, as well as to vote for the most original one. The community represents a change in Mulino Bianco's communication models, aimed to avoiding the confinement of consumers into passive viewers by turning them into active participants, thus enabling them to enrich the world of references of the brand with their ideas, experiences, emotions and conversations [25].

Starbucks is the first roaster and retailer of coffee in the world. Starbucks purchases and roasts high-quality whole bean coffees and sells them, along with fresh, rich-brewed coffees, Italian-style espresso beverages, cold blended beverages, a variety of complementary food items, a selection of premium teas, and beverage-related accessories and equipment, primarily through Company-operated retail stores. Through the Starbucks Entertainment division brand also markets books, music and film.

The Company's objective is to maintain Starbucks standing as one of the most recognized and respected brands in the world. To achieve this goal, the Company plans to continue disciplined global expansion of its retail and licensed store base, to introduce relevant new products in all its channels, and to selectively develop new channels of distribution.

The online communication of Starbucks uses a variety of traditional and Web 2.0 tools.

Alongside an institutional showcase website divided into six main areas, each one with its own blog, there are direct links to all major social media, like Twitter, Facebook, and YouTube. A number of links to the co-creation community called "MyStarbucksidea" is clearly visible and accessible from the various pages.

4 Data Analysis

"Nel mulino che vorrei" is divided into six areas: 1. discover the project; 2. propose an idea; 3. rate other people's ideas; 4. see ideas in assessment; 5. read the blog; 6. answer to Mulino. The community aims to collect ideas, analyze them, and actualize them if they are consistent with the mission, vision and company values.

Mystarbucksidea.com site is divided into three macro-areas: "Got an idea", "View ideas" and "Ideas in action". To propose an idea you must be a registered user; however, the registering process is fast and users can easily insert the idea description through a user-friendly/rich text interface. The area called "View ideas" is divided into "Popular", "Recent", "Top of all time" and "Comments". This distinction allows new ideas to emerge. For every idea members can vote thumbs up or down, and this is why it is possible for some ideas to get a negative score. Finally, the "Ideas in action" area is divided into four sub-areas: "Under review", "Reviewed", "Coming soon" and "Launched". All areas pages are have links to major social media and Rss feed tools.

The analysis of the community website design highlights a minimalist and very clean structure in both cases. Community members are not distracted by flashy graphics and banner ads. The typography is sober. Starbucks divides its front page in three sections (propose, ideas in action and see list) while Mulino Bianco adds a section devoted to the explanation of the project, a link to the official Mulino Bianco blog, and a section dedicated to surveys, researches and focus groups.

Table 2 Effectiveness of crowdsourcing community idea generation

Items	Nelmulinochevorrei.com	Mystarbucksidea.com
Ideas generated	3,846	112.331
Ideas in evaluation	14	640
Ideas launched on the market	6	156
Community members	130.000	450.000

Participating in these groups allows registered users to obtain tokens that entitle them to be rewarded with various Mulino Bianco products. This last section represents an element of discontinuity between the two communities, using traditional 1.0 marketing methodologies alongside the new 2.0 crowdsourcing strategies. The motivations behind this choice are not clear.

The type of ideas that can be submitted is different between the two websites. While in the Mulino Bianco site it is more focused on products, promotions, packaging, and social commitment, Starbucks proposes "Experience ideas" and "involvement ideas": the first refers to ordering, payments, and tips on the location and furnishings of their shops, while the second is about social responsibility involvement, and ideas and tips on community-building in a wider, more global sense (charity, social commitment etc.).

In both cases, and for all the sections, there are no tools aimed at democratizing innovation, such as dedicated software. In particular, there are no tools to design the packaging of products, recipes, products, locations, and new furnishings. The interface, in both cases, is very similar.

Transparency is a key element for both communities; in the Mulino Bianco one, however, the ranking of new ideas is done by internal company members, thus leading to a failure in the discovery of the evaluation criteria involved. In both communities, you can browse through the latest, most popular, most consulted and most commented ideas.

Despite the numerous and obvious elements of homogeneity, the analysis of the results achieved by the two communities immediately shows some substantial differences. Even though its registered members are about four times lower than the Starbuck ones, the number of ideas generated within the Mulino Bianco community is in proportion dramatically lower. The protocol used makes it impossible to tell if the Mulino Bianco community generates fewer ideas, or if the top management operates a more strict selection. Moreover, it is clear that the number of ideas contributed is much higher in Starbucks, and the datum which appears to be more striking is the fact that Mulino Bianco selected and launched only six new ideas (Table 2).

4.1 Design Evaluation

The analysis of the IT platforms tests the four dimensions of Usability, Interactivity, Functionality and Accuracy previously identified in the design science framework. The scores displayed in Tables 3, 4, 5, 6 display a zero value when the

Table 3 Usability of crowdsourcing community

Items	Nel mulino che vorrei	Mystarbucksidea.com
Multiple language	0	0
Glossaries of technical term	0	0
Audio access for visually impaired	0	0
Sitemap	0	0
A to Z index	0	0
FAQs	1	1
Search engine	0	0
Total scores	1	1

items analyzed do not appear in the two communities, and shows a one when they do. The global score in Usability, Interactivity, Functionality and Accuracy tables has been obtained by adding up the individual scores for every relevant item in each dimension.

Meta Design and Crowd Integration

To evaluate the intersection between meta-design and crowd integration we used Gant and Gant's description [12] of the ease of use in accessing information (usability) and browsing the web portal by users (Table 3).

From a first examination of crowdsourcing communities, the insufficient level of usability is immediately noticeable in all the dimensions assessed. Two cases show a low degree of development aimed to promote a high level of inclusion, i.e. the lack of an internal search engine or multiple languages browsing.

Meta Design and Efficiency of Creative Process

To evaluate the intersection between meta-design and efficiency of creative process we derive measures from Pina et al., description [15] of the development of interactive services that improve the bidirectional communication between companies and customers.

As can be seen from Table 4, two cases show a high degree of interactivity. Crowdsourcing communities are designed to enable the bi-directional communication between companies and users. The structure of the website explicitly allows users to write their ideas and follow the early idea-generation phase. In this case, the communities are able to collect individual knowledge.

Meta Design and Community Structure

To evaluate the intersection between meta-design and the community structure we derive measures from Leimeister et al. [16]. These measures are related to

Table 4 Interactivity of crowdsourcing community

Items	Nel mulino che vorrei	Mystarbucksidea.com
Propose an idea section	1	1
Rate other people's ideas section	1	1
Ideas in action section	1	1
Comments section	1	1
Total Scores	4	4

technical functionalities and explain how an IT platform supports users' activities (Table 5).

In both cases and for all the sections there are no democratizing innovation tools, such as dedicated software. In particular, it is not possible to design, for example, neither the packaging of products, nor recipes, products, locations, and new furnishings. The interface is very similar for both sites.

From a first analysis of these crowdsourcing communities, the insufficient level of functionality (Table 5) is immediately noticeable in the entire dimension assessed. The level of technical components in each IT platform in not sufficient to supports user's activities within business processes, and to maximize their productivity.

"Mystarbucksidea.com" shows better results in terms of technical functionalities' dimension: each submitted idea, in fact, can be connected to the personal profile of the user who submitted it.

Meta Design and Open Culture

To evaluate the intersection between meta-design and the open culture we derived measures from Wand and Wang's description [20] of the capacity of an IT artifact to provide the right data and the right level of detail (accuracy).

As highlighted in Table 6, the crowdsourcing communities present a sufficient degree of accuracy. The IT platform that shows the worst results is "MyStarbucksidea.com".

Designers should focus on improving site features such as the possibility to embed rich media content, as well as designing functions that encourage users to spend more time on the website.

5 Discussion

From our analysis, we believe that the crowdsourcing approach adopted by Starbucks and Mulino Bianco is currently particularly effective in creating innovative new products. MyStarbucksidea model is a powerful sample of how to manage co-creation strategies and web-communities best practices, while Mulino Bianco

Table 5 Functionality of crowdsourcing community

Technical functionalities	Description	Nel mulino che vorrei	Mystarbucksidea.com
Democratizing innovation tools	Provide specific tools or software that help users to describe and design their ideas	0	0
User profile	Tools that enable users to present themselves and their knowledge and skills.	0	1
Idea description	Section that enable members to describe and submit their ideas.	1	1
Linking people to ideas	Tools that enable users to contact the ideas' authors.	0	1
Total scores		1	3
Organizational functionalities			
Cash prizes	Provide monetary rewards for the best idea.	0	0
No cash prizes	Provide non-monetary rewards for the best idea.	1	1
Addressing tutors	Functionality that allow members to access technical aid.	1	0
Career application	Possibility to contact the career office and submit a job application	0	1
Rank ideas	Possibility to vote other people's ideas.	1	1
Addressing expert	Functionality that allow users to directly communicate with specialized personnel.	0	0
Peer communication	Functionality that allows bi-directional communication between users.	0	0
Total scores		3	3

Table 6 Accuracy of the crowdsourcing communities

Items	Nel mulino che vorrei	Mystarbucksidea.com
Protocols and rules	1	1
No broken links	1	1
Audio/video files	0	0
Customer consultation	1	1
Content arranged by topic discussed	1	1
Ranking of ideas proposed	1	0
Total scores	5	4

appears to have relevant difficulties in implementing what its own community produces.

A thorough analysis of the results obtained from the platforms shows that the two companies have achieved very positive results in terms of collaborative marketing (as demonstrated by traffic statistics). Moreover, even in terms of quantitative analysis, it is shown that the number of ideas is in line with major American business models that make use of crowdsourcing. In fact, about 1 % of community members actively propose ideas, while about 10 % of them comments and votes.

Regarding the Mulino Bianco community, some doubts arise from the decrease in contributions in the last few months (the number of ideas remained virtually unchanged, and this trend could be explained by a decrease in motivation among the contributors, as they are not rewarded by the launch in the market of any product or idea proposed). As for the efficiency and effectiveness of the business model, some problems must be taken into consideration. In fact, as shown on the platform, Mulino Bianco has launched only six new products while Starbucks new product launch is constantly increasing.

Both websites appear to encourage and promote participation based on the sense of community belonging, while they appear to fail in exploiting the main reasons underlying crowdsourcing success, such as direct compensation, social motivation, self marketing, learning, and competition.

The absence of a monetary reward for the best ideas appears to be a questionable choice. There is no evidence in literature about high quality, unrewarded voluntary contributions in fields different from charity, ethical issues or open source environment.

When Mulino Bianco created a new site area for internal surveys, offering brand gifts as a reward, contributions increased significantly.

The choice not to reward contributors appears more questionable in the light of the management of intellectual property adopted by Mulino Bianco. Mulino Bianco, in fact, retains full rights on all the contents generated within the community, but without establishing any of the motivations that lead to behaviors typical of gift economies [26].

Ranking in both communities is a powerful tool to lever social motivation high, as for example by means of appreciation by organizers and peers.

Another interesting aspect is the way in which communication between members is handled. In the community, members can communicate only indirectly by commenting on other people's posts. These links do not seem to be particularly effective, and help maintaining the diversity of the contributions of consumers.

The possibility to create an accurate profile page is available in both cases, but Starbucks allows customers to add more detailed information. Starbucks' design components seem to be more effective on leveraging self marketing motivation. in their profiles. Career options are offered in both communities.

The weaknesses about leveraging the learning of new skills are the same between the two analyzed communities. Both platforms do not provide any models of democratizing innovation, i.e. tutorials, training and software to facilitate and improve the quality of the contributions by community members [25]. The lack of such instruments, associated with the lack of remuneration, does not seem to exploit some of the main success reasons of crowdsourcing, such as competition, new skills learning, and reputation fostering (e.g. the phenomenon of open source as crowdsolving first experiment). For example, some competitors adopted strategies based on the implementation of specific software to create shapes, or to create new recipes and new ingredients. The absence of these factors results in the absence of one of the reasons that Benkler considers essential to the free assistance to projects: the gratification arising from learning new skills, and from knowledge sharing [12]. Moreover, no tool for accessing the knowledge of experts, mentors or peer is implemented.

6 Conclusion

Our findings offer some interesting conclusions, and this research makes a contribution to the limited literature in this field, thus enabling the development of more general works on the same subject. In particular, the notion of crowd integration, efficiency of creative process, community structure and open culture, which are the driven concept of this article, provide us a set of design principle for directing theory and performing research and development aimed at enhancing our understanding of the link between the firms design choices and the behaviour of the online crowdsourcing community.

References

1. Chesbrough, H. W. (2003). *Open innovation: The new imperative for creating and profiting from technology*. Boston: Harvard Business School Press Books.
2. Von Hippel, E. (1994). Sticky information and the locus of problem solving: Implications for innovation. *Management Science, 40*(4), 429–439.
3. Cassiman, B., Di Guardo, M.C., & Valentini, G. (2009). Organizing R&D projects to profit from innovation insights from co-opetition. *Long Range Planning*, *42*, (2) 216.

4. Von Hippel, E. & Von Krogh, G. (2003). Open source software and the Private-collective innovation model: Issues for organization science. *Organization Science 14* (2), 209–223.
5. Carmel, E. (2006). Building your information systems from the other side of the world: How infosys manages time zone differences, *MISQ Executive 5* (1), 43–53.
6. Carmel, E., & Agarwal, R. (2001). Tactical approaches for alleviating distance in global software development. *IEEE Software* , *18* (2), 22–29.
7. Cabiddu, F., Castriotta, M., Di Guardo, M.C., Floreddu, P. & Pettinao, D. (2012). Combining exploitation and exploration through crowdsourcing. In M. De Marco, D. Te'eni, V. Albano, S. Za (Eds.), *Information Systems: Crossroads for Organization, Management, Accounting and Engineering*, Heidelberg: Springer.
8. Spagnoletti P., Resca A. (2012). A design theory for IT supporting online communities. *Proceedings of the 45th Hawaii International Conference on System Sciences (HICSS-45), 4–7 January 2012*, Grand Wailea, Maui, Hawaii, (pp. 4082–4091).
9. Walls, J. G., Widmeyer, G. R., & El Sawy, O. A. (2004). Assessing information system design theory in perspective: How useful was our 1992 rendition? *Journal of Information Technology Theory and Practice, 6*(2), 43–58.
10. Walls, J. G., Widmeyer, G. R. & El Sawy O. A. (1992). Building an information system design theory for vigilant EIS. *Information Systems Research, 3*(1), 36–59
11. Lakhani, K.R., & Wolf, R.G. (2003). Why hackers do what they do: Understanding motivation and effort in free/open source software projects. MIT Sloan Working Paper no. 4425–03, Cambridge.
12. Gant D.B. & Gant, J.P. (2002). Enhancing E-Service Delivery. *E- Government Series, State Web Portals: Delivering and Financing E-Service*. Pricewaterhouse Coopers Endowment 2002.
13. Chesbrough, H., & Crowther, A. K. (2006). Beyond high tech: Early adopters of open innovation in other industries. *R&D Management, 36*(3), 229–236.
14. Amabile, T. M. (1998). How to kill creativity. *Harvard Business Review*, 77-87.
15. Pina, V., Torres, L., & Royo, S. (2007). Are ICT's improving transparency and accountability in the EU regional and local development. *Public Administration, 85*(2), 449–472.
16. Leimeister, J.M., Huber, M., Bretschneider, U. & Krcmar, H. (2009) Leveraging crowdsourcing—activation-supporting components for IT-based idea competitions. *Journal of Management Information Systems, 26* (1), 197–224.
17. Von Hippel, E. (2005). *Democratizing innovation*. Boston: MIT Press.
18. Surowiecky, J. (2004). *The wisdom of crowds: why the many are smarter than the few and how collective wisdom shapes business, economies, societies and nations*, New York: Random House.
19. Seffah, A., Donyaee, M., Kline, R., & Padda, H. (2006). Usability measurement and metrics: A consolidated model. *Software Quality Journal, 14*, 159–178.
20. Wand, Y., & Wang, R. Y. (1996). Anchoring data quality dimensions in ontological foundations. *Communications of the ACM, 39*(11), 86–95.
21. Goodhue, D. L. (1995). Understanding user evaluations of information systems. *Management Science, 41*(12), 1827–1844.
22. Kozinets, R. V. (1998). On netnography: Initial reflections on consumer research investigations of cyberculture. In J. Alba & W. Hutchinson (Eds.), *Advances in Consumer Research* (vol. 25, pp. 366–371). Provo, UT: Association for Consumer Research.
23. Kozinets, R. V. (2010). *Netnography. Doing ethnographic research online*. Thousand Oaks: Sage Publications.
24. Yin, R. K. (1984). *Case study research: Design and methods*. Beverly Hills: Sage Publications.
25. Dahlander, L., & Magnusson, M. G. (2005). Relationships between open source software companies and communities: Observations from nordic firms. *Research Policy, 34*, 481–493.
26. Fichman, G. (2004). Going beyond the dominant paradigm for IT innovation research: emerging concepts and methods. *Journal of the Association for Information Systems, 5* (8), 314–355.

New Internet-Based Relationships Between Citizens and Governments in the Public Space: Challenges for an Integrated System Design

Alessio Maria Braccini and Tommaso Federici

Abstract This paper deals with the recent phenomenon of original and official data about the activity of governments and public administrations distributed through the Internet by private subjects. In this paper, adopting a design research approach, we discuss four recent cases and the software artifacts that were used in them. The aim of the paper is that of deriving a descriptive design theory for a software artifact for improving citizens' capacity to act in the public space.

Keywords Transparency · Internet · Explanatory design theory · Government · Public administrations · Citizens · E-participation

1 Introduction

A new phenomenon that embodies a great potential of altering the way organizations manage the relationships with their stakeholders is currently emerging: publishing of original or official data regarding the activity of an organization or the behavior of its leaders is no more a monopoly of the same organization. Such phenomenon stems from the network, and finds in the network, particularly in the widespread diffusion of the Internet and of web 2.0 technologies, its foundations. In recent years the total number of Internet users grew up to the number of 2 billions. About one third of the total world population is now using the Internet. The growth rate of the number of

A. M. Braccini (✉) · T. Federici
Dipartimento di Economia e Impresa, Università degli Studi della Tuscia, Viterbo, Italy
e-mail: abraccini@unitus.it

T. Federici
e-mail: tfederici@unitus.it

R. Baskerville et al. (eds.), *Designing Organizational Systems*,
Lecture Notes in Information Systems and Organisation 1,
DOI: 10.1007/978-3-642-33371-2_9, © Springer-Verlag Berlin Heidelberg 2013

users reached the level of 500 % over a ten years basis [1]. The increase in the amount of Internet users goes in parallel with the increase in the amount of Internet resources and services available.

Among the several tools and services on the Internet, web 2.0 technologies allow a greater interaction of users with the network. Web 2.0 technologies are commonly understood as those technologies that allow users to have an intense interaction with online, Internet based, resources, permitting not only content fruition, but also content production. These technologies have further developed the natural-born capability of the Internet in acting as a powerful channel for information and data distribution. These technologies gave birth to a wide number of different, and differently capable, information channels and sources. Users animate indeed various on-line communities like, to name a few, Facebook, Twitter, e-Bay, Wikipedia, YouTube, and others. These communities are open repositories where scoring, ranking, and rating mechanisms, are used to balance and judge information providers' trustworthiness, and/or community interest on specific information resources. Currently several independent subjects access the Internet and use such web 2.0 technologies to act not only as information consumers, but also as information providers and producers.

In this behaviour the phenomenon we are addressing in this paper can be recognized. The diffusion of original data and information, or data and information from direct sources, through various channels to a potentially wide audience, is an affordance of the Internet and of web 2.0 technologies. This might affect the way governments and public administrations, and their leaders, relate with citizens, and vice versa. The idea is that more informed citizens can force public organizations to be more transparent, reducing corruption [2] and strengthening governors' and managers' accountability [3], promoting then a stronger social control.

Data and information diffused in this way can be used by other subjects to confront, confute, or compare official data released by governments and public administrations, or even policies adopted by their leaders or managers. Moreover original data concerning a phenomenon of public interest (i.e. in the case of a natural disaster or an accident) can be collected by independent actors and shared through the Internet even in the absence of official declarations/actions of administrations and governments involved in the specific event.

All this has already happened in some cases that will be later described. In such cases people made use of a set of different tools and technologies that were often designed for other purposes, or however, were not always ready to support all the possible interactions with both content providers and content consumers.

1.1 Citizens Capacity to Act in the Public Domain

The scenario described in the previous section points to the possibility of citizens to act in the public space by providing information to confute, confront, or evaluate declarations, actions, and policies of governments and public administrations through the use of Internet technologies.

To give a short definition of the mentioned phenomenon, we concern with all the cases where citizens, few or many, and possibly unfamiliar among themselves, deliberately and spontaneously want to share with everyone else interested data or information about the real acting of their government. The intention of such citizens is that of promoting the increase of transparency on governments' actions and, in this way, of improving their policies.

The use of information and communications technologies, like the Internet to manage relationships between public administrations and citizens, usually goes under the hat of e-government [4]. E-government is defined as "utilizing the Internet and World-Wide-Web for delivering government information and services to citizens" [5]. Applications of such technologies to the activities of public administrations can span from service delivery, which is of no interest for this paper, to transparency and accountability [4]. Within the e-government domain, the use of technologies to allow citizens to interact and participate in the public space, which constitutes the context in which this paper is framed, goes under the name of e-participation [6]. E-participation is usually described as a way of involving citizens in public decision making, promoted and supported in a top-down fashion by the government [6]. The phenomenon we refer to in this paper is a possible new face of e-participation, in which the process is fully bottom-up, promoted and performed by citizens, in all probability contrasting their leaders with this action.

1.2 The Aspect of the Design

We argue that this phenomenon shall be investigated not only under the organizational perspective [7], but also with the perspective of the design of Internet technologies that shall be used to support the above described network of actors and actions. Adopting a design research approach, in this paper we discuss some recent cases and we aim to contribute proposing meta-requirements for the design of such an artifact, also formulating considerations for the necessary surrounding organizational context. The paper will answer the following research question: how shall an Internet based technological artifact be designed to improve citizens' capacity to influence and act in the public domain?

The planned aim of this paper is that of starting the design of a set of web technologies capable of supporting users in such action, facing all the conditions and issues which might occur. Moving towards this perspective, the paper singles out a set of meta-requirements, which could orient further steps.

The intended audience of the paper is then composed, as practitioners, by groups of citizens (already members of associations or not) who want to develop a set of sound web integrated tools to promote this new form of participation in monitoring of governments' activities and in addressing them. At the same time, the results of the paper may concern researchers interested in evolving and extending the e-participation field of research.

The structure of the paper is as follows: in Sect. 2 we will describe the methodology and the research design adopted for this paper, in Sect. 3 we will present and describe the kernel theories used to frame this research effort, while in Sect. 4 we will introduce some recent cases that testify the phenomenon briefly described in the introduction. In the light of the evidences of these cases the findings of our paper will be discussed in Sect. 5; some final considerations will conclude the paper in Sect. 6.

2 Methodology

This section provides the necessary methodological information underpinning the research effort. In particular this section will discuss the design research framework adopted as guidance for the overall research effort, and the case study methodology followed to collect data pertinent to the empirical cases discussed.

2.1 Design Research

As a methodological guidance for the research described in this paper we followed a design research approach. This paper represents a first step towards the definition of principles for the design of specific software tools capable of supporting the processes of information diffusion involving the groups of actors in the scenario depicted in the introduction.

In an attempt to structure a design research effort, in their article [8], Walls et al. state that a design theory is composed by (a) a design product, and (b) a design process. The design product is in turn composed by meta-requirements, meta-design, kernel theories, and a set of testable design hypothesis. The design process is instead composed by the design method, the kernel theories, and a set of testable design process hypothesis. The contribution of Walls' et al. was later extended by Gregor and Jones [9] who proposed a new skeleton for IS design theories based on the components of: kernel theories, meta-requirements, meta-design, design method, and testable design product and process hypotheses.

In this framework, kernel theories are at the core of the design research effort composing the necessary justificatory knowledge. The kernel theories can derive both from natural and design sciences. The kernel theories form the basis on top of which prescriptions for meta-requirements, meta-design, design method, and testable design product and process hypotheses can be formulated. The kernel theories also provide explanations for the design. The meta-requirements are the class of goals to which the theory applies. The meta-design is the abstract blueprint or architecture that describes an IS artifact, being it either a product or a method of intervention. The design method is a description of the processes for implementing the theory (either a product or a method) in specific contexts. Finally the testable propositions are truth statements about the design theory.

Since the focus of this work is on the design product within the overall structure of a design theory, we found particularly useful the contribution of Baskerville and Pries-Heje [10], who distinguish between practice theories and explanatory design theories. In particular they affirm that an explanatory design theory explains why a generalized set of requirements is satisfied by a generalized set of object components. The essence of an explanatory design theory can be captured by representing the general requirements, which can be conditions or capabilities, the general components, and the relationships between the two [10].

In this paper we are then focusing on an explanatory design theory. We provide a descriptive theory for functionally explaining the features that shall be included in a set of technological web tools capable of supporting the information exchanges among several actors within the scenario depicted in the introduction, then improving citizens' capacity to act in the public space.

2.2 *Multiple Case Study*

To inform the design effort described in this paper we analysed four complementary empirical cases that according to us are useful to provide evidences of the phenomenon described in the introduction.

To deal with these cases we followed Yin's multiple case study method [11]. The cases that will later be described are: the Mayor of Bari and his Facebook profile, the Cablegate and WikiLeaks, the Fukushima crisis, and the Kenya riots and Ushaidi. In all these cases, a specific (and different in each case) technological artifact was used by different groups of people to disseminate information from direct source (i.e. directly taken from the origin), to confute other information disseminated by official sources (i.e. public administrations), or to provide information not known, not available to them, or not disclosed by them.

The choice of adopting a multiple case study method was due to the fact that the four cases differ in terms of technological artifacts used, of groups of people involved and of goal to be reached, but altogether they consistently provide a rich representation of possible different manifestations of the phenomenon in question.

In each of the four cases we focused on the specific characteristics of the technological artifact(s) (i.e. web applications, or other Internet technologies) that were used in each case to manage and support the information and communication sharing processes among the involved actors. In describing each case we focused on the sequence of events and on the actions of actors involved in the communication processes observed, in the circumstance of a specific event or on its aftermath.

Due to the heterogeneity of the cases analysed, a mix of direct and indirect sources were used in each case for data collection. Table 1 clarifies the sources used in each case. When the source is marked as "direct" we mean that the source

Table 1 Information sources used in the four cases

Case	Event	Sources
Mayor of Bari	Potential inefficiency in public sweeping services	Facebook profile of the Mayor of Bari (direct) Newspapers (indirect)
WikiLeaks	Disclosure of confidential cables	WikiLeaks website (direct) WikiLeaks cables (direct) Newspapers (indirect)
Fukushima	Detection of radiation level after a massive earthquake	Website of the Italian embassy in Tokyo (direct) Fukushima nuclear accident update log of the International Atomic Energy Agency (IAEA) (indirect) Reports of the Japan ministry of education (indirect) Reports of the Japan ministry of economy, trade and industry (indirect) Various blogs (eBuroggu, GiappoPazzie, RischioCalcolato) (direct) Newspapers (Repubblica, and Sole 24 Ore) (indirect)
Ushahidi	Report of abuses and human rights violations	Ushaidi website (indirect) Newspapers (indirect)

reports information from people directly involved in the phenomenon usually in real-time, while when it is marked as "indirect" we mean that the source reports information from people not involved in the phenomenon, usually not in real time.

3 Kernel Theories

The phenomenon of the diffusion by private subjects on the Internet of official data and information referred to governments' and public administrations' activities, is brand new and at a first glance very differentiated, with multiple tiers to be considered. As already mentioned, it involves a group of persons, possibly not in touch among themselves, who deliberately and spontaneously want to share data with everyone interested, in order to increase the transparency and improve the policies of their government, in all probability contrasting with this action their leaders.

More in detail, we then identified three main topics to be investigated in the selected cases:

1. The community of citizens essential to nurture each initiative on the Internet and, at the same time, to use it;
2. The capacity of the users to profit by data and information made available;
3. The risk of misbehaviours by other subjects, like media operators or service providers, which are critical for the diffusion of data and information, but may impede such activity [12].

For this reason, we believe that in order to inform our design process an interpreting framework based on a single kernel theory would be inadequate, as it could not shed light on all the facets of such specific phenomenon. As regards the first topic, we relied on the large body of the Social Capital theories. We recurred to the Absorptive Capacity Theory to deal with the second topic. We, finally, borrowed some concepts from the Agency Theory for the last topic.

Considering the novelty of our field of interest, we recall these theories not to proceed to an operationalization of any of them, even less of the three, but just to get some thorough guidelines to interpret as many single aspect emerging in the cases. The collected definitions and assumptions altogether build a multifaceted set of elements worth analyzing the different aspects taken into account to orient the design.

3.1 Social Capital Theories

Under the name of Social Capital a large and multi-faceted body of theories is available. Several scholars, mainly sociologists, nurtured this body. Not all the propositions stated by such scholars are worth investigating the phenomenon in question. Nevertheless, we found quite a lot of suggestions that seem coping the main instances of the selected cases. We then used such suggestions to identify and discuss some characteristics of the cases.

As stated above, a community of people needs to stay behind any initiative devoted to diffuse original or official data and information about the activities of a government or a public administration, in order to increase transparency on its actions and control over it. This statement recalls many assertions present in Social Capital works. Firstly, in general terms, Bourdieu [13] states that the social capital is composed by two elements: the social relationship, which makes accessing associates' resources possible, and the quantity and quality of the shared resources. Putnam [14] says that the social capital is a prerequisite for effective public policy, while citizens have accepted that public policy derives from a campaign strategy, rather than from a collective deliberation, thence changing the conception of democracy. Social capital is a public good, arising from some social activity [14], and it is a kind of resource that increases (and not decreases like others) its value when being used [14].

More detailed hints however could be also singled out. Granovetter, in a famous work [15], posits that whatever has to be diffused (information in our case) reaches a greater number of people, even at greater distance in social terms, when it passes through the weak ties, rather than the strong ones, of a network. Burt [16] reinforces such statement, saying that dense networks share redundant information, while weak ties may be sources of new knowledge.

Putnam [14] states that the collaboration on a new theme is easier when a community already exists with its own stock of social capital, ties, and norms. Such pre-existence may be worth also when the new collaboration involves a different social setting [14].

Individuals who share a same condition (i.e. a same team membership) can assume an altruistic mutual disposition, reserved only to their peers. Other members may appropriate in the same way such disposition, which works only within the original group, and for this reason is called “bounded solidarity” [17]. The identification with the group of its members is a strong source of motivation, which for Coleman can also lead towards excessive forms, like “zeal” [18]. This is a possible source of social capital.

Social capital can also stem from someone’s motivation to be part of a certain community. In this case, the donors give something to people they probably do not personally know, not because they expect to be repaid directly by the recipients, but because they are interested in what the common social structure might give them in the future [17].

3.2 Absorptive Capacity Theory

Absorptive Capacity Theory encompasses a wide and long-lasting body of works, with different perspectives and also definitions of the key concept of “absorptive capacity”, which is mostly referred to a firm. In this case however we adopted the definition by Mowery and Oxley, which is more suitable to our setting, being it centred on individuals. They state [19] that absorptive capacity is a set of skills necessary to handle the tacit component of transferred knowledge and to elaborate a foreign sourced technology. Another contribution worth of mention in our study is that of Cohen and Levinthal, who posit that absorptive capacity is a multidimensional concept, as it incorporates the ability to value, assimilate and apply knowledge [20].

Zahra and George, also building on other authors’ works, propose a model [21] where the absorptive capacity results as a combination of:

- *Antecedents*: multiple complementary sources of knowledge and experiences which increase the capabilities to assimilate knowledge;
- *Activation triggers*: events, both positive or negative, which stimulate exploring, learning and acquiring knowledge;
- *Social integration mechanisms*: organizational structures facilitating interaction among the members of a community, or even the free flow of information.

As regards these latter, the undergoing idea is that knowledge acquisition is a social process, which asks for lowering the barriers in information sharing among different subjects, and for increasing the easiness of assimilation and transformation of new knowledge.

3.3 Agency Theory

The Agency Theory describes the general relationships where one part (the principal) delegates a piece of work to another part (the agent), and the latter performs the work that has been assigned to him/her [22]. The relationship between the principal and the agent is seen by the agency theory with the metaphor of a contract. Agency theory thus describes the interactive relationships amongst several subjects playing the role of agents and principals within a network of contracts.

The agency theory was originally proposed to explain the hostile relationship between the management and the ownership of enterprises [22, 23]. Nevertheless, such theory was also applied to other contexts, and can anyhow be generally applied in the scenario where two different subjects, in a specific relationship, occupy the positions, respectively, of principal and agent. Under this perspective, the agency theory can be applied to investigate cooperation relationships where the involved parties have different goals and division of labour [24].

The differences in terms of objectives and risk proneness of the two parties involved in the relationship may foster conflicts and then turn the relationships between them in a hostile one. Two main problems then arise: the so-called agency problem, and the risk-sharing problem. The agency problem arises in case of conflicts between goals, respectively desired by the principal and the agent, and when the principal is in a difficult position to verify what the agent is actually doing [22], or to act in order to secure his/her own goal. The risk-sharing problem arises instead as a consequence of the different risk proneness of the principal and the agent. What happens then is that the principal and the agent, following their different risk proneness, might in the end prefer different actions.

4 Cases Description

This section describes the four cases we are addressing in this paper. These cases concern: the use of Facebook by the Mayor of Bari, the so-called "Cablegate" case involving WikiLeaks, the events in the aftermath of the Fukushima dai-ichi nuclear crisis, and the campaign carried on using the Ushahidi website during some recent riots in Kenya. The cases we are describing here are a selection of a larger number of cases we investigated. The specific four cases are reported here since, in spite of their differences in terms of geographical location, actors, and underpinning problems, they all deal with the sharing among the Internet of original data and information regarding governments' or public administrations' activities. Moreover in all these cases specific software tools or Internet based technologies were used to support the actions and processes that took place. While looking at the events happened in all the four cases we also look at the different software tools used to derive design principle for a unified collection capable of supporting all the processes described in the cases.

4.1 The Mayor of Bari

The Mayor of Bari (Italy) recently decided to use Facebook as an open forum to communicate with his citizens. In doing so he decided to open his Facebook profile and to use it to provide information to citizens and, more important, to receive information from them.

On January 2011 one of the citizens of Bari sent the Mayor a picture depicting a group of dustmen chatting down the streets. The meta-data revealed that when the picture was shot, the dustmen were just in the middle of their working hours. From the picture it is not immediately evident whether the dustmen are just messing around or organizing their work. The Mayor anyhow immediately posted the picture on his Facebook profile. Such event caught the attention of many persons: both citizens and trade unions. In a series of posts and comments to the picture published in the Facebook profile of the Mayor, several citizens complained about the poor efficiency of the sweeping service and about the poor professionalism of the dustmen. Trade unions, on their side, blamed instead the Mayor for his possible will to run down the work of honest workers. On his side the Mayor, since the picture came directly from the citizens, invited all parties to confront their position, either on Facebook or anywhere else.

Other examples of this kind of usage of Facebook from the Mayor of Bari are for instance the reports of protests related to town hall employers' cars being parked on pedestrian crossing, or even double-parked in the streets hindering regular traffic passage, private cars parked in dangerous conditions close to road intersections and neither fined nor removed by the police, or trash cans on pedestrian crossing or on passages reserved to disabled persons or pregnant women.

In this cases the software platform used to support the process of information exchange among all the parties involved was, as already mention, the social network Facebook, which was of course not specifically designed to support such kind of relationships.

4.2 "Cablegate" Case on WikiLeaks

WikiLeaks is an international non profit organization that receives and subsequently shares on its website confidential documents from large organizations or governments. WikiLeaks takes care of the anonymity of whistleblowers and also guarantees the truth of the contents of document disclosed.

On November 2010 WikiLeaks went to the fore for the publication of 251.287 documents containing confidential information on the work of the government and the diplomacy of the USA in the world covering the period from 1966 to 2010. These documents were made available through its website and, at the same time, were sent to the daily El Pais, Le Monde, The Guardian, The New York Times, and to the weekly Der Spiegel.

The disclosed documents were confidential but not top-secret. Their content was related to critiques and appraisals of the policies of the hosting countries of various US embassies in the world. The reactions of authorities and persons addressed by the documents being disclosed (mainly the US government but also some leaders of most prominent western democracies) were a mixture of strong criticism, commendation, bewilderment [25], dismay, and quiescence.

Explicit attacks were instead moved against the WikiLeaks website and the founder, the journalist Julian Assange. The US government described the disclosure of these documents as an attack on America's foreign policy and legal actions were taken against WikiLeaks. Congressmen, senators and members of other organizations exercised a relevant pressure on WikiLeaks and also on its service provider, which, in a short time, discontinued their services to WikiLeaks. The operational activity of WikiLeaks was impeded thanks to a massive financial blockade and also thanks to the imprisonment of Julian Assange for sexual related crimes.

In a tentative of protecting his integrity, and those of his coworkers, Assange used also peer-to-peer technologies (Torrent) to distribute over the Internet a huge encrypted file potentially containing all the leaks in possession of WikiLeaks. The file is encrypted with the AES algorithm. The decryption keys will be automatically made public if and when physical threats would be moved against Assange or his coworkers so that all the leaks could then go public.

Regarding the software used by WikiLeaks to support all the information exchange processes, a wide gamut of different technologies were employed. Besides web technologies necessary to run the WikiLeaks website, cryptography technologies were used to warrant whistleblowers' anonymity, as well as peer-to-peer technologies were also used to diffuse cryptography cable contents through the Internet.

Finally, it must be noticed that the disclosed documents, even though formally available to everyone in the world, actually are not immediately usable by most people. The language used in the documents (English), as well as their huge amount represent hard barriers to overcome for most potentially interested users in the world.

4.3 The Fukushima Crisis

On March 2011 a massive earthquake stroke the area of Sendai in Japan and subsequently triggered highly destructive tsunami waves. One of these waves hit the Fukushima Dai-Ichi nuclear power plant, and a consequence of events caused one of the most relevant incidents in the history of nuclear technology for energy production. Right after the earthquake reactors were automatically de-activated for security reasons, but the tsunami waves damaged both the main and the backup cooling systems. Following the over-heating of the reactor, and as a consequence of explosions involving the building surrounding them, nuclear radiations were released both into the air and into the sea.

The gravity of the situation emerged quite clearly since the very beginning, but there was a lack of precise information regarding security and safety. There were difficulties in restoring in a short time a safe condition for the reactors. At the same time, the suspect that the government was not telling the whole truth on the incident arose, mixed with the speculation of media and newspapers regarding safety conditions around the power plant and in Tokyo (about 250 km far from the power plant). Such situation created a big concern, not only in Japan but also worldwide, on the safety of nuclear technology, and also on possible local and global consequences of the incident.

In response to this uncertain and debated situation, several individuals and organizations started to publish information on blogs and websites concerning: the radiation levels around the nuclear power plant and in Tokyo, the daily life of people in Tokyo. Following these voluntary activities public authorities later started to regularly detect and publish official data on radiations levels, and to provide regular information on the evolution of the Fukushima nuclear crisis. At first it was the Italian civil protection that measured radiations levels near the Italian embassy in Tokyo. Later both the Japan Ministry of Economy Trade and Industry, and the Ministry of Education, started to publish official data on radioactivity level (both for air and water). In the end, the International Atomic Energy Agency started to publish regular and detailed reports, with explanations also for non expert users, on the evolution of the incident.

In the Fukushima case the technologies in play were regular web tools used to run personal websites and blogs. Web 2.0 technologies were also used to allow users commenting and syndicating contents provided in private blogs.

4.4 Kenya Riots on Ushahidi

Ushahidi (witness in Swahili) is a non profit company that develops open source software for information collection, visualization, and its interactively mapping. Ushahidi created a website to collect reports and eyewitnesses of violence sent by e-mail or short messages (even with photos or videos) from mobile phones, and eventually placed on a Google map. The website was firstly created and used in the aftermath of Kenya's disputed 2007 presidential election when President Mwai Kibaki was declared the winner while supporters of his opponents alleged electoral manipulations. An increasing number of violent protests from the opposition supporters leaded to fights in several parts of the country. During these protests the police shots a number of demonstrators, including a few in front of TV cameras.

Ushahidi later became an open collection of web tools, available for every group of citizens or associations who wants to report politicians misbehaviours. The software merges the combination of social activism, citizen journalism, and geospatial information to map actions of specific protesters or activists. Ushahidi allows local observers to submit reports using mobile phones and portable devices with Internet access, simultaneously creating a temporal and geospatial archive of events.

Besides the abovementioned events related to Kenya's presidential elections, Ushahidi was also used in many other cases also following natural disasters (i.e. the earthquake in Haiti or of Christchurch), or to track protests (i.e. during the so-called "Arab spring" in middle east) or administrators misbehaviours (i.e. the tracking of corruption cases in the Republic of Macedonia).

Regarding the technological aspect Ushahidi mainly makes use of web based multimedia blog technologies (involving thence not only text and pictures but also audio and video documents). Geo-tagging, geo-referencing, and representation on maps are possible for all the kind of contents managed on the Ushahidi portal. This collection continues to be evolved, through the offer of new tools to the users.

5 Discussion

5.1 Characteristics of the Technological Artifact

All these cases are witnesses of the phenomenon we were mentioning. Thanks to the usage of Internet technologies users turn into data and information providers. Data intended to be kept confidential can now be easily and cheaply revealed. Moreover incomplete data can be completed, integrated, or confuted with similar data directly gathered by users and shared on the Internet.

Moreover citizens can put more pressure on politicians or large organizations thanks to the availability of more information on their work, accessible at low cost. As mentioned in the introduction, by doing so citizens can force public organizations to be more transparent, reducing corruption [2] and improving accountability [3]. This phenomenon has then the potential to challenge the management style of public or large organizations, and the way they manage the relationships with their stakeholders. Possibly, the same organizational constructs on which governmental bodies are presently based may be rethought or profoundly modified, asking for new theoretical perspectives, as the traditional power of broadcasting official information may result limited, and the periodic cycle of being judged by citizens only through ballots may prove to be no more adequate.

While this emergent phenomenon is already provoking some changes, in this research paper we would like to point our attention to the software artifacts that were used, and could be used in the future, to support such processes. In some of the cases briefly described above a set of different Internet technologies were designed (like in the case of WikiLeaks and Ushahidi) or used, sometimes against their intended purpose (like in the case of Facebook for the Mayor of Bari, or the generic use of blogs for the Fukushima nuclear power plant accident). In this paper we argue that, to support processes like the ones described above, and to improve transparency and accountability in the relationships between citizens and governments or public administrations, specific software artifacts should be designed.

In order to draw hints out of our cases, we firstly tried to identify the main characteristics of the technological artifacts used in each of them (see Table 2). For each case we figured out the "spirit" of the initiative, the involved technological components, the type of managed data, the spatial dimension of the audience that the promoters wanted to reach, the languages used for texts or documents, and finally the forms of interaction reserved to the users.

As regards the characteristic we named "spirit", we referred to the use of this term by DeSanctis and Poole [26], who posit that the spirit is the general intent with which a technology is used in a specific context, related to the values and the goals underlying a given set of structural features. The spirit is the official line with which the technology is presented to the people by its designers. In the absence of procedures and norms that clarify how a certain technology has to be used, the spirit helps users in interpreting the features and understanding how to use them. In such perspective, the spirit is a sort of proposed goal, clearly readable between the lines by users even when not declared, to be reached through the use of the technology.

5.2 *Analysis of Instances in the Cases from the Adopted Kernel Theories*

We proceeded our analysis by identifying how the main aspects of the three kernel theories took place in the selected cases. We first drew Table 3 following Social Capital theories. We identified, as relevant items for our work: the existence of a community before the activation of the initiative related to the case, the density of the network built by the users after the start of the initiative, the prevalent presence of strong or weak ties in the relationships among users, the level of the members' (in this case the users of the technological artifacts) identification with the group (in this case the community of users), and the level of interest of the users to be part of the community.

With the exception of the case of the Mayor of Bari, where the community of Facebook already existed, and the particular situation in the Fukushima crisis, where we found some former little communities, in the other cases there was no pre-existing community before the starting of the respective initiative. The pre-existence of a community, even though devoted to different aims and with other rules, is considered by Putnam [14] a promising condition to create collaboration on a new theme. In our cases, however such situation does not seem to have been a problem.

The density of the network was generally low, again with the exception of the Mayor of Bari case on Facebook, that is to say networks built around each initiative do not ask for a tight community and each member (a node) may also have few (or even none) relationships with the other members. In the Burt's view [16], this is a characteristic worth circulating new knowledge. Moreover, ties in the relationships among users are always weak, which in this case means occasional, almost always not based on a reciprocal acquaintance. Following Granovetter [15],

Table 2 Main characteristics of the artifacts in the selected cases

Case	Spirit	Technology used	Type of data	Intended audience	Language	Users' interaction
Mayor of Bari	Open dialogue with citizens	Social network Blog	Text posts and photos	Local	Italian	Posting content Reading posts Commenting posts
Cablegate case on WikiLeaks	Promoting transparency on governments' and companies' activities	Website Cryptography Peer-to-peer Mirroring	Document files (mainly scanned) with text and figures	Worldwide	That of documents (mainly English)	Anonymously submitting (but not publishing) leaks Reading documents
Fukushima crisis	Informing on nuclear radiations	Websites Blogs Syndicating technologies	Technical figures Text posts and photos	National	Japanese English Italian	Publishing data/posts Reading data/posts Commenting data/post Syndicating data/post
Kenya riots on Ushahidi	Supporting local communities in being informed about democracy violation or disasters aftermath	Website CMS (even from mobile phones) Open source released code Geo-tagging Multimedia management system	Figures Posts Video	National	Local	Publishing data/posts/video Reading data/posts, watching videos

Table 3 Instances from social capital theories in the selected cases

Case	Based on pre-existing community	Density of the network	Strong or weak ties	Level of identification of users	Motivation to adhere
Mayor of Bari	Yes	Medium	Weak	Low	Medium
Cablegate case on WikiLeaks	No	Low	Weak	Low	Low
Fukushima crisis	Partially	Low	Weak	Medium	High
Kenya riots on Ushahidi	No	Low	Weak	High	High

this is another essential condition for giving a greater impulse to knowledge exchange. Our cases, where a lot of knowledge was transferred, seem to correspond to both these conditions.

In two out of four cases, those of the Fukushima crisis and of the Kenya riots, users had a medium or high level of identification with the community that was developing around the respective initiative. This happened perhaps also because the urgency of the crisis to be managed in both cases. A high level of identification is maintained by Coleman [18] as a condition which reinforces the members' collaboration. This seems confirmed in our cases. In fact, in the remaining cases, whose information was important, but not urgent, users do not much identified themselves with a community.

Also the users' motivation to adhere to a community expecting some kind of benefit in the future, is considered by Putnam [14] a positive factor for increasing collaboration in the community. In our cases, we observed that the motivation was high again in the cases of Fukushima crisis and Kenya riots, while lower in the other ones.

We then composed Table 4 on the basis of Absorptive Capacity Theory main elements for our analysis. First we addressed two set of skills necessary to a user for, respectively, moving the content (in both directions: uploading and downloading), and elaborating it (interpreting, summarizing etc.). After we mentioned the event(s) which caused a large convergence of users around each initiative. Finally, we presented the structures that, in each case, facilitated interaction of users, among them and with the technological artifact, and extend the information flow. In these latter columns we distinguished (between brackets in italic) the solutions not included in the set of proposed tools at the case time, which could however facilitate interaction of users.

Handling the knowledge asks for some skills which the users need to have [19]. In our cases this firstly means that users must have confidence with computer and Internet technologies (but in the Riots in Kenya case), and simple competences, like uploading files, data or photos, sending SMS or MMS through a mobile phone, or posting brief texts, to provide content to a web repository. The lower the competences asked to the users to interact with an artifact, the greater its usability. At the same time, users should not be too qualified for deriving benefits from the

Table 4 Instances from absorptive capacity theory in the selected cases (N.B. *structures not present at the time of the studied case*)

Case	Set of necessary skills to		Trigger events	Organizational structures to	
	Handle content	Elaborate content		Facilitate interaction	Free flow information
Mayor of Bari	Using a social network	Reading	Launches on newspapers	Common social network platform	SN page open to everybody Internal search engine
Cablegate case on WikiLeaks	None	Language	Launches on media	Website	Internal search engine Translator *Open format* *Summaries*
Fukushima crisis	Uploading data	Radiation measures	Earthquake	Blogs, websites	Internal search engine Tool for replication Guides to use data
Kenya riots on Ushahidi	Sending SMS or MMS Posting text	Reading	Riots	Interface toward mobile (even legacy) phones Multichannel access Platform ready to reuse	Possibility of localization *Tools to search and filter information*

content when are intended for local users, and then is based on a local language, and offer easy to be interpreted data, like in the cases of the Mayor of Bari and the Riots in Kenya. Users have instead to be more skilled in the case of Fukushima crisis, to interpret data on nuclear radiations measures expressed in millisieverts per hour or becquerel, or in the Cablegate case where, even though regarding the whole world, all the documents are in English.

Some events, like an important innovation, an emergence or a change in government policy, are considered activation triggers for knowledge exchange [27], stimulating who has already some form of knowledge to connect to a possible source of other knowledge. Moreover, the intensity of the stimulus positively influences the search of a source and the exchange with it [21]. In two of our cases (the Fukushima crisis and the Kenya riots) as many emergences provoked a quick and relevant participation by the users. In the other two cases, the new source of knowledge, even though represented a great innovation, needed a launch on newspapers or other media to become interesting for several users.

Knowledge exchange is a social process that requires organizational structures, like technological tools [21]. The simpler, the more accessible and the more powerful the tools, the greater and more valuable the exchange. Tools may serve both to let the users interact with the artifact and its content, and to make easier the information circulation.

By observing the four cases, we noticed different tools to facilitate interaction, which was never a big issue, even if some tools appear more addressed to a wide interaction than others. The case of the Mayor of Bari is fully based on the Facebook platform, then allowing its same form of interaction. The Cablegate case do not ask a great interaction by users (normally few whistleblowers send documents to WikiLeaks and many users read or download available documents), then the usual website functions of WikiLeaks seem sufficient. The Fukushima crisis case also requests simple tools, like a blog or website allowing posting, even though in this case information were available in several different Internet sources (i.e. personal blogs and websites) and integration and completion of the (sometimes partial) information available were left to users' will and to the use of Internet search engines. The Kenya riots case, based on Ushahidi, seems to have the richer and more developed set of tools for facilitating usability, as the portal can be accessed, at least partially, by multiple even legacy devices, like old mobile phones. This probably determined the so rapid diffusion of such initiative in a country where digital divide is a serious issue.

We also considered tools devoted to support the free flow of information, remarking this time the absence of some essential tools. While in the case of the Mayor of Bari, the usual Facebook page with its features can satisfy the exigencies, in the Cablegate case the WikiLeaks website do not provide tools to search and extract information, also taking into account the huge amount of documents, in a foreign language for most users, and in a scanned pdf format, not automatically searchable, neither translatable. Then, beside the current presence of an effective translator and a search engine, the provision of documents in an open format would increase the information usability. At the same time, the huge amount of documents asks for the presentation of summaries, keywords etc. In the case of Fukushima crisis, tools for replicating on multiple locations data posted on a blog help to disseminate information. In this case, however, an issue is also the interpretation of figures: even though some form of explication was some time provided, an easy-to-use and authoritative guide to read and interpret data may be worth. Finally, in the Riots case on Ushahidi, data is easy to read and interpret, and a tool for geo-mapping each data helps users to obtain information on their own zone. However, also considering the great amount of data collected, a tool to make research in the database or to extract synthesis of data would add a great benefit. A similar tool, not present at the case time, is actually now (March 2012) presented as a new feature on the Ushahidi portal.

Table 5 reports the elements we identified with regard to the Agency Theory: who are the principal(s) and the agents in each case; what kind of impediments the agents may cause to the principals, then hampering their initiative; and finally if or not such impediments already happened.

The principals (the persons or the organizations who delegate) are in each case the promoters of the initiative and the users who provide data to the common repository. Agents are in this context the intermediaries of different nature who are

Table 5 Instances from agency theory in the selected cases

Case	Principal	Agents	Possible impediments by agents	Already happened?
Mayor of Bari	Mayor	Facebook	Closure of the page	No
		Service providers	Blockade of the connection	No
Cablegate case on WikiLeaks	WikiLeaks	Media operators	Deny for new documents' announce	No Yes
			Presentation of partial or incorrect synthesis	Yes Yes
		Service providers	Website obscuration	Yes
			Connection interruption	
			Financial blockade	
Fukushima crisis	Citizens	Service providers	Website obscuration	No
			Connection interruption	No
Kenya riots on Ushahidi	Citizens	Service providers	Website obscuration	No
			Connection interruption	No

in charge of some activity essential for the principals to reach their users. Agents are [12]: media operators, like newspapers or TVs, service providers, both technological (connection providers, hosting providers, etc.), or financial (banks, credit cards, etc.), and the platform provider (a social network) in the case of the Mayor of Bari.

Because the divergence of aims, and the correlated different risk perception, between principals and agents, these latter may not correspond to their assignment when they perceive a risk too significant for them [24]. Media operators may decide not to announce an initiative, in order to fail to disclose it, or to propose partial or incorrect synthesis of data, in order to hidden some news. Technological providers, when exposed to external pressures, may suddenly obscure a website, or a page, interrupt a server connection and so on. Financial providers, for the same reasons, may quickly halt a bank account operations, suspend a credit card position, up to a financial blockade to the principal. All the examined principals are under many swords of Damocles, because each agent may rapidly change his/her behavior, provoking serious, or even fatal, issues to an initiative. As a demonstration of such danger, most of the above problems already happened to WikiLeaks, just during the Cablegate case, as a consequence of pressures on service providers by politics and governments [12]. Other initiatives did not suffer the same troubles, but in order to protect their initiatives from similar menaces, principals should consider some kind of solution.

5.3 Proposal of an Explanatory-Design Theory

Following the considerations formulated on the four cases and on the four different software tools used to support the information exchange processes in them, we can now discuss our proposal of meta-requirements. Figure 1 shows the two components of an explanatory design theory according to Baskerville and Pries-Heje [10].

The four cases described and discussed in this paper showed that the information and data exchange happened in the vast majority of cases originating from a single central repository (like in the case of Facebook for the Mayor of Bari, Ushahidi, and the website of WikiLeaks), or more than one (like in the case of the Fukushima crisis), which are open for contribution by the users. In a case (WikiLeaks) peer to peer technologies were also used. The data and information are exchanged through a network of users who were usually not previously in contact among each other. Even when a social networking dynamic was already in place before the event (i.e. the Facebook profile of the Mayor of Bari), we argue that weak ties largely dominate such network. Nonetheless, the social networking approach embedded in the adopted technology directly stimulates confrontation and interaction among users through the recourse to posts and comments.

In most cases data and information are transmitted on an open channel, where the sender is clearly identified (i.e. Facebook, Ushahidi). In other cases the sender is not immediately identified (i.e. like in the case of the authors of blogs in the Fukushima case) but is not kept secret while in other cases he/she is completely kept anonymous (like in the case of WikiLeaks). In this latter case anonymity is a specifically wanted feature that safeguards the identity of the subject who initially distribute the documents. Because the specific nature of the content disclosed, such subject might be in a vulnerable position against the organization to which the documents disclosed refer to. Still regarding this latter issue, replication and mirroring technologies could also be used to prevent against unwanted blockades of the repository.

Regarding the content usually exchanged, data and information can be in the format of written textual documents, visual representation of the reality (mainly figures and pictures, but also audio/video footages), and/or table with figures. Beyond data from original and direct source, another source of exchanged content is constituted by comments formulated by authors on the documents disclosed. Such kind of content are made available only when a specific tool explicitly support them (i.e. in the case of Facebook for the Mayor of Bari, and in the case of the blogs used in the case of the Fukushima crisis), but proven to be powerful in stimulating the social control of citizens over the actions of administrations (especially with regard to the dustmen in the case of the Mayor of Bari). Specific software functionalities like the sharing of posts among members of a social network, or posts and comments syndicating, are capable of fostering the diffusion of data and information exchanged among actors. Documents geo-referencing is used in some cases (i.e. Ushahidi), and would be necessary in others (i.e. in the cases of the blogs of the Fukushima crisis).

Finally such data and communication exchanged, besides being represented by different set of documents, can also be expressed in different languages, and can be presented in huge amounts, sometimes also containing non-trivial data and information for the interpretation of which authoritative guides should be provided to users. Specific searching and, potentially, translating functionalities together

General Requirements

Communication and data exchange takes place either in a broadcast fashion or through peer to peer channels using potentially several different communication channels

Communication and data exchange flows through weakly tied social networks either pre-existing or of novel constitution

Communication and data exchange contain original data, comments on original data or comments on other comments

Users participating into communication and data exchanges show intermediate level of identification and generally medium/high motivation to adhere

Information and data exchanged can be of different format and written in different languages and retrieval has to deal with such diversity

Data and information may be in huge amount; the possibility to search through all of them, as well as to summarize them are then helpful

When presented data are not trivial, users should be helped in interpreting them

Anonymity on data and information exchanged might be in place

Communication and data exchange processes might be impeded or hampered by opportunistic behaviours of service providers, media operators, or other bodies/authorities

General Components

Social networking functionalities

Blog posting functionalities

Blog posts syndicating functionalities

Peer to peer data/information transmission

Mirroring functionalities to protect integrity and independence

Management of multi-media contents

Possibility of geo-referencing contents

Search features and tools

Fig. 1 Explanatory design theory

with the presentation of documents in a searchable format, can aid users in information search and retrieval. Data and information summarizing features would also help users in information retrieving and interpretation. Even more than in other cases, in this context artifacts should be designed to avoid the marginalization of any group of citizens, paying attention to those impeded by the lack of updated and powerful technological resources, or by cultural barriers. However, particularly these latter can hardly fully overcome by only making recourse to automatic tools: careful policies should then later be adopted to manage the artifact and its content.

Under the point of view of the used tools, as already mentioned, a plethora of different software technologies are adopted: with the exception of WikiLeaks and Ushahidi, they are not always intended for the specific purposes. When formulating the exploratory design theory in Fig. 1 we argued that a single unified collection of technological tools would be better capable of supporting all the information exchange processes identified in the cases. The choice of a unified collection of tools would probably have the merit of simplifying the choice concerning the identification of a specific technology to be employed in an initiative like the ones described, and would also lower potential barriers of participation by users in different initiatives.

We eventually wondered what, amongst the several different software technological artifacts used in the four cases discussed and described in this paper, is the one that more closely matches the identified meta-requirements of a unified collection of tools that could support all the different information exchange processes so far described. Even though lacking some need (i.e.: anonymity of submitter in certain circumstances, and protection against possible misbehaviours by agents), Ushahidi seems the one that mostly covers such meta-requirements, particularly when considering the new offered tools.

6 Conclusion

This paper deals with the recent phenomenon of original or official data about the activity of governments and public administrations being distributed through the Internet by private subjects. Its aim is that of drawing an explanatory design theory for a unified technological set of tools able to support the various processes that a similar communication may involve, in order to both facilitate the knowledge exchange among users and make the artifact adequate and robust.

We recurred to the design research approach proposed by Baskerville and Pries-Heje [10], identifying as kernel theories the social capital body of theories, as regards the collaboration promotion to increase knowledge exchange, the absorptive capacity theory, with regard to the potential barriers for users in contributing or using new knowledge, and the agency theory, to single out possible impediments coming from some actors in this kind of initiatives.

By adopting the multiple case-study methodology, we proceeded analysing four cases, which, because of their differences in terms of context, aims, geographical wideness, features, may provide an ample set of clues for our objective.

The resulting explanatory design theory represents a first step in the design process of an integrate set of technological web tools capable to correspond to the arising demand of more information for a greater transparency, and can provide useful hints for future steps. Starting from this design theory it would be possible in the future to detail the specified requirements and to validate the design theory.

Possible limitations of this work may derive from the isolation of a single phase of the design process, performed without interacting with users. Such way of acting is however confirmed as appropriate by the adopted theoretic approach.

References

1. InternetWorldStats. (2001). Internet usage statistics the internet big picture. Retrieved Dec 22, 2011 from http://www.internetworldstats.com/stats.htm.
2. Kaufmann, D., & Bellver, A. (2005). Transparenting transparency: initial empirics and policy applications. *Working Paper Series*, The World Bank. Retrieved Dec 22, 2011 from http://ssrn.com/abstract=808664.
3. Gant, D. B., Gant, J. P., & Johnson, C. L. (2002). Enhancing E-Service delivery state web portals: Delivering and financing E-Service. Technical Report. PricewaterhouseCoopers Endowment. http://www.businessofgovernment.org/report/state-web-portals-delivering-and-financing-e-service
4. Yildiz, M. (2007). E-government research: Reviewing the literature, limitations, and ways forward. *Government Information Quarterly, 24*(3), 646–665.
5. United Nations, & American Society for Public Administration (ASPA). (2002). *Benchmarking e-government: A global perspective*. New York, NY: U. N. Publications.
6. Phang, C. W., & Kankanhalli, A. (2008). A framework of ICT exploitation for e-participation initiatives. *Communications of the ACM, 51*(12), 128–132.
7. Federici, T., & Braccini, A. M. (2012). How internet is upsetting the communication between organizations and their stakeholders: A research agenda. In: M. De Marco, D. Te'eni, V. Albano, S. Za (Eds.), *Information systems: crossroads for organization, management, accounting and engineering*. Springer: Berlin, Germany.
8. Walls, J. G., Widermeyer, G. R., & Sawy, O. A. E. (2004). Assessing information system design theory in perspective: How useful was our 1992 initial rendition. *Journal of Information Technology Theory and Application, 6*(2), 43.
9. Gregor, S., & Jones, D. (2007). The anatomy of a design theory. *Journal of the Association of Information Systems, 8*(5), 312–335.
10. Baskerville, R. L., & Pries-Heje, J. (2010). Explanatory design theory. *Business & Information Systems Engineering, 2*(5), 271–282.
11. Yin, R. K. (1994). *Case study research: Design and methods*. Thousand Oaks, CA: Sage Publishing.
12. Federici, T., & Braccini, A. M. (2012). Internet, citizens, and public organizations: The power of service providers in fostering or hampering transparency. In *Proceedings of the IADIS International Conference on Information Systems*, Berlin, Germany, March 10–12.
13. Bourdieu, P. (1985). The forms of capital. In J. G. Richardson (Ed.), *Handbook of theory and research for the sociology of education* (pp. 241–258). New York: Greenwood.

14. Putnam, R. D. (1993). The prosperous community: Social capital and public life. *American Prospect, 13*, 35–42.
15. Granovetter, M. S. (1973). The strength of weak ties. *American Journal of Sociology, 78*, 1360–1380.
16. Burt, R. S. (1992). *Structural holes: The social structure of competition*. Cambridge, MA: Harvard University Press.
17. Portes, A. (1998). Social capital: Its origin and applications in modern sociology. *Annual Review of Sociology, 24*, 1–24.
18. Coleman, J. S. (1990). *Foundations of social theory*. Cambridge: Harvard University Press.
19. Mowery, D. C., & Oxley, J. E. (1995). Inward technology transfer and competitiveness: The role of national innovation systems. *Cambridge Journal of Economics, 19*, 67–93.
20. Cohen, W. M., & Levinthal, D. A. (1990). Absorptive capacity: A new perspective on learning and innovation. *Administrative Science Quarterly, 35*, 128–152.
21. Zahra, S. A., & George, G. (2002). Absorptive capacity: A review, reconceptualization, and extension. *Academy of Management Review, 27*(2), 185–203.
22. Eisenhardt, K. M. (1989). Agency theory: An assessment and review. *Academy of Management Review, 14*(1), 57–74.
23. Hung, H. (1998). A typology of the theories of the roles of governing boards. *Corporate Governance, 6*(2), 101–111.
24. Jensen, M. C., & Meckling, W. H. (1976). Theory of the firm: Managerial behaviour, agency costs, and ownership structures. *Journal of Finance and Economics, 3*, 305–360.
25. Governo Italiano: Il Governo Informa (2011). Retrieved Jan 19, 2012 from http://www.governo.it/Presidenza/Comunicati/dettaglio.asp?d=61569.
26. DeSanctis, G., & Poole, M. S. (1994). Capturing the complexity in advanced technology use: adaptive structuration theory. *Organization Science, 5*(2), 121–147.
27. Bower, J., & Christensen, C. (1995). Disruptive technologies: Catching the wave. *Harvard Business Review, 7*(1), 43–53.

Part III
Design and Evaluation of Organizational Practices

Designing Teams for Enhancing Individual Added-Value Use of Technology

Stefano Basaglia, Leonardo Caporarello, Massimo Magni and Ferdinando Pennarola

Abstract This paper focuses on the team contextual characteristics that may support or hinder individuals' exploration of a new technology. By adopting a multi-level framework we show how team-level and individual-level attributes influences individual exploratory behaviors. Moreover, we show how team level and individual characteristics interact in shaping individual exploration. Our paper offers directions for future research and insights for managers supporting them to design teams that are going to adopt a new system.

Keywords Team · Technology introduction · Added value use

1 Introduction

Despite significant gains in explaining and predicting individual usage intentions and behaviors toward information technology (IT), organizations are still facing problems related to the underutilization of implemented technologies [1].

S. Basaglia
Bergamo University, Bergamo, Italy
e-mail: stefano.basaglia@unibg.it

L. Caporarello · M. Magni (✉) · F. Pennarola
Bocconi University, Milan, Italy
e-mail: massimo.magni@unibocconi.it

L. Caporarello
e-mail: leonardo.caporarello@unibocconi.it

F. Pennarola
e-mail: ferdinando.pennarola@unibocconi.it

R. Baskerville et al. (eds.), *Designing Organizational Systems*,
Lecture Notes in Information Systems and Organisation 1,
DOI: 10.1007/978-3-642-33371-2_10,

In particular, previous research has found that individuals often underutilize newly introduced technologies, interacting with only a limited set of features that may support their work tasks [2]. Unfortunately, the limited use of new technology features by employees obstructs potential IT-related job performance improvement and hampers organizational efforts to realize returns from their IT investments. Notwithstanding the important contributions of the empirical findings related to user acceptance of technology, the implicit assumption of this stream of research is the passive role of users. In fact, Nambisan and colleagues put it quite succinctly when they state that, "users have only to decide whether to accept or not to accept an application that has already developed" [3]. According to Nambisan et al. [3] many issues have to be addressed about user's creative behaviors in the identification of new applications for already implemented technologies and the active role that users play in interacting creatively with a new technology. As noted by Agarwal [4], "it is necessary to investigate and understand how to promote added value use of technology rather than how to influence individuals to use a technology." The need to study explorative behavior toward technology relies on the assumption that organizational long-term survival is tied to managers' ability to develop a creative environment to facilitate employees' ideas generation. Since IT is a crucial aspect of today's fast-paced environment, it is necessary to explore the creative role that users play in the deployment of existing technologies. Although the importance of this issue is recognized by managers and researchers [5], less work has specifically investigated the determinants of users' innovative behavior toward technology [3]. As noted by Nambisan et al. [3], one of the main aspects concerning users' innovative behavior revolves around the intention to explore a technology, which represents a user's willingness to find new applications for the system.

Unfortunately, relatively little research has focused on the factors that affect users' willingness to actively explore new technology features. Instead, with relatively few exceptions [6–8], prior research has tended to view end-users as being fairly passive in their stance toward new technology—i.e., users are ready to adopt a new technology as is [1]. Agarwal [4] emphasizes the need for more research investigating how to promote an added-value use of technology rather than simply studying the determinants of technology use *per se*. Similarly, Burton-Jones and Straub [9] recently highlighted the need to understand deep structure usage of new technology. Clearly, a deeper understanding of the determinants of intention to explore is needed.

Facilitating conditions have emerged as an important precursor to new technology usage [1]. These conditions have traditionally been linked to organizational provision of resource and infrastructure support for system use [1]. However, an important gap in this extant literature is the role of localized facilitating conditions—specifically in the context of work teams. The organizational reality is that, increasingly, organizations are moving toward a team-based structure for organizing work. Recent estimates suggest that over 80 % of Fortune 500 companies are utilizing team-based structures to organize work. Thus, a majority of employees are involved in some form of team work as a fundamental part of their jobs. A critical consideration under such work structures is that employees' behavior towards novel situations (including new technology use) is likely to be shaped by shared experiences and interpretations among team members. Indeed, according to Seibert et al. [10], individuals belonging to the same team are likely to be exposed to the same goals, strategies, and work environments, which leads to a shared perception of the contextual conditions within the team that is distinct from those of other teams.

Unfortunately, there is currently a dearth of research that examines the intersection of team-level conditions and individual drivers of intention to explore new technologies. Klein and Kozlowski [11] have lamented the lack of such meso-level theories, arguing that greater attention to models that span multiple levels of analysis can significantly expand our understanding of organizational phenomena. Further, Burton-Jones and Gallivan [12] have underscored the need for multilevel research that sheds light on technology usage. Thus, the purpose of this research is to understand the role of team-level conditions and individual characteristics in predicting employees' intention to explore new technology. Specifically, we draw on the team climate as well as on team creativity to understand how exploration intentions can be promoted within team-based structures. This foray into the role of team climate is coupled with an examination of individual attributes and attitudinal predictors of employee intention to explore. Previous research has highlighted the importance of individual attributes as predictors of technology usage [1].

We test our research model in a sample of 410 members and leaders of 69 organizational work teams adopting a new communication technology. Through an empirical test of the research model, this research contributes to the technology adoption literature in two important ways. First, by examining individual-level and team-level antecedents, we extend research on intention to explore—a construct that has hitherto received limited attention. Second, by examining the role of team climate, we contribute more broadly to technology adoption research. Previous research has pointed to the importance of adopting a multilevel perspective on the technology adoption and use phenomenon. This research takes a step in that direction.

The remainder of this paper is structured as follows. The next sections describe the theoretical background and research hypotheses. Next we describe the method and the findings. Then, we conclude by outlining the theoretical and pragmatic implications of our study.

2 Theoretical Background

2.1 Intention to Explore and Creativity

Recent theories define creativity as the production of novel and useful ideas in any domain [13]. Amabile's [13] compositional theory posits that in addition to individual characteristics, context plays a critical role in enhancing creativity. The model proposed by Amabile has been extended by the interaction theory proposed by Woodman, et al. [14], which builds upon the assumption that contextual factors affect individual creativity. More importantly, Woodman's et al. [14] theory highlights the multilevel nature of creativity by suggesting that individual creative behaviors are influenced by individual characteristics as well as by group influences.

According to the theories presented above, personal characteristics and contextual facilitating conditions affect individual creativity, ultimately influencing a person's willingness to explore and experiment with new ideas and approaches toward a certain stimuli [13, 14]. The ability to explore new cognitive pathways grants individuals the freedom to investigate alternative solutions enhancing the probability of generating creative ideas. However, the level of individual engagement toward exploration can vary in relation to personal characteristics and contextual situations [15].

Focusing on the information systems' domain, we can consider the use of technology not as a choice among a set of predefined possibilities, but as a situated and recursive process of constitution, which may also ignore such conventional uses or invent new ones. This means the use of technology has a certain level of flexibility, which is limited by the properties comprising the technology artifact [8]. Although continued habitual people's use of a technology tend to reinforce it over time, technologies-in-practice are changed as people modify the properties of their technology, and how they interact with it [8, 16].

Consequently, the user's intention to explore represents the individual's willingness to find new ideas related to the system deployment in her day-to-day activities. Intention to explore is defined as a user's willingness to explore a new technology with the purpose of finding potential applications to their work [3]. There are distinct differences between intention to explore and intention to use a new technology. Intention to use reflects a user's conscious plans to use a technology. It does not necessarily reflect how one plans to use the technology—i.e., the nature of use. In contrast, intention to explore reflects a user's conscious plan to actively survey the various features of a new technology [3]. This exploration behavior can lead to the discovery of methods for leveraging the technology to support one's work [6].

Unfortunately, there is currently a paucity of research on the antecedents and outcomes of user intention to explore.

Thus, building on the works of Amabile [13], we argue that individual, and contextual dimensions affect an individual's intention to explore a technology. At the individual level, a user's relationship toward technology is not invariant across users. Individual characteristics such as gender and age shape user's perceptions, and behaviors toward technology [3], ultimately influencing her willingness to explore the system. Moreover, users who belong to a team will exchange gossip, stories, rumors, and develop new interpretive frameworks related to the system. The quality of this exchange process may act as a stimulus to find new applications for the system. Finally, an environment which is oriented toward innovation will provide the necessary resources and recognition for employee results to facilitate a nurturing environment for exploration of new technology deployments. According to Triandis [17] a behavior cannot occur if environmental conditions constrain it and harnessing innovation and entrepreneurship amongst employees will lead to an organizational environment that support a 'transformational' competencies.

Although the creative process can be affected by contextual factors, Unsworth [18] underscores the importance of considering the kind of driver which initiates the individual willingness to generate novel ideas. According to Deci and Ryan [19] an individual's behavior can be initiated either through self-determined choice (i.e. individual desire to achieve a goal) or because of external demands (i.e., R&D project needs). Most of the empirical studies concerning creativity focus on externally driven generation of new ideas, exploring individual responses to given problems. Many researchers have investigated the role of creativity in certain professional figures such as engineers, architects, and R&D scientists [18]. In the information systems field, the importance of creativity has been recognized in the development of a new information system to enable organizational change [20]. In this work, Cooper states that a lack of creative thinking, from the definition of the system requirements to the program design, facilitates the creation of a new information system which reinforces the organizational status quo rather than enhancing the process of change [20]. Few studies, with notable exceptions, have analyzed self-determined creative thinking, which is related to a proactive behavior toward a certain situation or problem—such as the individual attempt to discover problems to solve [18]. People spontaneously try to look at an object or a situation through a different point of view not because it is required by their formal task, but because it is a self-determined attempt to generate new ideas. These insights may also occur in the IS domain when users try to discover new applications for a system, even if their formal task does not include the discovery and development of new technology functionalities. The present paper focuses on the self-determined individual's intention to explore a technology, rather than on external demand.

2.2 Individual Attributes Differences

Several researchers have pointed to the importance of individual attributes in the prediction of technology use [e.g. [3]). In particular, gender and age have emerged as important individual attributes in the prediction of technology use. These individual attributes have consistently been found to influence the way individuals view and approach technology. For instance, previous literature on gender points out that dissimilarity in outcomes between men and women can be traced back to different decision making processes [21]. Gill et al. [22] argue that men are more oriented toward individualistic tasks than women. Moreover, other studies in the technology adoption domain [23] point out that men are more task oriented than women, indicating that instrumental factors are more likely to influence men's likelihood to adopt a new technology. Other studies point out that the occurrence of preferences and orientation changes in the human life cycle lead to differential outcomes among individuals of different ages. For example, Sharit and Czaja [24] find that older workers are more likely to resist change than their younger counterparts. Although the effects of gender and age have been examined in predicting behavioral intention, we believe it is instructive to understand the implications of such individual attribute differences for the less-well-understood intention to explore.

2.3 Team Climate

Climate represents a shared perception of the types of behaviors, practices, and procedures that are supported in a specific setting [25]. The underlying perceptions that form climate can be shared at various levels of social collectivity, including organizational, unit, department, and team. As numerous studies have found, climate influences the behaviors of individual employees. According to [26] climate influences individual behavior through a social information processing mechanism, thus leveraging the way individuals think and feel about a certain aspect of their environment. Moreover, the conceptualization of organizational climate represented a source of debate when compared with the concept of organizational culture. Consistent with recent studies, we consider climate and culture interchangeably, given the overlap in conceptualizing the influence of social context within organizations [27]. We consider the distinction between the two as more a matter of perspective rather than substance. Team climate is defined as shared perceptions of the kinds of behaviors, practices, and procedures that are supported within a team. Indeed, teams have been conceptualized as social entities that develop shared attitudes and behavioral patterns through social interaction and through the exposure of team members to the same procedures, policies and experiences. In a team-based setting, one's teammates are the more proximal source of influence for their colleagues. Consequently, team members are likely to rely on cues from their team environment to interpret events, develop attitudes, and understand expectations concerning their behaviors [28]. For example, when there exists a climate for service, team members are more likely to engage in behaviors that foster a favorable relationship with the customer and for achieving higher customer satisfaction. The importance of climate in the context of technology introduction is consistent with the Adaptive Structuration Theory (AST), which looks at the structures that actually emerge in human action as people interact with these technologies. In particular, AST advocates that "atmosphere" concerning the relative formality or informal nature of interactions in a social system can play a pivotal role in shaping the technology itself as well as its use [29]. Therefore, the climate that pertains to the team as a social system represents a critical aspect that should be taken into account when investigating individual use of technology.

In the context of new technologies, two specific types of climate are important within teams: team innovative climate and team competitive climate. *Team innovative climate* reflects the extent to which team members have a shared perception that the team supports experimentation, innovation, and development of new ideas [30]. This type of team climate is important for individuals dealing with new technologies because it recognizes that the process of exploration of various system features may not necessarily yield immediate tangible returns. Rather, the innovative process may lead one down many unfruitful paths before the discovery of value-adding use of technology features is made.

Team competitive climate reflects the extent to which there is a shared perception of behaviors that promote individual achievement. It is important to note that competitive climate differs from subjective norm in two key ways. First, competitive climate refers to a shared perception, while subjective norm refers to an individual-level perception. Second, competitive climate refers to the characteristics of the contextual environment, while subjective norm directly refers to the pressure related to performing a target behavior. Competitive climate induces team members to search for opportunities for self-enhancement in work performance. Indeed, in environments characterized by the norm of competition, individuals are more likely to be oriented toward personal outcomes rather than on the interaction with other team members. Therefore, through a collective expression of competitiveness, team competitive climate increases the focus on tangible resources leading team members to take advantage of opportunities that may emerge and competitive intrateam structures have been found to lead to improved team performance [31].

3 Hypotheses Development

In this section, we develop the theoretical arguments for developing our research hypotheses. We first present the hypotheses related to individual attributes, followed by the hypotheses related to team climate. We then discuss the interaction of these various predictors of intention to explore.

3.1 Individual Attributes and Intention to Explore

Age. Recent psychological studies argue that when individuals grow older they experience changes in their cognitive abilities and their preferences [32]. In particular, extant research points out that older individuals have limited personal resources for framing organizational events and changes in a positive light, thus inducing a high sensitivity to stressful situations [33]. Older individuals have fewer cognitive resources for processing complex technologies. When the potential work applications of a new technology are not well understood, a great deal of cognitive effort is required for the search and discovery process. Consequently, such individuals are less likely to make an effort to explore new technology features. This is not unlike the challenges that older individuals face when adopting a new technology [23]. Thus, we hypothesize:

Hypothesis 1 Age will be negatively related to individual intention to explore a new technology.

Gender. Men and women have demonstrated different attitudes toward the use of technology [3]. Specifically, prior studies suggest that women are more likely to exhibit anxiety in interacting with technology [34] and are less likely to enjoy using technology [35]. Such differences are likely to be manifested in the individual proclivity for exploring the various features of new technologies and finding potential applications for supporting work tasks. In contrast to women, men—who have a task-achievement orientation—are more likely to explore new technology features so as to find efficient ways of achieving their work tasks. Therefore, ceteris paribus, we expect women to have a lower level of intention to explore when compared to men.

Hypothesis 2 Women will exhibit a lower intention to explore a new technology than men will.

3.2 Team Climate and Intention to Explore

Team innovative climate. Team innovative climate reflects a positive stance toward experimentation with new technologies [36]. Such a team climate emphasizes the importance of supporting and encouraging the development of novel ideas, as well as challenging traditional ways of doing things. Team members are able to explore various features and potential applications of the technology without fear of reprisal from making errors. Team members can reflect on their actions and revise their thinking to improve work outcomes. Individuals who perceive that the team recognizes their effort in taking the initiative for finding new potential uses for the newly introduced technology are more likely to engage in exploratory behaviors [30]. Thus, we expect that team innovative climate will foster an environment conducive for individual experimentation.

Hypothesis 3 Team innovative climate will positively influence individual intention to explore a new technology.

Team Competitive Climate. As noted earlier, a competitive team climate encourages team members to find ways of improving their own performance. Under such climate, team members continuously search for various sources of advantage in completing their work tasks. To the extent that they believe the technology will boost their work efficiency, team members are likely to explore various features of the technology. Such exploration may present an opportunity to outperform coworkers through the identification of new features and applications. Indeed, empirical evidence suggests that in the workplace, attitudes toward using a technology are closely tied to instrumentality. Further, exploration of the technology can enhance one's level of sophistication when it comes to using the technology, potentially improving one's image [37]. Therefore, we expect that team competitive climate will increase the individual intention to explore a new technology.

Hypothesis 4 Team competitive climate will positively influence individual intention to explore a new technology.

3.3 Team Climate and Individual Attributes

Team innovative climate. Older users of a new technology are more likely to engage in exploration behavior when they perceive a climate that supports such behavior. As noted earlier, exploring various technology features requires significant cognitive effort for older users. They are unlikely to engage in such behavior unless there is a context that supports it. Given their natural curiosity and abundance of cognitive resources, younger users do not rely on a supportive climate for experimentation with technology as older users might. Thus, we expect the relationship between team innovative climate and individual intention to explore to be stronger for older individuals. Women are highly sensitized to contextual factors that support technology use. In particular, women have been found to respond well to social influences that promote technology use. We expect that team innovative climate will encourage women to be less timid in exploring various technology features in their work. Given their instrumental focus, men are less likely to rely on the influence of team innovative climate. Consequently, we expect team climate to be more important in forming women's intention to explore a new technology.

Hypothesis 5 Team innovative climate will interact with age in its influence on intention to explore a new technology.

Hypothesis 6 Team innovative climate will interact with gender in its influence on intention to explore a new technology.

Team competitive climate. Given the drain that new technology exploration places on individuals' cognitive resources, older individuals are unlikely to explore the features of a new technology unless they feel compelled to. Team competitive climate creates conditions that favor such exploration. Older individuals may feel the need to explore various features of the technology merely as a competitive necessity. Hence, we expect team competitive climate to be more important for older users. As noted earlier, women hold less favorable attitudes toward new technology [38]. However, a competitive team climate can prompt women to explore various features of technology to ensure that they perform their work effectively. Such a climate is more important as a catalyst for intention to explore technology among women than is the case for men. Since men generally have an instrumental view of technology, the need for a competitive environment is less urgent [1]. Thus, we hypothesize the following:

Hypothesis 7 Team competitive climate will interact with age in its influence on intention to explore a new technology.

Hypothesis 8 Team competitive climate will interact with gender in its influence on intention to explore a new technology.

4 Methods

4.1 Study Context and Measures

Data were collected in two large European companies which introduced a new communication technology. The technology was introduced to manage all technology-mediated communications among individuals in an integrated manner. The technology was needed to support activities such as agenda sharing, information sharing, mobility management, and event coordination. In addition to offering more information that can be accessed and managed by users, this system embodied the convergence of different communication capabilities, enabling individuals to communicate with colleagues within and outside their team. This is particularly relevant because individuals, through a unique platform, are allowed to chose among different communication channels that match their synchronicity needs (e.g., voice, instant messaging, conference call, and e-mail). In particular the new system allowed to integrate all the communication tools in one single system, allowing individuals to use one single integrated system to send e-mail, messages, text and by maintain up to date all the information necessary to interact with other colleagues. In this particular case, while the use of the system was strongly encouraged, there was no policy in place for non-compliance and no actions were being taken as a result of the usage reports, suggesting that system use was voluntary. Indeed, users would have been allowed to use the stand alone systems used in the past for managing their communications and to interact with others. Data were collected using a survey methodology. The questionnaire was developed using a multi-stage iterative procedure. First, an initial set of items was constructed drawing upon prior work. Next, we conducted interviews with the IT managers responsible for the implementation project. This helped ensure that the questionnaire was appropriate for the organizational setting and the technology introduced. One week before the launch of the survey, CIOs at the participating organizations sent an e-mail memo explaining the importance of the study to all potential respondents.

Data were gathered through a web survey containing five-point Likert-type scales. To obtain more reliable ratings of the team-level constructs under

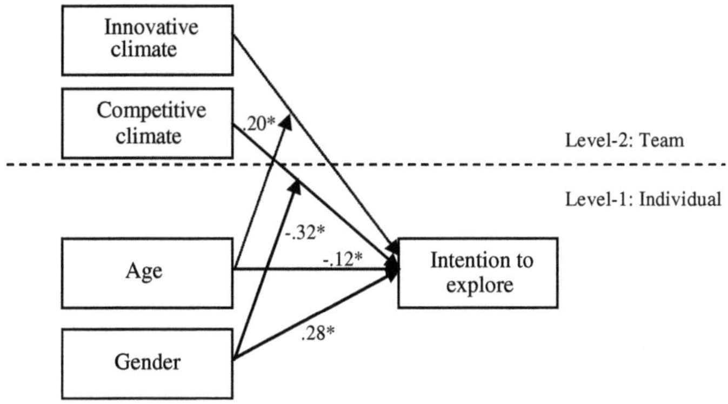

Fig. 1 Model results. *Dotted lines* represent not-significant relationships

consideration, multiple respondents from each team participated: the team leader and at least three team members. To ensure data validity, only teams returning at least three questionnaires (the team leader and two team members) were considered. Of a total of 810 individuals and 129 teams targeted for the survey, 410 usable surveys referring to 69 teams were completed, yielding response rates of 50.6 % (individuals) and 53.4 % (team). Data for the team-level independent variables were gathered through the assessment of items formulated explicitly at the team level.

In order to test our model we used scales derived from previous literature. We employed a scale from Nambisan et al. [3] to assess individual intention to explore the new technology. A scale adapted from [30] was used to measure team innovative climate. Individual scores were aggregated to the team level. The team competitive climate scale included items adapted from [39]. Consistent with previous research respondents were asked to self-report their age. We used a dummy code for gender (0 = female, 1 = male). Given consistent findings linking perceived usefulness to behavioral intention, we included this measure as a control variable. We adapted the scale from [23]. Before testing our model we also ran a confirmatory factor analysis that showed that items loadings were higher on their respective factor in comparison to cross-loadings.

5 Results

Given the hierarchically nested structure of the data and the research model, it was necessary to use a random coefficient modeling (RCM) technique. RCM enables researchers to examine relationships that span levels of analysis and can meaningfully partition the variance components in outcome variables [40]. The results of the analysis are presented in Table 1 and Fig. 1

Table 1 Models predicting intention to explore

IV: Intention to explore	Model 1	Model 2
Perceived usefulness	0.29**	0.28**
Age	−0.12*	−0.14**
Gender	0.28*	0.30**
Competitive climate	0.20*	0.46
Innovative climate	0.06	0.35
Interactions:		
Competitive climate x age		−0.04
Competitive climate x Gender		−0.32*
Innovative climate x age		−0.07
Innovative climate x Gender		0.05
R^2	0.27	0.34
ΔR^2		0.07

Notes: † $p < 0.10$, *$p < 0.05$, **$p < 0.01$, ***$p < 0.001$

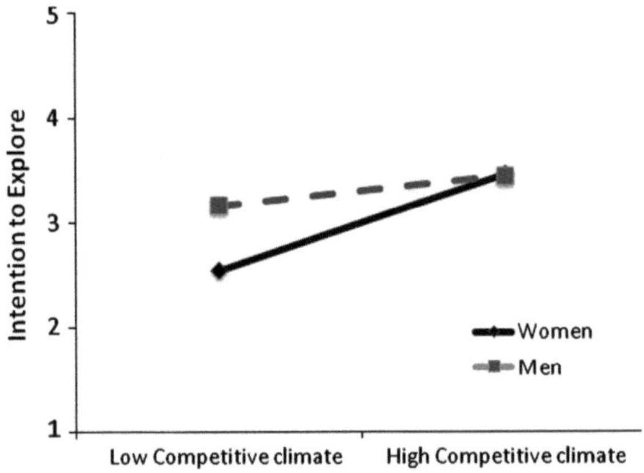

Fig. 2 Interaction effect between competitive climate and gender

As Model 1 in Table 1 illustrates, the main effects model explains 27 % of the variance in intention to explore. Age has a negative influence on intention to explore (coeff. = −0.12, $p < 0.05$). Thus, hypothesis 1 is supported. The coefficient for gender is positive and significant (coeff. = 0.28, $p < 0.05$) providing support for hypothesis 2, thus supporting the fact that age and gender are important aspects that should be taken into account when dealing with the introduction of a new technology. Team innovative climate has no significant effect on intention to explore (coeff. = 0.06, $p > 0.10$). Hence, hypothesis 3 is not supported. Finally, in support of hypothesis 4, the coefficient for team competitive climate is positive and significant (coeff. = 0.20, $p < 0.05$).

In the second model, we entered the interaction terms. As Model 2 shows, the interaction model explained an additional 7 % of the variance in intention to explore. Only hypothesis 8 is supported (coeff. = −0.32, $p < 0.05$). Hypotheses 5, 6, and 7 are not supported. To better understand the form of the cross-level moderation, we plotted the interaction. As Fig. 2 illustrates the slope of team competitive climate is steeper (more positive) for women than for men. This is consistent with our prediction that team competitive climate would be more important for women than for men in predicting intention to explore a new technology.

6 Discussion and Implications

This research contributes to the literature on technology adoption and use in several ways. In order to shed some light on the intention to explore predictors, we adopted a creativity-based approach because it allows one to consider individual, and contextual factors collectively, answering the call by Hofmann [40] who urges to consider the hierarchical nature of organizations.

First, our paper goes beyond the traditional IT acceptance literature by emphasizing a more active and creative role for users in looking for emergent use of newly introduced technology, thus, answering the call by Agarwal [4] who encourages researchers to depart from simply looking at the acceptance of a new technology. Our examination of users' willingness to explore various IT features represents an important step in overcoming the underutilization of new systems through a creativity-based approach.

Second, our research confirms the importance of individual attributes as drivers of users' cognitions about, and behavior towards, new technologies. In particular, the current research reveals that men are more willing to perform exploratory behaviors than women. The role of gender in driving individual intention to explore technology was hither to not well understood. Prior research has primarily focused on the role of gender in predicting acceptance of new technology. We also found that age affects the individual willingness to explore a new technology, with older individuals being less likely to explore a newly introduced technology. The nature of this relationship is not unlike that hypothesized by previous studies [41]. However, we suggest that the mechanism that leads older workers to be less likely to explore a new technology is substantially different. Morris and Venkatesh [41] point to differences in exposure to technology as the reason for age differences. In contrast, our conceptualization of the relationship is linked to motivational mechanisms. We reasoned that older individuals find it more difficult to increase the effort required to comprehend and experiment with features of the new technology. Consequently, such individuals would be less likely to have the motivation to explore new features.

In order to shed some light on the intention to explore predictors, we adopted a creativity-based approach because it allows one to consider facilitating conditions at the team level of analysis. Our results indicate a strong influence of competitive climate in shaping individual intention to explore a new technology. This finding suggests that the competitiveness among team members is a catalyst for individuals' exploration behavior. This result is particularly interesting because it represents a counterintuitive aspect in technology introduction processes. Such a result could be traced back to the fact that individuals in a competitive environment are more likely to explore a technology in order to reap advantages in comparison with other colleagues by leveraging on the ability to find more effective and way to use the technology and to better perform their tasks. We also found that competitive climate at the team level of analysis interacts with gender in shaping individual intention to explore a new technology. In particular, when team competitive climate is low, men are more likely than women to explore a new technology. However, increasing team competitive climate serves as a catalyst for exploration behavior among women.

Another important contribution of the present study is related to the adoption of a multilevel perspective for studying individuals' interaction with technology. A multilevel perspective allowed us to address the limitation of previous studies which mainly rely on one level of analysis. Thus, we respond to calls for considering the hierarchical nature of organizational phenomena [40] with a specific focus on multilevel models for explaining creativity-oriented behaviors [13].

The results of this study have substantial implications for organizations that introduce new technologies. It has long been recognized that the introduction of new technologies is not enough for realizing gains in performance; and the underutilization of technology does not allow for the full exploitation of its potential in supporting organizational processes. Thus, to the degree that it facilitates the discovery of new sources of value for the technology, active exploration of system features is a desirable behavior.

Based on our findings about team climate, managers may consider creating competitive team structures that emphasize a tight integration of technology use into employee work practices. While previous research underscores the need to design team-based structures, our results point out that the individual exploration of a new technology is influenced by a climate that fosters individualism within the team. However, we stress the importance of exercising caution in fostering such climate as it may have unintended consequences for employee outcomes (e.g., satisfaction). On one hand it could trigger desirable exploratory behaviors. On the other hand it may lead to negative outcomes such as opportunistic behavior or information hoarding which may threaten overall team performance. The use of such climate should be aligned with desired exploration behaviors.

Our research also points to a need for managers to be sensitive to the compositional makeup of the teams in which technological innovations are being deployed. To the degree that individuals have different approaches to using a new technology, team composition should be based upon a balance in individual attributes for facilitating the emergence of technology "creative explorers" within each team. Teams composed primarily of men may not require a competitive climate. However, a team composed primarily of women may require such a climate in order to foster greater exploration of the system.

7 Limitations and Future Research Directions

As with any work our research has limitations that should be addressed in future studies. Because of the cross-sectional nature of the study we were unable to test for true causality, although causality is theoretically implied in some of the proposed relationships. A longitudinal study can provide some more relevant considerations and implications. Therefore, this study should be reiterated over time in order to catch the temporal effects of depicted variables on the individual intention to explore. Moreover, we did not have access to the demographic data of non-respondents and were thus unable to verify the existence of any significant differences between respondents and non-respondents. Some issues for future research emerge from this study. Although the system we examined embodied characteristics that are common to other systems, future research should validate our results in other settings in order to increase the generalizability of our findings. Moreover, the results are based on the Italian context, suggesting the need for future research in other national and cultural settings. Consistent with these directions future research should also analyze if there are any differences between individual biological gender and psychological gender in influencing individual intention to explore. Moreover, we focused on the shared contextual perception of climate, while future research should also take into account the relational aspects among individuals belonging to the same team. For example dimensions connected to teamwork quality and team connections should be taken into account. Finally, whereas our paper took into account a positivistic perspective, we urge future research to embrace also an hermeneutic perspective in looking at the way through which individuals use and explore a technology on the basis of the social structure in which they are embedded. We believe that taking such a perspective would be complementary to our view and would contribute to a better understanding of the technology exploration phenomenon.

References

1. Venkatesh, V., Morris, M. G., Davis, G. B., & Davis, F. D. (2003). User acceptance of information technology: Toward a unified view. *MIS Quarterly, 27*(3), 425.
2. Ross, J. W., & Weill, P. (2002). Six IT decisions your IT people shouldn't make. *Harvard Business Review, 80*(11), 84–91.
3. Nambisan, S., Agarwal, R., & Tanniru, M. (1999). Organizational mechanisms for enhancing user innovation in information technology. *MIS Quarterly, 23*(3), 365–395.
4. Agarwal, R. (2000). Individual acceptance of information technologies. In R. W. Zmud (Ed.), *Framing the domains of IT management: projecting the future from the past* (pp. 85–104). Cincinnati: Pinnaflex Educational Resources.
5. Ciborra, C. U. (1991). *From thinking to tinkering: The grassroots of strategic information systems*. Paper presented at the 12th International Conference on Information Systems, New York.

6. Ahuja, M., & Thatcher, J. B. (2005). Moving beyond intentions and toward the theory of trying: Effects of work environment and gender on post-adoption information technology use. *MIS Quarterly, 29*(3), 427–459.
7. Boudreau, M. C., & Robey, D. (2005). Enacting integrated information technology: A human agency perspective. *Organization Science, 16*(1), 3–18.
8. Orlikowski, W. J. (2000). Using technology and constituting structures: A practice lens for studying technology in organizations. *Organization Science, 11*(4), 404–428.
9. Burton-Jones, A., & Straub, D. W. (2006). Reconceptualizing system usage: An approach and empirical test. *Information Systems Research, 17*(3), 228–246.
10. Seibert, S. E., Silver, S. R., & Randolph, W. A. T. (2004). Taking empowerment to the next level: A multiple level model of empowerment, performance, and satisfaction. *Academy of Management Journal, 47*, 332–349.
11. Kozlowski, S. W. J., & Klein, K. J. (2000). A multilevel approach to theory and research in organizations: Contextual, temporal, and emergent processes In K. J. Klein & S. W. J. Kozlowski (Eds.), *Multilevel theory, research, and methods in organizations* (pp. 3–90). San Francisco: Jossey-Bass.
12. Burton-Jones, A., & Gallivan, M. (2007). Toward a deeper understanding of system usage in organizations: A multilevel perspective. *MIS Quarterly, 31*(4), 657–679.
13. Amabile, T. M. (1988). A model of creativity and innovation in organizations. *Research in Organizational Behavior, 10*, 123–167.
14. Woodman, R. W., Sawyer, J. E., & Griffin, R. W. (1993). Toward a theory of organizational creativity. *Academy of Management Review, 18*(2), 293–321.
15. Shalley, C. E., & Gilson, L. L. (2004). What leaders need to know: A review of social and contextual factors that can foster or hinder creativity. *Leadership Quarterly, 15*(1), 33–53.
16. Barley, S. R. (1986). Technology as an occasion for structuring: Evidence from observations of CT scanners and the social order of radiology departments. *Administrative Science Quarterly, 31*, 78–108.
17. Triandis, H. C. (1971). *Attitude and attitude change*. New York: Wiley.
18. Unsworth, K. (2001). Unpacking creativity. *Academy of Management Review, 26*(2), 289–297.
19. Deci, E. L., & Ryan, R. M. (1987). The support of autonomy and the control of behavior. *Journal of Personality and Social Psychology, 53*, 1024–1037.
20. Cooper, R. B. (2000). Information technology development creativity: A case study of attempate radical change. *MIS Quarterly, 24*(2), 245.
21. Bem, D., & Allen, A. (1974). On predicting some of the people some of the time: The search for cross-situational consistencies in behavior. *Psychological Review, 81*, 506–520.
22. Gill, S., Stockard, J., Johnson, M., & William, S. (1987). Measuring gender differences: The expressive dimension and critique of androgyny scales. *Sex Roles, 17*, 375–400.
23. Venkatesh, V., & Morris, M. G. (2000). Why don't men ever stop to ask for directions? Gender, social influence, and their role in technology acceptance and usage behavior. *MIS Quarterly, 24*(1), 115–139.
24. Sharit, J., & Czaja, S. J. (1994). Ageing, computer-based task performance, and stress: Issues and challenges. *Ergonomics, 37*(4), 559–577.
25. Schneider, B., White, S. S., & Paul, M. C. (1998). Linking service climate and customer perceptions of service quality: Test of a causal model. *Journal of Applied Psychology, 83*, 150–163.
26. Glomb, T. M., & Liao, H. (2003). Interpersonal aggression in work groups: Social influence, reciprocal, and individual effects. *Academy of Management Journal, 46*(4), 486–496.
27. Smith, K. G., Collins, J. C., & Clark, K. D. (2005). Existing knowledge, knowledge creation capability, and the rate of new product introduction in high-technology firms. *Academy of Management Journal, 48*(2), 346–357.
28. Liao, H., & Chuang, A. (2004). A multilevel investigation of factors influencing employee service performance and customer outcomes. *Academy of Management Journal, 47*, 41–58.

29. DeSanctis, G., & Poole, M. S. (1994). Capturing the complexity in advanced technology use: Adaptive structuration theory. *Organization Science, 5*(2), 121–147.
30. Van der Vegt, G. S., Van de Vliert, E., & Huang, X. (2005). Location-level links between diversity and innovation climate depend on national power distance. *Academy of Management Journal, 48*(6), 1171–1182.
31. Beersma, B., Hollenbeck, J. R., Humphrey, S. E., Moon, H., Conlon, D. E., & Ilgen, D. R. (2003). Cooperation, competition, and team performance: Toward a contingency approach. *Academy of Management Journal, 46*(5), 572–590.
32. Kanfer, R., & Ackerman, P. L. (2004). Aging, adult development, and work motivation. *Academy of Management Review, 29*, 440–458.
33. Mroczek, D. K., & Almeida, D. M. (2004). The effect of daily stress, personality, and age on daily negative affect. *Journal of Personality, 72*, 355–378.
34. Bozionelos, N. (1996). Psychology of computer use: Prevalence of computer anxiety in British managers and professionals. *Psychological Reports, 78*, 995–1002.
35. Gefen, D., & Straub, D. (2000). The relative importance of perceived ease of use in IS adoption: A study of E-commerce adoption. *Journal of the Association for Information Systems, 1*(8), 1–30.
36. Edmondson, A. C. (1999). Psychological safety and learning behavior in work teams. *Administrative Science Quarterly, 44*, 350–383.
37. Venkatesh, V., & Davis, F. D. (2000). A theoretical extension of the technology acceptance model: Four longitudinal field studies. *Management Science, 46*(2), 186–204.
38. Ahuja, M. (2002). Information technology and the gender factor. *European Journal of Information Systems, 11*(1), 20–34.
39. Erdogan, B., Liden, R. C., & Kraimer, M. L. (2007). Justice and leader-member exchange: The moderating role of organizational culture. *Academy of Management Journal, 40*(2), 395–406.
40. Hofmann, D. (1997). An overview of the logic and rationale of hierarchical linear models. *Journal of Management, 23*(6), 723–744.
41. Morris, M. G., & Venkatesh, V. (2000). Age differences in technology adoption decisions: Implications for a changing work force. *Personnel Psychology, 53*, 375–403.

Design Principles at the Edge of the Designable: Non-formal and Informal Learning in SMEs

Nunzio Casalino

Abstract Informal learning is defined as the learning process which occurs in the workplace and is neither determined nor designed by an organization. Designing a methodology for identification and recognition of non-formal and informal learning could help managers to give employees a better autonomy and better forms of experiential learning and skills. So the main goal is to explore and describe in depth the organizational concept of informal learning. It is fundamental also to understand and improve in depth the recognition of non-formal and informal learning acquired by employees in SMEs, as a central part of lifelong learning processes. This is an essential feature to find the designability edge at which organizational systems designers can effectively operate to enable learning to occur. The reflections transpired have important implications about the development of detailed procedures for the accreditation of informal learning in the workplace.

Keywords Working environment · Experiential learning · SME · Non-formal learning · Informal learning · Social control

1 Introduction

Many important organizational processes lie beyond the realm of formalization. It is an intractable problem to formalize such processes because people are unique individuals who will engage in unique behaviors in unique organizational settings.

N. Casalino (✉)
Dipartimento di Strategie di Impresa e Innovazione Tecnologica,
Università degli Studi Guglielmo Marconi, Via Plinio 44, 00193 Rome, Italy
e-mail: n.casalino@unimarconi.it

R. Baskerville et al. (eds.), *Designing Organizational Systems*,
Lecture Notes in Information Systems and Organisation 1,
DOI: 10.1007/978-3-642-33371-2_11,

Although in the best interests of the organization, the behavior may not even seem rational. Though impossible to specify such processes formally, it is completely possible to design organizational settings that enable or promote informal (or even irrational) processes that are of benefit. Such designs are at the edge of the designable because they require designers to create environments and position resources that facilitate these important processes, while avoiding the temptation to design the informal processes themselves. Designers must understand how they can design the edges of these organizational systems, while allowing the exact configuration of the actual processes to unfold, change, and evolve according to the nature of the human actors actively engaging in the process.

Informal learning at the workplace is an example of such an informal process. Certainly such learning can take place in formal environments, such as classrooms. Learning that takes place in formal education and training environments is the most visible and have dominated educational policy and practice for a long time. But it more often occurs in different settings and contexts, non-formal and informal environments, and can be conceived as the social organization of learning activities. In recent years, however, there has been a growing understanding that learning in non-formal and informal settings are fundamental for the lifelong learning achievement, thus requiring new strategies for recognition and validation of more invisible learning environments [1]. This essay has the purpose to explore and describe in depth the organizational concept of informal learning, which was once described as an iceberg: mostly invisible at the surface and immense in its mostly submerged informal aspects [2]. The main goal is to better understand and improve the recognition of non-formal and informal learning acquired through work experience in SMEs, as an important part of lifelong learning. Such an understanding is required to find the designability edge at which organizational systems designers can effectively operate to enable learning to occur.

Informal learning at the workplace is defined as the learning process which occurs in the workplace and is neither determined nor designed by an organization [3]. By using this definition it can be distinguished between the goals of the learning and the process of learning. This description clarifies that an organization has to distinguish informal learning features and facilitate the occurrence of such learning, without making it formal.

The effectiveness of a learning event is determined by the relation of learning contents and the worker's needs. Informal learning generally emerges from specific worker needs, therefore it is particularly relevant. Formal learning may vary from extremely relevant to completely irrelevant to workers' needs. This changing worker role demands technical knowledge as well as skills in interpersonal communication and teamwork. High-performance jobs require on-going learning about changing technology, business relationships, and the perspectives of all members of the work community, including management, customers, and suppliers [4, 5]. The main drive for informal learning in the workplace is the need to meet organizational objectives that hang down on employees in the form of incentives, such as increased employee contribution in decision making and extended job responsibilities. Another drive for informal learning is the desire to meet individual goals such as financial and psychological goals of recognition and personal achievement. Through cross-training, trainees learned new job-specific skills; the character of co-workers (personality and work ethic); how to integrate feedback; and effective social skills. As well, cross-training expands an employee's perspective of observation—when an employee learns another task within the entire production process, particularly when it takes place out of his/her department, the employee's understanding of the task is redefined within the context of the whole process [6]. It is important to identify also employers, employees, SME owners, SME managers, HR managers and SME consultant's needs, because each of them is involved, from the organizational point of view, in informal learning from a different aspect.

Organizational studies specify that current instruments always require either a solid base in scientific knowledge about organizational design or support for a sociotechnical systems perspective on organizational design [7]. The research and the considerations that will be described might be considered as a first step in this direction, bringing a patrimony of data and practices, with whom it will be easier design upcoming researches with comparable objectives.

2 Theoretical Background and Research Methodology

In the context depicted in the introduction, the research has followed a learning centered approach, identified as a distinct stream of research that differs from the psychological orientation of cognitive-perceptual research. This approach has been motivated by educationists addressing the diversity of the environment in which learning takes place [8], and driven by process-based concerns relating to meeting individual differences and learning needs. The focus has been shifted from concentrating on the hypotheses of capacity and processing of information, to an increased interest in learners' active response to the learning assignment and the knowledge situation. Learning centered organizational studies have grown out of process-based models of learning in workplace such as:

- the learning process as a form of experiential learning [9];
- learners' orientations to learning [10, 11];
- workplace cognitive skills and strategy development [12].

This stream of research on learning style shows that learners are dynamic and open to adaptation according to the particular context of learning. Reproaches have been stated about the learning-centered tradition of research on learning styles, on the basis that it represents an uncertain relationship between learning style and cognition and that concepts are poorly defined and used loosely [8].

First of all the research team has focused on the identification of a taxonomy mainly related to the learning-centered tradition and focused on individual adjustments and approaches that arise while learners are engaged in the learning process. Learning at the workplace should become increasingly more popular for companies to achieve their short and long-term goals [13], but it is essential to address two sets of problems related to recognition of non-formal and informal learning.

The first group of problems is related to SMEs and their owners. On the one hand, SMEs are poorly informed about the benefits of and need for assessment of competences acquired in a non-formal and informal way. On the other hand, the lack of human, temporal and financial resources very often is a major obstacle in adopting procedures for assessment of competences and skills as practiced by large enterprises.

The lack of knowledge on these problems weakens the competitiveness of SMEs and is a barrier for the transition to knowledge based economy.

The second group of problems is related to employees in SMEs. Vocational education and training of staff in SMEs often happens through on the job-training and practically performing a job.

Since the acquired skills and competences are often difficult to transfer, the taxonomy adopted was focused on the scope of project research and was integrated by the following categories:

- building and improving a solid baseline knowledge;
- promoting operational efficiency also supported by collaborative tools and customized approaches;
- collaborating to create tangible solutions to organizational complex problems;
- improving employee performance with several kinds of resources;
- helping employees to quickly resolve concrete issues;
- fostering collaboration and an innovative mindedness;
- expanding learning opportunities beyond what can be provided through formal training;
- understanding corporate knowledge gaps and transform them in opportunities.

Designing a methodology for identification and recognition of non-formal and informal learning could help managers to give employees a better autonomy and better forms of experiential learning and skills. People tend to develop learning strategies in order to deal with learning materials and therefore learning strategies can be regarded as cognitive tools, which enable learners to complete tasks and solve problems. By relating the research on learning strategies to the design of learning environments it is possible to investigate how learners approach their learning, how they perceive of themselves as learners and what they value in the learning experience [10, 11].

In the last years, validation of non-formal and informal learning has become a key-element in national and European strategies for lifelong learning [14]. More and more countries have moved from a stage of initial testing and experimentation to full scale implementation where validation has become an integrated part of mainstream education, training and learning systems. Lifelong learning is defined as: all learning activity undertaken throughout life, with the aim of improving knowledge, skills and competence, within a personal, civic, social and/or employment-related perspective.

Learning is assumed here in terms of the social organization of learning activities which facilitate the communication and acquisition of knowledge and skills, also supported by information systems [15]. While there has been an increasing revitalization of informal learning aspects in recent years, can be evidenced several difficulties for employers to manage these aspects in the workplace. During the last twenty years, networks have provided the basis for different tools, such as e-mails and search engines, to develop corporate informal learning [16]. More recent developments include the application of social media to support informal learning activities through the virtual social networking among employees. Individuals in organizations have always exchanged their views, during lunch or informally during work, and after, but both small and large firms are now encouraging their employees to become involved in virtual social networking. This raises a series of ethical questions with regard to the management of social networking as a part of informal learning. Employers now make use of Facebook and such other social networking platforms. Many companies now require existing employees to demonstrate their activities on professional networks such as LinkedIn or distinctive groupware platforms. It is clear that these "social" technologies can also be used for the social control through the tracking of messages in order to verify and disciple individual employees in organizations [17].

According to Markus et al. [7] there are several design problem of providing IT support for emerging knowledge processes (EKPs). They are defined as: "organizational activity patterns that exhibit three characteristics in combination: an emergent process of deliberations with no best structure or sequence; requirements for knowledge that are complex, distributed across people, and evolving dynamically; and an actor set that is unpredictable in terms of job roles or prior knowledge."

Organizational requirements about the emergent knowledge design are critical processes for manufacturing sector, since it is known to be associated with good or poor performance on such measures as productivity, cost, quality and cycle time [7].

The reflections above have important implications about the development of procedures for the accreditation of informal learning in the workplace. On the one hand, the recognition of intentionality in informal learning offers a number of opportunities to adopt and develop instruments such as learning portfolios and learning diaries which provide opportunities to record the significant learning experiences and accomplishments of individuals. On the other hand, incidental learning, and, in particular tacit learning, gives rise to important issues about the recognition of learning experiences and social control within organizations. For this reason it was decided to apply the well-known model of the learning process derived from the Kolb's theory of experiential learning as the basis for design of traditional learning contents and to combine this with other information gained about the target learners [9]. The core of it is that learners progress through a learning cycle in which experience leads to observation and reflection, which then leads to concept formation (Fig. 1).

Fig. 1 Learning cycle steps according to Kolb theory of experiential learning

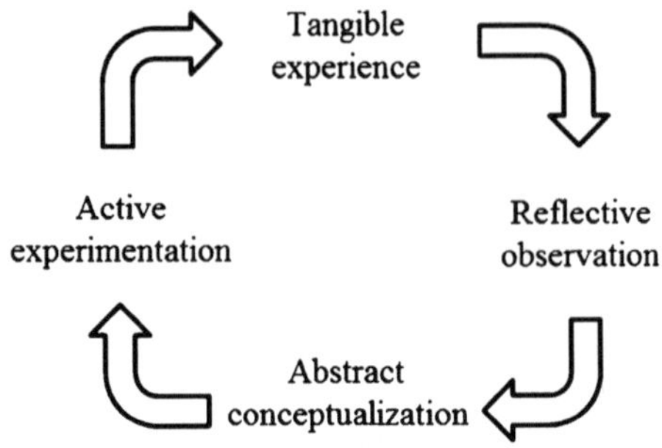

Kolb's learning theory sets out four distinct learning preferences, which are based on a four-stage learning cycle. In this respect Kolb's model is particularly relevant, since it offers both a way to understand individual people's different learning styles, and also an explanation of a cycle of experiential learning that applies to us all. In his studies, Kolb considers the cycle of learning as an essential principle in which "immediate or concrete experiences" deliver a basis for "observations and reflections."

These "observations and reflections" are assimilated and distilled into "abstract concepts" producing new implications for action which can be "actively tested" in turn creating new experiences. Kolb says that ideally this process represents a learning cycle or spiral where the learner "touches all the bases", i.e. a cycle of experiencing, reflecting, thinking and acting. Immediate or concrete experiences lead to observations and reflections. These reflections are then assimilated into abstract concepts with implications for action, which the person can actively test and experiment with, which in turn enable the creation of new experiences.

The involvement of SME employees in learning activities means it remains challenging due to several obstacles. Employers and employees have different expectations, while the lack of managerial attention to the subject can lead to confusion among employees about the extent of company support.

Regarding the boundaries of the research, the research activity included the collection and the study of results of the two year (2009–2011) Leonardo Da Vinci Partnership project, financed by EU Lifelong Learning Programme and entitled "Evaluation and Recognition of Non-formal and Informal Learning"—EARN-FILE [18].

The partnership involved was composed by a network of research institutions and vocational training organizations to reach the goals established from different perspectives. The research team included the following partners:

- a private consultancy company that provides vocational training to SMEs in quality management systems and implementation of EU financed projects—"European Center for quality"—ECQ, Bulgaria;
- an university research center that studies and adopts innovative learning methodologies—Research Center on Information Systems of LUISS University—CeRSI, Italy;

- a private non-profit research center—MERIG, Austria;
- a private company that provides trainings, adult education and consultancy services related to career guidance—Roemeling Projectleiding—The Netherlands;
- a public non-profit organization—a department within the Ministry of Education of Belgium, French speaking community—CCG, Belgium [18].

Given the scope of the research and the investigation method chosen (interviews and multiple case study analysis), it was not easy to find suitable SMEs willing to participate in the study. More features of the sources has been identified by the adoption of a research strategy based also on the information available on web-sites and with the performing of an electronic survey.

First approaches to companies led to arrangements to talk to ten SMEs, five in the manufacturing sector and five in the services sector (business-to-business). The research team selected two for each partner Country from several business employing less than 50 people (50 % of SMEs interviewed in the project); and 50 or more but less than 250 people for a medium business (50 % of the remaining SMEs).

Many of the employers contacted initially, stated that they had no information on their employees' informal educational activities. After in-depth interview of each case following also the Yin methodology [19], the research team understood that there was a complex mosaic of learning issues in that SMEs. The research question was addressed by conducting an exploratory analysis of that SMEs situation and the cases analyzed provided a light, but well differentiated, picture of employer-supported formal training.

In total the project research group has done 125 phone calls and has sent about 250 emails: on average 125 phone calls have been made and 25 emails have been sent to each SME. The number of direct contacts needed, testifies the troubles faced in the identification of the exact person of reference and the delay in the return of a filled survey. In most cases the inertia of the process can be addressed to the set of steps necessary to directly interact with the head of the identified person.

The investigation had some important practical implications for the research team, as it furthers the understanding of how to maximize relationship performance in SMEs environments, thanks also to the adoption of online collaboration environments (CMS, emails, e-voting tools, etc.).

3 At the Designability Edge: Enabling Non-formal and Informal Learning

The initial results provide insight into the designable aspects of these organizations that would lead to non-formal and informal learning. These results also confirmed the importance for the organizations of the benefits of robust non-formal and informal learning processes. This motivation makes it difficult for an SME manager to oppose an employee's wish to improve his education, because there are too many obstacles which delay the participation of employees in education [20]. As any behavioral model, for Kolb's study nevertheless people clearly exhibit clear strong preferences for a given learning style. The ability to use or change frequently learning styles is not one that we should assume comes easily or naturally to many people. Simply, people who have a clear learning style preference, for whatever reason, will tend to learn more effectively if learning is orientated according to their preference. So how much informal learning is actually occurring in companies analyzed?

The project investigation highlighted the following aspects: uncertainty about the return on investments; time pressures; mismatch between training needs and training supply. In terms of the widely accepted "iceberg metaphor" of learning activities, only 20 % of learning activities are formal and 25 % non-formal, while 55 % of other learning activities are informal. Informal learning represents a largely overlooked dimension of learning activities in the workplace and enhancement of performance on the job [16].

The outcomes achieved also reveal that the difficulties in participation are often interconnected. These difficulties are opportunities for design-at-the-edge. Removing such limitations requires a detailed understanding of all factors, taken not only separately but also as a cluster of arguments that influence the enterprise's training policy or training culture. For instance, a lack of time, funds and other similar constraints might lead to a lack of interest in education for employees. According again to the study, part of the problems relating to SME involvement can be attributed to the different expectations of employers and employees towards lifelong learning. Both employers and employees seem to consider participation in informal education primarily as a way to strengthen knowledge, know-how and productivity and regard such education as goal-oriented. For employees, however, this view is complemented by a broader lifelong learning expectation particularly in terms of self-development as well as career enhancement. Because most of the SMEs involved in the study have a rather informal training policy, their managers risk becoming preoccupied with day-to-day concerns and failing to pay attention to learning and education, or becoming reluctant to acknowledge the need for it. Another risk is that, due to the lack of training measures, employees may no longer know what support to expect from the company or where to turn to with their specific learning demands. Although this project has its time limitations, it adds some new perspectives to current knowledge of the skills and training challenge within SMEs. The most remarkable perspective is that a lack of managerial attention has the additional effect of leaving employees not knowing what to expect in relation to training and showing an increasing lack of interest in the matter [20].

Organizational learning is mediated by several factors, both personal and environmental in nature. Everybody learns in accordance with their unique, individualized blend of personal and environmental factors. Few organizations have been able to pervade organization design expertise throughout their standard industrial processes because of the characteristics of emerging knowledge processes (process development, irregular user types and usage frameworks and spread skilled knowledge) [7].

Personal factors measured by the online questionnaires were initially some individual factors like motivation, interests and abilities which predispose an individual towards learning [21]. They are the following aspects:

- interaction aptitude;
- interests;
- readiness;
- experience;
- motivation;
- self-concept;
- attitudes;
- values;
- level of aspiration;
- learning style;
- workplace setting.

Environmental factors on the other hand, are those contextual factors which highlight the role of the environment in learning, such as the socio-emotional, social and cultural factors.

For the research, the team identified and formalized some environmental elements that can summarize the different contexts. These elements constitute the designable: principles available to an organizational system designer. These are examples of elements that lie at the edge of designability, aspects of the organization that can be designed in order to facilitate the evolution of organizational processes that cannot be designed. They can be classified into the following categories [18]:

- *existing resources* learning is really improved when needed resources are available. Making knowledge available to employees communicates management's commitment to and value of learning and knowledge;
- *incentives structure.* providing incentives for learning is one of the most important factors affecting informal learning in the workplace. Incentives reinforce the desired learning behaviors and greatly increase their occurrence;
- *promotion criteria and recognition.* the conditions by which organizations determine who gets promoted communicates to employees the importance of learning. Organizations that promote on the basis of merit reinforce the value of quality performance. Employees will try to learn and improve if their efforts are recognized;
- *financial incentives.* learning, that is economically remunerated, is appreciated and sought out by employees. Also providing incentives for learning communicates the value that the organization places on learning activities;

- *job security*. when employees feel their job is secure and the possibility of getting fired is low they may be unmotivated to expand their job scope. When job security is paired with reinforcement for job performance or career advancement, employees are motivated to learn, try new things and explore new opportunities. When job security is low, employees will attempt to perform their job in the best possible way avoiding any risks or standing out in the crowd in any way perceived as threatening;
- *management employee relationships*. relationships between management and employees affect the overall atmosphere in the workplace. Management usually wants employees to produce more and employees want higher wages. The extent of the tension between the two depends to a large extent on the mutual understanding and acceptance of each other's goals. The greater the overlap in the understanding and goals, the lesser the tension between the two. The alienation between the individual and the company creates an atmosphere where learning is perceived as contributing to the company and rather than to the individual;
- *size of organization*. the organization's size contributes to the sense of community level of understanding of one's place within the organization. In small organizations employees will know each other and this will increase the level to which they can ask each other questions and learn more from another;
- *working environment*. the physical characteristics of the working environment should ideally be of such quality that no offence is given to any of the five senses (well-being at work, noise, vibrations, lighting, air quality, work space). Louder noise for example may lead distraction. The concentration on the work at hand may be more or less hampered by the environmental noise. Conversely, extremely low levels of noise may also be experienced as irritating and thereby have an adverse effect on attention;
- *social control on work meetings*. learning originates from interaction through direct seminars in which people debate different things. The topics discussed between colleagues can be improved when there is someone who supervises the meeting;
- *learning culture*. to develop a learning organization is fundamental to consent a set of attitudes, principles and practices that allow the process of continuous learning within an organization. Through learning, individuals can re-interpret their world and their relationship to it. A true learning culture continuously challenges its own methods and ways of doing things. This ensures continuous improvement and the capacity to change. According to Senge [22] learning organizations are: "…organizations where people continually expand their capacity to create the results they truly desire, where new and expansive patterns of thinking are nurtured, where collective aspiration is set free, and where people are continually learning to see the whole together."

The learner and the learning process can only be completely understood with reference to the interaction of both environmental and personal factors.

4 At the Designability Edge: Evaluating Non-formal and Informal Learning

The initial results of this study imply certain significant future considerations for designing at the edge of non-formal and informal learning. Organizational learning addresses ways in which information processing affects the behavioral capacities of organizations [23]. Organizations also learn "vicariously" by picking up information from external sources, for example by adopting technical solutions practiced by competitors or advised by regulators. Frequent repetition of activities leads to acquisition of tacit knowledge. The literature has also discussed whether learning is incremental or radical. However, Miner and Mezias have argued that it is no longer an issue of concern and pointed that there is a consensus that learning can be both incremental and radical. Among the recent debates in the field was also the distinction between organizational learning and learning organization [23]: very close to SMEs context.

This post hoc, critical regard for non-formal and informal learning in organizations clarifies the way in which organizational system designers must also consider how to evaluate the outcomes of such undesignable processes. Such evaluation processes embody a different aspect of the designability edge. While designers may be unable to effectively design informal or irrational processes, they may be able to design evaluation mechanisms to identify expected or unpredicted outcomes from these processes.

For example, in the research case at hand, a first outcome regards if employees should use an accreditation process in order to get their newly acquired skills certificated so that they can take their achievements to provide evidence for formal qualifications or for entry to new programs of study. In the at-the-edge-design of such evaluation processes there are different methods to collect evidence of learning, skills or competences [18]. They can be divided into five categories:

- *examination* participants answer questions on a particular domain of study. They can focus on a domain or be interdisciplinary in nature. Questions can be open or closed (essay, multiple-choice). The evaluator can be a third party. Apart from the classical regular (written and or oral) examination (which can take various forms, from tests to essays), there are cases in which non-formal and informal learning are taken into consideration;
- *declarative* participants declare and justify that what they can do corresponds to particular parts of the curriculum taught in the education or training program for which they would like to obtain credit. A panel (third party) gives the final judgment. Once evidence is collected, it needs to be documented. Examples have been examined for non-formal and informal learning and have been classified into three categories: the check-up of competence; the portfolio and the certification of competences. The portfolio presents a synthesis of the personal, social and occupational experiences to highlight competences. It contains elements from the Curriculum Vitae, relevant information on the career,

education, training and other experience. A good portfolio is needed to showcase one's work and to help to demonstrate one's skills to prospective employers;

- *observation.* succeeding certain rules and strict methods, a third evaluator observes candidates and judges whether they have the competence described in a standard. Observation is a more demanding exercise than one can imagine. Methodology and training are required for the assessor to properly collect relevant and reliable observations. Direct observation of competences is used for the assessment in practical work situation. So, the observation of activities can take place in real work settings, or it can be based on past experience with the candidate or on a simulated work situation;
- *simulation* participants are placed in a context that presents all the characteristics of the real work (or other) situation and are then able to demonstrate their competences. Simulation requires a large amount of studies and job analysis to be prepared properly. Frequently decision is by a third evaluator. The major difficulty is the job analysis needed to support a simulation to be valid and reliable;
- *evidence extracted* founded on the descriptions of assessment standards, participants collect evidence of skills and competences in a real work situation.

These methods constitute a different kind of design principles for designing at the edge of non-formal and informal learning: evaluation elements rather than enabling elements. But such post hoc processes are complex. Because the informal processes themselves are unpredictable, any evaluation of the results should readily capture unexpected benefits (or costs) from the unique human behavior in the enabling context. In the case at hand, the research group noticed a certain degree of approximation and incompleteness of the information provided by the workers, but clearly understand that they need to be co-participants in learning, not simply receivers. In a recent study a researcher explained the training industry interest in informal learning [24] saying: "Training professionals are paying attention to informal learning because formal learning has run out of steam. Workers do not have time for the inefficiencies of old-style training. For years, we have talked about giving people what they need, when they need it. Internet makes it feasible to deliver on that promise. Learning often is distributed and includes both general expertise and local context knowledge."

The essence of many jobs is routine and doesn't offer any challenge to the employee. So it is important to give employees challenges, problems to solve, new activities in their existing job which challenge them to learn new skills and knowledge. Non-formal and informal learning creates interest and commitment of employees and leads to formal learning as well. Another idea is to give employees the opportunity to have their skills, knowledge and competencies recognized, initiate procedures for this, encourage employees to be involved in this, give support to the process and when finalized, reward employees appropriately (salary, job level, position); to allow employees to have access the required resources like time, opportunities, learning contents, learning vouchers, Internet access, etc.

Processes that evaluate the unexpected might, for example, account for the important role social media now plays in the learning and development of today's business professionals. Ignoring social media's informal learning influence is equal to ignoring the fact that a new generation of workers adept at and immersed in social media are beginning to flood the market. It is important to identify and evaluate the outcome of social media tools that are beneficial to enterprise and promote them as workplace-friendly learning resources. For example, if employees know that LinkedIn is considered a work-friendly workplace tool, but not MySpace or Facebook, they have guidelines for their informal learning choices. Some businesses especially those with heavy regulatory restrictions will choose to create internal collaboration and social media applications that allow for the rich networking and information-sharing abilities while minimizing security and confidentiality risks [25].

Designing evaluation at-the-edge of such informal learning must inevitably provide feedback for the design of enablement at-the-edge. When an evaluation captures important learning benefits from social media, an enabling design could align social media sites and tools with the organization's learning needs and guide employees to the resources that offer the most learning potential. Even the nature of the media used to circulate information can be used instrumentally when designing systems at-the-edge. For example, if e-mail is the main tool for time-consuming "official" communications in the organizations, learning opportunities through social media could be promoted using instant messaging.

5 Conclusions

Learning in organizations is important, but traditional models of training are often insufficient for continuous skills update and upgrade. Such training can be cumbersome and confine learners to prescribed and closed systems. It is nearly impossible to envisage in advance in each case who will take part in the process and which platform they will adopt. Organizations benefit from the perspective of informal and non-formal learning, because key organizational competencies are learned, updated and retained. But such informal processes can be unique to the individual and even partly irrational. It is the nature of the informal to defy prescriptive design.

Organizational systems designers confronted with the need to design the undesignable must operate by designing at the edges. In the example above, it may be impossible to design informal learning, but quite possible to design organizational elements that promote such learning and elements that capture the results from such learning.

In such a way, the designers design the before- and the after-edge of the informal processes.

For informal and non-formal organizational learning, the before-edge design elements could include tools such as instant messaging, e-learning support groups, expert communities, mentor and coaching networks, personal learning portals and moderated chats. Other design elements could promote an incentive structure of learning culture in the company by communicating to all employees in the organization that new ideas are highly valued and that each new idea shall be responded to, regardless of its worth to the organization. Innovative employees can be promoted when teams find a way to improve the information processes in an organization [25]. Employers can be open-minded and assure their employees that their door is always open for new suggestions and opinions. Organizational systems can be designed to improve transparency by implementing a better horizontal and vertical communication in management skills and especially by explaining career development opportunities [26].

The after-edge design elements could include many methods and a variety of techniques to collect evidence to provide a basis for judgments about whether learning (skills and competences) has been acquired [27]. Learning and knowledge support systems have to transform professional knowledge in actions for non-specialists; designers should assume to need many functional samples, instead of a few non-functional exemplars.

Understanding how organizational system designers can achieve design-at-the-edge is critical for developing and applying useful design principles for informal, but important processes in organizations. The research case described above demonstrated such usefulness in the context of designing informal and non-formal learning in SME organizations. It offers a first step in the direction of designing at the edge of informal organizational processes and thereby bringing an important set of design practices for a set of heretofore intractable organizational system design problems.

References

1. Feutrie, M. (2009). *Validation of non formal and informal learning in Europe: Comparative approaches, challenges and possibilities*. France: Université des Sciences et Technologies de Lille.
2. Livingstone, D. W. (1999). Exploring the icebergs of adult learning: Findings of the first canadian survey of informal learning practices. *Canadian Journal for the Study of Adult Education, 13*, 49–72.
3. Marsick, V. J., & Watkins, K. E. (2001). Informal and incidental learning. *New Directions for Adult and Continuing Education, 89*, 25–34.
4. Walton, R.E. (1985). Toward a strategy of eliciting employee commitment based on policies of mutuality. In R. E. Walton, & P. R. Lawrence (Eds.), *Human resource management: Trends and challenges*. Boston: Harvard Business School Press.
5. Marshall, G. (1994). *Concise Oxford dictionary of sociology*. England: Oxford University Press.
6. Agarwala, T. (2003). Innovative human resource practices and organizational commitment: An empirical investigation. *International Journal of Human Resource Management, 14*(2), 175–197.
7. Markus, M. L., Majchrzak, A., & Gasser, L. (2002). A design theory for systems that support emergent knowledge processes. *MIS Quarterly, 26*(3), 179–212.

8. Riding, R., & Rayner, S. (1998). *Cognitive styles and learning strategies*. London: David Fulton Publishers.
9. Kolb, D. A. (1984). *Experiential learning experience as a source of learning and development*. New Jersey: Prentice Hall.
10. Entwistle, N. J. (1997). Reconstituting approaches to learning: A response to Webb. *Higher Education, 33*, 212–218.
11. Biggs, J. B. (1979). Individual differences in study processes and the quality of learning outcome. *Higher Education, 8*, 381–394.
12. Keefe, J. W., Monk, J. S. (1986). Learning style profile examiners' manual. Reston. In *National Association of Secondary School Principals*. (pp. 291–300).
13. Baert, H. (2005). Lifelong learning in a changing working environment. In *Labour Market Research and Policy Making in Flanders, Conference Book* (pp. 195–224). Garant
14. Sargeant, A. (1996). Training for growth: How can education providers assist in the development of small businesses? *Industrial & Commercial Training, 28*(2), 3–9.
15. De Marco, M. (2004). *Le metodologie di sviluppo dei sistemi informativi*. Milan: Franco Angeli.
16. Vermeersch, L., De Rick, K. (2008). *SMEs and the participation of workers in formal learning*. Country report: Belgium, Lifelong Learning 2010 subproject 4, Leuven, HIVA, University of Leuven.
17. Casalino, N., D'Atri, A., Fadda, C. (2005). Organisational impact and exploitation of the results of an Italian research project for e-health and medical training. In *Proceedings of ECIS 2005—European Conference on Information Systems*, Regensburg, Germany.
18. EARNFILE project results (2009–2011). In Final report *Evaluation And Recognition of Non-formal and Informal Learning*, project number LLP-LDV-PA-09-IT-0276, Leonardo Da Vinci Partnership project, financed by EU Lifelong Learning Programme.
19. Yin, R. K. (2003). *Case study research: Design and methods*. London: Sage Publications.
20. Johnston, K., & Loader, K. (2003). Encouraging SME participation in training: Identifying practical approaches. *Journal of European Industrial Training, 27*(6), 273–280.
21. Overwien, B. (2000). Informal learning and the role of social movements. *International Review of Education, 46*(6), 621–640.
22. Senge, P. M. (1990). *The fifth discipline: The art and practice of the learning organization*. New York: Doubleday/Currency.
23. Miner, A., Mezias, S. (1996). Ugly duckling no more: Pasts and futures of organizational learning research. *Organization Science*, *7* (1), 88–99.
24. Cross, J. (2006). *Informal learning. Rediscovering the natural pathways that inspire innovation and performance*. San Francisco: Pfeiffer.
25. Baskerville, R., Lee, A. (1999). Distinctions among different types of generalizing in information systems research. In *New IT Technologies in Organizational Processes: Field Studies and Theoretical Reflections on the Future of Work*, New York: Kluwer Academic Publishers
26. Casalino, N., D'Atri, A., Manev, L. (2007). A quality management training system on ISO standards for enhancing competitiveness of SMEs. In J. Cardoso, J. Cordero, J. Filipe (Eds.), INSTICC, *Proceedings 9th International Conference on Enterprise Information Systems – ICEIS 2007* (pp. 229–235). Funchal, Madeira.
27. McLoughlin, C. (1999). The implications of the research literature on learning styles for the design of instructional material. *Australian Journal of Educational Technology, University of New England, 15*(3), 222–241.

Designing Innovative Learning Spaces in Higher Education at a Turning Point: Institutional Identities, Pervasive Smart Technologies and Organizational Learning

Chengzhi Peng

Abstract The provision of innovative learning spaces has become increasingly a critical mission to many higher education institutions around the world. This paper sets out testing an on-going research proposition that designing learning spaces in higher education is at a turning point, and it calls for a more open participatory system approach to better managing the tension arising from (a) the continuing trend of institutional quests for branding and re-branding distinctive visual identities to compete nationally and globally, (b) rising expectations of pervasive smart ICT provision, and (c) the need to sustain organizational learning from campus planning and design projects as the knowledge base for evaluating and envisioning innovative learning spaces. The paper reports and reflects on the findings from the design and deployment of a larger-scale Web-based 3D architectural and data visualization platform aimed at supporting collaborative modeling of present and future learning spaces in two real institutional contexts. A critical discussion of the prospect of the interactive 3D visualization platform for supporting organizational learning in designing innovative learning spaces is presented.

Keywords Interactive 3D architectural and urban modeling · Innovative learning spaces · Organizational learning · Context-sensitive data visualization · Organizational system design · Location sensing · Web3D

C. Peng (✉)
School of Architecture, University of Sheffield, Sheffield, UK
e-mail: c.peng@sheffield.ac.uk

R. Baskerville et al. (eds.), *Designing Organizational Systems*,
Lecture Notes in Information Systems and Organisation 1,
DOI: 10.1007/978-3-642-33371-2_12,

1 Introduction

The first decade of the twenty-first century has left the world with many legacies not encountered previously: ever increasing speed of globalization, the boom and bust of digital commerce, impacts of climate change on global security, global financial crises, the dramatic rise of mobile pervasive technologies, to name just a few. Some of these legacies have one way or the other induced profound effects on university education on a global scale. At the beginning of the second decade of twenty-first century, the United Kingdom in particular is an example showing how a nation's higher education sector is currently under unprecedented pressures and demands for change [1, 2]. Drawing on the UK scene, this paper aims to put forward a thesis that designing new learning spaces fit for the twenty-first century higher education is at a turning point, and it calls for a more open participatory system approach to addressing and managing the tension arising from (a) universities' continuing quests for branding or rebranding institutional identities to compete nationally and globally, (b) stakeholders' and users' rising expectations of pervasive smart ICT provision, and (c) the need for universities to engage organizational learning from on-going campus planning and design projects as the knowledge base for evaluating and envisioning innovative learning spaces.

To researchers working in the fields of architectural and educational design, the rationale underpinning the recent developments of new university campus, buildings and spaces need to be articulated in new concepts—they are now seen as examples of new *Learning Landscapes*, rather than new building or program types [3, 4]. Clearly, the rapid growths in the ICT industries and universal uptake of digital technologies have induced profound changes in how twenty-first century university students and teachers go about their learning and teaching. The current examples of new learning landscapes emerging from the UK higher education scene seems to suggest a paradigm shift in conceiving what was used to be called libraries: spatial informality (as in the practice of informal social learning), an emerging ICT ecology (blending of fixed physical and mobile virtual resources), inhabitation (24/7 open access and greater student-centered occupation and ownerships), inter-personal interactions (social networking and group working), service-oriented (more than provision of static information and learning contents), and spatial views (both interior and exterior views provided by the building and urban surrounding). As an example of this new trend of learning space design, Fig. 1 shows interior views of the Information Commons at the University of Sheffield which was opened in 2007 [5].

"Learning Landscapes in Higher Education", a project recently carried out by researchers at the University of Lincoln in collaboration with DEGW, a major international planning and design practice, has conducted a set of 12 case studies of new developments in teaching and learning spaces recently commissioned by the participating UK universities.[1] As seen from the case studies, the creation of

[1] http://learninglandscapes.lincoln.ac.uk/

Fig. 1 The information commons, University of Sheffield (*Source* University of Sheffield, Photographer: Andy Brown)

Fig. 2 Characterizing organizational learning in designing innovative learning spaces, adapted from Argote & Miron-Spektor (2011) with more specific constituents mapped out in Table 1

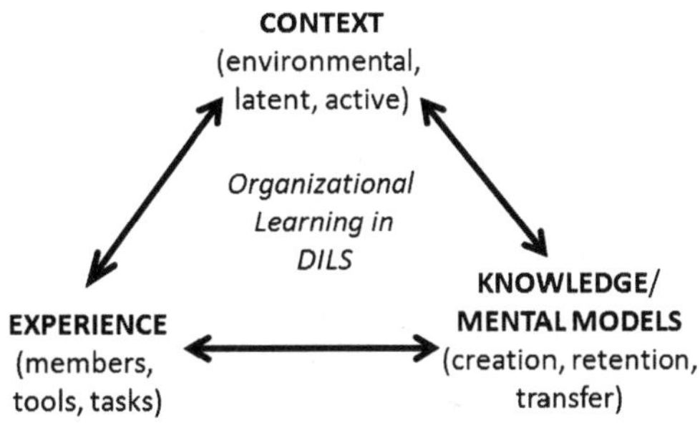

innovative or creative learning spaces has been embraced by the institutions as opportunities for strengthening or rebranding the institutions' reputations and visual identities. The Great Central Warehouse University Library at the University of Lincoln, for example, has clearly been defined to play the role of not only providing the state of the art library and learning spaces but also creating a new visual identity and brand for the Brayford Pool Campus due to the rapid expansion of the university [6]. Since the completion of the Learning Landscapes in Higher Education survey, there have been further new developments commissioned by various institutions such as the Gateway (Buckinghamshire New University), the Law & Management Building (University of York), and the Wolfson Centre for Medical Education (University of Birmingham), which are yet to be evaluated to reveal how they perform as landmark innovative learning and teaching spaces.

Previous UK JISC-funded studies have shown that the growing need of integrating information and communication technologies into the design of physical learning spaces has been more widely recognized and addressed through attempts at innovative designs [7, 8]. More recent dramatic rises in students' ownership of smart mobile devices (phones, tablets, and netbooks) have demanded the facility to connect to a university's wireless or cable networks anytime anywhere. In an age of pervasive computing in higher and further education, an institution's high-speed broadband Wi-Fi provision is no longer considered exceptional but norm.

However, as experienced by many, conventional or new learning spaces are not necessarily compatible with free uses of personal mobile devices for accessing digital learning materials and inevitably, social networks. As Poole and Wheal pointed out recently [9], “However, are learning centres culturally ready for mobile devices, even when they ring and are answered?”

None the less, the emerging practice of Learning Landscapes as driven by institutional aspirations and learners’ as well as educators’ needs is particularly interesting and challenging from an architectural research point of view. Boys, an architect, educator and Senior Research Fellow of Learning Spaces at the Centre for Excellence in Teaching and Learning through Design, has proposed a multi-perspectival framework for re-thinking the relationships between learning and spaces: architectural, educationalist, and estates planning [10]. How do we know that a learning space has been designed, built and inhabited to its intended purpose, i.e., a space for learning? Who is to judge the effectiveness of a learning space? And, perhaps more importantly, how do universities as institutional client bodies learn to define and deliver innovative learning spaces as a sustainable reality? Based on the earlier works by Lave and Wenger [11, 12], Boys draws our attention again to “communities of practice” as a model for conceptualizing learning space. She writes ([10], p. 73):

> It is a space that must enable motivation and develop involvement through an iterative and relatively systematically organised sequence of encounters, towards the absorption of a specific set of social and spatial practices.

Therefore, we have reasons to believe that designing innovative learning spaces fit for the twenty-first century higher education is at a turning point which calls for a more open participatory system approach to addressing the complex requirements of institutional identities, digital provision, and organizational learning. In short, there is an urgent need for organizational systems capable of facilitating universities as communities of practices to learn what innovative learning spaces are and how to make them perform as lived spaces valued by their users. A research proposition set out here is that the creation and social uses of a Web based 3D virtual campus modeling system could evolve into an institutional knowledge base for supporting organizational learning in designing innovative learning spaces (OL in DILS).

The remaining of the paper presents a case study of how such an organizational system could be developed in view of the outcomes from the weCAMP project funded by the UK JISC Institutional Innovation Programme.[2] The weCAMP project team have designed and implemented a bespoke Web-based 3D interactive campus visualization modeling platform called uCampus intended to effect wider participation and collaboration in planning and design of future learning spaces. In the next section, previous related research is summarized which informs our methodological approach. Before introducing the design of the uCampus system in

---

[2] http://www.jisc.ac.uk/whatwedo/programmes/institutionalinnovation.aspx

Sect. 4, a closer look into the requirements of organizational learning in the context of DILS is presented in Sect. 3 by consulting the theoretical frameworks put forward by some of the leading scholars in organizational learning. Section 5 gives an account of how stakeholders and users engagement throughout the project have been played out in testing and informing the usability of the campus modeling system including a pilot application of uCampus at another higher education institution. Drawing on the empirical studies of uCampus in real uses and the theoretical framework of OL in DILS, a generalization of how uCampus can be used to facilitate organizational learning is presented. Finally, in Sect. 6, the paper is rounded off with concluding remarks and pointers to further research.

2 Related Research

Among others, *The Oregon Experiment* was one of our key references in search for a methodological proposition. In the early 1970s, a team based at the Berkeley Center for Environmental Structure led by Christopher Alexander was commissioned by the University of Oregon to redesign the University's master planning system [13]. Instead of producing yet another campus master plan as a solution to the problems encountered by the various constituents of the university, Alexander's team developed and deployed a user-centered participatory planning and design framework which had a pattern language at its core. In the end, the Experiment stipulates six principles: *organic order, participation, piecemeal growth, patterns, diagnosis*, and *coordination*. Our revisiting this set of principles concludes that they are still highly relevant today from the perspective of institutional learning and innovation. For instance, the *Principle of Diagnosis* requires that "The well-being of the whole will be protected by an annual diagnosis which explains, in detail, which spaces are alive and which ones dead, at any given moment in the history of the community" [13, p. 6]. Given the radical changes in how UK universities will be funded from 2012 onwards, one would argue that the kind of recurrent diagnosis of spaces across a university campus could lead to significant efficiency savings as well as improved student experiences even if exact readings of dead or alive spaces are subject to local contexts. However, a genuine fulfillment of the diagnosis principle will demand a well-designed social-technical system such that annual diagnoses are properly carried out, recorded and made openly available to a university community as a whole.

All universities are constantly undertaking projects of new build or redevelopments. Yet, the question is if institutions are learning from projects over time as the basis for achieving innovation in planning and design. Retrospectively, what the Alexander's team did not have is the universal access to the digital world technology that most universities nowadays are well equipped with. Could the development and wider uses of a virtual campus modeling system as a shared spatial representation of the campus lead to an institutional learning process akin to the Oregon Experiment principles? Assuming that an institution is committed to grow the virtual campus modeling application over a sustained period of time, we could ask if the institution would ever need to invest on master planning every now and then, which has not really led to substantial institutional learning in the end? Could meaningful interactions of parts and whole of a campus environment be played out over time more transparently through university-wide uses of an easily accessible and usable virtual campus modeling system?

Another key conceptual framework for guiding our research and development was sought from the Meta-Design approach developed by Gerhard Fischer and co-workers [14]. They are interested in exploring how users of information systems or digital design environments could be enabled to continuously adapt the systems/environments once they have been created initially by the software developers. A particular approach to supporting the meta-design was formulated as the "SER" process model: *Seeding*, *Evolutionary Growth* and *Reseeding* [15]. Following SER, a seed is initially introduced as "a piece of knowledge, content, or code that can be fundamentally created, evolved and recombined by means of mechanisms that allow its sharing and modifications"; evolutionary growth occurs when users generate additional domain-specific information at use time which may not be well integrated with the existing system information or functionality contained in the seed; and reseeding is the phase where large-scale evolutionary changes occur in order to reorganize and formalize the information artifact resulting from the evolutionary growth. Clearly, the SER process model of meta-design is concerned with the development and use of social-technical systems where 'social creativity' cannot be anticipated and encapsulated completely in the initial production of the software. Indeed, open source software has been identified by Fischer as an exemplar of meta-design that allows for a more community approach to system development and evolutionary changes [16].

However, we consider that attempts at reseeding a 3D campus modeling system as an institutional application need not always involve large-scale changes but piece-meal extensions and/or enhancements open to institution-wide participation from academic and professional departments such as Computer Science, Landscape, Architecture, Estates, Computing and Learning Resources Services etc. The extent to which a 3D campus modeling system could be embedded in university's planning and decision-making processes ought to be in consultation with a wide range of stakeholders including architectural practices employed by the university. It could be suggested however that at least in theory a synthesis of the Oregon Experiment principles and the seeding-reseeding meta-design framework could lead to development of organizational information systems as social-technical resources to facilitate institutional learning in planning, design and management of innovative learning spaces.

On the 3D virtual world modeling front, we looked at a number of 3D virtual modeling projects applied to university campuses attempted recently. For instance, employing MultiGen-Paradigm's MultiGen and Vega, Alexei Sourin led a team to build a VRML-based model of the real campus of Nanyang Technological University (NTU) in Singapore [17]. Apart from being a university social media space, the NTU model has been used for research on crowd simulation and shared cyberspaces [18]. More, recently, as a part of the "City in the Palm of Your Hand" project,[3] the Liverpool University virtual campus model was tested on mobile devices [19]. For promoting the Lancaster University campus, an interactive 3D model has been developed by Arup Manchester in association with the university's Facilities Division. The Lancaster model is designed to be accessed through a Web browser installed with the TurnTool Viewer on a PC platform.[4] Meanwhile in Canada, 3D virtual photorealistic model of the Keele and Glendon Campuses of York University in Toronto was developed by the iCAMPUS project where an in-house 3D reconstruction software system was developed to derive photo-realistic 3D cityscapes from airborne LIDAR datasets [20, 21]. The Google Earth platform has attracted world-wide participation in the "Model Your Campus Contest", resulting in sixteen winning entries of university campuses in 2007 and 2008.[5]

Having seen the previous attempts at 3D university campus modeling, it seems reasonable to ask in an age of Google Earth (GE) and Second Life (SL): Why is it necessary to create yet another 3D virtual world modeling platform? Why can't we simply adopt GE/SL as the underlying platform to host a university campus models? One of the main reasons that we decided not to use GE/SL in this project was the issue of representation and visualization of the campus environment. Adopting existing 3D modeling platforms such as GE/SL means that we have to subscribe to the graphic conventions, rendering technologies and other usability decisions imposed by the existing platforms, which we and, more importantly, end users may not necessarily agree with. To use GE, for instance, one has to model with Google SketchUp[6] and comply with the rules specified in the uploading procedure which can take up to weeks' waiting for an administrative decision to accept or reject the 3D models to be displayed on the GE platform. We also find that 3D navigation on GE becomes very difficult, if not impossible, towards small scale spaces such as building interiors; GE is not designed for immersive viewing of intimate architectural interiors. Likewise, SL has a specific approach and design about the set of visual media features afforded by the virtual world platform that is complicated and difficult to remember for infrequent authors and visitors.

In the next section, leaving the precedents of technical systems aside, we will look more into the nature and requirements of fostering organizational learning in the thinking and making of innovative learning spaces, taking the institutional context of University of Sheffield as an example.

---

[3] http://www.liv.ac.uk/lsa/caadru/projects/city.html

[4] http://www.lancs.ac.uk/facilities/lancaster_university_3d/home.php

[5] http://sketchup.google.com/intl/en/competitions/index.html

[6] At the time of writing this, the home of SketchUp has changed from Google to Trimble; more details of this change are published on http://sketchupdate.blogspot.co.uk/2012/04/new-home-for-sketchup.html (accessed 25 May 2012).

3 Organizational Learning in Designing Innovative Learning Spaces

Like many other Higher Education institutions in the UK, The University of Sheffield (TUOS) has undergone an intense period of campus regeneration during the past 15 years. The University's Strategic Plan,[7] demands to take a holistic view of the student experience, facilitated by partnership working between the academic and service departments. The TUOS Learning and Teaching Strategy takes account of, and has informed, its Estates Strategy, and it is recognized that in order to achieve this, and to facilitate the development of innovative learning and teaching approaches, developments in the estates need to be included in its strategic planning. This was confirmed by a recent review of teaching spaces carried out in the University, which concluded that the University needs to increase the amount of flexible space it can provide for learning and teaching purposes. Although more and more new learning spaces have been designed, constructed and inhabited, there are several areas of research, development and practice need to be enhanced in order that the new learning space projects can really contribute to long-term sustainable institutional innovation.

Drawing on the specific context of TUOS, we have identified a number of areas where organizational learning is required in planning and design of future learning spaces which could also be of a common interest to the wider higher and further education communities:

- The capacity for interlinking an institution's Learning and Teaching Strategy with its Spatial Estate Strategy more transparently and effectively;
- The ability to better manage the creative tension between open participatory planning and design processes and financial-time constraints;
- An organizational knowledge base to ensure that new learning spaces are designed and built, and existing ones re-fitted, to meet the current and anticipated future needs;
- The capacity for maintaining accurate and up-to-date records of an institution's estates assets over time in a cost-effective way and to make them easily accessible as the institution's knowledge base for effective planning and design of future learning spaces;
- The ability to retain collective memory of learning space projects from inception, commissioning and evaluation such that the provision of learning and other related spaces as a whole will not evolve into isolated individualistic pieces but a holistic macro learning environment; and
- The need for senior managers and decision-makers to be well-informed of new trends and developments in the design of technology-rich learning spaces.

---

[7] http://www.shef.ac.uk/strategicplan

According to Argyris and Schön, two pioneering scholars of organizational learning since 1970s, learning takes place only when new knowledge is translated into visibly changed pattern of behavior that is replicable [22, 23, 24]. In one of his classic expositions, March pointed out that organizational learning takes place at two levels competing for resources allocation: the exploration of new possibilities and the exploitation of old certainties [25]. Adopting an action-theoretical perspective on the nature of organizational learning, Daniel H. Kim defined learning as "increasing one's capacity to take effective actions" and that "Organizational learning is more complex and dynamic than a mere magnification of individual learning" [26, p. 34]. In Kim's view, the link between individual and organizational learning is the transfer mechanism brought about by members' making explicit and sharing individuals' mental models of the things they do. Kim argued that "each mental model is a clustering or an aggregation of data that prescribes a viewpoint or a course of action" and that "mental models are where a vast majority of an organization's knowledge (both know-how and know-why) lies" [26, pp. 41–42]. Following Kim's proposal, it is crucial for an organization to engage learning through cultivating and maintaining a common language and toolset for its members to make explicit and share their mental models over time.

More recently, Linda Argote and Ella Miron-Spektor proposed a theoretical framework for analyzing organizational learning which can be characterized by examining the interaction between task performance experience and environmental, organizational and active context in terms of three sub-processes: creating, retaining, and transferring knowledge [27]. If one considers also the tacit dimension of knowledge as expounded by Polanyi [28], there seems to be an extent of overlap between knowledge and mental models as the terms used here for analyzing organizational learning. The field of organizational learning research is vast and under active development in the age of Digital World; it is beyond the scope of this paper to arrive at a rigorous survey of the current consensus regarding what constitutes organizational learning and how it might be analyzed and measured. However, restricting to the area of planning and design of learning spaces in higher education, we could apply some of the key concepts as introduced above to map out a working definition of organizational learning in DILS (Fig. 2 and Table 1).

The above framework, adapted mainly from Argote & Miron-Spektor (2011), is not meant to be prescriptive but probable in trying out a systematic study into the complex interaction between Experience and Context associated with the business of designing innovative learning spaces. A further elaboration of the Members subsection is drawn out in Table 2 using the TUOS context as an example. However, the collection of specific constituents mapped out for Knowledge (or, Mental Models) is particularly useful in highlighting problematic scenarios where the dynamisms, distributed and transient nature, varying durations, languages and tools affect how knowledge is created, retained and transferred. For instance, are there any known schemes of mental models that we could attribute to social communication of shared meanings of innovative learning spaces when the discourse is about some real buildings or proposed designs?

Table 1 Mapping specific elements of context, experinece and knowledge of organizational learning in desiging innovative learning spaces based on the digram in Fig. 2

Context	*Environmental context*: national higher education funding council; local government development framework including local city planning and building codes; External professional services agreements (architects, engineering consultants, surveyors, project management, building construction contractors, furniture equipment suppliers, etc.); National/international heritage conservation organizations; International/national green building directives or certification schemes;
	Latent organizational context: The institution's internal/national standing and educational ethos; Shared vision statements and propositions; Academic strategies; Estates strategies; Community relations and social responsibilities; Health, safety and security directives; Greening campus initiatives;
	Active context: Faculties and academic departments; Profession services (Finances, Estates, Computing, Library, Teaching & Learning, Students' Services etc.); Students' Union;
Experience	*Members*: Senior management group, Project specific internal task and focus user groups; Appointed external professional teams; Local government authorities;
	Tools: Project management protocols; Planning and design decision-making; City data and information portals; Institutional databases/archives; Consultation and communication;
	Tasks: Project briefs formulation; Selection and appointment of external professional services; Design proposals generation, consultation and iteration; Planning permission application;
Knowledge/mental models	*Creation*: Stakeholder and user requirements understanding; Project briefs and programs; Design responses to the constraints presented by the environmental, organizational and active contexts; Stakeholders and users responses to the design proposals presented by the design teams; New procedures in project management, consultation, communication; Creativity in sustaining interaction between the constituents of Context and Experience;
	Retention: Project documents, Design drawings/models, Records of project meetings; Members' email/phone messages; Members' explicit/implicit memories; Procedural forms or guides; Written articles about the projects undertaken;
	Transfer: Flow of memberships among the various layers of Context; Reuse of conceptual, pictorial, procedural or simulation devices/frameworks across project or institutional boundaries;

During our preliminary consultation exercise for setting out the weCAMP project, we found that most representative users appeared in favor of 3D modeling of the campus environment as it supports intuitive understanding of spaces by a wider population of the community without special skills of reading and interpreting 2D technical drawings as representation of the university's learning spaces. This was then recognized as one of the main objectives to facilitate widening participation and collaboration in the design decision-making processes as well as in recording lessons learned from campus development projects. As such, a number of more specific questions regarding 3D modeling arose from the initial survey:

1. How can we model a university campus as a common 3D visual reference easily accessible to a wide cross section of stakeholders and end users in knowing more about the campus and its surrounding environments?
2. Can we build 3D campus models useful not only to the Estates Department's facility management team but also to other user groups such as professional architectural practices or architectural students when developing their design projects on campus sites?
3. Can Web-based 3D virtual campus models be linked with social media as a means for expressing, gathering and sorting public opinions and comments on particular learning spaces on campus?

By conjoining our observation of what is required of organizational learning and consideration of potential usefulness of 3D interactive virtual modeling, we have formulated the following proposition of designing interactive 3D virtual campus as the core of an organizational learning system:

- Most universities in the European tradition are deeply rooted in the city fabrics where they were founded and therefore 3D university campus modelling is not dissimilar to 3D modelling of real cities;
- 3D digital or analogical representation of buildings and spaces are more accessible to viewers/users who have not been trained to interpret 2D architectural (technical) drawings to arrive overall spatial understanding;
- The architectural professions worldwide are changing their workflow from 2D drawing/drafting based to 3D modelling based in response to the demand of achieving a higher level of efficiency; and
- Proprietary or open-source 3D graphics now provides facilities to construct 3D models as "information holders," allowing value-added pre- and/or post-processing to take place and to deliver data or information-rich virtual models, offering not only 3D graphic scenes but also valuable mark-up datasets and information links.

In response to the above system design proposition, a number of practical steps were taken in developing a bespoke 3D university campus modeling platform: (a) use of open source Web friendly data standards, (b) use of a variety of 3D modeling tools in generating source models, (c) supporting rapid acceptance of user-generated content, (d) extensibility of interactive domain-specific data visualization, and (e) simple yet memorable user experiences of 3D navigation at varying scales of virtual landscapes from walking through a large section of the campus to looking around a seminar room. We have since opted for Java and XML-based technologies to build and test a Web-enabled 3D campus modeling platform which are explained in Sects. 4 and 5.

4 Design of a Web-Based 3D Campus Modeling System

It was clear that in order to satisfy all requirements the application needed to be Web-based with both a client and server side implementation. The salient factors influencing the choice of platform proved to be interoperability, concurrency, a unified development language and scalability. It was envisaged that there may be several hundred users at a time, so scalability through concurrency was particularly important. For these reasons, the Java Enterprise Edition (Java EE)[8] environment seemed the best fit. It's Servlet based architecture would provide the concurrency that was required and the software development work at present and in the future would benefit from both the client and server sides being developed in a common language with the potential for the use of a common source-code base and shared libraries [29]. A three-tiered system architecture was devised to guide the subsequent design and implementation of uCampus (Fig. 3).

Web Front End (Presentation Tier). The Front-End tier is for supporting user interaction and navigation. System components produced on this tier are mainly to deliver graphical user interface with which the users can navigate and interact with a range of Web-based contents. On this presentation tier, the user interface has been designed to be superficially simple but also facilitate more complex 'use cases' posed by the more advanced users of the platform. Since the project is about 3D visualization, maximizing the rendering space available to users is paramount and it is important that the data retrieval tools provided don't overly impinge upon the visual client space. An important aspect of the user interface is that 3D models can be retrieved using either a visual 2D interactive map representation of the data or through layered selectable items. Regardless of which method is preferred by the user, both methods are mutually consistent, equivalent and synchronized to each other so that a change in state is immediately reflected throughout the application.

Users can register a username and password to their own private account to which they can then upload their own models. These can be shared and discussed with other members of their working group or subsequently 'published' to a public area, making them visible to everyone. The Interactive map is the main point of visual reference and the aim is to make this very user friendly as the system progresses. The uCampus map is the main interface to the platform, hosting a primary piece of data content (Fig. 4). This is the first visual artifact that users see when launching uCampus and is the means by which they can visualize the area covered by the system and then go on to interact with it. Therefore, while designing the map interface it was crucial to keep in mind user friendliness and clarity in illustration. The uCampus interactive map was initially drawn in Adobe Illustrator and then exported as the Scalable Vector Graphic (SVG) format to be overlaid on top of a GIF image depicting the larger urban region. Our experience shows that the SVG engine provided by the SVG Salamender Project was

[8] http://www.oracle.com/technetwork/java/javaee/overview/index.html

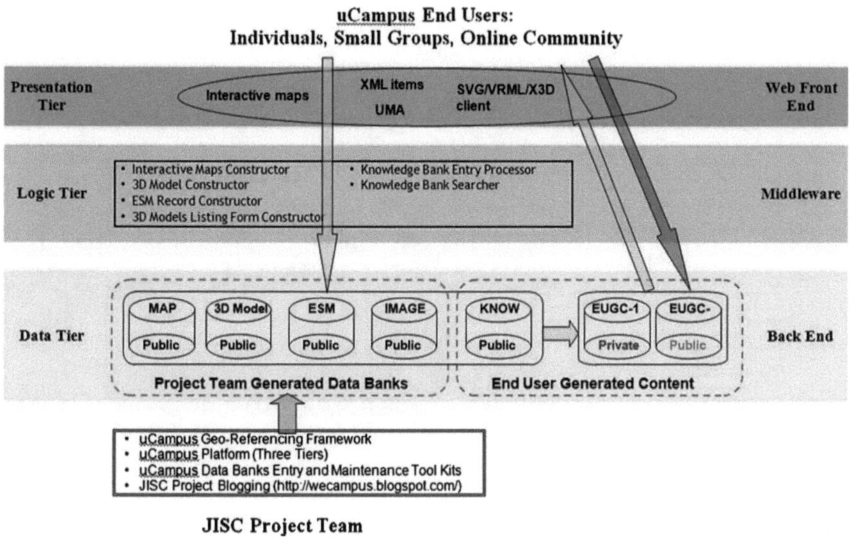

Fig. 3 Three-tiered system architecture as a blue print for the design and implementation of the uCampus platform

particularly suited to drive uCampus's small size interactive map.[9] The uCampus map covers the central area of the University of Sheffield campus. A 3D DWG model of city landscape and building surfaces was initially acquired from Zmapping Ltd to serve as a base model for extensive 3D editing. This area is then divided into terrain squares pertaining to the UK Ordinance Survey national grid naming system with each square covers an area of 100 by 100 m. These grid squares also represent the geographic terrain respective to the area which is selectable through the uCampus interactive SVG map.

Middleware (Logic Tier). The Middle tier is for creating dynamic Web contents constructors. The middle tier is the place to develop a pool of intelligent software components to construct a variety of dynamic Web-based contents in response to user requests submitted over the Web. Multiple clients connect to the server through our Presentation tier which is implemented using Java Servlets [30]. These provide the front end interfaces to the client for services such as model retrieval, upload and user account management. They manage requests and responses to and from the Logic tier. The middleware tier contains the application service logic for managing model retrieval, manipulation and storage. It also contains modules for 3D model on-demand assembly and user account management.

Back End (Data Tier). The Back-End tier is for depositing campus data resources. The 3D models and their associated data and metadata are retrieved from the Data tier. XML is used for metadata and the Data tier manages the

9 http://svgsalamander.java.net/

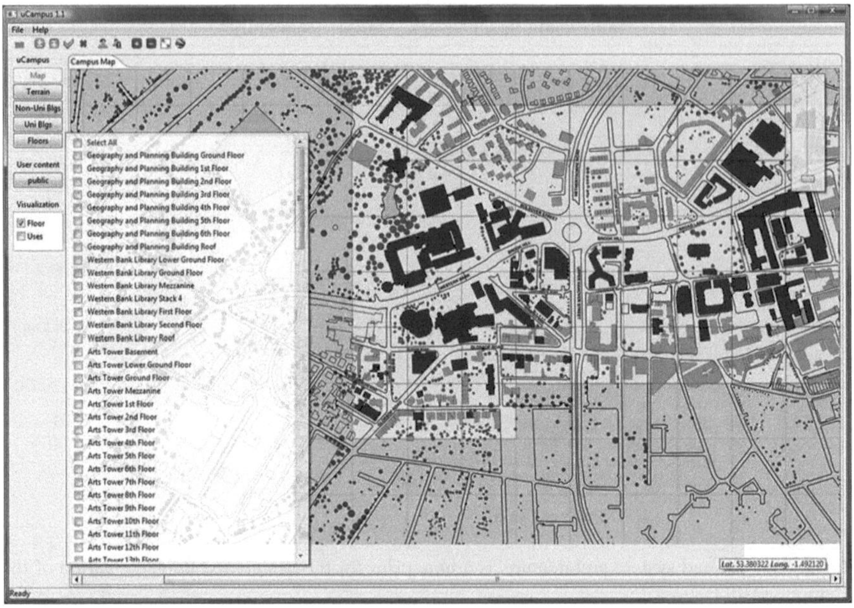

Fig. 4 The user interface of uCampus 1.1 featuring menu and SVG-based retrieval of X3D content

manipulation, instancing and retrieval of these objects using SAX and DOM parsers where appropriate. The interface reflects the internal organisation of the model data sets. A distinction is drawn between project generated (uCampus) models and models that can be submitted by users as part of a larger community.

The development of 3D University building models was undertaken in two phases. The first was a less detailed phase, which allowed us to populate the entire uCampus area, creating an initial prototype for demonstrations, and progressing with other areas of the project that were dependent on the building modeling method. From early on, a decision was made to adopt the latest X3D (eXtensible 3D Graphics [31]) open standards file format in the production of all uCampus models (Figure 3). The second phase was for more detailed modeling of the university buildings which were constructed from the drawings provided by the University's Estates Department. The detailed modeling of major university buildings generated a significant volume of workload, which called for participation from the postgraduate students at the School of Architecture to work on the project as extra 3D modelers.

Following the X3D model data standard, an important design for the Data Tier is the uCampus 3D Estates and Data Modeling Specifications (3D-EDMS) which are essentially the knowledge bases of how the 3D virtual models created in the X3D open standard could be a shared representation of the campus environment including its spatial taxonomy. Just like the Presentation and Service tiers, the uCampus 3D-EDMS can be adapted by other institutions to create their own X3D model and data content to be maintained on their own campus modeling visualization applications.

A number of exemplar models, covering the basic building typologies, were developed by the project team, which was then standardized into a number of technical specification documents which, in combination with a number of workshops, allowed the students to contribute to 3D building modeling effectively. All 3D models submitted by the student participants were checked and corrected according to the specifications before being entered into the system. In order for the platform to communicate with the data sets, a data-feed structure had to be set. The chosen format for the data-feed structure was XML due to its usability and adaptability, as well as its compatibility and similarity in design philosophy to X3D [32]. On the basis of the three-tiered architecture and the specification of content development, we have further experimented with 3D visualization modeling operations afforded by uCampus to be accessible to a wide range of stakeholders and end users with relative ease and flexibility:

(a) Contextual Architectural Modeling. This is a straightforward operation for users to perform on the uCampus interactive map and/or the left-hand content dropdown menu showing the model sets under categories such as Terrain, Buildings, and Floors etc. With the selection tools, users specify an area of interest and/or specific model entries and submit the request. A 3D contextual campus model is then assembled and delivered to the users in real-time for immersive 3D viewing. All contextual models are built by the weCAMP team in accordance with the initial 3D CAD master model and the 2D architectural drawings provide by the university's Estates Department. Here an existing university building is represented as, firstly an overall 3D volumetric mass, and, secondly, more detailed constituent open-top building floors and roof with footprints of interior partitions added for each floor. The intention was to provide enough architectural details for high legibility of the virtual models without resorting to full-blown photorealism (Fig. 5).

(b) Domain-Specific Data Visualization Modeling. Creating 3D visualisation for the University's space usage was seen as a continuation of the detailed building modelling process; it however involved developing a separate methodology from the aforementioned contextual architectural modelling, which we named Spatial Taxonomical Modelling (STM). Based on the datasets provided by the Estates Department, the basic categories of room uses were established and colour-coded, for instance, blue to indicate rooms used as academic offices. The specification for making the colour-coded volumes to build up the STM datasets was simple to follow, and required only basic 3D modelling skills (Fig. 4). To covey the University's current spatial usages more efficiently, we simplify the entire range of spaces into six basic categories: Teaching, Learning Support, Offices, Shops & Leisure, User Support and Building Services. The colour assigned to each space category and sub-category as currently implemented on uCampus is entirely arbitrary which is subject to further reviews.

(c) Overlay of (a) and (b). If users retrieve instances from both *(a)* and *(b)* as described above, the results will be overlaying of data visualization models and

Fig. 5 An assembly of (official) uCampus models built in X3D

contextual architectural models (Fig. 6). We believe such an overlay facility will significantly increase the accessibility and readability of abstract datasets even they are in visual form.

5 Prospect of uCampus as an Organizational System for Learning in DILS

Since its inception, the weCAMP-uCampus project has taken the form of institution-wide inter-departmental collaboration. A Project Board chaired by the Pro-Vice-Chancellor for Learning and Teaching was convened at the beginning with board members drawn from various departments including Estates, Learning and Teaching Services, Corporate Information and Computing Services, and the Library. Regular meetings between the Project Board and the Project Team were held to review progress and to steer emerging issues of the software and content developments. User engagement and evaluation activities were rolled out to coincide with stages of software implementation and content development. This institution-wide collaboration has proved highly effective in delivering project outcomes far beyond originally anticipated [33]. By the project end time, there have been three major releases of uCampus and rapid deployment of 3D models covering 48 + hectares of the campus terrain, 38 clusters of Non-university buildings, 71 University buildings, 124 detailed University building floors, and 79 case studies of spatial usage of selected University building floors, which we believe has delivered a solid foundation for future growth. The research has also tested the capabilities of the X3D open data standards and the 3rd-party X3D browsing technologies in delivering high-quality 3D visualization modeling and

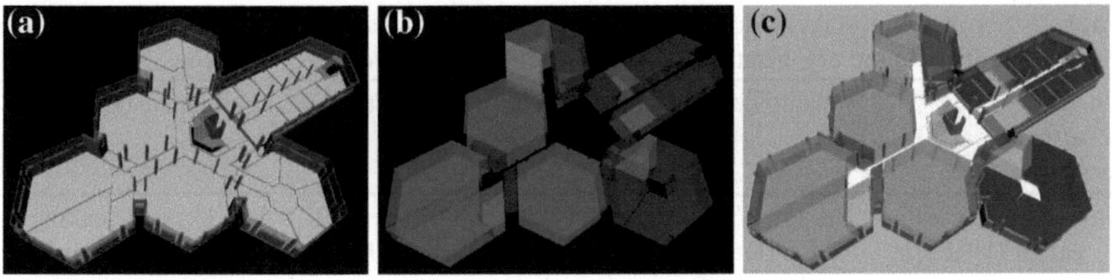

Fig. 6 An example of combining a contextual architectural model with a spatial taxonomical model freely controllable by end-users on-demand. **a** A 3D building floor as an architectural context, **b** A colour-coded spatial taxonomy model of the building floor indicating its usage, **c** Overlay of **a** and **b**

rendering no less than those provided by proprietary high-end 3D CAD packages. The following key figures extracted from the uCampus server indicate the extent of usage in the past 2 years (as accessed on 31 July 2012):

- Number of X3D models built by the we-CAMP project team: 673 (74.4 MB)
- Number of end-user accounts registered on uCampus: 94
- Number of X3D models uploaded by users to uCampus: 2,817 (785 MB)

Given that no high-profile campus-wide promotion of uCampus was ever launched, we consider the above figures a positive result in terms of its usage since its public release. As only active users are likely to register private user accounts, the actual usage should be of a higher reading if casual accesses were tracked and included. Clearly, more stakeholder and user engagement is needed to kick-start a more vibrant uCampus user community.

Table 2 show a summary of the scope of stakeholder and user engagement rolled out during the uCampus development time and how sustainability may be achieved post project funding.

5.1 Applying uCampus to the Augustine House Experiment

Through a separate funding awarded by the JISC Institutional Innovation Benefits Realisation Programme, the Augustine House Experiment (AHE) project was later undertaken by the uCampus team in collaboration with the iBorrow project team based at the Canterbury Christ Church University [34]. The AHE project aims to produce a synthesis of the outcomes from the weCAMP and iBorrow projects to further demonstrate how patterns of spatial uses in a technology-rich learning center could be captured and better understood. An important part of the iBorrow

Table 2 Scope of the stakeholder and user engagment with uCampus development representing the key members in the organizational learning in DILS framework set out in Fig. 2 and Table 1

University departments and services	Stakeholder/user engagement	Post project funding sustainability
University Executive Board (UEB)	The Pro-Vice-Chancellor for Learning and Teaching will chair the Project Board throughout the project life-time. The PVC will represent the project on UEB	The UEB is the decision making body responsible for all major institutional projects. The "Learning Hub" project will form the basis of good practice and link to the UEB
Department of Estates (DoE)	The Head and the Space & Strategy Manager are on the Project Board representing Estates' needs; the IT Manager is on the Project Team to advise on accessing the digital datasets maintained at the Estates	uCampus will be embedded in DoE's services as a modeling platform in the development of the University's Estates Strategy and in collaborating with internal/external practices on planning/design of future learning and other spaces
Corporate Information and Computing Services (CiCS)	The Assistant Director (Customer Services) is on the Project Board contributing to design of ICT-rich learning spaces; the Assistant Director (Technical Services) is on the Project Team to advise on implementation of uCampus on the University's ICT networks	CiCS will continue to provide the ICT infrastructure for the daily running of uCampus. Contribution to the development of Technology-Rich Learning Spaces as organizational knowledge and memory will also continue
Learning and Teaching Services (LeTS)	The Director and Deputy Director are on the Project Board to review progress on achieving more effective interaction between Academic Strategy and Estates Strategy through uCampus	LeTS will continue to advise uCampus' further development in relation to their work on the University's Learning and Teaching Strategy, and specific projects
The University Library	The Assistant Director is on the Project Board representing the library to contribute to the development of the Knowledge Bank concerning pedagogically informed planning of future learning spaces	uCampus will be used by the Library Service in connection with the restoration of the Western Bank Library. The Library will continue to contribute to the planning and design of new learning spaces
Students' Union	The Education Officer is on the Project Board representing Union's needs who will also help to recruit students across the University to take part in user evaluation	The Union will continue to promote public awareness of the uCampus resources among current and prospective students as a virtual forum to feedback their experiences of the campus spaces

(continued)

Table 2 (continued)

University departments and services	Stakeholder/user engagement	Post project funding sustainability
School of Architecture (SoA)	A Senior Lecturer is the Project Director. A Professor in Sustainable Architecture is on the Project Board to advise on sustainable campus design as part of the Knowledge Bank development	uCampus as open-source software will be maintained by SoA with contributions from other academic departments such as Landscape and Computer Science. uCampus will be used by staff and students at various departments as teaching, learning and research resources
Bureau of Design Research (BDR)[10]	The Director is on the Project Board representing the view of a University-Based Design Consultancy. Two Associate Directors are on the Project Team to act as the Lead Usability Evaluator and the Project Manager	BDR have been working closely with DoE on several campus projects including the current re-fit of the Arts Tower. Design consultants will continue to advise on all new build and refurbishment projects

project was concerned with how the Augustine House performed as the University's brand new learning center, which was awarded the UCISA[11] Higher Education Award for Excellence 2010. The iBorrow project provided a large-scale demonstrator of the use of tracking software and location-aware technology to aid the configuration of facilities within flexible learning spaces, and eventually an insight into the way students use flexible learning spaces. By overlaying location information with additional data it can provide insights into the way students use digital resources at an individual level or within a group context and thus answer the questions that arise when designing new learning spaces. On the basis of uCampus, our method of visualising the iBorrow dataset can be summarised in the following steps.

5.2 *Architectural and Urban Context Visualisation of the Augustine House*

An aerial-photo derived 3D urban model with the Augustine House at the center was used as the urban context of creating 3D models in the X3D format. A user

[10] BDR is a multidisciplinary design consultancy based in the School of Architecture at the University of Sheffield, specializing in sustainable school building and landscape projects through innovative participative processes.

[11] Universities and Colleges Information Systems Association, http://www.ucisa.ac.uk/

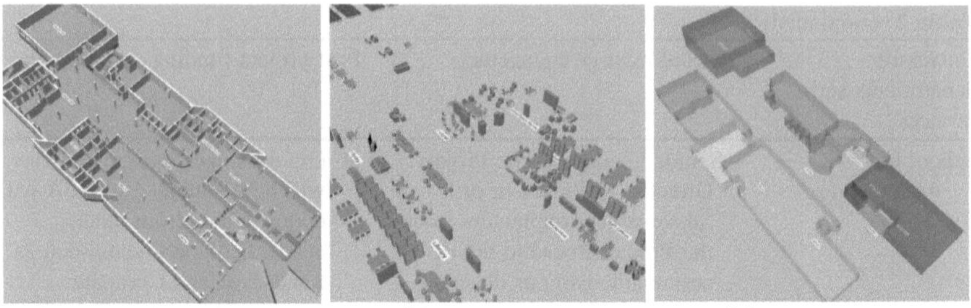

(a) architectural floor layer (b) furniture layer (c) spaces layer

Fig. 7 Architectural visualization of the Augustine House (Ground Floor) (**a**) Architectural floor layer, **b** Furniture layer, (**c**) Spaces layer

account "AUGUSTINE" was registered on uCampus to host all the X3D models produced at this stage. For each floor of the Augustine House, three X3D models were built to represent (a) architectural floor, (b) furniture, and (c) spaces (Fig. 7). Through the uCampus user interface, these models can be freely combined to construct rich architectural contexts for displaying data models with reference to the AH floors.

6 3D Visualization of the iBorrow Location Sensing Data

A bespoke software tool "xml2x3d" was developed to convert the iBorrow datasets into X3D models with location reference to the architectural floors modeled previously. Each tracked position is represented as a colored geo-referenced sphere positioned 50 cm above each floor. Various schemes of data visualization were devised to work with different combinations of data fields such as Male–Female, Times of a Day, PG-UG level of study, Full-Part Time etc. Due to software development limit, generating the iBorrow X3D data models remains a combined software and manual process: XML files need to be manually created according to a specific format as inputs to the xml conversion tool. Meaningful viewpoints of the resultant X3D iBorrow data models are inserted manually before uploading onto the uCampus accounts.

6.1 Overlay of the iBorrow Data Models on to the 3D Augustine House Floor Models

We use the user account facility provided on uCampus to set up a number of accounts for uploading the X3D models created in the previous stages into different user content folders. Overlaying iBorrow tracking data models on the AH

Fig. 8 An example of navigating an iBorrow datascape with the BS Contact VRML/X3D viewer

floor models into final 3D iBorrow datascapes can be performed simply by selecting relevant data and floor models from the lists established in the hosting accounts. A user can navigate an iBorrow datascape freely at any viewing position with a web browser that has an X3D viewer plug-in installed (Fig. 8).

6.2 Further Presentation of the AHE Datascapes on Web Browsers

On the basis of the 3D modeling approach described above and the uCampus platform, it is relatively straightforward to construct a website that lists the Augustine House Experiment results according to the selected data fields, for instance, "Female-Male, 01/03/2010, Ground Floor" or "Disable-Able, 01/03/2010, 2nd Floor." The current AHE website contains links to 33 pre-assembled X3D models in 8 different groups of data fields.[12] For each X3D data model, a set of color-coded keys is provided to aid user reading of the relevant user information and location sampling time. This further presentation enables end-user direct access to the AHE data visualization models without installing and logging into the uCampus accounts. Although, there were several technological limitations experienced through the AHE project, we found that inspections of the iBorrow datascapes can contribute to the discussion in a way that is helped by a strong grasp of large complex datasets. The synthesis of location sensing and context-rich

[12] http://www.wecamp.group.shef.ac.uk/AHE/

data visualization as piloted in this experiment can be developed into a creditable research apparatus with which we could probe deeper into the emerging learning landscapes to inform design of future learning spaces.

6.3 How Can uCampus be Used to Generate Organizational Learning?

The empirical studies of the Sheffield University Campus Experiment and the Augustine House Experiment as reported above can be seen as initial tests of uCampus as a potential platform for enabling organizational learning in design innovative learning spaces. Relating the uCampus-TUOS and uCampus-AHE experiment outcomes to the theoretical frameworks discussed in Sect. 3, a generalization regarding how organizational learning in designing innovative learning spaces may be facilitated by uCampus is summarized in Fig. 9. Here an interaction takes place whenever members attempt at fitting new or revised design proposals into the three layers of context. Interactions generate organizational learning if they initiate the sequence of data collection, data interpretation/visualization, creation, retention or transfer of knowledge, and action taken leading to visibly changed but replicable pattern of behavior. Within the context of DILS, such visible changes of pattern of behavior include shifts in planning and design thinking (shared mental models of experiencing innovative learning spaces), revised campus pattern language (assuming that an institution has developed a pattern language similar to the Oregon Experiment [13]), new procedures of evaluating and judging design proposals, improved interlinking between academic and estates strategies, identification of new external professional service providers or educational technology suppliers, new schemes for enhancing an institution's visual identities, new modes of operating learning spaces and facilities, to name but a few.

The visual language and modeling tools developed as an integral part of the system is essential for the layers of context to be represented in such a way that it can be interacted with tasks performed by various organizational members. The language and tools can also be conducive to resolving individual mental models into shared ones through context-sensitive domain-specific data visualization modeling. uCampus can also play a role in knowledge management not as a centralized institutional repository but as virtual hub offering mechanisms for members to link existent or new pieces/chunks of knowledge to the 3D virtual campus models, no matter where and when the knowledge is created, retained or transferred (Table 1). Some distinctive organizational learning outcomes could in turn redefine the existing layers of context as well as inform/enrich future task performance experiences.

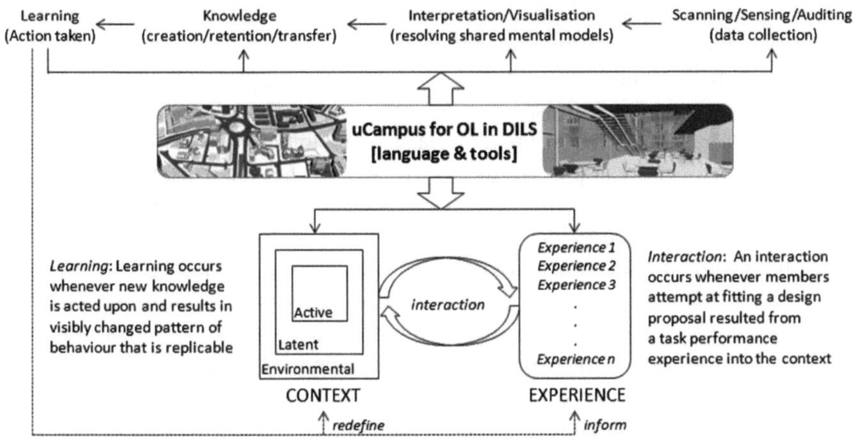

Fig. 9 uCampus as a platform for organizational learning in designing innovative learning spaces (DILS)

7 Conclusion and Further Research

The provision of new learning spaces on a university campus is a physical manifestation of a complex organization. As shown through the weCAMP-uCampus and AHE projects, the 3D digital spatial and data modeling processes required to achieve information-rich virtual campus models is not dissimilar to modeling a small city. The research projects reported above have presented us opportunities to explore how an interactive 3D virtual campus modeling platform could be built with Web-based open source technologies as an experimental organizational system. Given the constraint of a relatively short period of design time, why did not we just use Google Earth and Street View instead? We have demonstrated that uCampus offers both interior spaces and exterior features of buildings and information on how individual spaces are used on a building floor basis, allowing different perspectives to be gained and explored in desktop/laptop immersive 3D virtual worlds. The accuracy of the uCampus 3D campus context models allows them to be used for a variety of purposes such as domain-specific data visualization. Users can upload 3D architectural and data models in real time and decide whether their models should be in private or public domain.

Working with two university campuses as real user/stakeholder contexts, we tested the methodology of combining rapid software and content development with user engagement in iterations. One of the key features achieved in uCampus is free juxtaposition of 3D spaces in rooms (at the micro-scale), between buildings (meso-scale), and among different parts of the university (at the macro-scale). This varying scale of applications enables visualizations modeling to be performed by users across the entire campus or just a single building floor. Another feature of overlaying 3D data visualization on architectural floors and masses has been extensively applied to visualizing the spatial uses of building floors in the Sheffield campus context and the spatial–temporal locations of the iBorrow netbooks in the Augustine House context. In both applications, 3D architectural representations of the campus real estates are intended as contextual support for intuitive understanding of complex domain-specific datasets.

The uCampus platform has proved robust, adaptable and extensible. It has been deployed across the campus by the University of Sheffield Managed Desktop Service and is publically available on the Web. The concepts of the platform were well received by a wide range of stakeholders and users, with each group seeing opportunities to store, access and visualize domain-specific data that could have a direct impact on organizational learning. The exact impact of uCampus on organizational learning is yet to be assessed according to some rigorous measures (see, for instance, [35, 36]). However, by relating the present experimental data to the theoretical frameworks proposed by some of the leading organizational learning scholars, we could at least draw some inferences and theoretical implications as how such system can support campus-wide organizational learning in designing innovative learning spaces. By providing the visual language and modeling tools, uCampus is seen to support the interaction between members' task performance experience (e.g., developing and reviewing design proposals) and the layered context; further system extensions in information processing and linking mechanisms will enable distributed creation, retention and transfer of knowledge or shared mental models across the contextual boundaries, leading to visibly changed institutional policies or procedures that are sustainable. The methodology developed through the projects has resulted in several exemplars of how the individual learning and possibly many other types of spaces can be accurately modeled and visualized as a common visual representation the campus context in parts and whole. We also see that this methodology can be further adapted by other higher education institutions' for similar initiatives. However, like many other individual and organizational learning systems developed previously, the sustainability of the uCampus platform will depend on how it will remain open to a community approach to system development and evolutionary changes.

Reflecting on the question if uCampus as a social-technical system could be deployed to support institutional learning and innovation in campus planning and design, we consider how the wider issues of participation and sustainable platform development could be addressed after the project funding came to an end. A potential strategy is drawn on synthesizing the principles identified by the Oregon Experiment and the SER process model based meta-design framework reviewed in Sect. 2. The proposition is that if the growth of a real physical university campus environment can be sustained through the six principles found in the Oregon Experiment so does a virtual campus environment created as social-technical resources for institutional learning and innovation, and that a university community is ideally suited to apply the seeding-reseeding meta-design framework for growing the uCampus platform into future both in terms of virtual campus modelling capabilities and scope of content development. Since the public release of uCampus 1.1, several possible further extensions and applications have been suggested by internal and external reviewers:

1. *Incorporating user comments into 3D virtual campus model sets*—users' comments on their experiences of the exterior or interior campus environments could be potentially useful to planning and design if the comments elicited, aggregated and analyzed can be further linked up with 3D models. A new multi-modal user interface is required to enable interactive overlay of 3D virtual navigation and textual commenting.
2. *Raising social awareness of energy uses in university buildings*—As smart metering technologies are getting deployed more widely, energy uses in buildings can now be tracked more extensively and efficiently to give accurate spatial and temporal profiling of energy consumptions. Similar to the Augustine House Experiment, real-time data visualization of energy uses across campus buildings could be widely accessible on a system like uCampus as a means to raise campus-wide awareness of areas in need of greening behavior change.
3. *Connecting uCampus modeling to professional digital design workflow*—As mentioned earlier, a limited user evaluation of uCampus by a professional architectural practice has been carried out. We consider that further possibilities lie in the kind of "new hybrid design workflows" as reported by Christian Derix at the Aedas R&D in which an "in-between system of light applications" has been implemented to aid communication and sharing across workflow stages [37]. However, a more in-depth collaborative study is required to explore how open source based virtual campus modeling could benefit both institutional documentation and professional digital design workflow.
4. *uCampus for mobile devices*—The opportunity to make uCampus an application for smart mobile devices would enable the platform to be used 'on the move' and further enhance the range of uses for the system. Being able to use GPS to track a device and even visualize its location within a space on uCampus could aid way finding and navigation as well as the possibility of locating resources such as finding a specific book on a shelf in a library or bookable venues in buildings nearby.

Such probable extensions will need to address the fundamental requirement of organizational learning by facilitating the interaction between context and experience leading to visible changes in pattern of behavior that is replicable. A key criterion for future augmentation of the virtual campus language and modeling tools is its effectiveness for participants to derive shared mental models—What are innovative learning spaces and how will learners experience in the spaces? Furthermore, the complex situation faced at this turning point cannot be addressed adequately through discrete experimental projects within a single discipline. Following the uCampus and AHE studies, we consider further broader interdisciplinary research is required to advance the synthesis of pedagogical studies, locative-social media, context-rich data visualization, spatial–temporal language processing and Web3D as the foundation of an organizational system for learning from the new learning landscapes:

- Open-source shared representation of learning spaces in higher education to sustain truly interdisciplinary discourses on innovation in learning spaces participated by technologists, educationalists, designers, learners and researchers;
- Interlinking social commenting media and opinions mining capability with virtual world modelling to build up a multi-modal knowledge base allowing annotated 3D interactive navigation;
- Development of better tuned micro-scale indoor and outdoor location sensing coupled with context-rich data visualization into a credible research apparatus for uncovering leaners' footprints afforded by the learning spaces; and
- Business models and processes of knowledge exchange/transfer between higher education institutions and professional planning, design and management practices to promote intra-organizational learning.

References

1. Greenaway, D., & Haynes, M. (2003). Funding higher education in the UK: the role of fees and loans. *The Economic Journal, 113*(485), 150–166.
2. Barr, N., & Crawford, I. (2005). *Financing higher education: answers from the UK*. London and New York: Routledge.
3. Dugdale, S. (2009). Space strategies for the new learning landscape. *EDUCAUSE Review, 44*(2), 51–63.
4. Neary, M., Harrison, A., Crellin, G., Parekh, N., Saunders, G., Duggan, F., Williams, S., & Austin, S. (2010). Learning landscapes in higher education. centre for educational research and development, University of Lincoln, Lincoln.
5. Leiws, M. (2010). The University of Sheffield library information commons: a case study. *Journal of Library Administration, 50*, 161–178.
6. Glancey, J. (2010). University architecture shapes up for a revolution. The Guardian, Tuesday, 31 August 2010
7. JISC (2006). Designing spaces for effective learning: a guide to 21st century learning space design. Bristol: JISC. Retrieved from. May 25, 2012. http://www.jisc.ac.uk/media/documents/publications/learningspaces.pdf
8. JISC (2006). Technology-rich physical space design: An overview of JISC activities. Bristol: JISC. Retrieved from. May 25, 2012. http://www.jisc.ac.uk/ media/documents/publications/bpelearnspacev1final.pdf
9. Poole, P., & Wheal, A. (Eds.) (2011). Learning, spaces and technology: Exploring the concept. Canterbury: Canterbury Christ Church University. Retrieved from. May 25, 2012 http://www.canterbury.ac.uk/iborrow/book/
10. Boys, J. (2011). *Towards creative learning spaces: rethinking the architecture of post-compulsory education*. London: Routledge.
11. Lave, J., & Wenger, E. (1991). *Situated learning: legitimate peripheral participation*. Cambridge: Cambridge University Press.
12. Wenger, E. (1998). *Communities of practice: Learning, Meaning and Identity*. Cambridge: Cambridge University Press.
13. Alexander, C., Silverstein, M., Angel, S., Ishikawa, S., & Abrams, D. (1975). The oregon experiment. Oxford University Press, New York.

14. Fischer, G. (2010). End-user development and meta-design: foundations for cultures of participation. *Journal of Organizational and End User Computing, 22*(1), 52–82.
15. Fischer, G., McCall, R., Ostwald, J., Reeves, B., Shipman, F. (1994). Seeding, evolutionary growth and reseeding: supporting the incremental development of design environments, Proceedings of the SIGCHI conference on Human factors in computing systems: celebrating interdependence, pp. 292–298.
16. Fischer, G., Giaccardi, E., Ye, Y., Sutcliffe, A. G., & Mehandjiev, N. (2004). Meta-design: a manifesto for end-user development. *Communications of the ACM, 47*(9), 33–37.
17. Sourin, A. (2004). Nanyang technological University virtual campus. *IEEE Computer Graphics and Applications, 24*(6), 6–8.
18. Sourin, A. (2005). From a small formula to cyberworlds, proceedings of international conference on computational science and applications, Singapore, May 9–12, 2005, Lecture Notes in Computer Science, Vol. 3482, Springer, Heidelberg, pp. 983–992.
19. Brown, A., Knight, M., & Winchester, M. (2005). *Representation and delivery of city models, proceedings of the 10th international conference on computer aided architectural design research in Asia* (pp. 344–352). New Delhi: University of New Delhi.
20. Armenakis, C., & Sohn, G. (2009). *iCAMPUS: 3D modelling of York University campus*. Baltimore, Maryland: American Society for Photogrammetry and Remote Sensing Annual Conference.
21. Li-Chee-Ming, J., Gumerov, D., Ciobanu, T., & Armenakis, C. (2009). Generation of three dimensional photo-realistic models from LiDAR and image data, IEEE international Toronto conference—science and technology for Humanity, Ryerson University, Toronto.
22. Argyris, C., & Schön, D. (1978). Organizational learning: A theory of action perspective, Mass: Addison Wesley Longman Publishing.
23. Argyris, C., & Schön, D. (1995). Organizational learning II: Theory, method, and practice, FT Press, London.
24. Argyris, C. (1999). On organizational learning, Oxford: Wiley-Blackwell.
25. March, J. G. (1991). Exploration and exploitation in organizational learning. *Organization Science, 2*(1), 71–87.
26. Kim, D. H. (2004). The link between individual and organizational learning, How organizations learn: Managing the search for knowledge. In K. Starkey, S. Tempest, & A. McKinlay (eds.), 2nd edn, London: Thomson Learning.
27. Argote, L., & Miron-Spektor, E. (2011). Organizational learning: from experience to knowledge. *Organization Science, 22*(5), 1123–1137.
28. Polanyi, M. (1966). The tacit dimension, Doubleday & Co.
29. Horstmann, C. S., & Cornell, G. (2008). *Core java volume II: Advanced features* (8th ed.). San Francisco: Sun Microsystems Press.
30. Hunter, J., & Crawford, W. (2001). *Java Servlet programming*. Sebastopol, CA USA: O'Reilly Media.
31. Brutzman, D., & Daly, L. (2007). *X3D: Extensible 3D graphics for web authors*. San Francisco: Morgan Kauffman.
32. Harold, E. R., & Means, W. S. (2001). *XML in a nutshell: A desktop quick reference*. Sebastopol, CA USA: O'Reilly & Associates Inc.
33. Hart, D., & Pinder, J. (2012). weCAMP external evaluation report. Retrieved from. May, 30 2012. http://www.wecamp.group.shef.ac.uk/weCAMP _ExternalEvaluationReport.pdf
34. Poole, P., Ellery, I., & Wheal, A. (2012). iBorrow final report, JISC Institutional innovation programme. Retrieved from. May, 25 2012. http://www.jisc.ac.uk/whatwedo/programmes/institutionalinnovation/iborrow.aspx
35. De Marco, M., Imperatori, B., & Isari, D. (2010). IS, organization and strategy: convergence or divergence? In A. D'Atri., M. De Marco., A. Maria Braccini., & F. Cabiddu (Eds.), *Management of the interconnected world: ItAIS*, Physica-Verlag, Heidelberg, pp. 275–282.

36. Ardimento, P., Baldassarre, M. T., Cimitile, M., Mastelloni, G. (2010). Key performance indicators to relate knowledge governance with knowledge process, In A. D'Atri., & D. Saccà (Eds.), Information systems: people, organizations, institutions, and technologies. Physica-Verlag, Heidelberg, pp. 147–156.
37. Derix, C. (2009). In-between architecture computation. *International Journal of Architectural Computing, 4*(7), 565–585.

Performance Management Systems as Driver of Public Administration Improvement: A Dream?

Debora Tomasi, Stefano Scravaglieri and Maurizio Decastri

Abstract Recently the Italian Government required public administrations to manage organizational and individual performance and to implement pay for performance systems. Actually each Italian public administration has to adopt Performance Management Systems (PMS). The Reform recalls the New Public Management framework in several points even if there's a great controversy in the literature concerning the effective implementation of PMS in public administrations: for some authors PMS would run well while for others they need an adaptation to the public context. In this scenario, we assess the design of PMS on the basis of the empirical evidence collected in an Italian public administration and we indentify which parts of the literature are consistent with the empirical results. Our aim is to contribute to knowledge base on performance management in public administrations through an action design research approach based on the empirical evidence collected in the design of a PMS in Italy.

Keywords Performance management · Public administration management · Design science methodology

D. Tomasi · S. Scravaglieri (✉) · M. Decastri
Faculty of Economics, University of Rome "Tor Vergata", Via Columbia 2, 00133 Rome, Italy
e-mail: stefano.scravaglieri@uniroma2.it

D. Tomasi
e-mail: debora.tomasi@uniroma2.it

R. Baskerville et al. (eds.), *Designing Organizational Systems*, Lecture Notes in Information Systems and Organisation 1,
DOI: 10.1007/978-3-642-33371-2_13,

1 Introduction

The attention on public administrations' performance, intended as debureaucratization and achievement of efficiency and effectiveness [1], arose between the 1980 s and 1990 s [2] merging into the stream of New Public Management [1, 2]. One of the most important implication concerns the introduction of Performance Management Systems (PMS) [3], which would lead to an increase of efficiency and effectiveness [2, 4] and, consequently, to a better and faster accomplishment of the public administrations' mission. The introduction of PMS in public administrations requires not only the planning and control of organizational and individual performance, but also the introduction of pay for performance criteria trough which a part of workers' wage depends on their contribution to the organizational performance [5]. This represents an absolute innovation for many public administrations, since these structured performance processes are seldom implemented. Furthermore, PMS require a large amount of information and the possibility of analyzing and evaluating it [6].

In order to achieve performance it is necessary to plan and control activities and/or results both on organizational and individual level [1, 3, 7], and to introduce pay for performance systems [5]. Even though this framework appears very simple, comparative analysis shows that the effective application of PMS presents a wide range of diversity in Europe [2, 8, 9]. Furthermore, PMS implementation has generated several controversies. Some scholars underline that performance management systems do not suitably consider the difficulty of measuring and evaluating public administrations results [2]. Others notice that the mere incorporation of private principles in public administrations may be at odds with the concept of "public value" [10, 11]. Moreover, some scholars saw in this process of reform a great movement of rebureaucratization [12–14], rather than debureaucratization. This means that PMS cannot be transferred from private to public sector *tout court*, but have to be adapted to the specificity of the management of the public administration.

In this research we aim to contribute to the knowledge base on performance management systems in public administrations through a design research approach based on the empirical evidence collected in the design of a PMS in Italy. In the design research paradigm, knowledge is achieved through the design and evaluation of artifacts, which can be constructs, models, methods and instantiations [15]. According to a design research framework grounded in the Information Systems literature, we generalize the outcomes of an action design research project by taking into account both relevance and rigor constraints. Relevance is achieved through the understanding of business needs from the "environment". On the other hand, rigor is related to the analysis of the "knowledge base" which is the collection of methods, experiences, expertise and any other elements already produced in the specific domain [16].

The field problem addressed in this paper is related to the implementation issues of PMS in public administrations. First, which characteristics of a PMS are suitable for addressing the needs of public administrations? Second, which process should be followed by public administrations for implementing such PMS? These questions are addressed in the empirical setting of our study which refers to the design and implementation of a PMS in the context of an Italian public administration, ISPRA,[1] whose mission concerns the scientific research on and the protection of the Italian environment. From this perspective ISPRA is a really interesting subject because it has never been applied a PMS before (relevance) as well as the majority of Italian public administrations. Indeed, in order to address the problem of the compliance with Decree n. 150/2009, which requires that most of the Italian public administrations implement PMS, the authors of this paper were involved to support ISPRA in the design and implementation of its PMS. Multiple methods, techniques, and previous experiences in the areas of management control, human resources management, Italian regulations, and information systems were utilized during the project (rigor).

In other words, we formulate the following research question: which characteristics should PMS design have in a Public Administration? By answering to this question we evaluate if the newly produced artifact, e.g. a PMS model designed in compliance with the legislative decree and according to the knowledge base, responds appropriately to the environment needs and, at the same time, strictly follows the existent knowledge base. The empirical evidence collected during the project justifies the proposed design theory for performance measurement in public administrations.

The paper is structured as follows. Firstly, we describe the process through which we formulate the design theory for PMS in public administrations. Then we introduce the knowledge base elements on which the artifact requirements are grounded. Afterward we present the PMS model and its implementation process. Finally, we discuss the case findings and the research contribution.

2 The Design Research Framework

Design science is grounded in the H.A. Simon's book "The Science of the Artificial" [17] in which a distinction is made between the natural sciences and the sciences related to man-made artifacts. These artifacts are necessarily material and can consist of any form of designed intervention that can solve a field problem. The key characteristic of natural sciences is that they are explanatory in nature, being engaged in the quest for truth. On the other hand, design sciences, like architecture, engineering, medicine and law, are prescriptive in nature and are engaged in solving field problems through the creation of new and innovative

[1] ISPRA is the Italian acronym of "Istituto Superiore per la Protezione e la Ricerca Ambientale".

artifacts [18]. The ultimate goal of design science is to develop knowledge that can be used to develop solutions to problems.

This scientific knowledge, which is prescriptive in nature, complements behavioral knowledge and can be applied to the design of solutions for management problems. The concept of "technological rules" is used for meaning knowledge that links an intervention or artifact with a desired outcome or performance in a certain field of application. With these premises vanAken [19] advocates that the relevance problem of academic management research can be mitigated by creating space for Management Theory research, based on the paradigm of the design sciences, next to the more traditional Organization Theory research, based on the paradigm of the explanatory sciences.

Although the design of the information system supporting the PMS in public administrations represents only a small part of the broader managerial problem, in this paper we adopt a design research framework grounded in the Information Systems literature. This choice is motivated by the fact that Management Information Systems is an interdisciplinary field of research to which many design-oriented disciplines, such as engineering and computer science, contribute. These influences have led to the development of a number of design research models, processes and evaluation criteria that have been applied to several IS design problems.

The framework is based on the Action Design Research (ADR) method [20]. The Design Theory concept has been introduced Walls et al. [21, 22] and is divided in two main components: the design product and the design process. The design product is composed by meta-requirements, meta-design, kernel theories and a set of testable design product hypothesis. Differently, the design process components are the design method, kernel theories and a set of testable design process hypothesis.

In this paper we present the four stages of our ADR project. We begin by framing the problem in the public sector environment and by adopting NPM as a theoretical premise for our intervention (stage 1). The environment contributes to the kernel theories through both the characteristics of public administrations in terms of resources (i.e. people, organizational and technical systems) and the external constraints (i.e. legal framework, political objectives). The knowledge base refers to scientific theories and methods in the fields of human resources, organizational systems and information systems, together with more practical knowledge based on previous experiences and expertise and artifacts in use in the private sector.

As a second stage we present our organization building, intervention, and evaluation process in which the evidence collected in the ISPRA case is analyzed through the organizational performance, the individual performance, and the information system perspectives. Furthermore, we describe our reflection and learning stage along the same perspectives (stage 3). Finally we generalize the outcomes by presenting a design theory for PMS in public administrations by using the constructs of the Walls et al. [21] model.

3 Stage 1: Problem Formulation

3.1 A Practice-Inspired Research: The Public Administration Environment

Public administrations are characterized by unique dynamics in terms of motivations of managers and employees due to contractual conditions, the lack of competitive pressure, and the negative impact of bureaucratization. Free riding, inefficiencies and opportunistic behavior in public administrations are at the forefront of media and newspapers. The increasing demand for timely and effective public services together with the scarcity of economic resources have recently put in the agenda of politicians and public managers the need for implementing new mechanisms to manage and control the performances in public administrations.

In Italy, the Decree n. 150/2009, more than previous reforms, formally introduced performance management in public administrations. It seems to be a great change in particular because public administration would be now under "*goal pressure*" as private sector organizations. In this landscape, moreover, it seems to be very difficult for public administrations to avoid the request to introduce long-lasting organizational innovations.

The Decree n. 150/2009 has an international perspective, both in the language and in the contents. It follows the roadmap tracked by, among the others, the American "Government Performance and Results Act" (1993), the British "Comprehensive Performance Assessment" (2003) and the French "Loi organique relative aux lois de finances LOLF" (2001).

The first part of the Decree n. 150/2009 (articles 2–31) introduces the themes of performance and transparency in all Italian public administrations. In particular, the Decree allows passing from a perspective of performance measurement to a perspective of performance management [23, 24]. Performance is intended in two ways:

- As *organizational performance*, related to the whole organization in term of structure, processes, products and services provided.
- As *individual performance*, related both to management and to employees, in term of professional results and behaviors.

While the organizational performance influences individual performance and vice versa, this two kinds of performance are closely related. Furthermore, the theme of *performance* appears as one of the "main concepts" in the pattern of the reform. As a proof, consider that in the Decree the term "performance" occurs 98 times in 49 pages.

Another main theme in the Decree is transparency. It is mainly associated to access to any relevant information for stakeholders included the performance results. Therefore, performance and transparency are considered and evaluated as linked goals: to give the possibility of a social control to stakeholders might lead to a road of continuous improvement of performance.

The Decree also provides prescriptions related to the need to integrate performance management systems with the Information Technology (IT) infrastructure of public administrations. Indeed, a number of IT governance processes such as planning, demand management, software development and procurement are also involved in this change program. It must be noted that IT governance in the Public Sector is constrained by particular norms and regulations which are mainly related to the procurement procedures and to security and privacy issues.

3.2 A Theory-Ingrained Artifact: The New Public Management Framework

In OECD countries, the traditional way of understanding the "performance" was by translating policies into laws and regulations. Anyway, this system worked well only in less complex environments with an easy task to achieve [25]. Moreover, because of the general decline in the availability of financial resources [1], today public administrations are expected to become more efficient and reliable and to offer better services for less money [2]. In other words, public administrations are expected to be "performers" differently, encompassing a broader concept of performance based on efficiency and effectiveness.

This new concept of public administrations' performance is one of the flags of New Public Management. Performance, in fact, is among the seven pillars of New Public Management [1]. In this frame, Hood suggested that public sector organization must be "performance-driven" and not "rule-bound". To reach performance, afterward, public administrations need to plan and to control activities and/or results both at organizational and individual level [1, 3, 7].

For several scholars, the implementation of performance systems [3], would increase efficiency and effectiveness [2, 4] and, consequently, would lead to a better and faster accomplishment of the public administration's mission. However, other scholars noticed that performance systems do not adequately take into account some difficulties such as setting standards, measuring and evaluating certain types of public results, especially in sensitive fields such as culture and environment [2, 26].

As already mentioned, we draw the requirements from a mix of knowledge base and environmental elements. Since the design of PMS requires competences from three different fields of research and practice, in the next section, after a brief presentation of the Decree n. 150/2009, we deal with the organizational performance, the individual performance and the information system perspectives by illustrating their general principles as well as those principles tailored to the public administration which contribute to the requirements definition.

4 Stage 2: Building, Intervention and Evaluation: Evidence from the ISPRA Case

In 2010 the authors of this paper were involved in the design and implementation of a PMS in the context of ISPRA, an Italian Public Administration whose mission concerns the scientific research on and the protection of the Italian environment. In particular, the role of the researchers was to support the staff members of the control management department in the change process for the adoption of a PMS compliant with the legislative Decree n. 150/2009. The main issue faced by the project team was creating instantiations of general concepts such as performance, goals, KPI, etc. into specific elements characterizing the ISPRA context. With this purpose, multiple methods, techniques, and previous experiences in the areas of management control, human resources management, Italian regulation, and information systems were utilized during the project.

In this section we present a set of prescriptions related to both the characteristics of a PMS in a public administration and to the process for its successful implementation. In terms of Design Research [21] our objective here is to summarize the meta-design and the design method through which it is possible to satisfy a set of meta-requirements that allow to solve the field problem of implementing an effective PMS in a public administration. In fact, a meta-design is the abstract "blueprint" or architecture that describes an artifact (be it either a product or a method/intervention), while a design method is a description of processes for implementing the theory (either a product or a method) in specific contexts. The design theory resulting from the logical flow linking kernel theories and environmental requirements to meta-design and design method components can be expressed through a set of testable hypotheses representing true statements about the design theory.

4.1 The Design of PMS from an Organizational Performance Perspective

The objectives of the intervention, from the organizational performance perspective, were to design a PMS compliant with the request of the decree 150/2009 and able to guarantee an effective planning and control of ISPRA's goals and the right distribution of resources, according to the plans and relative actions. These are what are called "Meta requirements" in Design Science theory.

To accomplish this mission, we need of course to design a plan and control cycle, following the main prescriptions of the literature. This cycle, named "performance cycle" in the decree, should generate two main outputs: a three-year plan and a report on results evaluation. According to what we said before, we designed a system able to link the plan phase to the control phase and, at the same time, to take into account the specificity of ISPRA context.

For the first purpose, we also designed a control management system. This system, starting from the goals stated in the three-year plan, had the mission to link performance planned with performance obtained, through the measurement and the evaluation of results and the use of KPI. To use this system we worked together with the control management department, in particular with the organizational unit responsible for the entire implementation of the process. We designed a PMS starting from what ISPRA had already done in term of planning and control, bridging the gaps to be compliant with the decree.

To be as much consistent as possible with the ISPRA context, we designed a PMS through interviews to all middle and top managers. These interviews had a double function: first of all, they allowed to define together with ISPRA's people some pivotal points of the systems such as, among the others, stakeholders, goals and standards for control. Secondly, interviews were useful to disseminate the main aim of the reform, to train managers enabling them to be ready with the next request by the control management department.

Moreover, PMS were designed to link organizational performance to individual performance.

4.2 The Design of PMS from Individual Performance Perspective

As regards to the Individual Performance, the meta-requirements are the compliance with Decree n. 150/2009 (the same of the Organizational Performance), the effective distribution of incentives and the behavior assessment.

In order to reach these objectives, we designed the individual performance appraisal system for both managers and non-managers. We followed the directions of Decree n. 150/2009 and the main findings from the literature. For these reasons the two systems are quite different, especially with respect to the appraisal objects.

Both performance appraisal systems are characterized by a multifactorial approach based on:

1. competences (organizational behavior). They have been identified with reference to the standard role;
2. organizational performance of the organizational unit of the evaluated employee.

As regards to managers, they will be evaluated on: (a) indicators of performance relative to the organization's aims for which they have direct responsibility; (b) individual goals; (c) quality of their contribution to the general performance of the structure, level of managerial and professional competence demonstrated; (d) capability to evaluate their own staff, to be demonstrated by means of significant differentiation in their assessments.

As regards to non-managers, they will be evaluated on: (a) organizational performance; (b) professional behavior, since it denotes the use of the competences necessary to ensure efficient coverage of the role. The professional behaviors evaluated were grouped into four areas of expertise, corresponding to the following capabilities: relational, organizational, realization and improvement.

We produced a handbook for the appraisal of individual performance that provides a methodological and operating guide for those who, on the basis of Decree n. 150/2009, are called to appraise the individual performance. It also constitutes a source of information for those who are undergoing assessment. It includes: (a) an overview of the Decree n. 150/2009 regarding the section of measurement and evaluation of performance; (b) the appraisal process with the description of the main steps, the responsibilities of actors and the instruments in support of the assessor; (c) the performance appraisal systems for managers and for non-managers. We illustrated the main features of the two rating systems, differentiated on the basis of the recipients of the evaluation; (d) the two appraisal forms, one for managers and one for non-managers. We provide their description of and some guidelines for the compilation.

Having in mind the meta-requirements, the two systems were designed taking into account the real situation in ISPRA and the design process was shared as much as possible. In particular we designed and delivered a training course for technical staff in order to develop their competencies on performance appraisal system and process. The training course covered the following topics: introduction to management, performance appraisal system and control management system. Moreover, we made meetings with top management and technical staff to design the individual performance appraisal system, since they know the structure and culture of ISPRA very well. Finally, we made sample interviews to the staff in order to identify the main activities, the responsibility, the competences and, consequently, the appraisal objectives.

4.3 The Design of PMS from Information Systems Perspective

The role of the information system is to provide an appropriate information workflow to ensure that PMS run well. To do so, first of all we need to consider the compliance of IT systems not only with the decree, but more specifically with the IT governance regulations. In Italy, several regulations on the information system were in force when we developed the PMS. We also need to consider indirect effects as those due to privacy laws.

From an operational point of view, we designed IT systems to allow the integration of different data sources, since each ISPRA department obtains information from its own sources and, therefore, there was a considerable lack of integration. In order to achieve this integration, it was also necessary to take into account both internal and external data. At the same, time we faced a problem of interoperability of existing applications.

Our solutions, oriented towards the integration of individual and organizational performance, foresaw the design of:

- a multidimensional dashboard able to create reports;
- a tool for modeling goals, activities, resources, organizational units, KPI, KPI thresholds;

Proceeding in this way, a participated process is once again necessary since, from the one hand, we have to collect functional and non-functional requirements from the control management department, while, from the other hand, we need to identify all the present data sources and different information needs, also considering the demand of new data due to the implementation of the decree.

5 Stage 3: Reflection and Learning

5.1 The Organizational Performance Perspective

The Decree n. 150/2009 contains several elements closely related with the New Public Management perspective of organizational performance. First of all, the Decree provides a more specific definition of "performance" and extends its evaluation in breadth and in depth. In fact, it is no longer enough to manage the organizational performance of the whole public administration as previously, but it becomes necessary to manage the performance at both intra-organizational (department, team, etc.) and individual level. This means that all the public administration components must be involved in the process of planning and control.

Secondly, according to the Decree, each public administration has to implement a process, called "Performance Cycle". It is substantially a process of planning and evaluation of organizational performance and individual performance [27]. In these models, in fact, there is a distinction between the planning macrophase and the control macrophase.

The planning macrophase starts from the forecasting of strategic and operational goals. The goals should be S.M.A.R.T. and have to satisfy stakeholders request and to address performance in terms of efficiency, satisfaction, equality, resources development and effectiveness of outputs and outcomes.

In order to do so, it is important to define what are the most important needs to be met and which activities can satisfy these needs. So, the definition of the organizational mission, the awareness of internal and external stakeholders needs and the knowledge of the cause–effect relationship between objectives and actions become a fundamental means to manage performance [24, 28].

The definition of strategic goals and operational goals is the output of a process of negotiation between governing bodies (political dimension) and public managers (management dimension). To accomplish this phase, public managers need the definition of explicit standards and of precise measures of performance. These features overlap with Hood's description of performance features [1].

This macrophase of Performance Cycle might generate a three-year plan, tracked in a formal document named "Performance Plan".

The control macrophase includes three main activities: measurement, evaluation and reporting, according to the scientific literature [24, 28–30]. To implement these activities, the management has to constantly measure and evaluate the gap between the performance planned and the performance realized. In the reporting phase, in particular, the results of the performance are reported to internal and external stakeholders.

In order to support the control and evaluation phases, the Decree foresees a tool called "Monitoring and Evaluation System". It is substantially a collection of people, processes and Information Technology with the task of monitoring progress in achieving the performance and of providing data for evaluation of results.

So, it is clear that each public administration needs a system able to link the planning macrophase with the control macrophase. This system has also to be related with the evaluation of individual performance, as a piece of the whole performance [5, 28, 31, 32], and with IT tools, as a means to plan and control the performance [33–35].

At the same time, the PMS should deal with the specificities of the public administration's context, such as the lack of profit, transparency, accountability and, more generally, the permeating spirit of being a civil servant. This means that the simple incorporation of tools coming from private enterprise management can result in a mismatch with the public value emerging from this context [15].

Considering these elements we formulated the following propositions:

(1) to be effective and compliant with the laws and consistent with the main findings from the literature, PMS should create a relationship between planning and control phases;
(2) to be effective and compliant with the laws and consistent with the main findings from the literature, PMS should apply tools coming from the private sector to the context of public administrations.

5.2 The Individual Performance Perspective

Following the New Public Management approach, public administrations are invited to design, among other models and tools, a human resources management system characterized by mobility and a salary based on merit and providing performance incentives [36–38].

In this frame, the claim for a broader discussion on the application of individual performance appraisal system was always a relevant issue for research and practice relating to public sector management, since, in most countries, government organizations employ a substantial part of the workforce [39].

In public administration there are different problems related to the performance appraisal system, such as the employment of non-sophisticated systems [40, 41] and a more specifically cultural problem, that is the fear which people have of the appraisal, since they frequently perceive it as a form of control. They do not see the potential that appraisal systems actually have and the different purposes they can pursue [42, 43]. In Italian public administration, the only purpose for which the individual performance appraisal system has been used up to now and that consequently, people have been able to see, is the Management purpose that, basically, produces a variable reward related to the contribution [44–48]. But there are other two purposes: the Organizational purpose and the Development purpose [49–51]. In Decree n. 150/2009 (art. 3) the legislator refers to different purposes.

With reference to the different purposes that an organization can pursue, it is evident the necessity to differentiate between the concept and the steps of measurement and appraisal. Although in the literature there are definitions with different shades, the performance appraisal is generally considered as the process through which organizations define, measure, evaluate and reward (economically and not) the contribution of a person, through a comparison between the expectations of the organization and the actual output over a period of time, by using a method which ensures fairness and consistency with the objectives and the organizational and cultural context [43, 52–55].

In this frame, while the measurement procedure employs shared criteria that allow the elimination of uncertainty to obtain a result considered "objective", the appraisal presupposes an element of judgment that inevitably produces a subjective result. In order to reduce this subjectivity, the organization should adopt specific methods of analysis, procedures and evaluation tools. For these reason, an individual performance appraisal system consists of two main parts [43]: the object of appraisal and the process (actors, tools and steps).

Generally, there are two main types of appraisal objects: (a) quantitative and qualitative goals [56]; (b) behaviors [57, 58].

These objects of evaluation are mentioned in Decree n. 150/2009 (art. 9) distinguishing between managers and employees. The Decree also refers to group objectives with reference to appraisal of non-managers. Contrary to theoretical suggestions [39], the Decree does not formally indicate the job analysis as a foundation for individual appraising performance and as a preliminary step to formalize the job description with individual duties and responsibilities, or the job profile with the list of individual expected behaviors. Instead, we assume that the job analysis, and therefore job descriptions and job profiles, are important tools in the appraisal process.

In an individual performance appraisal system, in addition to the objects of appraisal, another important element is the "process" (actors, tools, steps).

The actors involved in the appraisal process are many: the Head, the Director of Human Resources, and the Supervisor [43]. Usually the superiors are in charge of the rating, but also colleagues, subordinates, other managers or even the worker him/herself could be [55, 59, 60]. The raters should follow an evaluation process which includes different steps [61]. All steps are important for defining the final appraisal and are relevant to the success of the whole performance appraisal process [62].

There are many kinds of appraisal tools that can be used to evaluate employees' performance. A very important tool for the boss-rater is the appraisal form. It should outline the employees' goals and expected behaviors.

Considering the theoretical framework, we formulated the following propositions:

(1) to be effective and compliant with the laws and consistent with the main findings from the literature, PMS should link individual performance with organizational performance;
(2) to be effective and compliant with the laws and consistent with the main findings from the literature, PMS should adopt specific methods of analysis, procedures and evaluation tools.

5.3 The Information System Perspective

With respect to the general objectives of managing performance and to ensure transparency, information systems play a key role enabling the exchange of information within the organizations and between an organization and its stakeholders. Performance management systems need to collect information from the operational processes in order to measure their inputs and outputs and to provide feedback that supports decisions at different levels. The capability of ITs to support such feedback loops can be easily recognized due to the pervasive role of ITs in many organizational and individual activities. Also transparency is based on information flows through which data on the resources allocation and process outcomes are communicated beyond the organizational boundaries, thus activating further feedback loops with citizens, businesses and other external stakeholders.

Despite a thorough transformation of public administrations into process oriented organizations is still an ongoing process, in the last two decades new IT capabilities, software applications and IT platforms have been introduced as fundamental parts of the public administration organizational systems. The expected advantages of such investments are related both to the efficiency of internal work practices through automation and workflow support and to the effectiveness of public administrations in satisfying the needs of citizens and businesses by providing services through multiple channels (i.e. e-government).

The achievement of these goals for public administrations is a non-trivial process that must take into account many issues in the design of IT systems and in the selection and procurement of software products and other solutions from IT vendors. For instance, PAs must be aware of vendor lock-in risks and of the importance of safeguarding data privacy and security when they implement new systems. In Italy several norms regulate this domain by providing rules and guidelines for IT governance[2] such as the rules fostering the adoption of open source software [63].

From the architectural point of view, supporting a Performance Management System with IT does mean collecting data and information from the operative processes and elaborating them for obtaining the values of the key performance indicators which have been defined for measuring the organizational and individual performances. The complexity in implementing an IT system with such functionalities is highly dependent on the structure of the whole organizational system, in terms of number of organizational units and their interactions, and on the maturity level of the overall IT architecture. In this context a critical phase is the information gathering which must be matched with available information supply, prioritized, homogenized and integrated into the 'global' conceptual data schema of the decision support system [64].

Considering the previous analysis, we formulated the following proposition:

(1) to make PMS run well, information system design should be adapted to the new requirements of individual and organizational performance.

The design theory resulting from the generalization of the ISPRA case is summarized in Table 1.

6 Formalization of Learning

In this paper a prescriptive theory for successfully implementing a PMS in a PA is illustrated through the lens of a research framework based on the design research. In the literature there is a great controversy, among both scholars and practitioners, on the adoption of PMS. On the one hand, there are "supporters" of a *tout court* adoption of PMS, in order to avoid the traditional problem of efficiency and effectiveness in public administration management; on the other hand, others support a careful adoption of PMS paying particular attention to the specific environment of the public administration.

We participated in the design of a PMS in an Italian Public Administration, following a "road map" that started from the literature analysis and the assessment of the environmental impact.

Our experience was useful to evaluate the proposition we formulated before. In particular, focusing on proposition 1 (to be effective and compliant with the laws and consistent with the main findings from the literature, PMS should create a relationship between planning and control phases) we identified a system able to link past performance results with a new planning phase. This approach results very useful to improve efficiency, since the planning phase does not start from a

[2] CAD Codice dell'Amministrazione Digitale, Decreto legislativo 7 marzo 2005, n. 82, art. 69 (2005).

Table 1 A design theory for performance management system in an Italian public administration (ISPRA)

	Organizational performance	Individual performance	Information systems
Meta-requirements	Compliance Effective planning of goals and resources Control results	Compliance Effective distribution of incentives Behavior assessment	Compliance with IT governance regulations Integration of different data sources Interoperability of existing applications
Meta-design	Performance cycle Performance plan and results evaluation Monitoring and evaluation system	Individual performance appraisal system for managers Individual performance appraisal for non-managers	Multidimensional dashboard and report generation Modeling goals, activities, resources, organizational units, KPI, KPI thresholds Internal and external data collection and aggregation
Design method	Work together with control management department Interviews to middle and top management Stakeholders and goals definition Definition of standards for control	Training technical staff to develop their competencies on performance appraisal system and process Meetings with top management and technical staff to design the individual performance appraisal system Sample interviews to staff in order to identify the appraisal objectives	Collecting functional and non-functional requirements from the control management department KPI and multidimensional model definition Interoperability issues with existing systems Make or buy choice (i.e. SaaS, etc.)
Testable hypotheses	The effective implementation of a PMS in Public Administrations depends on the capability to successfully link organizational performance with individual performance within a given context and to support the monitoring process through IT The implementation of an effective PMS in a Public Administration requires: (1) to develop the awareness on the principles and mechanisms of the overall control cycle in the top and middle management, (2) to carefully analyze the relationships between goals, activities, resources, organizational units, and KPI, (3) to successfully integrate an IT-based monitoring system within the existing IT infrastructure		

"tabula rasa" any more. It also indicates guidelines for performance, because it allows to define indicators and target of performance and control in the remaining management period. Therefore, we can confirm proposition 1.

Proposition 2 states that, to be effective and compliant with the laws and consistent with the main findings from the literature, PMS should apply tools coming from the private sector to the context of public administrations. This is particularly true for ISPRA and, we think, generally for any public administration. We need to avoid the rejection of new systems and to facilitate the organizational change related to their adoption. For this reason, we acted in two ways: first of all, we stimulated the comprehension of the new systems through training interventions; secondly, we involved top and middle managers in the PMS design, through interviews and document analysis. In this way we succeed in adapting PMS to the specific context and in developing a commitment to implement it. We can consequently confirm proposition 1.

Proposition 3 states that to be effective and compliant with the laws and consistent with the main findings from the literature, PMS should link individual performance with organizational performance. One of the objects of the individual appraisal we have identified is exactly the organizational performance of the organizational unit. In particular, each manager has the responsibility for achieving the expected result for its organizational unit; moreover the performance appraisal for non-managers is also influenced by the overall result achieved by the organizational unit. In our experience, proposition 3 is confirmed.

Proposition 4 states that to be effective and compliant with the laws and consistent with the main findings from the literature, PMS should adopt specific methods of analysis, procedures and evaluation tools. In ISPRA we adopted the typical evaluation tools adapted to the specific situation: we identified the evaluation process (definition and communication of the expectations, intermediate observation and feedback, performance appraisal, performance feedback); we designed the appraisal form containing the personal details of the worker and especially the areas of responsibility. We also produced an individual appraisal performance handbook with all the information for the evaluator and the evaluated. This was accompanied by a training path designed to act both on content and on the organizational culture. Consequently, we collected elements to confirm proposition 4.

Finally, we can confirm proposition 5 as well, since we operated to identify old and new requirements in order to guarantee the functionality of the PMS and, in particular, the possibility of creating a linkage between individual and organizational performance.

Considering all these elements we can respond to our research question. PMS design in Public Administration should pay attention to effectiveness and efficiency, to planning and control, to linking individual and organizational performance, as well as to the specific context in which this system should be adopted, by involving people in order to increase comprehension and commitment. This means that, considering the before mentioned controversy in the literature, we have elements to support the careful adoption of PMS, to take care of the environment.

In conclusion, the emerging research propositions are related to the components of a successful PMS applied to a PA, and to the necessary steps to take for the PMS implementation. First, the effective implementation of a PMS in Public Administrations depends on the capability to successfully link organizational performance with individual performance within a given context and to support the monitoring process through the ITs. Second, the implementation of an effective PMS in a Public Administration requires: (1) to develop the awareness on the principles and mechanisms of the overall control cycle in the top and middle management, (2) to carefully analyze the relationships between goals, activities, resources, organizational units, and KPI, (3) to successfully integrate an IT-based monitoring system within the existing IT infrastructure.

These results are based on the evidence collected in the PMS implementation within an Italian Public Administration. Further works will provide additional elements for justifying the design theory on the basis of actual performance results and of a more analytic description of the ISPRA evidence.

Acknowledgments We acknowledge the ISPRA control management department and the participants to the ISPRA PMS project for their contribution to this research.

References

1. Hood, C. (1991). A public management for all season. *Public Administration, 69*, 3–19.
2. Pollit, C., & Bouckaret, G. (2004). *Public management reform: A comparative analysis*. Oxford: Oxford University press.
3. Emery, Y. (2004). Rewarding civil service performance through team bonuses: findings, analysis and recommendations. *International Review of Administrative Science, 70*, 157–168.
4. Kettl, D. (2000). *The global public management revolution*. Washington: The Brookings Institution.
5. Varone, F., & Giauque, D. (2001). Policy management and performance related pay: comparative analysis of service contracts in Switzerland. *International Review of Administrative Sciences, 67*(3), 543–565.
6. Neely, A., Gregory, M., & Platts, K. (1995). Performance measurement system design: A literature review and research agenda. *International Journal of Operations and Production Management, 15*, 80–116.
7. Emery, Y., & Giauque, D. (2005). Employment in the public and private sectors: toward a confusing hybridization process. *International Review of Administrative Science, 71*, 636–657.
8. Gualmini, E. (2008). Restructuring Weberian bureaucracy: Comparing managerial reforms in Europe and the United States. *Public Administration, 86*, 75–94.
9. Kickert, M. (1993). Complexity governance and dynamics: Conceptual explorations of public network management. In J. Kooiman (Ed.), *Modern governance*. London: Sage.
10. Ingraham, P., James, R., & Elliot, F. (1995). Political management strategies and political/ career relationships: Where are we now in the federal government? *Public Administration Review, 55*, 263–272.
11. Thompson, J. (2006). The federal civil service: The demise of an institution. *Public Administration Review, 66*, 496–503.
12. Grey, C., & Garsten, C. (2001). Trust. *Control and Post-Bureaucracy. Organization Studies, 2*, 229–250.
13. Hodgson, D. (2004). Project work: The legacy of bureaucratic control in the post-bureaucratic organization. *Organization, 1*, 81–100.
14. Kallinikos, J. (2004). The social foundations of the bureaucratic order. *Organization, 1*, 13–36.

15. March, S., & Smith, G. (1995). Design and natural science research on information technology. *Decision Support Systems, 15*(4), 251–266.
16. Hevner, A., March, S., Park, J., & Ram, S. (2004). Design science in information systems research. *MIS Quarterly, 28*, 75–105.
17. Simon, H. (1996). *The sciences of artificial*. Cambridge: MIT Press.
18. Hevner, A. (2007). A three cycle view of design science research. *Scandinavian Journal of Information Systems Information Systems, 19*(2), 87–92.
19. van Aken, J. (2004). Management research based on the paradigm of the design sciences: The quest for field-tested and grounded technological rules. *Journal of Management Studies, 41*(2), 219–246.
20. Sein, M., Henfridsoon, O., Purao, S., Rossi, M., & Lindgren, R. (2011). Action design research. *MIS Quarterly, 35*(1), 37–56.
21. Walls, J., Widmeyer, G., & El Sawy, O. (1992). Building an information system design theory for vigilant EIS. *Information Systems Research, 3*(1), 36–59.
22. Walls, J., & Widmeyer, G. (2004). Assessing information system design theory in perspective: How useful was our 1992 initial rendition. *Journal of Information Technology Theory and Application, 6*(2), 43–58.
23. Otley, D. (1999). Performance management: A framework for management control systems research. *Management Accounting Research, 10*, 363–382.
24. Bouckaert, G., & Halligan, J. (2008). *Managing performance. International comparisons*. Oxon: Routledge.
25. OECD. (2004). Public sector modernisation: Governing for performance. Paris: OECD Publishing.
26. Plant, R. (2003). A public service ethic and political accountability. *Parliamentary Affairs, 56*, 560–579.
27. Flamholtz, G. (1995). Il sistema di controllo come strumento di direzione. In F. Amigoni, *Misurazioni d'azienda*. Milano: Giuffrè.
28. Boivard, T. (1996). The political economy of performance measurement. In *A. Halachmi* & G. Bouckaert (Eds.), *Organizational performance and measurement in the public sector: Toward service, efforts and accomplishment reporting*. Westport: Quorum Books.
29. Hinna, L., & Monteduro, F. (2003). *Trust in local authorities : The role of social reporting to citizens*. European group of public administration, Oeires.
30. Mussari, R. (2000). La valutazione dei programmi nelle aziende pubbliche. Giappichelli, Torino.
31. Ford, J., & Schellenberg, D. (1982). Conceptual Issues of linkage in the assessment of organizational performance. *Academy of Management Review, 7*(1), 49–58.
32. Bannister, B., & Balkin, D. (1990). Performance evaluation and compensation feedback messages: An integrated model. *Journal of Occupational Psychology, 63*, 97–111.
33. Heeks, R. (2000). The approach of senior public officials to information technology-related reform: Lessons from India. *Public Administration and Development, 20*, 197–205.
34. von Waldenberg, W. (2004). Electronic government and development. *European Journal of Development Research, 16*, 417–432.
35. Madon, S. (2006). IT-based government reform initiatives in the indian state of Gujarat. *Journal of International Development, 18*, 877–888.
36. Ferlie, E., Ashburner, L., Fitzgerald, L., & Pettigrew, A. (1996). *The new public management in action*. Oxford: Oxford University Press.
37. Hood, C. (1995). Emerging issues in public administration. *Public administration, 73*(1), 165–183.
38. Pollit, C. (1990). *Managerialism and the public services: The Anglo-American experience. Mass*. Cambridge: Basil Blackwell.
39. Daley, D. (1992). *Performance appraisal in the public sector—Techniques and applications*. CT: Quorum, Westport.
40. Pynes, J. (1997). *Human resources management for public and nonprofit organizations*. San Francisco: Jossey-Bass.

41. Kellough, J., & Selden, S. (1997). Pay-for-performance systems in state government: Perceptions of state agency personnel managers. *Review of Public Personnel Administration, 17*(1), 5–21.
42. Guion, R. (1997). Criterion measures and the criterion dilemma. In N. Andreson & P. Herriot (Eds.), *International handbook of selection and assessment* (pp. 287–302). Chichester: Wiley.
43. Fletcher, C. (2001). Performance appraisal and management: The developing research agenda. *Journal of Occupational and Organizational Psychology, 74*, 473–487.
44. Kessler, I., & Purcell, J. (1992). Performance related pay: Objectives and application. *Human Resource Management Journal, 2*(3), 13–33.
45. Campbell, D., Campbell, K., & Chia, H. (1998). Merit pay, performance appraisal, and individual motivation: An analysis and alternative. *Human Resource Management, 37*(2), 131–146.
46. Beer, M., Cannon, M. (2004). Promise and peril in implementing pay for performance. *Human resource management, 43*(1), 3–20.
47. Kim, J. (2010). Strategic human resource practices: Introducing alternatives for organizational performance improvement in the public sector. *Public Administration Review, 70*(1), 38–49.
48. Latham, G., Almost, J., Mann, S., & Moore, C. (2005). New developments in performance management. *Organizational Dynamics, 34*(1), 77–87.
49. Daley, D. (1993). Performance appraisal as an aid in personnel decisions. *American Review of Public Administration, 23*(3), 201–213.
50. Li, L. (2000). An analysis of sources of competitiveness and performance of Chinese manufacturers. *International Journal of Operations and Production Management, 20*(3), 299–315.
51. Roback, T. (1989). Personnel research perspectives on human resource management and development. *Public Personnel Management, 18*(2), 138–162.
52. Baron, A., & Armstrong, M. (1998). Out of the box. *People Management, 23*, 38–41.
53. DeNisi, A. (2000). Performance appraisal and performance management: A multilevel analysis. In K. Klein & S. Kozlowki (Eds.), *Multilevel theory, research and methods in organizations* (pp. 121–156). San Francisco: Jossey-Bass .
54. Mondy, R., Noe, R., & Premeaux, S. (2002). *Human resource management*. Upper Saddle River: Prentice Hall.
55. Roberts, G. (2002). Employee performance appraisal system participation: A technique that works. *Public Personnel Management, 31*(3), 333–342.
56. Locke, E., & Latham, G. (1990).Work motivation: The high performance cycle. In U. Kleinbeck & et al. (Eds.), *Work motivation*. Hillsdale: Lawrence Erlbaum.
57. Guest, D. (1997). Human resource management and performance: A review and research agenda. *International Journal of Human Resource Management, 8*, 263–276.
58. Murphy, K., & Cleveland, J. (1995). *Understanding performance appraisal: Social, organizational, and goal-based perspectives*. Thousand Oaks: Sage.
59. Brown, M., & Heywood, J. (2005). Performance appraisal systems: Determinants and change. *British Journal of Industrial Relations, 43*(4), 659–679.
60. Soltani, E. (2005). Conflict between theory and practice: TQM and performance appraisal. *International Journal of Quality and Reliability Management, 22*(8), 796–818.
61. Hodgetts, R. (1993). *Modern human relations at work*. New York: Harcourt Brace College Publishers.
62. Reinhardt, C. (1985). The state of performance appraisal: A literature review. *Human Resource Planning, 8*(2), 105–110.
63. Spagnoletti, P., & Federici, T. (2011). Exploring the interplay between FLOSS adoption and organizational innovation. *Communications of the Association for Information Systems, 29*(15), 279–298.
64. Winter, R., & Strauch, B. (2003). *A method for demand-driven information requirements analysis in data warehousing projects*. Annual Hawaii International Conference on System Sciences.

Part IV
Design and Evaluation of Managerial Strategies

Design on a Societal Scale: The Case of e-Government Strategic Planning

Carlo Batini, Gianluigi Viscusi and Marco Castelli

Abstract In this chapter, we discuss the case of the instantiation and development of a methodology for e-Government initiatives design and planning in the specific context of Mediterranean Countries. The methodology aims to support the definition of strategy implementation roadmaps that consider the fitting of e-Government vision principles, policies and the context of intervention. Moreover, the methodology aims to provide a contribution to design science research on a societal scale, by dealing with the obstacles that Simon recognized as a "budget of obstacles or alternatively as a budget of planning requirements", even with restraint and simplification typical of a complex decision making process. Taking these issues into account, the Chapter discusses the case of the methodology application to an information systems integration initiative of the Tunisian Ministry of Agriculture and Hydraulic Resources in 2008–2009. The focus of the case is on problem representation and organizations in social design as challenges for information systems design on a societal scale.

Keywords Design science · Information systems planning · policies · e-Government

C. Batini · G. Viscusi (✉) · M. Castelli
Department of Informatics, Systems and Communication (DISCo),
University of Milano-Bicocca, Viale Sarca 336-U14-20126 Milan, Italy
e-mail: viscusi@disco.unimib.it

C. Batini
e-mail: batini@disco.unimib.it

M. Castelli
e-mail: castelli@disco.unimib.it

R. Baskerville et al. (eds.), *Designing Organizational Systems*,
Lecture Notes in Information Systems and Organisation 1,
DOI: 10.1007/978-3-642-33371-2_14,

1 Introduction

Design science is recognized as one of the main paradigms of research in information systems [1, 2]. At the state of the art, the major issue for design science in information systems concerns the result of the research: the IT artifact [3, 4]. Indeed, while *constructs*, *models*, *methods*, and *instantiations* are included in broader definitions of IT artifact [1], these latter seem strictly related to a narrow perspective on design of information systems, mainly focused on micro and meso organizational dimensions. In particular, at the state of the art it seems still missing, or at least not yet fully investigated, what Simon [5] called the complexities of designing artifacts on a societal scale (e.g. American Constitution or the voyages to the moon).

It is our belief that the focus on such a societal scale of the design of information systems is currently mainly concerned with e-Government research. Furthermore, we point out that design in e-Government research may provide contribution both for practitioners and academics, on the one hand, resulting in models and methods for systemic policy making and strategic planning; on the other hand, investigating the appropriateness for public sector of recognized models and methods for planning of information systems, mainly defined and applied to private sector.

Taking these issues into account, in this Chapter, we discuss a methodology developed for e-Government initiatives design and planning in the specific context of Mediterranean Countries [6, 7]. The methodology aims to support the definition of strategy implementation roadmaps that consider the fitting of e-Government vision principles, policies and the context of intervention. Moreover, the methodology aims to provide a contribution to design science research on a societal scale, by dealing with the obstacles that Simon recognized as “a budget of planning requirements” [5], even with restraint and simplification typical of a complex decision making process; such obstacles refer to the following issues:

1. problem representation (*Bounded Rationality*);
2. accommodating to the inadequacies that can be expected in data (*Data for planning*);
3. the nature of the clients affects planning (*Identifying the client-Society as the client*);
4. organizations in social design (*Change management both at organizational and societal level*);
5. limits on the planner’s time and attention (*The discounting of time, defining progress*);
6. ambiguity and conflicts of goals in societal planning (*Designing without final goals*).

In this chapter we mainly discuss the methodology as a design artifact valuable for issues such as 1 and 4–6 that Simon considered less formal than issues 2–3, and more specific of the societal design [5]. Nevertheless, as to issue 2, it is worth noting that usually in the design of an e-Government strategy implementation plan or roadmap, data and documents related information are often not inadequate but too adequate in terms of details; in summary, the problem is that public managers have too much information than their capacity of transforming it in appropriate requirements for the planning process. The methodology in this case aims to provide an accessible and appropriate document plan as instantiation and result of the design process.

The chapter is structured as follows. In Sect. 2 we discuss related work on information systems design and planning for e-Government initiatives. In Sect. 3 we introduce the methodology as resulting from a design science research, while in Sect. 4 we present the experience made while using and instantiating the methodology in the specific context of the Tunisian central public administration. Section 4 provides a further discussion of the challenges, the benefits, and the limitations of the instantiation of the methodology in the considered specific context. Conclusion and future work bring the chapter to a close.

2 Related Work

Planning is a relevant area for the design of Information Systems. At the state of the art the research has been focused mainly on business and private sector information systems planning [8], while e-Government and public sector information systems received less attention. Not withstanding, as to the topic of societal level design, public sector information systems and e-Government are a relevant field: in particular this field may provide contribution to the design research in considering less formal tools for managing uncertainty and governance issues [9]. In the e-Government area most of the efforts have been devoted to produce maturity models [10, 11] and frameworks to understand the adoption and diffusion of technology in government and the public sector [12, 13], whereas design models and methods for planning and implementation have been considered by a smaller number of scholars [14–17].

As pointed out by [18] from a design perspective maturity models are mainly a way of ranking e-government initiatives evolution, while obscuring the fact that policy[1] and design choices are instantiated in the form and functions of e-government projects. In the planning literature this is called the issue of *IT strategy alignment* [19]: as to this issue, understanding the homology with policy and design choices represents a relevant open path for design science in e-Government. Indeed, e-Government applications "emerge from the intersection of what is

[1] In general terms, policies can be considered as intention(s), action(s) or as made up of intention(s) and action(s). Principles are "general views about how public affair should be arranged or conducted" (a principle can be considered a specific policy intentions) [30]. Finally, public policy can be considered synonymous with law, rule, statute, edict, and regulation, when considered as "an officially expressed intention backed by a sanction" [31].

possible to do with information and communication technologies at any given point in time and what decision makers choose to accomplish with that technology" [18, p.158]. As to these issues, design in e-Government planning is receiving a growing attention with the diffusion of technologies that increase the user participation and content generation (such as e.g. social network and Web 2.0 technologies) and the need for policies that allows the enactment of open government.

3 The eG4 M Methodology

The methodology, called eG4 M after the e-Government for Mediterranean countries project, where it was conceived and built [6, 7], considers both how ICTs affect organizations and how the social context and the organizations influence the use of technologies in e-Government initiatives. The focus of the analysis is on the ways the different stakeholders interact when introducing ICTs and how these interactions can affect institutions and society at large. On the one hand, the design and development of e-Government initiatives must take into account both the constraints and the opportunities in terms of potential incentives offered by the institutions. As pointed out, e.g., in [20] e-Government is not only about service delivery, but also about a set of innovative institutions. Thus, the evolution of e-Government is a process of institutionalization. On the other hand, the eG4 M methodology considers how social phenomena develop in social contexts characterized by emerging information and communication technologies. These issues impact on the potential contribution of ICT-based initiatives to the efficiency and effectiveness of administrative reforms, where the main challenges are ICT adoption, application, and management [21]. As a consequence, ICT-related strategic choices in the early planning phase are more and more relevant for the effectiveness of the final deployment of the e-Government initiative.

Taking these issues into account, starting from the awareness of the lack of state of the art methodologies specifically designed for e-Government planning [7], eG4 M has been developed to analyze from a systemic perspective the institutional and socio-economic context under review, and to propose interventions, which fit the environment and accompany the changes required for their implementation.

The systemic perspective proposed considers both the outer and the inner context to preserve context diversity in planning e-Government initiatives [22], where the starting point is made up of the available services and the requirements of constituencies (i.e., citizens and businesses). According to this analysis, the planning activity results in the choice of projects which, starting from the current features of the social/technological system, better fit the achievement of new target requirements considered in terms of quality impact for the different layers (legal, socio-economic, processes, resources, and technological layers). The focus on quality in eG4 M is related to the perspective on public value that can be considered not only as the result of a cost-benefit evaluation but also as the degree to which public policies improve the quality of life of constituencies (namely citizens and businesses), by improving the quality of public services and of the public administration organization and processes.

The methodology is made up of two main phases (1) strategic planning and (2) operational planning, which we detail in the following. The strategic planning is made up of four main steps: (1) e-Government vision elicitation, (2) state reconstruction, (3) eReadiness, and (4) quality assessment. In particular we now briefly discuss the (1) e-Government vision elicitation, and the (2) state reconstruction steps, that are relevant for the topics of this Chapter (for a detailed discussion of the methodology we refer to [7]).

The e-Government vision elicitation aims to provide as output a structured policy documentation eliciting the e-Government vision in terms of macro- and micro-objectives to be reached. The inputs to the step are

- a set of principles and policies underlying the intentions and strategies of the political vision declared by public decision makers;
- the legal framework of the context of intervention;
- the available enabling technologies.

The goal of state reconstruction is to provide a clear understanding and knowledge of the general context in which the e-Government intervention takes place. During this step, the knowledge on the social context, laws and rules, services delivered (and administrative processes that produce them), information flows, and technological infrastructures is collected and related. The outputs are a set of matrices, a simple but expressive graphical representation, showing the relationships among the types of knowledge described before.

Taking these issues into account, the eG4 M methodology is a Design Science (DS) artifact whose building and evaluation processes have been carried out under an Action Research (AR) perspective [23]. This is coherent with the debate on similarities and differences between DS and AR [24, 25], which has pointed out a significant overlap in solving "a socio-technical problem by developing a new solution technology and evaluating it in an organizational context" [24]. Indeed, in the course of the eG4 M project, the building of the methodology and the evaluation processes have been carried out by means of a strict interaction with public managers involved in the field work. Furthermore, the different steps of the methodology have been designed on the basis of their appropriateness and effectiveness in contributing to solve the planning problems raised by public managers of the countries involved in the project activities (in particular, Tunisia and Morocco). In this context, enabling the access of population to government services is critical in particular to avoid forcing rural residents to travel to major cities for certification or other core administrative services [1]. In the cited countries, a second critical issue concerns provision of services for the urbanization phenomena, supporting the movement of citizens from rural areas to cities and suburbs of cities. Due to their complexity, these issues require planning activities which consider the social context both at the macro and micro level. This is necessary in order to promote a broad consensus among officials and citizens, and to provide a holistic perspective to senior government leadership, thus promoting their active involvement and commitment.

In the following, we discuss the case of the methodology application to an information systems integration initiative of the Tunisian Ministry of Agriculture and Hydraulic Resources in 2008–2009. Thus, the focus will be on how the methodology can be applied in a specific context for the aims of planning requirements, and in particular for facing (1) problem representation and (2) organizations in social design (see the discussion of the six issues identified by Simon in the introduction to this Chapter).

4 Case Study

In this Section we discuss a case study, from the field work at the Tunisian central public administration. The case study [26] aims at showing "how" the instantiation of the methodology has been carried out, and to point out the challenges of moving from policies to designing an e-Government initiative at societal scale.

The case study has been carried out following an interpretive approach to Action Research [27, 28], aiming to understand how participants interpret their context and act on the basis of their interpretation of institutional constraints, influencing also the subjective construction of the interpretation of observations by the researchers. Thus, the research team has had access to the field through the e-Government Unit of the Tunsian Prime Ministry. The research activities have been carried out from June 2007 to April 2009. Moreover, the access to the field of the main experimentation at the Ministry of Agriculture (started in February 2008) required the following preliminary actions:

- two preliminary seminars to Chief Information Officers and Executives of Tunisian Central Public Administration;
- the signature of a memorandum of understanding between the coordinator of the eG4 M project and the Minister Delegate to the Prime Minister for Public Service and Administrative Development (December 14th, 2007), with the involvement of Italian Embassy in Tunis;
- a further set of introductory seminars in French to the eG4 M methodology and the related topics (IS Planning, Data Governance, Business Process Management, e-Readiness, etc.); the seminars participants were mainly Chief Information Officers and Executives of Tunisian Central Public Administration (January 2008).

It is worth noting that the e-Government Unit was in charge of the supervision, coordination, and control of all the e-Government initiatives and of the e-Government strategy definition. As to these issues, the e-Government vision elicitation step of the methodology has considered as input for the state reconstruction step the guiding principles of this strategy [29]:

- efficiency and effectiveness of the Public Administration procedures and services;
- cost reduction;
- transparency;
- accountability and reporting.

These principles were related to a set of policies [29], guiding the initiatives at the Tunisian Ministry of Agriculture and Hydraulic Resources (MAHR in the following), such as the following ones:

- strengthening communication and information exchange within the different units and departments at central, regional and local levels;
- strengthening the capacity of public servants with regard to e-Government.

It is worth noting that the above mentioned set of introductory seminars to the eG4 M methodology raised the awareness of the IT executives of the MAHR about the fitness between their strategic needs of the MAHR and the goals of the eG4 M research activity. This issue facilitated the involvement of the MAHR by the E-Government Unit, which coordinated, organized, and supervised all the sessions of the participatory design activities. The E-Government Unit acted as a mediator with the local context and a facilitator for the eG4 M researchers; on the other hand, these latter were in charge of the planning activities and related documentation in French. Thus, the use of Arab or French language represented a requirement for the access to the field. Indeed, while English was spoken by E-Government Unit members and IT staff in most of the ministries, the administrative staff used to adopt Arab and French as official languages of the Tunisian bureaucracy, as most of the laws and technical documents were written in these two languages.

Taking these issues into account, we now consider the strategic challenge for the Tunisian MAHR, which was the integration at a horizontal level of databases of the central administrative departments; the goal is to have an integrated vision on the whole set of activities and matters the Ministry is in charge of, supporting strategic and political decisions and forecasts, e.g., on the productivity of the agricultural sector. Because of their role in MAHR core processes, four major administrative departments were given priority, namely:

- the department in charge of the restructuring of agricultural state-owned domains, owner of the agricultural state property database;
- the department of veterinary services, owner of the veterinary services database;
- the department of water resources, owner of the water resources database;
- the department of agricultural production, owner of the agricultural production database.

As for the current information systems of the four departments, it is worth noting here that the requirements collection and the technical design were outsourced to local private companies. Considering these issues, the MAHR has been the focus of the application of the eG4 M methodology mainly for the strategic planning phase. In the following, we first focus on the use of the methodology as a tool for solving problem representation issues (Simon's issue 1).

4.1 Problem Representation

The state reconstruction step of the eG4 M methodology has been focused on the reverse engineering of the current logical database representations, resulting in the production of a conceptual representation for each database and of an integrated conceptual representation in terms of a global schema; this has been done with the initial goal of conceiving a new target database architecture and the final goal of offering integrated services to internal and final users. The "new database architecture" activity has been developed through participatory design workshops involving four teams composed of three civil servants (one senior manager and two middle-level managers) from the four departments. A three days a week workshop had a monthly frequency. ICT skills and computer literacy among the participants were not homogeneous, where a major divide was mainly related to the age of the attendees and to their functional roles in the organization (some departments being represented by the IT staff while others by non-IT human resources). Thus, the main goal here has been to build with the collaboration of the public managers a complete and integrated view of the information content managed by MAHR. To achieve this goal, we applied data governance methods as complimentary steps of the eG4 M methodology strategic planning phase [7].

The final result is shown at a high level of abstraction in Fig. 1. A different type of line is associated with each schema, which will also be used in the following to distinguish the different schemas.

Among other results, the participatory analysis performed on the integrated schema (Fig. 1) allowed making public servants aware of the presence of different entities common to several schemas. In Fig. 1 the multiplicity of schemas in which an entity is involved is graphically highlighted by the number of incoming/outcoming edges. This situation usually leads to redundant representation of data and high risks of misalignment among the different copies of the same data. As a consequence a recommendation by the eG4 M researchers has been that of considering in the future architecture a cooperative publish and subscribe layer among schemas that disciplines and aligns the updates of the entity instances in different databases.

As for this recommendation, the IT executives agreed to carry out a set of further analysis and participatory activities concerning:

- the data quality evaluation of the databases, in terms of their accuracy, currency, and completeness, in order to assess the effectiveness of the current administrative processes and services provided by the public administration;
- the representation of the interactions between organizational units of MAHR in terms of services and related processes, together with the types of information

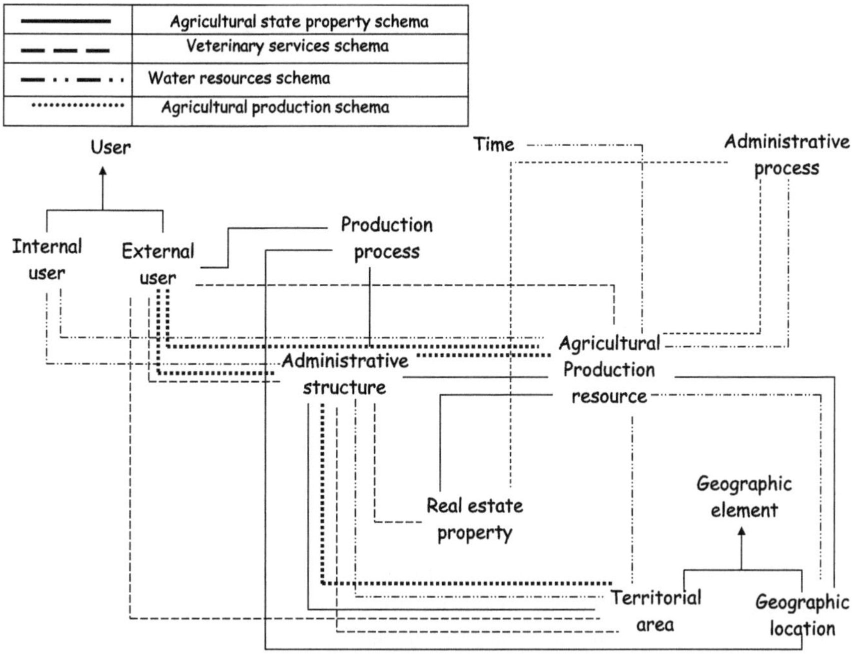

Fig. 1 The integrated schema with the four local schemas in evidence

involved and the ownership of the databases; the goal here was to define the priority intervention areas in the integration initiative.

The analysis moved from the databases to the information systems of the four departments mentioned above, where the focus at this stage concerned the following topics: (1) agricultural state property; (2) veterinary services; (3) water resources; (4) agricultural production. These topics were investigated in terms of interactions between different department units for specific processes or information flows.

In the following, we first provide an example of problem representation issues having an impact on the organizations in social design (Simon's issue 4). Then, we discuss the results of the above mentioned second set of participatory activities for the information systems of the four departments of the MAHR.

4.2 Organizations in Social Design

The MAHR jurisdiction was in practice on all the territory of the country. Not withstanding, while all department databases need to represent the territory in their schemas, only one database, the Water resources database explicitly represented the geographic localization. This choice resulted in heterogeneities in the

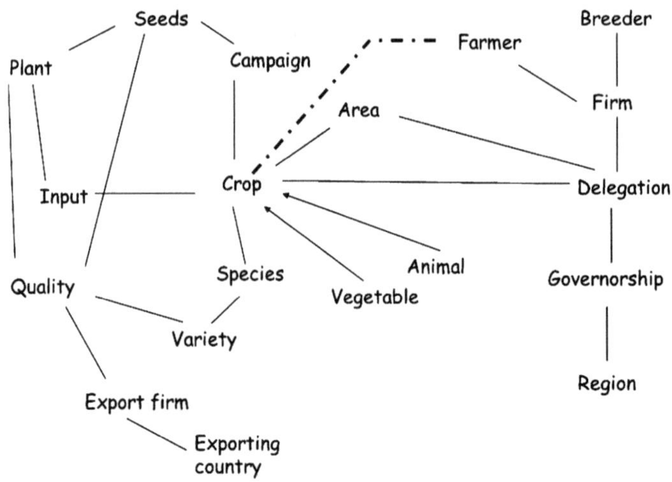

Fig. 2 Conceptual schema of the department of agricultural production information system

representation of the territory and led to limited integration in the representation of the different entities grounded in the territory, e.g., the state property resources cannot be correlated with the cadastral databases, which another ministry is in charge of. A design decision has been to move to a homogeneous representation of the territory in the four databases, by means of a spatial DBMS, namely a DBMS that allows representing natively in the logical model spatial objects (such as points, lines, polylines, areas). The participatory analysis activities emphasized other problems.

As an example, once designed the re-engineered conceptual schema of the information system of the department of agricultural production (Fig. 2), one of the senior managers (educated as computer engineer) attending the workshop pointed out that the schema was wrong, due to the lack of a relationship between the entity Farmer and the entity Crop (a kind of strategic information in the case of MAHR).

As a consequence, in order to validate and check the issues emerged from the participatory design activities, we first checked with the help of other attendees the correspondence between schemas produced with the ones produced by the outsourcer company: the result was negative. At this point all the attendees became aware of the fact that in order to maintain the control over the outsourcer companies, the methodology and the participatory work can be very helpful in providing an effective instrument for managing information and knowledge of interest for the administration. Furthermore, among the participants awareness arose that in strategic and operational activities on the whole information system of the administration it may be worthwhile to leave the deployment and maintenance activities to the market (namely, private vendors), while the public administration has to retain the planning, design, and quality monitoring of the e-Government projects, with particular attention paid to data

Table 1 Indicators and dimensions for the choice of integration technologies

Indicator	Dimension
Condition of use (strategy)	Economic value of the integration
	Costs of heterogeneity
	Relevance of historical data
Condition of use (organization)	Autonomy of management
	Management complexity
Condition of use (processes)	Relevance of queries with respect to transactions
	Query complexity
Condition of use (information flows)	Volatility of queries
	Relevance of currency of data in queries

governance decisions. These conclusions guided the second set of participatory activities mentioned in the previous (Section 4.1), which supported a shared choice of integration solutions by the four department of the MAHR.

We chose first a set of indicators and related dimensions (see Table 1), to be used in the decision table that would guide the integration choices. Further, to represent the relationships between the various aspects of the information system we produced matrices relating the following issues:

- Services-Laws-Processes
- Processes-involved organizations
- Involved organizations-databases owned/managed.

For each matrix, the participants were asked to provide information such as:

- number of levels of intervening management between staff and managers in the organizational structure of the considered departments;
- number of organizational units involved in the information flow/process;
- number of yearly updates for each database table involved in the considered information flow/process;
- number of instances for each database table involved in the considered information flow/process.

The filling of the matrices and the related information was supported by a further set of seminars and joint work with the eG4 M researchers. This joint work has been carried out partly at the MAHR and partly by mail from December 2008 to April 2009. The main difficulty was related to the need for public managers to focus on a limited set of administrative processes and of related services provided by departments and to analyze separately the processes/services from specific units or functions involved inside departments. Another challenge was the retrieving of analytic data related e.g. to the number of queries in a given time unit required by a specific process. All of the above activities resulted in the production of a decision table, which provides the most relevant correspondences between values of the dimensions appearing in Table 1 and ICT and integration technologies to be adopted. As for integration technologies, we considered the following solutions:

Table 2 Indicators and required value for a set of technological solutions for information systems integration

Dimensions	Technological solutions			
	Data warehouse	Enterprise application integration/ publish and subscribe	Consolidation	Data integration
Economic value of the integration	High	High	High	High
Costs of heterogeneities	–	–	High	High
Relevance of historical data	High	–	–	–
Autonomy of management	–	High	Low	–
Management complexity	–	–	High	–
Relevance of queries with respect to transactions	–	–	–	High
Query complexity	High	–	–	–
Volatility of queries	–	–	–	High
Relevance of currency in queries	–	Low	–	High

(a) data warehouse, (b) enterprise application integration (publish and subscribe), (c) consolidation, and (d) data integration. The result of the overall activity identified Publish and Subscribe as a suitable technological solution for all the departments, these latter fulfilling dimensions such as high autonomy and low relevance of querying with respect to update operations; whereas a data warehouse solution was suitable and required by the department in charge of the restructuring of agricultural state-owned domains, the department of veterinary services, and the department of agricultural production, considering the relevance of historical data and the complexity of the queries executed on a yearly basis (Table 2).

5 Discussion of the Results

The success of public sector investments in e-Government initiatives strongly depends on effectively exploiting all aspects of ICT systems and infrastructures. The related objectives are hardly reachable without methodological frameworks that provide a holistic perspective and knowledge on the domain of application of e-Government initiatives. Yet public administrators usually have a mix of legal and administrative knowledge, while lacking an information systems background. As a consequence, the design of artifacts on a societal scale, such as e.g. in e-Government initiatives, represents a challenge for practitioners and a research path for scholars in the field of information systems design.

Taking these issues into account, the chapter discusses the case of the instantiation of a comprehensive methodology for e-Government planning, which as a design artifact has provided a contribution to problem representation in terms of having a shared and integrated schema of the information systems of the involved organization.

The participatory design of the integrated schema contributed to solve the problem of strengthening the communication and information exchange within the different departments of the Ministry of Agriculture. This activity allowed to create, on the one hand, a competence on conceptual modeling by public servants with no previous IT competencies; on the other hand, IT skilled public servants had the opportunity to share their views by leveraging on a common representation of the information system. Furthermore, the design activity allowed both IT and non IT skilled public servants to identify the problems in data representation with reference to the value of the information for e-Government services currently provided or yet to be designed, according to the political agenda.

As for the issue of organizations in social design, the use of the methodology enhanced the awareness of the relevance of a critical perspective on outsourcing and the need for a control by public managers of the core activities in e-Government, such as e.g. the conceptual modeling of information systems. The discussion on the conceptual schema of the department of agricultural production information system led to a proposal of outsourcing model, where public managers are in charge of strategic design and monitoring activities, and the vendors are in charge of deployment of the chosen project/solution.

Finally the participatory choice of the appropriate technological solution, on the one hand has shown how a certain solution (for example a middleware) does not fit for all the units (in our case departments) of a complex organizations, where advantages in adoption must be evaluated at different levels (strategy, organization, processes, information flows); on the other hand, a clear strategy (for example the need for integrating information systems) can provide a roadmap for technological solutions that seems unrelated. In our case, data warehouse and publish and subscribe may be considered a first step and a foundation for evolutionary processes that from a focus on information integration may move towards a focus on information as the core for complex transaction and services supported by enterprise application integration solutions. In this example, the focus is also on the costs and benefits in terms of capabilities and facilities enabled by a given technological solution. This cost-benefits analysis has not been performed; nonetheless we think that also this kind of analysis could result from a participatory design among the potential users and adopters.

As for the role of the eG4 M researchers, the main contribution consists in what at the state of the art is named as a facilitator, whose goal is to enable "conversations" that contribute to the definition of a shared view among different organizational units [32]. The steps and the tools (matrices, schemas, etc.) of the methodology represented an enabler of the activities of the facilitator, providing a configurable platform for the participatory design process. Finally, considering the practical implications of this analysis, a set of preliminary recommendations for action in design at societal level are provided as an output of the case study. In particular,

- the research activity and the related actions must be framed in a legal document that details the principles, the goals, the institutional constraints and duties of the partnership;
- the involvement and commitment of decision makers at higher political level is a necessary condition for having an effective participation of different Ministries and the engagement of the public managers (executive);
- the design activity must produce an elicitation of the goals that derive from the strategy principles and policies in order to frame further activities of state reconstruction of the information system in the current institutional setting. Clear policies are a necessary condition for effective design at societal scale;
- design activities must involve small teams (max ten persons) with mixed competences and roles (a half of the team made up of middle managers and project managers, a half of operational staff);
- the more the design artifact (in our case a methodology) is revised and perceived by public managers involved in the design activity as having an impact on their daily procedures and activities, the more the artifact is perceived as co-produced and suitable to solve the organizational problems;
- a preliminary capacity building activity is often necessary in order to align the different knowledge and disciplines to the current organizational culture and information literacy;
- a preliminary evaluation of the relevance of the language constraints is mandatory for the effectiveness of further collaboration and communication with all the stakeholders;
- the focus must be on enabling the building of a shared view on the problem where methodologies for planning must be considered as an active instrument [5] for enacting appropriate e-Government initiatives and satisfying solutions.

These recommendations are obviously limited to the results of the case study. Nevertheless, we think they are a starting point suitable to be extended and revised by other researchers interested in e-Government as a design activity at societal scale.

6 Conclusion and Future Work

The chapter discusses a case study of instantiation of a methodology for e-Government Planning at the Tunisian Ministry of Agriculture, focusing on some of the challenging issues mentioned by Simon [5] for design of artifacts on a societal scale: problem representation (issue 1), and organizations in social design (issue 4). The discussion in previous sections has pointed out the challenges and the benefits of using the methodology in the case of the Tunisian Ministry of Agriculture. Furthermore, a set of clear recommendations for action in design at societal level are provided as a result from the case study. As a conclusion, we now carry out a discussion on further applications of the methodology and some evidence as to further evaluation activities of the methodology as design artifact.

As for the first issue, we are currently applying the methodology in other MENA (Middle East and North Africa) countries, in particular for the definition of policies and implementation roadmaps [33]. As to evaluation of the design results, we are focusing in particular on limits on the planner's time and attention (Simon's issue 5) and ambiguity and conflicts of goals in societal planning (issue 6). As for issue 5 the methodology instantiation in Italy, Tunisia, Morocco and other MENA countries, has produced plans with different time ranges for completing the entire cycle of the methodology (strategic planning phase). Besides the experiences with public managers, from January 2010 to December 2011 nearly 40 Italian master students and 35 Mena Countries master students of Information Systems courses (these latter in July 2011) have been in charge of providing a final examination essay consisting in the instantiation of the methodology on a strategic planning proposal for local and central administrations e-Government services. The resulting plans required an average of two man-weeks.

The limitation of the evaluation is related to the sample, that is mainly composed of master students, whereas public managers involvement and engagement is required. In future work, we will improve the evaluation setting and we will extend it to a large set of public managers (in Italy as in MENA countries where we can have access to the field through current ongoing academic or institutional projects). In future work we will further develop design issues related to the convergence of policies, social context, and development practices. Finally, as for issue 2 (data for planning) we are currently investigating the factors influencing information value [34] in order to build a model for supporting both public and private managers in the evaluation of their information asset and to transform it in appropriate requirements for the planning process and strategy decision making.

References

1. Hevner, A. R., March, S. T., Park, J., & Ram, S. (2004). Design Science in information systems research. *MIS Quarterly, 28*(1), 75–105.
2. March, S., & Smith, G. (1995). Design and natural science research on information technology. *Decision Support Systems, 15*, 251–266.
3. Orlikowski, W. J., & Iacono, C. S. (2001). Desperately seeking the 'IT'in IT research: A call to theorizing the IT artifact. *Information systems the state of the field, 34*, 121–134.
4. Weber, R. (2003). Still desperately seeking the IT artifact. *MIS Quarterly, 27*(2), iii–xi.
5. Simon, H. A. (1996). *The sciences of the artificial* (3rd ed.). Cambridge: The MIT Press.
6. Batini, C., Viscusi, G., & Cherubini, D. (2009). GovQual: A quality driven methodology for e-government project planning. *Government Information Quarterly, 26*(1), 106–117.
7. Viscusi, G., Batini, C., & Mecella, M. (2010). Information systems for eGovernment: A quality-of-service perspective. Heidelberg: Springer.
8. King, W. R. (2009). Planning for information systems. Advances in Management Information Systems (AMIS), Armonk, N.Y: M.E. Sharpe.
9. Christensen, K. S. (1985). Coping with uncertainty in planning. *Journal of the American Planning Association, 51*(1), 63–73.
10. Layne, K., & Lee, J. (2001). Developing fully functional eGovernment: A four stage model. *Government Information Quarterly, 18*(2), 122–136.

11. Andersen, K. V., & Henriksen, H. Z. (2006). E-government maturity models: Extension of the Layne and Lee model. *Government Information Quarterly, 23*, 236–248.
12. Fountain, J. E. (2001). *Building the virtual state: Information technology and institutional change*. Washington, DC: Brookings Institution Press.
13. Cordella, A., & Iannacci, F.(2010) Information systems in the public sector: the e-Government enactment framework. *The Journal of Strategic Information Systems, 19*(1), 52–66.
14. Heeks, R. (2005). *Implementing and managing egovernment: An international text*. London: SAGE Publications.
15. Palkovits, S., & Wimmer, M. A. (2003). Processes in e-Government—A holistic framework for modelling electronic public services. In R. Traunmüller (Ed.), *Electronic government: Second international conference, EGOV 2003, Prague, Czech Republic, September 2003: Proceedings, LNCS* (Vol. 2739, pp. 213–219).
16. Jansen, A. (2006). What role has Scandinavian IS tradition in eGovernment implementations. *Electronic Government: 5th International Conference, EGOV 2006, Krakow, Poland, LNCS* (Vol. 4084, pp. 47–57). Heidelberg: Springer.
17. Grönlund, Å. (2002). *Electronic government: Design, applications and management*. Hershey: Idea Group Inc (IGI).
18. Harrison, T. M., & Zappen, J. P. (2010). Designing e-government: Exploring the potential of new information and communication technology paradigms for democratic purposes. In H. J. Scholl (Ed.), *E-government: information, technology, and transformation* (Vol. 17, pp. 156–178). M.E. Sharpe: Armonk, NY.
19. Luftman, J. N. (1996). *Competing in the information age: Strategic alignment in practice*. New York: Oxford University Press.
20. Yang, K. (2003). Neoinstitutionalism and e-government: Beyond Jane Fountain. *Social Science Computer Review, 21*(4), 432–442.
21. Misuraca, G., & Viscusi, G. (2010) E-Governance for development: Designing an operational roadmap for ICT-enabled public administration reform. In D. Piaggesi, J. Sund, W. Castelnovo (Eds.), *Global strategy and practice of e-governance: Examples from around the world*. Hershey: IGI Global Publishing.
22. Avgerou, C. (2001). The significance of context in information systems and organizational change. *Information Systems Journal, 11*, 43–63.
23. Baskerville, R. L., & Wood-Harper, A. T. (1998). Diversity in information systems action research methods. *European Journal of Information Systems, 7*, 90–107.
24. Iivari, J., Venable, J. R. (2009). *Action research and design science research—Seemingly similar but decisively dissimilar*. In proceedings of ECIS 2009.
25. Iivari, J. (2007). A paradigmatic analysis of information systems as a design science. *Scandinavian Journal of Information Systems, 19*(2), 39–63.
26. Yin, R. K. (2009). *Case study research: design and methods* (4th ed.). Thousand Oaks: Sage Publications.
27. Klein, H. K., & Myers, M. D. (1999). A set of principles for conducting and evaluating interpretive field studies in information systems. *MIS Quarterly, 23*, 67–93.
28. Walsham, G. (1995). Interpretive case studies in IS research: Nature and method. *European Journal of Information Systems, 4*, 74–81.
29. Zammouri, K. (2008). Les bonnes pratiques en Tunisie en matière d'e-gouvernement: Une administration électronique pour une administration communicante. In Workshop on E-Government strategic planning and best practices in the Middle East and North African region.
30. Page, E. C. (2006). The origins of policy. In M. Moran, M. Rein & R. E. Goodin (Eds.), *Oxford handbook of public policy* (pp. 207–227). Oxford, UK: Oxford University Press.
31. Lowi, T. (1998). Foreword: New dimensions in policy and politics. In R. Tatalovich & B. Daynes (Eds.), *Moral controversies in American Politics: Cases in social regulatory policy*. Armonk, NY: M. E.Sharpe.

32. Hansen, A. M., Kraemmergaard, P., & Mathiassen, L. (2011). Rapid adaptation in digital transformation: A participatory process for engaging IS and business leaders. *MIS Quarterly Executive, 10*(4), 175–185.
33. Viscusi, G. (2011). *OECD policy frameworks and instruments: How academics can contribute? Reflections from MENA experiences.* The 7th meeting of the OECD Working Group II on Open and Innovative Government "Open to be innovative: a new partnership between citizens and their governments", 28–29, November 2011, Seoul, Republic of Korea.
34. Batini, C., Cappiello, C., Francalanci, C., Maurino, A., & Viscusi, G. (2011). *A capacity and value based model for data architectures adopting integration technologies.* AMCIS 2011 Proceedings -Paper 327 .

Towards the Redesign of e-Business Maturity Models for SMEs

Paolo Depaoli and Stefano Za

Abstract This paper shows the results of the conceptual part of a research aimed at redesigning e-business stage models for small and medium size enterprises (SMEs). The literature review shows that these models are based mostly on a techno-centric perspective and are rather mechanistic in their approach to the development of e-business in smaller firms. Based on design science—which offers a methodology capable of understanding business needs deriving from the interplay of people, organization and technology—a non-linear stage model for the development of e-business in SMEs is proposed. Different levels of interaction in the exchange of information between a firm and its suppliers and customers characterize e-business: the model includes four levels and it outlines their main organizational implications. The model is not meant to be prescriptive, that is it is not intended to serve as an evaluation ladder for public administrations deciding to grant financial support to SMEs investing in e-business. Rather, it has an interpretive, organizational character: (i) entrepreneurs can be supported in their understanding and evaluation of the organizational needs connected with the exploitation of a given opportunity by means of different levels of digital interaction and (ii) policy makers can be guided in promoting the appropriate support (e.g.: training and advisory services) to different kinds of SMEs.

Keywords e-Business · SMEs · Maturity model · Non-linear stage model

P. Depaoli (✉) · S. Za
CeRSI – LUISS Guido Carli University, Rome, Italy
e-mail: pdepaoli@luiss.it

R. Baskerville et al. (eds.), *Designing Organizational Systems*,
Lecture Notes in Information Systems and Organisation 1,
DOI: 10.1007/978-3-642-33371-2_15,

1 Introduction

In the past decade information systems research has been studying the relationship between small and medium size enterprises (SMEs) and e-business identifying a number of factors that characterize this phenomenon. Outcomes indicate that the focus on customer motivations are most important in adopting e-business with smaller firms positioned at the early stages of e-business implementation [1]. Other research—based on a survey of North American and European SMEs—has found that Internet business solutions are adopted internationally to improve performance with tangible financial benefits achieved. Results show an uneven distribution across regions, industries, technologies, or size categories and suggest the adoption of a staged approach to maximize performance gains [2]. Improvements in the competitive position are reached when e-business investments are coherent with the environment and strategic objectives of SMEs and with their technology management capabilities [3]. The importance of the level of e-business assimilation on the part of the firm that intends to invest further in this area has been considered a decisive factor towards the use of maturity (or stage) models when evaluating investments in this area. In fact if, on the one hand, e-business investments are capable of containing the pressure of competitors, reducing costs and improving performance [4], on the other hand, there are instances of delay or failure in implementing the projects [5, 6].

Maturity models suggested for SMEs that are involved in e-business can be considered as road-maps in which these type of firms can measure their own actual conditions related to every stage, considering the relative barriers and facilitators for each one of them [7].

Some authors have questioned the appropriateness of the use of stage models in this context because such models are considered to be too generic, to overlook the diverse nature and needs of SMEs, and not to be supported by empirical evidence [8]. Other research suggests that there may not be a sequential path to e-business adoption after all [9]

Two are the aims of this contribution. First, to consider the present debate in the literature in order to categorize the pros and cons in the use of maturity models in the context of e-business and SMEs. Second, to propose a non-linear stage model for the development of e-business, not based on a techno-centric approach. A mechanistic and technology driven view seems in fact to pervade this type of models and literature (see below) so that the research gap addressed concerns the possibility of taking into account the interplay of technology and organization in the design of stage models.

The methodological approach adopted is based on an overarching approach, the conceptual Information Systems Research Framework [10] whereby research (meant to be both relevant and rigorous) includes the development, evaluation and refinement of theories and artifacts as the outcome of the analysis of both 'business needs' (deriving from the relevant environment as a combination of 'people', 'organization', and 'technology') and 'applicable knowledge' (resulting from the rigorous application of appropriate 'theories and methodologies'). Therefore, the following relevant areas are combined to pursue the research aims stated above: (i)'business needs' refer to the needs that SMEs ('organization')—led by their entrepreneurs and workers ('people' with their capabilities)—can satisfy by interacting digitally (e-business 'technology' as an enabler) with their suppliers and customers; (ii) applicable knowledge comprises the theoretical background on the interaction between technology and organizations and relevant research on maturity models.

As for the theoretical underpinnings, the interplay of technology and organization has been considered according to Orlikowski's principle of 'entanglement in organizational practice' of technology [11].

The research work started with an in-depth literature review to categorize strengths and weaknesses of stage models. They have been developed to depict the different stages that characterize the adoption of information systems [12] and specifically the path towards e-business in SMEs [7]. Relevant papers where searched on main e-libraries (ACM, AIS, EBSCO) using as key words 'SMEs', 'e-commerce', 'e-business', 'maturity model', and 'stage model'.

The paper is structured as follows. The first paragraph describes the main stage models developed in the literature (and specifically aimed at SMEs) classifying them into three groups according to the basic orientation chosen for describing the scope of e-business: towards either promoting 'integration' or managing 'customers' or harnessing 'interaction'. The following section comments on the findings and examines the criticisms that have been addressed to stage models and are specifically relevant for this paper. The third section introduces the proposed 'non-linear stage model for the development of e-business in SMEs'. The following section discusses the advantages of the proposed model. The final paragraph contains the concluding remarks and it outlines both present limitations and subsequent research work.

2 Literature Review: Exploring the Different e-Business Stage Models for SMEs

The eight stage models that have been examined can be grouped according to the prevailing scope of e-business that more or less explicitly the researchers have considered when subdividing the development of systems. Three groups emerge:

- Integration-aware models: they are mainly related to the technological integration between internal and external systems. In these three models e-commerce is one stage of e-business.
- Customer-aware models: e-commerce is the main focus even though it is considered as a part of e-business; they are mainly concerned with customer side communication and web-site development.

- Interaction-aware models: technology supports the interaction between different actors; even though centered once again on technology, they are closer to the model proposed in this paper.

2.1 Integration-Aware Models

The common objective of the three models is to drive SMEs towards increasing the integration level between internal and external systems, supported by the Internet (i.e. mail, web-presence, supply-chain integration, etc.). Since they are mainly focused on technology adoption, they basically show their value in their "capacity to offer a simple means of benchmarking ICT activity" ([13], p. 850)

From their multi-case study analysis, Poon and Swatman [14] propose a three stage model regarding three levels (minimum, limited and full) of Internet-to-internal application integration, taking into account some organizational process adjustments (such as passing from the traditional transaction methods to Internet-based payment systems). From a multi-case study they show that the standard applications (i.e. e-mail and web-browsers) are used by SMEs with little or no Internet-to-internal application integration (e.g.: if a customer sends a purchase order using e-mail, most firms need to process it manually). The full integration is only reached once SMEs identify apparent advantages, either direct benefits (e.g.: saving communication costs) or indirect ones (e.g.: advertising and marketing, new business initiatives).

Willcocks et al. [15] provide a four stage model on Internet technology adoption. In the first stage firms use basic Internet tools such as web pages to develop web presence on the Internet. The next stage (transacting business) requires a careful assessment of benefits that can be obtained through available resources. The firm moves to stage three (e-commerce context) when it acknowledges the fact that it needs to change processes, structures and skills in order to exploit the technology. Stage 4 (e-business) is reached when it is possible to use the Internet to develop new markets and products.

Martin and Matlay [16] describe and discuss a five stage model for e-business adoption by SMEs, (which includes the two preceding models) where the sets of functionalities for each stage are described: the use of e-mail for internal and external communication (stage 1), adopting a web-site (stage 2), implementing e-commerce features (order and pay on line—stage 3), developing e-business capabilities (integration in the supply chain—stage 4), opening the system to partners, supplier and customers (stage 5). This model, known also as the "adoption ladder", was proposed in the U.K. by the Department of Trade and Industry (DTI) to encourage SMEs in their e-commerce adoption at the beginning of the years 2000.

2.2 Customer-Aware Models

The two models described below are oriented to provide guidelines to SMEs when digital technology is adopted to improve the relationship with customers. It basically entails the development of a firm's web-site in order to enable customers to choose the products and services, to order them and to make online payments. Compared to the models in the previous group, these ones take into account only the stages for planning e-commerce adoption without even mentioning the successive steps concerning e-business.

Chaston et al. [17] adopt an eleven stage model for firms that decide to become more involved in e-commerce. They considered the model to be reliable since a focus group of entrepreneurs acknowledged its plausibility. The steps in the adoption of technologies (and their use) are the following: the starting point is email used for communication purposes with customers (stage 1) and then for promotion in advertising campaigns (stage 2). In stage 3 groupware systems are adopted, and in stage 4 the Internet is used to expand market knowledge. Promotional web-sites are designed in stage 5, their integration in the overall marketing strategy takes place in stage 6, and online purchasing is included in stage 7 while order tracking is achieved in stage 8. In stage 9 customers are involved to design web sites, to configure and price products (stage 10) and to customize extranet systems (stage 11). This stage model is strongly focused on customers, showing the evolution of the functionalities of web sites which become the most important communication channel.

Burgess et al. [18] use a case study (Australian wineries) approach to analyze the evolution of web sites for SMEs. They identify three main stages for measuring the maturity of the website development: information provision (general, product and business contact information); ordering and sales (order by email or online and online sales): creation of an online community for the SMEs customers (a sort of simple social network).

2.3 Interaction-Aware Models

The following three models have a main objective in common: to guide SMEs to e-business applications adoption so that a more efficient and effective interaction takes place between the firm and all the stakeholders (and not only customers). However, the interaction perspective in two models does not consider any organizational implication. Only Rao et al. [7] mention the existence of non-technological facilitators (e.g.: the commitment of the firm to reach strategic goals by means of e-business) and barriers (e.g.: costs, resistance to IS use by employees).

Daniel et al. [19], expecting SMEs to be involved in e-commerce (but they actually mean e-business) in a sequence of stages, perform a research based on surveys and define four distinct clusters. The first group of firms are developing their first e-commerce services (developers), those at the second stage of adoption were using e-mail to communicate with customers, suppliers and employees (communicators). Those at the third level of adoption had information-based websites operating and were developing on-line ordering facilities (web presence). The most advanced adopters (transactors) had on-line ordering in operation and were developing on-line payment capabilities.

Magal et al. [6] undertake a research to test the robustness of Daniels et al.'s [19] four-stage model by increasing the number of the e-business applications. By means of their cluster analysis, they find evidence for a three stage instead of a four stage model. In fact, their first level includes the characteristics of the first two stages in Daniel's model ('developers' and 'communicators'). In stage one firms devote minimal attention to e-business activities (probably because of their orientation to local markets); in stage two firms may be in a transitional stage (because they use supply chain functions but a moderate use of other applications). Stage three shows a more mature stage of e-business adoption, particularly for service-providing firms, with a higher intensity of use of a large number of applications.

Rao et al. [7] propose a four stage model and, as mentioned above, it is the only model to include facilitators and barriers in each stage of development. The first stage is named 'presence': showing company brochures and products on web site; 'portals' is the name of the second stage: introduction of two-way communication, customer or supplier order placing, the use of profiles and cookies; 'transactions integration' is the third stage: presence of financial transactions between partners requiring higher technical capabilities, and IT infrastructure; and 'enterprises integration' indicates the final stage: complete integration of business processes to the extent that old-line business is indistinguishable from online business. It involves high levels of collaboration between customers and suppliers using customer relationship management or supply chain management.

3 Discussion on the Models: Comments and Criticisms

The analysis of the literature shows that different definitions of e-business have been used by authors: in some cases they are considered to be the same as e-commerce [6, 7, 14, 19], in some other cases e-commerce is considered instead to be one of the stages of the e-business stage model proposed or analyzed [15, 16].

When the two words are used to indicate the same concept, e-commerce includes Internet technologies to support buying and selling activities and also other technologies—such as e-mail, web sites, and web portals—enabling the exchange or the sharing of information either within the organization itself or with external stakeholders [8, 19]. In some cases e-commerce is considered to be a business model whereby transactions and information exchange are conducted between organizations and people using information technology in order to conduct such processes in a more effective and efficient way [7].

As in the work by Taylor et al. [20] and Zheng et al. [21], in this paper e-commerce is considered as a part of e-business because the two concepts differ. As in Rodgers et al. [22], e-commerce refers primarily to buying and selling activities over the Internet, focusing on customer needs and including placing orders, making payments, and tracking the delivery of orders over the Internet. On the other hand, e-business generally refers to the use of the Web and Internet-related technologies to extend the connectivity of an organization beyond customers to include other actors such as suppliers, employees, and regulatory authorities. In sum, e-business is an area where "economic value creation and information technology (IT) come together and enable inter-organizational connectivity" [23]. In this paper, the term 'interaction' is preferred to 'connectivity' to underline the organizational character of exchanges (see below the paragraph on the proposed model).

As shown in the preceding section, in spite of the varying number of stages, there is a common view concerning the evolution of e-business adoption in SME. The adoption starts with the use of e-mail and static web sites containing basic product and service information and contact details, to reach the most mature stages where the business web site is fully integrated with back office systems (even though there is scant empirical evidence that this final stage is actually achieved in a significant number of cases). From the first to the last stages there are different levels of integration characterized by a progressive use of some applications for communicating with customers and suppliers, for finding business information, for e-retailing (buying and selling online), and also for supporting the order tracked on the web site. The assumption is that the higher the stage reached, the greater the benefits obtained (e.g.: reduction in communication costs, advertising and marketing for new business initiatives).

Another common characteristic that runs across the three groups of models is that they provide a sequential and progressive set of stages. For each one of them, specific technologies are suggested to implement specific e-business functionalities.

A critical appraisal of these models can be found in the literature: a growing number of authors have questioned the appropriateness of e-business adoption stage models in the context of SMEs [8]. Martin et al. [16] argue that the stage model based approach is misdirected and likely to fail. Indeed the UK government's target of 1 million SMEs trading online by the end of 2002 was missed by more than 50%: the Department of Trade and Industry had suggested to follow a five stage model (which became known as the 'adoption ladder'). According to Zheng et al. [21] stage models (like Willcocks') are more relevant and useful for large firms rather than for SMEs. The variety and uniqueness of smaller firms is not taken into account by these models.

In general, the literature review conducted for this paper has shown—as Taylor and Murphy [20] argue—that maturity models have considered e-business adoption only from a technological perspective. Furthermore, they often assume a sequential and progressive engagement with e-business information technology. Given the diversity of SMEs, it is necessary to better understand how these firms recognize and develop business opportunities in general, and not just the ones that might or might not be associated with a particular set of technologies [20]. Indeed, Levy et al. [9] argue that because SMEs may choose to only implement selected Internet applications (which coincide with their growth and business value goals), e-business adoption cannot be modeled as a sequential process. Also Zheng et al. [21] mention that e-business adoption by SMEs depends mainly on their strategic focus, on the owner's knowledge of IT opportunities, and on customer pressure, rather than on the requirements of a specific stage.

In sum, since SMEs often follow a discontinuous path concerning technology adoption instead of a linear, stage-by-stage progression [24], such a mechanistic view has to be overcome in order to build more realistic models.

4 The Proposed Nonlinear Stage Model Based on Levels of Interaction

In this paragraph the basic traits of the model are explained so that the reader can gain an overall view of the proposal. A more in-depth description of some parts of the model and the theoretical underpinnings of the proposal are addressed in the following section.

Four key aspects distinguish the proposed model so that the two main criticisms to existing stage models (their techno-centric and mechanistic character) are overcome. First, technology is to be considered as strictly connected with the acts of organizing (and vice versa) so that the following comment—a suggestion to improve existing e-business models—by Taylor et al. [20] p. 288) has been adopted here as a guideline: *"..it might be more productive if attention was redirected away from ICT as an end in itself towards ICT as a means to an end i.e. realizing business opportunities, generating profits and creating wealth"*.

Second, if technology is to be considered not as an end in itself but as an enabler which is enacted (modified by its use), then the purpose of e-business is the pursuit of different levels of (digitally supported) 'interaction' with the relevant actors (individuals and organizations inside and outside the firm) in order to exchange with them information and knowledge to perform business activities.

Third, different levels of interaction are possible (i.e.: technically feasible and organizationally rewarding) with different kinds of actors; this model presupposes that 'stages' reflect the number of actors involved in the interaction processes. That is, for example, a 'low' level of interaction identifies a situation where the exchange involves one party which can only access information or knowledge without any significant power to modify both the content and the modality of the interaction. Instead, a 'complete' level (stage) of interaction involves most of the relevant actors (i.e.: employees, suppliers, customers, public administrations) engaged by the firm in its activities with the possibility of active participation in most of the processes.

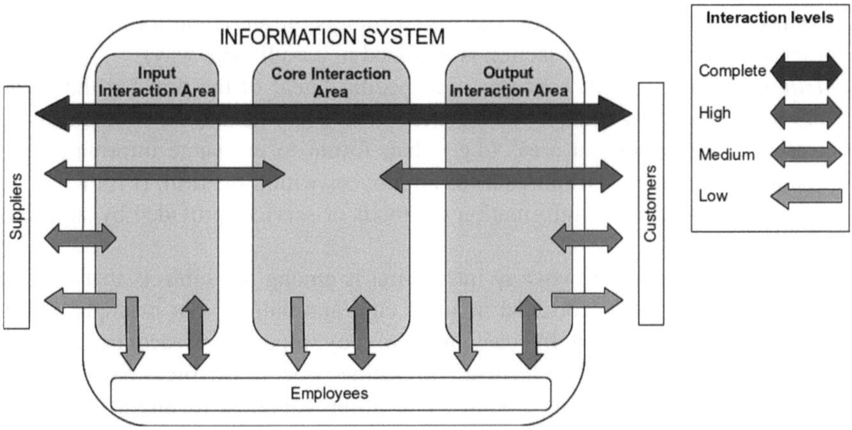

Fig. 1 The proposed nonlinear stage model and its interaction levels

Fourth, the model shows three areas of interaction: the 'input interaction area', the 'output interaction area', and the 'core interaction area' where the processes of the firm transform the relevant inputs in significant outputs. Of course, the higher the number of actors involved and the degree of active participation pursued, the more complex the technical and organizational implications become. Therefore, the four stages are certainly not to be considered as a sequence but as an articulation of how the individual firm interprets its approach to e-business (of course, the development of a complete level of interaction takes advantage of preceding experience acquired at lower levels). This articulation may change over time because the entrepreneurs modify their objectives as a consequence of the evolution of the business environment and of the available information technology.

The time factor and the non sequential nature of the stages (the non linearity of the model) are particularly important for SMEs which typically and flexibly change their level of interaction to pursue new opportunities with different partners. The model is represented in Fig. 1.

The model indicates that in e-business, the interaction levels within the firm matter (for example, people in the core area) because they are prerequisites for a proper interaction with external actors. In fact, it is reasonable to presume that higher levels of interaction for information and knowledge exchanges are possible with external actors if the internal ones have a level of interaction among themselves appropriate for such exchanges. It is a question of being accustomed to the techniques that improve social interaction and collaborative work especially when it is enabled by ICT-IS.

Having stated the general principles upon which the model is based, the four levels of interaction are described and exemplified as follows:

- *Low*. Interaction is kept at a minimal level and each actor has a 'one way' communication concerning one of the three 'areas' (input, core, output): information is published and can be accessed by authorized individuals or organizations.

Examples are: a brochure web-site for customers, or an online form to send an order to suppliers (the transaction is finalized in a traditional way).

- *Medium*. This level still concerns one specific ‘area’ of the firm but the interaction is ‘two ways’. Examples are: (i) interactive web-site functionalities for customers in the ‘output area’ (e.g.: chat, forum to exchange information on products or services); (ii) intranet for employees within the firm; (iii) the online procedures to exchange information on goods or services provided by suppliers in the ‘input area’.
- *High*. At this stage the two-way interaction is among the subjects that operate in two different areas (core and input or core and output). For example: (i) an e-commerce portal used by customers to buy products or acquire services involving the core area to finalize the selling process (invoice, payment and delivery); (ii) the software modules that allow suppliers to interact with the procurement office and finalize the purchasing process.
- *Complete*. A two-way interaction involves several actors and all the ‘areas’. For example: (i) through the e-commerce application customers can buy personalized products, this action triggers an information flow inside the firm and produces at the same time an order to one ore more suppliers; both purchase and sale made by the firm are finalized in the core area while customers can track the order that was placed; (ii) supply chain management systems if the firm is a node within the chain.

It should be noticed that the proposed model allows for different interaction levels in a single ‘area’ and between different ‘areas’. Indeed, it is possible to have a high interaction level involving two areas (e.g.: e-commerce functionalities need to have a high level of interaction between the actors only in the core and output areas) while the other ones can remain at a low or medium levels.

Furthermore, since the model does not suggest a preconfigured set of technologies, it is independent of “how” and “where” infrastructures and applications are managed. It is thus possible to evaluate what kind of technology to adopt in order to support a level of interaction appropriate for a given situation and decide whether to manage it internally or externally (IT-IS consultants, application service providers, outsourcers). Of course, this choice depends on the level of the available internal IT competences. In the following section this issue is considered in some detail.

5 Implications of the Model and Discussion

Some further comments are needed to better explain the theoretical bases of the model and its adherence to some specific traits of SMEs and some emerging opportunities for them. They concern: the interplay of organization and technology, the issue of competences needed to address e-business, and the concept of ‘stage’ in the context of this paper.

5.1 *On Technology, Organization and Computer Mediated Communication*

The remarks made in this paper in the sections concerning the literature review show the inadequacy of models built almost exclusively on technological options. In fact, technology is only in part a *datum* (exogenously set) and it is dynamically defined by (and it itself defines) the intertwining of organizations, individuals and artifacts. The adoption of this perspective avoids both techno-centric (technology as a given instrument) and human centered (technology is the way people involve themselves in it) viewpoints which are misleading since the first "black-boxes" technology and the second underestimates its role. In this respect, Orlikowski refers to the 'entanglement in organizational practice' of technology: "Humans are constituted through relations of materiality—bodies, clothes, food, devices, tools, which, in turn, are produced through human practices" ([11] p. 1438). The adoption of this approach seems to be particularly rewarding since "contemporary forms of technology and organizing are increasingly understood to be multiple, fluid, temporary, interconnected and dispersed" ([25] p. 137).

This is certainly the case with the phenomenon of virtual enterprises: a virtual enterprise (VE) can be defined as "a temporary alliance of enterprises that come together to share skills, core competencies and resources in order to better respond to business opportunities, and whose co-operation is supported by computer networks" ([26] p. 5). Undoubtedly, e-business is the basis to manage VE projects and the fact that the proposed model works with different levels of 'interaction' among relevant actors makes it a useful framework for a SME that has to decide whether or not to enter a VE set up. In fact, different levels of interaction can be envisaged and entrepreneurs have to evaluate whether their organizations have the necessary expertise or should instead either invest or renounce to a too costly endeavor. 'Interaction' in e-business raises the issue of computer mediated communication (CMC).

It is beyond the scope of this paper to examine this question; yet, some comments are useful in this context. In spite of the development of 'synthetic worlds' deployed by organizations to support distributed collaboration [25], a number of researchers remain skeptical and cautious when evaluating to what extent ICTs and IS can be expected to moderate 'distance' since certain kinds of collaborative work require presence [27]. It is acknowledged, however, that CMC interactions allow for a reduction in psychological distance among remotely located sites where face-to-face interactions are either too costly or unfeasible [28, 29]. Thus, the present evolution of technology poses new opportunities of interaction among firms and this raises the question of the competences needed to cope effectively with IS-IT. This is the topic considered next.

5.2 The Issue of IT Competences for Addressing e-Business in SMEs in Accordance with the Proposed Model

As mentioned above, a number of competences are needed when a SME considers information technologies and specifically e-business. Among several definitions of IT competences proposed in the literature [30–32], here the approach provided by Caldeira and Ward [33] is chosen because of its holistic nature. In fact, IT competences can be viewed as composed by three skill sets: technical IT skills, managerial IT skills, and business and general management skills.

Considering the proposed model, we exemplify some possible combinations of internal versus external IT competences and IT resources that a SME should consider when choosing an 'interaction level'. Of course, some factors are important and may radically change the "how" and the "where" of the combinations described below: they include the industry in which the SME operates (e.g.: IT vs shoe making), the firm size (a large number of innovative SMEs do not exceed 10 employees), and the quality and sophistication of the communication chosen for a certain level of interaction.

Combination A. Both competences and technology are located inside the organization (managing hardware and software within the firm). This can be the case with low or medium interaction levels, since only common software (browser web, mail, simple web editor or basic content management systems for a website creation) and hardware (personal computer, laptop, few servers and basic network devices) are needed.
Combination B. External competences and internal technology (i.e. involving a consultant). In medium or high interaction levels the use of specific software to support, for example, core activities for the interaction with customers, requires a highly specialized expertise that can be conveniently acquired from dedicated service companies. The technology employed can be instead rather common.
Combination C. Internal competences and external technology. (i.e. dealing with an Application Service Provider (ASP). This is another possibility at medium or high interaction levels if highly performing infrastructures and systems are required to manage high volumes on web portals "always running" to answer continual requests on the part of customers. Internal competences in this case concern the ability to manage the provider.
Combination D. Competences and technology are placed outside the company (i.e.: outsourcing). This can be the scenario in the high or complete interaction levels. A typical solution when supply chain management systems are chosen. In this case competences are needed to initiate and manage the relationship with the outsourcer.

As these combinations show, choices imply good managerial capabilities (which usually the owners of SMEs have) supported by some knowledge of the evolution of the IT-IS market (not so common instead) in order to choose the most appropriate solutions. This is the case where advisory services of public agencies help avoid that mere imitation affects e-business strategies (a sort of IT-IS isomorphism). The question concerning what competences are needed when addressing e-business poses the more general question of organizational learning. The following two sub-paragraphs address this issue.

5.3 Stages in a Nonlinear, Interpretive Model

Stage models are usually mechanistic because sequential steps (such as the ones depicted in the 'adoption ladder' introduced in the UK) are to be followed by any SME engaged in the development of e-business. The proposed model has an interpretive character instead because decision makers (entrepreneurs and public authorities) can interpret a given situation in the light of the previous (together with the possible) evolution of the interplay of ICT with organizing activities (including strategy and policy making) aimed at finding a rewarding level of 'interaction' among actors. In this sense, the proposed model is supportive rather that prescriptive. It may very well be that "SMEs are unlikely to follow a stages model" ([34], p. 181) because entrepreneurs decide to 'adopt Internet' on the basis of the expected business value rather than on a given maturity level. In the proposed model, however, 'stages' are 'reminders' that help entrepreneurs make sense of preceding experience [35] and/or imagine the most appropriate e-business solution for their organization in pursuing its business objectives.

5.4 The Proposed Model, Interaction, and Organizational Learning

A further problem with e-business linear models is that they reduce organizational learning to the acquisition of technological competences necessary to run (per each stage) a given set of e-business technologies. The multifaceted and often tortuous individual pathways that characterize the entrance and permanence in the e-business world cannot be properly understood since the combination of exploratory and exploitative activities, as defined by March in his pioneer work [36], loose much of their momentum. In fact, in those models the aims of the learning activities performed by firms can be summarized only as both the compliance with the technological requirements of a certain stage (exploitation) and the assessment of what is needed to comply to the successive set of requirements for the following stage (exploration). In the proposed model, instead, the focus on interaction shows a better fit with the 'mutual learning' that takes place between an organization (with all the components of its knowledge: languages, beliefs, practices, and procedures) and the individuals that belong to it, as March highlighted. Above all, there is no given set of options (the stages) that constrains the search for an appropriate balance between exploration and exploitation activities on the part of entrepreneurs. On the contrary, different levels of interaction can be chosen where the mutual engagement of people, organization and technology will produce different gains to both the collective and the individual knowledge. This perspective allows for a more holistic evaluation of the tangible and intangible investments needed to perform in a fast evolving environment such as e-business.

6 Conclusion

A nonlinear stage model has been designed to overcome the limitations of current maturity models, namely their techno-centric and mechanist nature. E-business is conceived as a multi-level IT-IS supported interaction among relevant actors of SMEs. The model has an interpretive and supportive character that can be of interest to entrepreneurs and their advisors engaged in understanding how they should approach e-business so that it is rewarding and coherent with their organizations.

In fact, the model restrains the role of technology by focussing the attention of decision makers on the relationship between business intents, organization capabilities, and communication requirements. This is an important issue for organizations (such as SMEs) where agency is usually not formally structured. Thus, entrepreneurs are supported in acquiring a better understanding of the desirable interaction levels among the relevant actors engaged in the accomplishment of the business objectives of their firms, while searching for the appropriate mix of digital and non-digital communication techniques to support them. In other words, the focus shifts from their asking to IT-IS suppliers, for example: "Since I want to sell my product on line, what technology do I need?" to a more articulated question: "Since I want a closer relationship (a higher level of interaction) with my clients even at a distance, what are the business and organizational implications of a computer mediated communication (interaction) within my organization and with my clients? Moreover, what are the critical IT-IS features and competences involved?"

Furthermore, policy makers can use the model to assess (without a technological bias) the current state of development of e-business in SMEs and, consequently, to design appropriate supportive actions for a digitally oriented business development of SMEs.

Finally, the model contributes to research because it introduces the interplay of technology and organization in the design of stage models.

Limitations of the proposed model concern the need for a better identification of the characteristics of SMEs based on organizational traits rather than on mere size.

In the following research work, the model will be evaluated and refined by means of a comparative analysis of successful and unsuccessful experiences by SMEs employing a data analytic strategy known as 'qualitative comparative analysis' (QCA) [37].

References

1. Levenburg, N. M., Magal, S. R. (2005). Applying importance-performance analysis to evaluate E-business strategies among small firms. *E-service Journal*, pp. 29–48.
2. Johnston, D. A., Wade, M., & Mcclean, R. (2007). Does e-Business matter to SMEs? A comparison of the financial impacts of internet North American SMEs. *Journal of Small Business Management, 45*, 354–361.
3. Raymond, L., & Bergeron, F. (2008). Enabling the business strategy of SMEs through e-business capabilities: A strategic alignment perspective. *Industrial Management & Data Systems, 108*, 577–595.
4. Oliveira, T., & Martins, M. F. (2010). Firms patterns of e-business adoption: Evidence for the European Union-27. *Electronic Journal Information Systems Evaluation, 13*, 47–56.
5. Kapurubandara, M., Lawson, R. (2007). SMEs in developing countries need support to address the challenges of adopting e-Commerce technologies. 20th Bled eConference.
6. Magal, S. R., Koslage, P., Levenburg, N. M. (2008). Towards a stage model for e-Business adoption among SMEs: Preliminary results for manufacturing and service firms. AMCIS 2008 Proceedings.
7. Rao, S. S., Metts, G., Monge, C. A. M. (2003). Electronic commerce development in small and medium sized enterprises: A stage model and its implications. *Business Process Management Journal, 9*, 11–32.
8. Alonso-Mendo, F., Fitzgerald, G., & Frias-Martinez, E. (2009). Understanding web site redesigns in small—and medium-sized enterprises (SMEs): A U.K.-based study on the applicability of e-commerce stage models. *European Journal of Information Systems, 18*, 264–279.
9. Levy, M., & Powell, P. (2003). Exploring SME internet adoption: Towards a contingent model. *Electronic Markets, 13*, 173–181.
10. Hevner, A. R., March, S. T., Park, J., & Ram, S. (2004). Design science in information systems reserach. *MIS Quarterly, 28*, 75–105.
11. Orlikowski, W. J. (2007). Sociomaterial practices: Exploring technology at work. *Organization Studies, 28*, 1435–1448.
12. Poeppelbuss, J., Niehaves, B., Simons, A., & Becker, J. (2011). Maturity models in information systems research: Literature search and analysis. *Communications of the Association for Information Systems, 29*, 505–532.
13. Beckinsale, M., & Ram, M. (2006). Delivering ICT to ethnic minority businesses: An action-research approach. *Environment and Planning C: Government and Policy, 24*, 847–867.
14. Poon, S., & Swatman, P. M. (1999). An exploratory study of small business Internet commerce issues. *Information & Management, 35*, 9–18.
15. Willcocks, L., & Sauer, C. (2000). *Associates: Moving to e-business*. London: Random House Business Books.
16. Martin, L. M., & Matlay, H. (2001). "Blanket" approaches to promoting ICT in small firms: Some lessons from the DTI ladder adoption model in the UK. *Internet Research, 11*, 399–410.
17. Chaston, I., Badger, B., Mangles, T., & Sadler-Smith, E. (2001). The internet and e-commerce: An opportunity to examine organisational learning in progress in small manufacturing firms? *International Small Business Journal, 19*, 13–30.
18. Burgess, S., Sellitto, C., & Wenn, A. (2005). Maturity in the websites of Australian wineries: A study of varying website content. *International journal of electronic business, 3*, 473–490.
19. Daniel, E., & Wilson, H. (2002). Adoption of e-commerce by SMEs in the UK. *International Small Business Journal, 20*, 253–270.
20. Taylor, M., & Murphy, A. (2004). SMEs and e-business. *Journal of Small Business and Enterprise Development, 11*, 280–289.
21. Zheng, J. (2004). Small firms and e-business: cautiousness, contingency and cost-benefit. *Journal of Purchasing and Supply Management, 10*, 27–39.

22. Rodgers, J. A., Yen, D. C., Chou, D. C. (2002). Developing e-business; a strategic approach. *Information Management & Computer Security, 10*, 184–192.
23. Robeiro, F. L., & Love, P. E. D. (2003). Value creation through an e-business strategy: Implication for SMEs in construction. *Construction Innovation: Information, Process, Management, 3*, 3–14.
24. Fillis, I., Johansson, U., & Wagner, B. (2004). A qualitative investigation of smaller firm e-business development. *Journal of Small Business and Enterprise Development, 11*, 349–361.
25. Orlikowski, W. J. (2010). The sociomateriality of organisational life: considering technology in management research. *Cambridge Journal of Economics, 34*, 125–141.
26. Camarinha-Matos, L. M., & Afsarmanesh, H. (1999). The virtual enterprise concept. In L. M. Camarinha-Matos & H. Afsarmanesh (Eds.), *Infrastructures for virtual enterprises: networking industrial enterprises* (pp. 3–14). Boston: Kluwer.
27. Olson, G. M., & Olson, J. S. (2000). Distance matters. *Human-computer interaction, 15*, 139–178.
28. Oh, H., Curley, S. P., Subramani, M. R. (2008). The death of distance? The influence of computer mediated communication on perceptions of distance. ICIS 2008 Proceedings
29. Schultze, U., Hiltz, S. R., Nardi, B., Rennecker, J., & Stucky, S. (2008). Using synthetic worlds for work and learning. *Communications of the Association for Information Systems, 22*, 351–370.
30. Davern, M. J. (1996). When good fit is bad: The dynamics of perceived fit. Seventeenth Annual International Conference on Information Systems ICIS96. pp. 112–121.
31. Feeny, D. F., & Willcocks, L. P. (1998). Core IS capabilities for exploiting information technology. *Sloan Management Review, 39*, 9–21.
32. Bassellier, G., & Reich, B. (2001). Information technology competence of business managers: A definition and research model. of management. *Information, 17*, 159–182.
33. Caldeira, M. M., & Ward, J. M. (2003). Using resource-based theory to interpret the successful adoption and use of information systems and technology in manufacturing small and medium-sized enterprises. *European Journal of Information Systems, 12*, 127–141.
34. Levy, M., & Powell, P. (2003). Exploring SME internet adoption: Towards a contingent model. *Electronic Markets, 13*, 173–181.
35. Weick, K. E., Sutcliffe, K. M., & Obstfeld, D. (2005). Organizing and the process of sensemaking. *Organization Science, 16*, 409–421.
36. March, J. G. (1991). Exploration and exploitation in organizational learning. *Organization Science, 2*, 71–87.
37. Ragin, C. C. (1987). The comparative method: Moving beyond qualitative and quantitative strategies. University of California: California Press.

Offline and Online Communities: Great Differences and Some Similarities

Andrea Resca and Maria Laura Tozzi

Abstract The concept of community has evolved considerably: from an essentially closed, spontaneous community based blood ties, space sharing, and spiritual connection to a planned community without clear borders. Due to the online communication phenomenon a traditional society is superseded by a virtual society. A society that is innovative because it involves a variety of cultures with their richness and diversity, and it is advanced because it requires ways of interactions that differ from the ones typical of traditional life. Then, can ICT create a real society? This is one of the questions at stake and the origin of the necessity to investigate online community. Further, does it reproduce the characteristics of a traditional community? An analysis of main organizational forms that typify the net suggests something different and community is representative only of a small number of such social groupings and a more precise terminology is necessary to identify them.

Keywords Online community · Offline community · Transactions cost approach · Governance structures · Collective action

1 Introduction

The spread of online communities has offered valuable insights to analyze the phenomenon of community. The point is due to the radical change of the space–time conception determined by the introduction of information and communication

A. Resca (✉) · M. L. Tozzi
Cersi—Luiss "Guido Carli" University, Rome, Italy
e-mail: aresca@luiss.it

M. L. Tozzi
e-mail: 618071@luiss.it

R. Baskerville et al. (eds.), *Designing Organizational Systems*,
Lecture Notes in Information Systems and Organisation 1,
DOI: 10.1007/978-3-642-33371-2_16,

technology (ICT). A complex and articulated debate characterizes the definition of online community and an unanimous agreement has not been reached so far. In this respect, different streams of thought have emerged: some have highlighted the great potential for establishing social relationships remotely and others have instead emphasized the risks associated with social fluctuation and the depersonalized characteristics of cyberspace.

This article is an attempt to provide a sufficiently exhaustive analysis of the concept of community on the basis of a dual perspective: a perspective derived from online communities, widely explored in studies related to ICT and Computer Mediated Communication, and a perspective derived from the offline community, a classical object of analysis of sociological studies.

One of the objectives of this paper, therefore, is to highlight the major differences between these two types of communities, through the comparison of their distinguished characteristics. Specifically, this goal will be achieved exploring specific aspects related to online and offline communities. Among them are: (1) factors and circumstances leading to the birth of both kinds of communities, (2) the space–time conception in social networks and in traditional networks, (3) the intensity of social ties that typify the net and how these differ from those face to face, and (4) the development of identity and personality of members of these two types of communities; (5) the characteristics of organizational forms that characterize both offline and online communities.

To the latter is dedicated the second part of this paper. The objective, here, is to identify the organizational arrangements that typify the cyberspace. In this proposal, the cornerstone is the community that is investigated according to different perspectives, both objectivist and subjectivist (agency/structure) [1]. However, in the end, the transaction cost theory is considered more appropriate to investigate these phenomena [2, 3]. This decision is based on the fact that the clan form represents communities whereas the market form and the bureaucracy form account for further organizational arrangements. The comparison of market, bureaucracy, and clan with organizational forms that characterize the cyberspace according to the current literature leads to the conclusion that community is far less preponderant than expected and other forms are developing.

The first two sections are dedicated respectively to the analysis of the existing literature on community within the sociological thought, economics and organization studies. The third section focuses on the concept of community in the digital age whereas the forth section covers the online communities' organizational arrangements. The paper ends with a discussion and conclusion.

2 The Concept of Community in Classical Sociological Thought

The concept of community, for centuries at the centre of the philosophical debate, dates back to the origins of human kind. Life of humans, in fact, is developed mainly within communities. In the social sciences, the term "community" is used with multiple meanings. In classical sociology, it defines social relationships that typify members of a closed area of people. The term refers to small village communities but it can also refers to the national community. In either case, community includes the family and any social unit that are highly integrated. In contemporary sociology, however, the term denotes the case of the local community, a social unity in which members share a territory where they carry out daily life. Therefore, the concept of community represents different meanings that have made problematic the use of the term, to the point that some authors have argued for banning it from the vocabulary of the social sciences. .

Approaches to communities are based on whether a community is conceived as a collection of individuals who, interacting, create it or as an autonomous entity able to influence the activities of its members. In the former conception, the agency of individuals is stressed, and, in the latter, the structure is privileged. In other words, the ontological dichotomy between agency and structure is the principle used to map community studies [1]. However, in both cases, community is envisaged as a whole of established relationships among its members even though in one case the focus is posed on the characteristics of relationships established by singular individuals (agency—individuals as agents of their own actions who produce relationships on the basis of this agency) and, in the other case, the system of relationships as a specific entity prevails (structure—the social unit determines the activities of its members).

The objectivist perspective (structure) is followed by Tonnies [4], whereby communities are social realities based on territory. Typical of rural areas of developing societies, such communities are characterized by high density and are strongly connoted by blood ties and attachment to the land. Hence, the embryonic forms of community emerge within the family, then extends to neighbourly relations and friendship. These relationships are characterized by intimacy, gratitude, and the sharing of language, meanings, practices, spaces, memories and experiences.

Blood-based, spatial (neighbourhood) and spiritual (friendship) ties, according to Tönnies [4], define organic social units (communities), in which individuals feel permanently attached by factors that make them similar to each other and within which inequalities can develop only within certain limits. Otherwise, relationships become so rare and insignificant as to overshadow the elements of community and sharing. The traditional concept of community, then, refers to a social entities that are characterized by:

- small size
- well-defined geographical boundaries
- a limited population
- an involvement in a common activity
- shared historical experiences
- shared beliefs and values.

For these reasons, traditional communities are relatively closed social units where it is very difficult to get in and out and the gap between those included and excluded is strongly felt. Further, Tönnies [4] contrasted the concept of community to that of society. A community takes shape when individuals express their intent to join in because of the shared ideologies, traditions and experiences. The members of a community are mutually related by pre-rational ties, such as those produced by feelings, customs and traditions. Goods and situations are shared, mutual protection is present, and a common defence is built. In different circumstances (i.e. society), individuals can consciously decide to pool their resources for the sole purpose of achieving certain goals or for establishing relationships that constitute the essence of society at large. In other words, nobody will do anything for each other, except in exchange for a benefit or reciprocal donations that are at least equal, if not more satisfactory, since only the possibility of obtaining an object that looks better that motivates individuals to deprive themselves of something.

The emergence of capitalism and the development of modern society would have gradually dissolved those social relations that are represented by community. But Tönnies [4] was not the only one to support the distinction between community and society, even within the subjectivist perspective (agency). According to Weber [5], social relationships are defined by community if, and insofar as, the condition of social action is based on a common membership, subjectively felt due to affection or tradition by individuals who participate. On the other hand, social relationships are defined by association if and insofar as the condition of social action it based on an identity of interest, or on common interests rationally motivated according to values or purposes. Weber [5], therefore, maintains that the social relations of community depend on the orientation of the mutual attitudes of individuals, based on the subjective awareness of a specific situation.

Durkheim [6], having an objectivist perspective, introduces the concepts of "mechanical solidarity" and "organic solidarity" for investigating the modernization process. For instance, pre-modern societies are organized according to the logic of mechanical solidarity as social integration is achieved by the sharing of a collective consciousness based on a strong emotional and cognitive harmony between individuals (the reference is clearly to the idea of community). Modern societies, however, are characterized by a greater heterogeneity among individuals and these differences are so significant that, to achieve social integration, it is necessary to turn to an imposed cooperation based on the division of labour (organic solidarity).

Fernback [7] points out that even Durkheim's notions of mechanical and organic solidarity fall into the influence of the Tonnies's ideal–typical construction. However, Durkheim [6] stresses how organic solidarity, based on the heterogeneity of individuals and result in a progressive division of labour, acquires a positive connotation in comparison with social entities characterized by traditional mechanical solidarity typical of pre-industrial society, based, on the contrary, on similarities of individuals. Tönnies [3], however, sees negatively the move away from the community since it represses tradition and collective memory in favour of progress and encouraged individualism.

In contrast to Tönnies, Simmel [8], following a subjectivist perspective, argues that modernity has helped to develop the personality of individuals making it more social thanks to the ability to form relationships without being completely absorbed in a community. The evolution of society, in fact, has made human life more complex and has led to the emergence of a multiplicity of communities which, despite having clearly defined boundaries, are connected by specific relationships. In modern society, individuals are no longer fully inserted in one social circle but they are able to enjoy greater personal freedom to strengthen their identities.

It may be noted that in the study of community, sociologists have interpreted the process of modernization of society using a dichotomous approach, referring to polarized social entities, such as the Tonnies's community/society, the Weber's community/association and so on. However, this interpretation has made difficult to conceptualize "intermediate" social entities and, above all, to explain the persistence of a social entity within the opposite entity. All these tensions have undermined the concept of community, both in its more general use, such as identifying a type of social unit, and in its more limited use, such as identifying specific social relations.

The "sense of community", in crisis because of the ongoing process of individualization in modern society, is reborn in the late twentieth century as a solution to anxiety, insecurity and contradictions that characterize contemporary society. In this period, in fact, communitarianism [9, 10] emerged as a socio-political school of thought in order to recover the "community feel".

To be part of a community becomes more and more an individual and conscious choice. This means that community is seen as an entity in which subjects, in one way or another, develop mutually beneficial ties, represented by the sharing of feelings, common beliefs, memories and a membership area. However, how these factors are actually rooted in individuals is unpredictable in a globalized era. In modern society, in fact, the traditional model of community is no longer able to represent actual social life as society has become increasingly urban, complex and based on articulated forms of division of labor and separation of roles.

Nevertheless, the alleged revival of the sense of community is founded not so much in the rediscovery of the emotional side of living together but as a defensive position exercised by groups of people who fear the uncontrolled flows of information, people and financial resources, typical of a globalized society.

3 The Concept of Community in Economics and Organization Studies

Community has been an object of study not only for sociologists but also for economists, even though in a far smaller scale. Unlike sociologists, economists tend to follow only the subjectivist perspective (agency), and Olson's work "The logic of collective action" [11] is considered a landmark in this respect. Within this framework, individuals are conceived as actors who privilege their own self-interest over common or group interest and free-riding is assumed. If public goods are available, individuals are not inclined to participate voluntarily in their production and, in contrast, take advantage of them without contributing to their cost. This means that public goods are available only in the presence of selective incentives, which reward givers and penalize free-riders, or if public goods are distributed among group members by assigning property rights to each of them. In this way the passage from public goods to private goods prevents opportunistic behaviors.

Ostrom [12, 13] maintains that neither of these solutions is optimal. The introduction of an external authority or the privatization of public goods are not the only method to prevent free-riding. Empirical studies have demonstrated that communities, autonomously and spontaneously, succeeded in establishing forms of collective action for managing public goods to exclude free-riders. Ostrom [12, 13] identifies a series of points in this respect: (a) members and non-members of the community have to be clearly separated (boundary rules); (b) adopted rules take into consideration local circumstances, whereas a central authority tends to standardize different situations; (c) benefits derived from the use of public goods have to be equally distributed according to a specific regulation; (d) members are entitled to participate actively in the decision making process related to the government of the community; (e) the necessity of a supervisor, recognized by the community and able to sanction behaviors that violate the regulation; (f) the presence of effective and efficient mechanisms for dispute-resolution that prevent undermining trust among members due to lasting conflicts; (g) a central authority recognizes members' self-regulation in order to envisage and impose new rules; (h) in case of public goods of a large entity, a multi-level governance is recommended where small local committees, ruled by specific regulations, cooperate.

The transaction cost theory envisages an organizational form that prevents free-riding as well. Ouchi [14] maintains that transactions can be governed not only through bureaucracy (the authority that promotes selective incentives and forms of control to prevent free-riding) and market (the passage to private goods) but also by clan. If in the market, transactions take place in the case of reciprocal satisfaction between the two parties involved in the exchange and in a hierarchy if one party decides to submit itself to an authority in exchange for a salary, in the case of clan transactions there is no reciprocity in the exchange but a so-called congruence of scope between the two parties. For congruence of scope is not intended a sharing but the presence of a common ground. Here, it is decisive to have a complete agreement on a paradigm among the actors involved in these transactions. Specifically, the congruence of scope represents a set of general assumptions and values, enabling the parties involved to identify the interests of their community and recognise that they overlap with their personal interests. The sharing of values, beliefs and goals, the strong identification of clan members with a specific context, the development of trust and reciprocity, the presence of traditional forms of authority, and the participation in a common process of socialization are factors that characterize a clan as well as a community. A high degree of reciprocal dependence between individuals is created within a collective consciousness.

According to Wilkins and Ouchi [15] conditions that allow the development of a clan are threefold: (1) actors involved in transactions, in addition to sharing a common history, should ensure a stable participation as clan relationships develop with difficulty in case of actors' replacement, (2) the absence of alternative institutional forms, and (3) a significant degree of interaction between actors. Regarding the first point, the authors believe that, referring to the work of Berger and Luckmann [16], the permanence of actors involved in transactions promotes the socialization process and consequently the emergence of shared meanings. The second condition indicates how the presence of alternative definitions of reality within a clan would derail its functioning, while the third condition stresses the importance of relationship frequency as a modality that tends to strengthen the clan's shared reality.

Table 1 integrates the two schemes proposed respectively by Ciborra [17] and Boisot [18] and captures the main characteristics of markets, bureaucracies and clans.

Even though the transaction cost theory has its roots in the economic discipline, it offers useful insights for organization studies as well. Specifically, Ouchi's work [14] seems to abandon the subjectivist perspective, which is typical of economics, to attempt to reconcile agency and structure. Berger and Luckmann's work [16], at the basis of the clan organization form, in turn, hinges upon Schutz's studies [19] that are seen as a relevant example for overcoming the agency/structure dichotomy [1]. In fact, following phenomenology, human action is subjectively meaningful and at its basis there is the consciousness of an actor—the actor who is driven by a project that he or she seeks to accomplish. However, human action is always embedded in a social context, which is taken for granted as a natural and factual environment. What emerges is an encounter between actors' desires and aims, on the one hand, and, on the other, the given situation in which they are involved. Common sense, a common ground for interacting and for developing relations is the result of this encounter. Actors are involved in continuous negotiations moved by respective motivations as they mould a context, which, in turn, organizes and manages social relations. According to Schutz [19], society has a structure but this structure substantiates in a sense-making process based on interactions of its members [1].

The notion of community of practise, at first proposed by Lave and Wenger [20], has been object of a considerable number of studies following a perspective that attempts to reconcile agency and structure. What is a community of practice? It represents a group of people who invest their interest or a passion in a specific topic and, on the basis of informal interactions, investigate and engage with this object of interest. Communities of practice are spontaneous social aggregations that emerge in order to deal with work practices or common problems to be managed through cooperative relationships. Members share the awareness that they are a part of a common undertaking and the way to advance it depends on mobilising common resources such as languages, routines, stories, values and whatever else characterizes the specific community.

Table 1 The main characteristics of Bureaucracy, Market, and Clan

	Market	Bureaucracy	Clan
Level of scope congruence	Low	Medium	High
Type of social relationship	Reciprocity Impersonal relationships prevail. Identity is not important	Reciprocity Authority Relationships tend to be impersonal. Identity is not relevant	Reciprocity Authority Shared values and beliefs Personal relationships prevail. Identity is important
Type of admittance	None	Selection followed by training and monitoring	Selection followed by socialization
Informational requirements	Information is abstract, codified, and spread. i.e. prices	Information is abstract, codified and underused (information diffusion is subject to a centralised control). I.e. regulations and formal rules	Information is concrete, uncodified, but enjoys limited diffusion—i.e., traditions and internalised norms
"Atmosphere" i.e. quality of the social relationship	"alienated"	Partially alienated	"Organic"
Form of control	Control is external, shared values and trust are not necessary	Control is external, shared values and trust are not necessary	Control is internalized, shared values and trust are necessary
Coordination	Co-ordination is horizontal and self-regulating (the invisible hand)	Co-ordination is hierarchical and formal	Co-ordination is horizontal and carried out through mutual adjustments e
Goals	Each player is free to pursue his/her own goals	Goals are imposed from above	Goals are negotiated between players
Core institutional values	Transactional freedom	Obedience to a rule	Loyalty to a group

At this point, one may wonder about the role of the communities of practice in organization studies. They are seen as forms of organizational self-learning because they are conducive to circulation and exploitation of developed know-how. These communities are present in any corner of society, not only in businesses—anywhere where there is a domain of knowledge to be explored and developed, where there is a group of people to interact with and share practices. Three elements characterize communities of practice [21]: (1) A specific domain or topic represents community members' common interests and promotes the establishment of a common identity and a sense of responsibility for the development of a specific practice. (2) A community creates a social fabric for learning and fosters proper conditions for encouraging interactions, trust, reciprocity, brainstorming and understanding. (3) Practice consists of common ideas, tools, information, languages, stories and documents. As such, it realises the knowledge developed, shared, and conserved by the community.

The life blood of these communities is not the pursuit of an objective but the commitment to a common path. It goes without saying that a common history is a prerequisite in this regard, as a common culture and a common knowledge are able to lead to a significant sense of cohesion and a spiritual connection. As a spontaneous phenomenon, communities of practice do not require an official acknowledgment by an organization, and, because they are not subject to formal controls, their existence depends on members' commitment and internal leadership.

These communities can be small and large. However, the latter, usually, are subdivided into sub-themes or geographical areas. The survival of these social units is strictly related to a continuous interaction among its members. Therefore, it is usual that communities originate among individuals who come from the same or a delimited geographical area. Nevertheless, the spread of ICT has determined an important change in this respect giving room also to distributed community of practice.

4 The Concept of Community in the Digital Age

The change promoted by information technology has profoundly and fundamentally altered human relationships and, consequently, forms of social structure. Today, thanks to the development of technologically advanced means of communication, it is possible to establish connections that exceed the traditional space–time constraints due to the creation of a network of personal relationships in which the cornerstone is the flow of information. The implementation of social relations in an imaginary space (defined as cyberspace—a term coined by the science fiction novelist William Gibson in the early 80) has led to the emergence of online communities.

The technological conditions that allowed such a development have been identified by Castells [22]:

- the digitization of all sources of information;
- the possibility to compress digital signals so that to optimize memory resources and the potential for transmission;
- the package transfer of information in numerical form in order to make flexible the traffic between the nodes of the network;
- the identification of a universal communication protocol (TCP/IP) for computers that transmit digital information.

This transition has also been favoured by the advent of the World Wide Web. Specifically, Marinelli [23] states that the emergence of online communities has been encouraged by some features of this architecture. For instance:

- it is a simple, flexible, decentralized, and articulated into autonomous nodes able to cooperate in the exchange of resources;
- it is a fully multimedia communication environment that supports the interoperability of communication formats originally separated;
- it is a virtual place that allows the experience of self-construction, as each identity is constantly put to the test in communicative interactions made possible by new forms of technological mediation (chat, forum, e-mail, instant messaging, SMS, MMS, video call).

However, it is not only due to technology that new forms of aggregation take place. The role of users is fundamental. The encounter between users' needs and technologies leads to situations in which some technologies are rewarded and not others as opportunities for communication and spending time.

Given the extent of the literature on online communities, it is not possible to provide a clear-cut definition of this phenomenon. According to Rheingold [24], online communities are social aggregations that emerge from the net when a significant number of people are involved in public discussions, if these discussions are sufficiently long and characterised by human emotions so that a network of personal social relationships takes place in the cyberspace.

Although this definition may be considered too generic, Rheingold's vision [24] on the nature of interactions through the Internet suggests a place for socializing, supporting creativity and altruistic action. It can be considered unrealistic to envisage such a primordial democratic community in which communication occurs due to the presence of social relations and not due to a common physical space. This view has been criticised for excessive optimism and technological determinism, since the author seems to say that it is sufficient to provide computer-mediated communication technologies and, automatically, a community comes out.

Wellman [25], a scholar of the sociology of the Internet, equates social relations created in the physical world and social relations that occur in a virtual environment, stating that online communities and real communities are not opposed to each other, but are coexisting. According to the author, the growing interaction and interdependence between online and offline favours the creation of a new social environment, characterized by membership in multiple networks of relationships, which Wellman called "personal communities" [25]. About the impact that communication via the Internet can have on offline social life, Wellman [25] believes that its impoverishment is not at stake since the creation of online connections (weak or strong) tends to strengthen rather than weaken traditional relations.

According to some authors, including Castells [22], innovative communication channels have encouraged the involvement of people who are usually excluded. In this respect, online communities represent an opportunity for expression, given the protection of personal details that the medium offers. A few years ago, Meyrowitz [26] pointed out the social function of new technologies, maintaining that electronic means of communication change the relationship between the location of individuals and access to information. In other words, people who live in isolated contexts, and therefore are excluded from access to a large variety of information, may, through new technologies, share experiences and interact with others, regardless of their location.

Other authors, however, have questioned the value of social units that develop in a virtual context, such as the Internet. Among these, Luke [27] argues that the development and dissemination of new technologies has created a new elite class, made up of those who have free access to the net. Now, according to this author, the concept of community is weak because of the division of interests, the loss of a common historical consciousness and the weakening of shared values. The fact that the advent of information and communication technology have overturned the geographical distances contributes to this phenomenon.

Turkle [28] in "Simulation and its discontents" seems to be in favour of this position. The dominant trend engendered by this technology would lead to the creation of a well informed and up-to-date upper class and to increasing disparities in the endowment of cultural capital, rather than to the development of an actual community. The electronic media are becoming places where it is possible to find refuge and to escape from the fears and uncertainties of life. Here, nostalgia that comes from a lack of a sense of community is replaced by a sort of social anonymity.

In the end, an analysis of the literature on online communities shows that there is no agreement on this topic yet. Online communities were opposed to face-to-face relationships, as their antithesis, and as a menace to personal identity and social relationships. The spread of these communities has generated a heated debate between those who believe that they can be a valuable tool to facilitate social relationships and expand the boundaries of the community and those who argue that relationships developed in the net do not represent actual forms of sociality.

5 Online Communities' Organizational Arrangements

The analysis of online communities continues taking into consideration their organizational forms. Following Kallinikos [29], the intention is not to limit the investigation to approaches that lead to structural configurations. For instance, let us think about the level of centralization or functional profiles (labour unions, business firms, etc.). In this respect, to compare Linux with Microsoft or Wikipedia with Encyclopaedia Britannica is not very significant, if the analysis is based on their structural configuration such as the level of centralization or the functional profile. To investigate an organizational form, it is more appropriate to investigate the whole of bonds that link individuals to collective arrangements [29]. A configuration falls short to account for what happens in an organization. In contrast, it is decisive to figure out the matching between individual contributions and collective agreements. Also according to this perspective, the intention is to reconcile agency and structure.

The transaction cost theory is selected as an appropriate approach for investigating the organizational arrangements of online community. Not only this theory casts light on the nature of the transactions within organizations such as communities (clan) but also of the transactions governed by markets and bureaucracies. Actually, both Ostrom's commons or Lane and Wenger's communities of practice would have been equally valid approaches for investigating online communities but their range of applicability is limited to a specific organizational form.

The challenge, now, is to envisage how individual contributions and collective agreements work out in the virtual world, a place where it is possible to meet, cooperate, communicate and be informed; where remote interactions are allowed and social and cultural borders can be overcome; where individuals who share interests, aspirations, ideals, or simply a hobby can experience a sense of mutual cohesion. So, the question is what organizational forms populate this environment.

The main sources for investigating governance structures that characterize this world refer to the work of Shirky [30] and to the work of Demil and Lecocq [31]. The latter deal with a specific activity: the development of open source software. The development of this software is part of a larger phenomenon known as common-based peer production [32–34].On the basis of studies on modalities through which open source software is produced, it has been possible to identify a new governance structure called bazaar.

Whereas market transactions take place when a reciprocal satisfaction is reached between the two parties involved in the exchange and whereas with the hierarchical transaction one party decides to submit him/herself to an authority in exchange for a salary, in the case of the bazaar, the contract states that what is produced remains available to all. In other words, you cannot exercise ownership rights to the developed part of the open source software even though there are different types of licenses that allow some forms of copyright .

However, contractual issues are not the only ones to define the bazaar governance structure. Also clan transactions do not differentiate significantly from bazaar ones. Yet, the fact that it is not possible to impose property rights on what is produced dramatically reduces actors' opportunistic behaviours. Besides, coordination occurs due to self-organizing, rather than due to an authority, as in the case of the hierarchy, or due to prices, as in the case of the market. Subjects' motivation, character, disposition and willingness are at the basis of the participation in this type of initiatives. There are conditions conducive to channelling effort toward an undertaking such as the production of free software. Two other factors, according to Demil and Lecocq [31], characterize the bazaar: the mode of control and the type of incentives. Both tend to be rather weak. Bazaar transactions are voluntary, spontaneity and freedom prevail so that it becomes difficult to impose stringent forms of control. Certainly, there are social norms that allow to influence behaviour and to promote an ethic of cooperation. Material incentives are not available because of the impossibility of appropriating what is provided. Nevertheless, intangible incentives, such as reputation, are supported as contributions are attributable to individual participants in some instances.

Shirky's work [30] partially overlaps with what is proposed by Demil and Lecocq [31] as the bazaar governance structure is incorporated into what Shirky defines as collaboration. Collaboration constitutes one of the three organizational forms that are present in the virtual world other than sharing and collective action. Therefore, the forms that characterise the net can be represented by:

1. sharing (actors make available their own contents—text, images, documents, etc.—on the net, creating in this way a resource available to all). This governance structure allows free participation. At its basis is the spontaneous action of the subject and no form of collaboration is required. What emerges is an aggregation of individuals who perform similar tasks but independently. The Flickr platform is a classic example in this respect;
2. collaboration (to follow rules and engage in activities that require greater coordination in comparison with the sharing governance structure). In this case, participants are required to adapt their behaviour to others, so as to be able, eventually, to have a group identity. A typical example of collaboration is represented by the conversation. It is in the conversation, even online, that individuals establish a continuous process in which questions and answers follow each other among the involved parties. What Demil and Lecocq [31] have defined as the bazaar governance structure becomes collaborative production for Shirky [30]. It is considered a more complex organizational form as it requires a greater alignment between the objectives of the group and the objective of the individual. Moreover, as pointed out above, individuals are in a situation where the personal appropriation of results obtained is not possible and, at the same time, the participation of a considerable number of actors is necessary to obtain those results. Therefore, in contrast to the sharing structure, it is imperative to make some collective decisions, and then put in place processes of negotiation. Wikipedia is a classic example of collaborative production in addition to the open source;
3. collective action (to follow a common goal and abide by common rules established by group membership). It represents a governance structure in which regulations are complex and a close coordination is required as highlighted by Ostrom's works [12, 13]. Decisions made by group members prevail over personal interests. A strong internal cohesion typifies collective action so that the individual has the opportunity to identify him/herself with this social unit. The applications of e-participation adopted by social movements, political parties and governments can be seen as examples in this direction.

The Table 2 compares the governance structure of offline communities (clan) with online communities (sharing, collaboration and collective action).

6 Discussion

The concluding task is to compare Table 1 with Table 2. In other words, the objective is to see if the characteristics of markets, bureaucracies and clans can be of some help for interpreting the organizational forms of sharing, collaboration (bazaar) and collective action.

At first, let us consider the characteristics of the sharing form. Except for the fact the sharing form, as other two organizational forms, are not subject to opportunistic behaviours of their members, the points of contact with market is striking. Even though the level of scope congruence is higher in sharing rather than in market (where, in contrast, they are opposite and reciprocity in the sharing form is absent), as far as the type of social relationship, type of admittance, informational requirements and up to core institutional values, there is a significant overlapping between these two organizational forms.

Both markets, bureaucracies and clans do not seem to be helpful to investigate the organizational arrangements that typify the collaboration form. The level of scope congruence is high like in a clan but the type of social relationships is diverse as the type of admittance, informational requirements, the "atmosphere", the form of control, goals, and core institutional level, whereas a similarity is present in the coordination modalities. On the other hand, the collaboration form shares with bureaucracy the "atmosphere" and the presence of a hierarchical coordination, even though in a context in which horizontal coordination prevails. Core institutional values are the same as in markets.

Finally, the collective action form shares a lot of characteristics with clan. From the level of scope congruence to core institutional values, an almost complete overlapping of characteristics takes place. The only partial differences can be seen in the informational requirements in which information is not only concrete and relatively diffused but also abstract, the "atmosphere" is only partially organic due to the fact that interactions are mediated by ICT, and the form of control and coordination are influenced by the possible presence of hierarchical and formal aspects.

To sum up, the interpretative framework provided by the transaction cost theory suggests how the organizational forms that characterize the so-called cyberspace are best articulated as the limit to the use of a concept such as that of community. Clan represents only marginally organizational arrangements that take place in the cyberspace. On the other hand, market, which at a first look seems to have no bearing on an environment such as this one, succeed to account for a specific kind of transaction. Only the collaborative form or bazaar comes out as a whole of governing principles very typical of the net as a combination both of market, bureaucracy and clan.

Table 2 The characteristics of the, sharing, collaboration and collective action governance structures

	Sharing	Collaboration	Collective action
Level of scope congruence	Medium	High	High
Type of social relationship	No reciprocity Impersonal relationships prevail. Identity is not important.	Limited reciprocity Relationships tend to be impersonal Identity is not important	Reciprocity authority Shared values and beliefs Relationships can be personal. Identity is important
Type of admittance	None	Self-selection, low level of monitoring	Selection followed by socialization
Informational requirements	Information is codified, abstract and diffused	Information is codified, abstract and diffused	Not only information is abstract but also concrete and relatively diffused
"Atmosphere" i.e. quality of the social relationship	"Alienated"	Partially "alienated"	Partially "organic"
Form of control	Control is external, shared values and trust are not important	Control is external, shared values and trust are not excluded	Control is substantially internalized but it can also be external. Shared values and trust are necessary
Coordination	Co-ordination is horizontal and self-regulating	Co-ordination is horizontal and self-regulating even though hierarchical and formal aspects are present	Co-ordination is horizontal and carried out through mutual adjustments. Hierarchical and formal aspects can be present
Goals	Each player is free to pursue his/her own goals	Each player is free to pursue his/her own goals even thug negotiations are not excluded	Goals are negotiated between players
Core institutional values	Participation freedom	Participation freedom	Loyalty to a community

7 Conclusion

The results of this analysis suggests that online communities differ significantly from offline communities. Factors such as physical contact, closeness, and social co-presence, which are prerequisites of offline communities, become irrelevant in online communities. Here, individuals are separated, they do not share the same place, they have difficulty experiencing the same social reality and there are many obstacles to creating shared values and meanings. The absence of physicality and corporeality give way to an environment in which non-verbal symbolism is absent. The expressiveness of the face, gestures and gaze, for example, lose their importance at the expense of language. Online communities meet in a common space, the cyberspace, but it is an imaginary space, non-physical, and it prevents its participants to share experiences beyond the experience of communicating online. The sense of belonging is likely to be precarious, unstable and focused on limited and transient objectives, since it is not based on socio-cultural values of a specific territory. Social interactions are often characterized by transiency, social ties tend to be loose and subject to vulnerability. This is due to the fact that they are based primarily on personal interests and the willingness to freely share, which can limit the free expression of emotions. Moreover, the possibility of "masking" individual identity involves an environment in which communications tend to be anonymous, leading to fragile and depersonalised social relations.

Now, the question is if aggregative phenomena that occur on the net are actually communities. The decision to adopt Shirky's [30] typology through which we have identified three main organizational forms (sharing, collaboration and collective action) is helpful in this regard. Indeed, only the collective action structure shares several characteristics of the clan structure that is considered an ideal–typical community. However, it can be implemented with difficulty because it requires that everyone is committed to a common goal. Besides, group-level decisions are binding. This means that the achievement of the necessary cohesion for collaborating online is a thorny question. As for the sharing form and the collaboration form, there are significant differences with communities especially in the first case. To consider the latter a community is not warranted as it shares several characteristics with the market.

Most of online communities are not as "solid" as communities based on face-to-face interaction are, but they are not less real than physical ones, as confirmed by many studies. Online communities reflected the need of socialization inherent to every human being and they should not be seen as simple alternatives to everyday life. It is not appropriate to think of the participation in a online community as a total escape from everyday life. "Online" and "offline" overlap with each other, and one sphere does not exclude the other. In most cases, virtual communities are a simple form of aggregation and personal enrichment. Here, it becomes possible to meet new people who share the same interests or to expand knowledge about a specific topic.

References

1. Walsh, D. F. (1998). Structure/agency. In C. Jenks (Ed.), *Core sociological dichotomies*. London: Sage Publications.
2. Coase, R. H. (1937). The nature of the firm. *Economica, 4*(16), 386–405.
3. Williamson, O. E. (1975). Markets and hierarchies: Analysis and antitrust implications: A study in the economics of internal organization. New York: Free Press.
4. Tonnies, F. (1955). *Community and association: (Gemeinschaft und gesellschaft)*. London: Routledge & Kegan Paul.
5. Weber, M. (1968). *Economy and society; an outline of interpretive sociology*. New York: Bedminster Press.
6. Durkheim, E. (1984). The division of labour in society. New York: Free Press.
7. Fernback, J. (1997). The indivividual within the collective: Virtual ideology and the realization of collective principles. In S. Jones (Ed.), *Virtual culture: Identity and communication in cybersociety* (pp. 36–54). London: Sage Publications.
8. Simmel, G. (1972). *Georg Simmel on individuality and social forms*. Chicago: University of Chicago Press.
9. MacIntyre, A. C. (2007). *After virtue: A study in moral theory*. Notre Dame: University of Notre Dame Press.
10. Sandel, M. J. (1998). *Liberalism and the limits of justice*. Cambridge: Cambridge University Press.
11. Olson, M. (1971). *The logic of collective action: public goods and the theory of groups*. Cambridge: Harvard University Press.
12. Ostrom, E. (1990). *Governing the commons: The evolution of institutions for collective action*. Cambridge: Cambridge University Press.
13. Ostrom, E. (2000). Collective action and the evolution of social norms. *The Journal of Economic Perspectives, 14*(3), 137–158.
14. Ouchi, W. G. (1980). Markets, bureaucracies, and clans. *Administrative Science Quarterly, 25*(1), 129–141.
15. Wilkins, A. L., & Ouchi, W. G. (1983). Efficient cultures: Exploring the relationship between Culture and organizational performance. *Administrative Science Quarterly, 28*(3), 468–481.
16. Berger, P. L., & Luckmann, T. (1967). *The social construction of reality: A treatise in the sociology of knowledge*. Harmondsworth: Penguin Books.
17. Ciborra, C. (1990). Mimeo. Bologna: University of Bologna.
18. Boisot, M. (1995). *Information space: A framework for learning in organizations*. London: Institutions and Culture. Routledge.
19. Schutz, A. (1962). *Collected papers*. The Hague: Nijhoff.
20. Lave, J., & Wenger, E. (1991). *Situated learning: Legitimate peripheral participation*. Cambridge: Cambridge University Press.
21. Wenger, E., McDermott, R. A., & Snyder, W. (2002). Cultivating communities of practice: A guide to managing knowledge. Boston: Harvard Business Press.
22. Castells, M. (1996). *The Rise of the network society*. Malden: Blackwell Publishers.
23. Marinelli, A. (2004). Connessioni. Nuovi media, nuove relazioni sociali. Milano: Guerini e Associati.
24. Rheingold, H. (1992). *Virtual reality*. Reading: Addison-Wesley.
25. Wellman, B. (1998). *Networks in the global village: Life in contemporary communities*. Boulder: Westview Press.
26. Meyrowitz, J. (1985). *No sense of place: The impact of electronic media on social behavior*. Oxford: Oxford University Press.
27. Luke, T. (1993). Community and ecology. In S. Walker (Ed.), *Changing community: The Graywolf annual ten* (pp. 207–221). St. Paul: Graywolf Press.
28. Turkle, S. (2009). *Simulation and its discontents*. Cambridge: The MIT Press.

29. Kallinikos, J. (2011). Bureaucracy under Siege: On information, collaboration and networks. In: S. R. Clegg, M. Harris, H. Hopfl (eds) Managing modernity: Beyond bureaucracy? Oxford: Oxford University Press.
30. Shirky, C. (2008). *Here comes everybody: The power of organizing without organizations*. New York: Penguin Press.
31. Demil, B., & Lecocq, X. (2006). Neither market nor hierarchy nor network: The emergence of bazaar governance. *Organization Studies, 27*(10), 1447–1466.
32. Benkler, Y. (2002). Coase's Penguin, or, Linux and the nature of the firm. *The Yale Law Journal, 112*(3), 369–446.
33. Benkler, Y. (2006). The wealth of networks: how social production transforms markets and freedom. New Haven: Yale University Press.
34. Tapscott, D., & Williams, A. D. (2008). *Wikinomics: How mass collaboration changes everything*. New York: Portfolio.

The Role of Network Governance Models in the Design of Local eHealth Policies

Valentina Albano

Abstract This paper aims to contribute to the rich debate over the obstacles to the diffusion of eHealth technologies by investigating the role of the institutional setting on the success or failure of an IT diffusion policy. This work focuses on the policy network perspective and it is based on the expectation that the internal characteristics of the policy network influence the policy design. The main goal of this paper is to investigate how eHealth policy networks operate and to determine whether a more effective network governance configuration exists that could improve the design and deployment of successful eHealth projects. This work presents a case study of three Italian healthcare networks with different models of network governance: a Region-governed network, an eHealth Local Board-governed network and a Local Health Agencies' Consortium-governed network. The focus of this investigation is on how the three models of network governance operate and influence the design of strategies to address the main challenges to eHealth implementation that have been identified by scholars and practitioners.

Keywords Policy design · Policy network · Network governance · eHealth

1 Introduction

According to Herbert Simon, "design" can be defined as "the process by which we [devise] courses of action aimed at changing existing situations into preferred ones" [1, p. 129]. Actually, the term "design" denotes a process made up of

V. Albano (✉)
Faculty of Economics, University of Rome III "Federico Caffè", Rome, Italy
e-mail: valentina.albano@uniroma3.it

R. Baskerville et al. (eds.), *Designing Organizational Systems*,
Lecture Notes in Information Systems and Organisation 1,
DOI: 10.1007/978-3-642-33371-2_17,

decisions and actions that are instrumental to the realization of an "artifact": not only physical objects but also logical and cognitive ones [2]. Consequently, understanding design choices involves the analysis of *who* or *what* drives the decision-making process and the *way in which* these drivers influence the process.

The debate about the characteristics of the decision-making processes that drive design has engaged many scholars in the field of organization studies. Against a typically positivist approach that recognizes a natural convergence toward a "unique optimal solution" based on predefined and external aims according to a perspective of absolute rationality, many scholars argue that in organized social systems, decisions are influenced by many players who frequently hold conflicting interests [3, 4]. These participants can influence the decision-making process at many steps, driving the decision toward design choices that could not be predefined ex ante [3, 5].

This issue of conflicting interests has received particular attention in studies of public management, where the design process concerns arrangements aimed at addressing public issues. The transition from the concept of "government" to the concept of "governance", which emphasizes the need for more participation and involvement from stakeholders, has encouraged public actors to use more horizontal forms of steering and to work together in a network with other public and private actors to achieve policy outcomes. Many scholars have converged on the concept of a policy network as a way to understand the dynamics of policy-making on complex issues (see [6–10]). Rhodes [11] defines the policy network as a cluster of organizations that are connected by resource dependencies, emphasizing the structural relationship between the political institutions. According to this approach, the design choices of policy arrangements are influenced by the internal characteristics of the network, such as the particular network structures linking actors and their concerns. Therefore, we can argue that different network structures could influence the decision-making process in different ways, leading to the definition of different "artifacts" or different policy outcomes.

The main goal of this paper is to investigate how the characteristics of the local policy network influence the design of the policy arrangements related to a complex issue such as the diffusion of eHealth. It is widely believed that the activities required to implement a health IT agenda involve the entire health care system [12–14], which is made up of various stakeholders (i.e. public entities, private sector companies, hospital systems and individual physicians) that hold different interests, ideas and values.

Electronic health (eHealth) refers to the delivery of health care with support from various information and communication technologies, such as electronic health records, telemedicine, clinical decision support systems, and computerized provider order entry [15]. The European Commission issued the eHealth Action Plan in 2004 [16], recognizing the pivotal role of eHealth with respect to the present and future socio-economic and financial challenges faced by national healthcare authorities in Europe. The importance of eHealth has been reiterated in the Digital Agenda for Europe [17] and in the preliminary consultations on the eHealth Action Plan 2012–2020.

It is widely believed that eHealth can address many of the problems currently faced by health care systems, improving the quality of care, increasing the efficiency of healthcare work, and improving the accessibility of healthcare services and the effectiveness of medical interventions and patient care [18–20].

Nevertheless, despite institutional programs and enthusiastic declarations of the potential of eHealth, its adoption has progressed slowly [21–23]. Moreover, there is significant variability among countries and local healthcare systems in terms of policy aims, priorities and stages of deployment [24].

This paper aims to contribute to the rich debate on the obstacles to the process of eHealth diffusion (see, among others, [21, 25, 26] by adopting the approach, not yet adequately explored, of deeply investigating the role of the institutional setting in the success or failure of an IT diffusion policy [27]. In fact, as Löfgren argues [27], traditional approaches explain the success or failure of public eService policies through the concept of "IT maturity", which is often based on fairly simple benchmarking based on technological aspects.

We argue that understanding the operation of eHealth policy networks can help verify whether it is possible to establish a network governance configuration—in terms of the mechanisms of coordination and control of network-level activities—that support the design and deployment of successful eHealth projects.

This paper reports a case study of three Italian healthcare networks with different models of network governance: a Region-governed network, an eHealth Local Board-governed network and a Local Health Agencies' Consortium-governed network. The focus of this investigation is on how the three models of network governance operate and influence the design of strategies aimed at addressing the main challenges to eHealth implementation identified by scholars and practitioners.

To address the aims described above, this paper first discusses the network governance approach by focusing on the eHealth and healthcare literature (Sect. 2) and the strategic challenges facing eHealth implementation (Sect. 3). The research approach adopted here is then described (Sect. 4), and the three policy networks studied are reviewed, leading to a discussion on their ability to face five main eHealth challenges: financial challenges; IT challenges; change management challenges; institutional challenges and sharing best practices and evaluation tools (Sect. 5).

2 eHealth Network Governance

The role of the network has not yet been sufficiently explored in the eHealth literature. While many studies argue that eHealth enables communication and both inter-organizational and inter-professional integration [28], the concept of "policy network" and its contribution to understanding the dynamics of eHealth policy-making remain unexplored.

Nevertheless, because the stakeholders involved in the eHealth decision-making process are the same as those involved in the local healthcare network, useful insights are provided by the literature on healthcare management.

In recent years, the success of the Integrated Care paradigm [29, 30] has contributed to a shift of the research focus from the individual health care organization—primarily the hospital—[31–33] to the healthcare delivery network [34]. This emerging literature on the healthcare network has examined its structures, processes and relational characteristics.

A first stream in the literature analyzes the network model and its strategic and organizational characteristics, considering nodes as the main units of analysis [35, 36]. These studies focus on analyzing the benefits that the model provides to organizations, e.g., a more rational use of resources or more learning opportunities.

A second stream prefers to observe the dynamics of coordination rather than the network nodes, aiming to describe the structure and operation of the network [37, 38]. A great deal of attention has been devoted to the exploration of the impact of the network structure on trust [39], innovation processes [40], and quality [41]. Other studies analyze the impact of the network structure on the political healthcare agenda [9, 42]. These studies mainly investigate the interconnections among participants in the policy process and explore their ability to influence policy development, while the relative effectiveness of different network structures has not been addressed. More investigation is required to determine how the network structure should be chosen and what impact the network structure has on the effectiveness of the political agenda.

Provan and Kenis [43] provide interesting insights to address these issues. The Authors focus on the governance of organizational networks—defined in terms of the mechanisms of coordination and control of network-level activities performed—and its impact on network effectiveness. Network effectiveness is defined as the attainment of positive network-level outcomes that could not be achieved independently by individual organizations. From this perspective, the eHealth policy network can be considered as a set of players working together to obtain the common outcome of the eHealth political agenda.

Provan and Kenis [43] identify three network forms with specific structural properties and the conditions under which each form is effective.

Lead organization-governed network. A network in which a lead organization takes a central coordinating role, facilitating and enabling collaboration. Power is generally centralized, and communication and decision making may be top-down. A lead organization provides administration to the network and/or facilitates the activities of member organizations in their efforts to achieve network goals. The goals of the member organizations may be closely aligned with the goals of the lead organization. The role of the lead organization may emerge from the members themselves based on what seems to be most efficient and effective; alternatively, it may be mandated.

Participants-governed network. A network in which the members themselves collaborate to achieve goals that would otherwise be outside the reach of individual organizations. The governance of a participant-governed network can be either formal (e.g., based on regular meetings) or informal. Power in the network is symmetrical, at least regarding network-level decisions, despite differences in resource capabilities, organizational size and performance. A participant-governed network is not characterized by the presence of a formal administrative entity, although some administrative and coordination activities may be performed by a subset of the full network.

Network administrative organization (NAO). A network in which a separate administrative entity is established specifically to undertake governance activities. This administrative unit operates as a central node for communication, coordination and decision making. More formalized NAOs typically have board structures that include all or a subset of network members addressing strategic-level network concerns, while the operational decisions are left to the NAO leader.

According to Provan and Kenis [43], the successful adoption of a specific form of governance is based on four structural contingencies: trust, the number of network participants, consensus on the goals of the network and the need of network-level competencies. These authors argue that as trust becomes less densely distributed throughout the network, as the number of participants increases, as the goal consensus declines and as the need for network-level competencies increases, networks governed by a lead organization or an NAO are likely to become more effective than a participants-governed network [43, p. 237].

Nevertheless, the Authors emphasize that moving from the potential of a model of governance to its success depends on the capabilities of the network managers: specifically, on how managers respond to three basic tensions inherent in network governance:

- *Efficiency versus inclusiveness*—the need for an inclusive approach is often at odds with the need to be efficient and responsive.
- *Internal versus external legitimacy*—because a network must be recognized both externally and internally as credible and representative of the members' interests, an effective network governance structure must be responsive to the need for both internal and external legitimacy.
- *Flexibility versus stability*—a trade-off exists between stability and being flexible enough to quickly address issues.

The stability of a network can contribute to its legitimacy, but it can also lead to rigidity in its governance process, structures, and culture.

3 eHealth Policy Challenges

The strategic importance of eHealth to increase the sustainability of the healthcare system and improve the quality of care, along with the pressures applied by the European Community encouraging the adoption of a cross-borders eHealth framework, have led to studies addressing the issue of eHealth policy making. Many of these studies describe countries' visions and strategies [14, 44–46], but most do not move beyond a basic description of the policy ideas and the actors behind them.

Both policy makers and scholars have discussed the challenges to and critical factors in the success of eHealth strategies [12, 13, 26]. These authors argue that the success of eHealth initiatives depends on both the selection of the right technology and the ability to manage a set of challenges and adopt appropriate strategies to overcome them. From this perspective, the effectiveness of the eHealth policy agenda, defined as the network-level outcomes, can be considered in terms of its ability to address these eHealth policy challenges.

Because these challenges are at the network level, a collaborative governance approach is considered essential [12–14]. The challenges can be clustered into five macro-categories:

1. Financial challenges
2. IT challenges
3. Change management challenges
4. Institutional challenges
5. Sharing best practices and evaluation tools

1. *Financial challenges*. Cost is often cited as the primary reason that the health care field has not embraced IT as quickly as other information-intensive industries [22, 23, 25]. Moreover, the realization of socio-economic benefits may require a medium to long-term time horizon that discourages further investment [13, 47]. Financial realities play an even more significant role when the healthcare system is based mainly on public support. Thus, the identification of new sustainable business models and innovative financial solutions, including public–private partnerships, is a critical factor in the development of eHealth [14, 26].
2. *IT challenges*. Scholars agree that the development of appropriate data structures and data definitions are critical to the success of an eHealth project, as are the definition of a plan for managing data and information products and quality assurance/compliance programs [12, 13, 48]. Nevertheless, as Gil-Garcìa and Pardo [48] note, the challenge in this area consists not only of obtaining agreement but also engaging the necessary partners in the development and adoption of common structures and standards. Another critical factor, especially due to the inter-organizational nature of eHealth applications, is the involvement of the healthcare network as a whole in addressing interoperability issues. Interoperability issues include both technical aspects, such as standards-enabling connectivity, and semantic aspects and political/organizational issues [12, 13, 48].

   Moreover, the presence of many competing IT vendors, each with its own product, makes the adoption of certification systems for vendor applications and the imposition of standards important strategic issues [25]. Finally, policy makers must address privacy and security concerns. In fact, many scholars and policy makers argue that successfully establishing a network for the exchange of health information depends on the ability to protect personal data and the trust in the system that people will hold as a result [12–14, 48].

3. *Change management challenges.* The pervasive adoption of technological solutions requires the development of change management interventions to affect the behaviors of individual users and, therefore, the degree of consensus around and involvement in the change [13, 14, 26, 48]. Change management interventions are particularly critical in the healthcare domain because the field is characterized by strong professional autonomy. Healthcare professionals are also frequently opposed to the influence of the computer culture embedded in Health IT because they do not recognize its legitimacy [49]. Thus, IS development should be oriented toward user participation [50], and training is critical to the success of eHealth projects [48]. Training can be instrumental to the development of the specific skills required to use the new system or implement new procedures, and it can also be used as leverage to build consensus and disseminate project results [26].
4. *Institutional and legal challenges.* Additional challenges are related to the institutional framework and the policy environment in which governmental organizations operate. Institutions are characterized by their laws and regulations and by the norms, actions, or behaviors that people accept as good or take for granted. In particular, the lack of regulations related to privacy, confidentiality, liability, and data protection led to a slowdown of eHealth deployment in several countries [13, 14, 25, 48]. Moreover, Gil-Garcìa and Pardo [48] argue that in many countries, government agencies and programs frequently act as independent and autonomous units without taking the actions of other public organizations into account. This can constrain efforts to use technology to integrate or share information across multiple agencies. Finally, scholars and practitioners agree that the length and complexity of eHealth projects requires a steady, long-term commitment by authorities and management [13].
5. *Sharing of best practices and evaluation tools.* A successful strategy fosters knowledge transfer [13, 26]. The use and dissemination of best practices can support decision making. Best practices can represent important information premises that drive policy makers and reduce the risk of investment. Moreover, sharing best practices is an excellent opportunity to encourage the greater rationalization of efforts by promoting the approach of "re-use". It is also important to create global agreement on how to coherently measure the adoption of health IT. Using joint assessment and evaluation tools, it is important to identify both factors in success and the reasons for failure and to record the difficulties experienced by participants [26].

4 Research Approach

As emphasized above, this paper investigates how the characteristics of the local policy network influence the design of eHealth interventions and studies whether it is possible to identify a model of network governance that leads to more appropriate strategies for addressing eHealth challenges.

An exploratory case study was undertaken to address these research questions. This study was based on a selection of three Italian healthcare networks that exemplify the different theoretical models of network governance established by Provan and Kenis [43]. This study focused on the Italian context because the decision-making process is disseminated across a wide set of stakeholders that make up the national healthcare system (i.e., Ministry of Health, regional governments, local health agencies, general practitioners, private healthcare providers, etc.), which has led to the development of widely varied patterns of innovation. In fact, the levels of computerization and innovation differ significantly between regions, as do the strategic, organizational and technological choices [51].

We first outlined the essential characteristics of each model of network governance. For each of these models, we analyzed the outcomes achieved at the network level, expressed here in terms of the eHealth political agenda, and assessed their effectiveness. For the purpose of this paper, network effectiveness is defined in terms of the ability to address the 5 categories of eHealth challenges identified in the literature review.

To better explain the different levels of effectiveness obtained by the three models, the findings are discussed in light of the conditions of effectiveness proposed by Provan and Kenis [43]. In this way, it is possible to evaluate their explanatory effectiveness with respect to the analyzed cases and to the issue of the eHealth policy network.

The case study was conducted by analyzing a set of documents, including eHealth and/or eGovernment plans, regulations, resolutions and technical reports. Since we focused on highly formalized institutional policies, the study of the available documentation was useful to reveal the paths taken by the three local healthcare networks with respect to their eHealth deployment.

5 Case Study

5.1 Background

In Italy, the Constitutional Reform of 2001 introduced a radical change in the relative roles and responsibilities of the State and the regional governments with respect to healthcare issues. In particular, the reform attributed legislative authority over health protection to the regional governments. The Ministry of

Health determines the essential principles and guarantees the system's fairness by monitoring the Fundamental Levels of Healthcare Services, i.e., the services that are guaranteed by each regional healthcare service as appropriate for specific clinical conditions and healthcare settings. In line with this new configuration of roles and responsibilities, eHealth policy is defined in each region by roadmaps developed through cooperative activity between the central and regional authorities. This activity is carried out within the Italian eHealth Board (Tavolo di lavoro permanente per la Sanità Elettronica). Active since 2004, the Italian eHealth Board is the official setting for discussion and consultation among regional governments, the Ministry of Health and the Ministry of Innovation for the harmonization of eHealth policies and for the implementation of the national and regional plans [52].

However, local eHealth policies are influenced by additional factors beyond the interactions between the central and regional governments. The regional governments must also interact with a variety of entities with different levels of operational and financial autonomy, which may exert a significant effect on eHealth choices. These entities include the local health agencies responsible for the organization of healthcare services in a geographical sub-area of the region, hospitals, pharmacies, private healthcare providers, and general practitioners. These individuals and entities make up the policy network that makes decisions related to eHealth adoption at the local level.

5.2 Three Modes of Network Governance

The first network mode suggested by Provan and Kenis [43], the lead organization-governed network, is exemplified by the Lombardy's healthcare network, in which the regional government (Lombardy Region) is the lead organization with the main responsibility for eHealth policy. The Lombardy Region aims to develop an integrated network that includes all the organizations and healthcare professionals working in the area through a centralized and systematic approach.

In this "Region-governed network", the eHealth strategy is carried out along with the development of a region-wide project, the CRS-SISS (Regional Services Card and Socio-Health Information System—Carta Regionale dei Servizi—Sistema Informativo Socio-Sanitario), which aims to develop an ICT infrastructure connecting all the healthcare providers in the region. The regional government has delegated the project development to a publicly owned IT service company (Lombardia Informatica) working as a technical partner, but it has retained responsibility for the "project government" and, therefore, its promotion, financing and direct management. The monitoring and governance of the project was initially assigned to a Technical Committee made up of representatives of the Regional General Directorates involved ("Health" and "Family and Social Solidarity") and of the Lombardia Informatica. Two years after the shift from the pilot phase to the implementation of the project in all the districts in the region, a

Users Committee was set up that consisted of all the stakeholders of the regional healthcare system.

The main goals of the Users Committee are as follows: to ensure alignment between users and the project team, to verify that the design assumptions fit with actual organizational processes, and to verify the functionality and the technical aspects of integration. These formalized tasks reveal that the involvement of healthcare stakeholders is essentially limited to issues related to the adoption of a project whose essential characteristics have already been defined. Thus, healthcare stakeholders are not directly involved in decision making related to the definition of eHealth policy.

However, in 2009, the project governance was redefined, and a strong emphasis was placed on greater user involvement: in particular, on involvement from local health agencies at both the operational and strategic levels. A Strategic Committee composed of members of the regional government and some general managers of local health agencies has been established with the missions of providing general guidelines, controlling the performance of services and making fundamental decisions.

The Apulian healthcare network exemplifies the second type of network identified by Provan and Kenis [43], the participant-governed network, hereafter renamed "eHealth Local Board-governed network". In fact this network is governed by the Apulian eHealth Board, a collegial body in which the main participants in the regional healthcare system discuss eHealth strategies. This Board was established in 2007 through a regional regulation to satisfy the need for a more collaborative structure governing technological innovation processes in healthcare. This need was highlighted in the Apulian Plan for eHealth, which was launched in 2006 by the regional government. In particular, the plan establishes that the Apulian eHealth Board features involvement from the Department for Health, the Regional Agency for Health, local health agencies, public hospitals, University hospitals (IRCCS) and private healthcare providers. The Board also includes a publicly owned IT service company (Innovapuglia) that provides technical and organizational support for the implementation of the electronic health plan.

The primary objective of the Apulian eHealth Board is the realization of an institutional steering committee for the real and continuous government of all eHealth plans, projects and initiatives realized by both the regional government and public or private healthcare providers.

Although in its initial formulation, the Apulian eHealth Board was defined to be representative of all the institutional players in the regional healthcare system, in reality, later regulations limited participation to members of the regional government (the Department for Health and the Regional Agency for Health) and the technical partner.

The other stakeholders, especially the local health agencies, are involved in Technical Working Groups working on specific issues or projects. Since 2007, 19 Technical Working Groups have been established, focusing on both strategic (e.g., the "IT Assessment" Technical Working Group and the "Fundraising" Technical Working Group) and technical issues (e.g., the "IT" Technical Working Group).

Most of the Technical Working Groups were established following the launch of the N-SISR project (New Regional Health Information System, Nuovo Sistema Informativo Sanitario Regionale). The N-SISR is the main regional eHealth project aiming to digitize 32 administrative and clinical processes. Technical Working Groups have been recognized as a way to ensure greater compliance between the system requirements and the actual needs of the healthcare professionals.

Provan and Kenis's third type of network, the NAO, is exemplified by the Veneto's healthcare network that is governed by a separate administrative entity, established by the local health agencies working in the regional area, called Consortium Arsenàl.it. The Consortium Arsenàl.it constitutes a spontaneous and voluntary aggregation of the 23 local health agencies and hospital trusts of the Veneto Region that has established an eHealth consultancy agency to serve its associated members. In this "LHA Consortium-governed network" the Consortium works to develop and coordinate eHealth projects involving the local health agencies, enabling the achievement of innovation objectives that were beyond the reach of the individual agencies. As shareholders, the members collaborate to establish the general guidelines and the governance system through general meetings of the associated members and by appointing members of the board, composed of general managers from all the provinces. The operational decisions are made by the General Manager of the Consortium, supported by the staff. The Veneto Region is not among the members of the Consortium Arsenàl.it. However, it is a privileged stakeholder because it informs the Consortium of the guidelines it intends to establish, requests opinions and technical investigations and develops special projects aimed at implementing regional policies. The Consortium represents all the health agencies in the Veneto Region and acts as a fundraising group, giving it a significant influence on the orientation of regional policy.

5.3 Findings

The case study clearly illustrates that the different networks can be effective in coping with eHealth challenges, with each model exhibiting different strengths and weaknesses in interpreting and promoting eHealth choices.

The first interesting differences between the networks are related to their strategic and technological priorities (Table 1).

The objectives that recur in all three networks are efficiency and cost reduction, the streamlining of organizational processes, quality improvements and accessibility of care, and professional growth.

All these objectives can be achieved through the adoption of the so-called Integrated Health Clinical Information Network [53] and especially through the development of distributed Electronic Health Record Systems, which is scheduled in all three regional strategies in line with the European and national roadmaps.

However, a more careful observation shows that there are significant differences between the priorities pursued by these models. In particular, both the

Table 1 Comparison of the strategic and technological priorities in the three analyzed networks

	Region-governed network	LHA Consortium-governed network	eHealth Local Board-governed network
Strategic priorities • *Efficiency and cost reduction*	High	Moderate	High
• *Quality improvement and accessibility of care*	Moderate	High	Moderate
Technological priorities • *Health Clinical Information Network*	High	Moderate	High
• *Telemedicine*	Moderate	High	Moderate

Region-governed network and the eHealth Local Board-governed network pay greater attention to the objectives of efficiency and the development of IT applications for the digitization of administrative processes and the monitoring of expenditures. The LHA Consortium-governed network appears to be more oriented toward ensuring the quality and accessibility of healthcare services than toward the economic issues. This focus explains the greater attention paid by local health agencies to the development of Telemedicine applications, i.e., personalized health systems and services (e.g., remote patient monitoring, tele-consultation, and tele-care) [53]. In fact, the Consortium Arsenàl.it was established to observe Telemedicine applications and only later developed competences in the broader domain of eHealth.

Table 2 summarizes how the three healthcare networks respond to the five eHealth challenges identified above.

Financial Challenges

While the three networks consider financial aspects to be critical, they adopt significantly different approaches. In the Region-governed network, the regional government directly financed the CRS-SISS project. However, to ensure sustainability, this network has also exploited the potential of public–private partnerships. In particular, the instrument of project financing provides the financial coverage for the project, allowing the Lombardy Region to pay only when the project is closed and on the basis of services effectively received and activated. Neither of the other two networks features a public–private financial partnership.

In the LHA Consortium-governed network model the Consortium Arsenàl.it approaches financial issues through a strong commitment to fundraising at both the regional and European Community levels. This has enabled the development of internal expertise that ensures the sustainability of the Consortium and enables the launch of new project activities. However, this orientation towards fundraising could have a considerable influence on decision making, favoring specific eHealth

Table 2 eHealth challenges addressed by the three governance networks

eHealth challenges categorie(s)	Region-governed network	LHA Consortium-governed network	eHealth Local Board-governed network
1. Financial	Highly	Highly	Moderately
• *Find adequate funding*	*Regional funding and exploitation of a Public–Private Partnership*	*Strong fundraising activity*	*Passive approach: management of received EC funding*
2. IT	Highly	Highly	Highly
• *Information and data quality*	*Project development delegated to a technical partner*	*The Consortium develops and coordinates projects*	*Project development delegated to technical partner*
• *Interoperability (technical, semantic and organizational aspects)*	Highly *Top-down development of a single regional project*	Poorly *Need to face interoperability problems among different projects. Research on interoperability issues vs eployment of integration strategies.*	Moderately *Previously funded initiatives merged in a broader intervention (N-SISR)*
• *Standardization*	Highly *Standards for the integration of local systems with the regional health information network; vendor certifications*	Poorly *Research on standardization issues vs. deployment of standardization strategies*	Moderately *Board responsible for the validation of local projects*
• *Security (identification & authorization systems)*	Highly *Developed*	Moderately *Issue addressed in each project*	Highly *Under development*
3. Change management	Highly	Moderately	Moderately
• *Resistance to change*	*Pervasive approach; user involvement in IT development; training & communication; economic incentives*	*Focused approach; user involvement in IT development; training, & communication*	*Pervasive approach; user involvement in IT development; training & communication*

(continued)

Table 2 (continued)

eHealth challenges categorie(s)	Region-governed network	LHA Consortium-governed network	eHealth Local Board-governed network
4. Institutional and legal	High	Low	Moderate
• *Institutional commitment*	*Regional government leads the eHealth policy network*	*Regional government is not a member of the Consortium*	*Formalization of the Board functions, clear regional eHealth plan*
• *Need for Regulations*	Highly	Poorly	Highly
	Robust legislative and regulatory framework establishing strategic objectives, roles, privacy issues & data protection…	*eHealth regulations are less developed*	*Robust regulation of privacy issues & data protection*
• *Inter-institutional relationship*	Highly	Poorly	Moderately
	Progressive integration in the regional IS of private HC providers and welfare institutions	*Issue not explicitly addressed*	*Inter-institutional integration planned but not realized*
5. Best practices and evaluation tools	Poorly	Highly	Moderately
• *Knowledge transfer*	*Regional project as an incubator of all other projects*	*Adoption of a "re-use" approach*	*Previous projects merged in the N-SISR*
• *Evaluation tools*	Moderately	Highly	Moderately
	IT partners assess the local IT projects and certify IT vendors	*Launch of a project on the topic*	*The Board evaluates the local IT projects*

projects over others depending on the funding opportunities identified for each. Furthermore, this approach can also present a significant obstacle to developing a long-term vision because projects are often short-lived and fragmented.

The main problem in the eHealth Local Board-governed network is not fund-raising but the need to funnel the available grants (mainly EC funding and national funding) into planning that is as systematic, long-term and homogeneous as possible. A first intervention involved the redefinition of the responsibilities for the management of these funds among the different regional units.

IT Challenges

The approach to IT challenges is strongly affected by the overall strategy for eHealth diffusion in the three networks analyzed here. In all three investigated networks, the policy makers are aware of the strategic importance of taking an integrated approach to eHealth to fully exploit its potential. Nevertheless, the specific strategies chosen are very different, and they have been adopted at very different times.

In the Region-governed network, the eHealth strategy has led to the development of a single large regional project that acts as an incubator for all new projects (the CRS-SISS project). Indeed, over the years, a number of initiatives and projects have been added to the CRS-SISS project with the aim of supporting the development of semantic standards and ICT architectures to extend and improve quality and data sharing at both the regional and national and European levels. A comprehensive IT infrastructure has been developed that integrates all the healthcare providers' information systems with the regional health network, enabling the access and exchange of patient data across the entire region. The Lombardy Region has adopted an incremental approach to integration based on the identification of relatively small issues at a time, but for the whole region. The initial activities included the development of a robust identification and authorization solution and support for the construction of local Information Systems. After the IT infrastructure was completed in 2006, the priorities shifted from administrative processes, which were now completely digitized, to clinical applications. The regional government's interest in combining the needs for unity, systematic intervention and control with the need to respect the operating independence of healthcare providers led to the adoption of a "non-invasive" approach. This approach views the structure of CRS-SISS as a model of a federated system based on the integration of already existing local systems and that respects the operational procedures in use. To ensure the proper functioning of the overall system, healthcare providers must integrate their local systems with the regional health information network according to the rules and standards defined by the technical partner (Lombardia Informatica). The company also supports healthcare providers in selecting between the different products available for integration and the various certified regional vendors.

In contrast, the Apulian eHealth Board was established in a context in which individual healthcare providers had already individually developed many IT applications, but these applications functioned only at the organizational or departmental levels (stovepipe). The Apulian eHealth Board has attempted to merge previously funded initiatives in a coordinated and systemic intervention called the New Regional Health Information System (N-SISR). Moreover, the board must oversee the regional governments' development of inter-organizational systems. Finally, it must define the integration requirements with the help of the technical partner, including the requirements for interfacing and interoperability with the regional Information Systems that must be followed by local health agencies when building their internal Information Systems. The Apulian eHealth Board is also responsible for the validation of projects initiated by individual healthcare organizations.

The Consortium Arsenàl.it adopts a different approach to IT challenges due to the lack of a strong regional intervention, which is associated with the need for the Consortium to meet its members' specific needs and associate its projects with fundraising activities. The Consortium faces the problem of interoperability between many projects launched at different times and often with different logics and purposes. Four projects form the cornerstones of the eHealth strategy of the Consortium Arsenàl.it; some of these are funded by the European Community, and others are funded by the Region. However, only one of these projects involves all the regional healthcare districts, while the others focus on pilot areas. The team drafted various solutions that were screened by and shared with suppliers and clinicians engaged in different projects with the involvement of qualified experts. A solution was identified that could be implemented over time, and it was chosen on the basis of efficiency, stability and reliability criteria. The cooperative platform and the standards applied in the new projects are in line with those of previously launched projects. Moreover, systems that had already been developed for other regional projects have been re-used in an advanced manner. However, this approach has contributed to a slowdown of the projects implementation and led to a greater effort in terms of the resources spent. Finally, note that the effort of the Consortium Arsenàl.it is more focused on fostering research on interoperability issues than on defining an effective strategy for integration between different network members.

Change Management Challenges

Significant differences exist between the realization strategies of the projects discussed here. One pervasive approach is that of the CRS-SISS project of the Region-governed network, in which all technological and organizational problems are addressed at the regional level.

The same approach was taken in the N-SISR project developed by the eHealth Local Board-governed network. The only region-wide project of the LHA Consortium-governed network is the result of the "re-use" initiative of a previous project that was successfully developed in an individual regional district. Consequently, we can argue that in this case, a focused approach was adopted.

All three networks converge on the same approach to change management. This may be due to the success obtained by IT scholars and practitioners using the participatory-design approach [50]. In all three networks, working groups composed of representatives of the IT providers and users were established to develop a constructive dialogue to identify actual user needs and translate them into system functionalities. As the Region-governed network shows, customer orientation is a key element of the success of an IT system and its sustainability. As soon as the Lombardy Region and its technical partner Lombardia Informatica began to engage healthcare professionals in the design, development and implementation of clinical guidelines, the systems' acceptance rate began to increase. Gradually, health professionals have begun to think actively about how to improve their working processes and about the role of ICT in this change.

Training is the second change-management tool used in all three networks. Training is used to ensure user familiarity with the system functionalities and as a powerful instrument to communicate the institutional commitment to eHealth. The Consortium Arsenàl.it uses e-learning and Web 2.0 tools to disseminate training. Web 2.0 is also exploited by the Consortium to communicate innovations to citizens, representing the third pillar of the change-management activities in the three cases analyzed here.

One significant difference distinguishes the Region-governed network from the others. To stimulate and promote the use of the eHealth system, to communicate its benefits to patients and to offset the disadvantages encountered in the early step of the SISS adoption process, in 2003 the Lombardy Region introduced a set of financial incentives for general practitioners. In 2008, similar financial incentives were introduced to promote eBooking functionalities among pharmacists. As soon as the system was completely established, the use of CRS-SISS services was explicitly imposed on all healthcare providers by a regional law.

Institutional and Legal Challenges

The strong institutional commitment that characterized the Region-governed network has fostered the introduction of a robust legislative and regulatory framework and a long-term vision. In particular, the legislative framework supporting the development of the CRS-SISS project establishes the clear and explicit inclusion of SISS in regional planning, a clear definition of roles and responsibilities of all the stakeholders involved, measurable strategic objectives, and agreements with public and private healthcare providers to adhere to the project. Critical issues related to privacy and data processing have also been adequately addressed by legislative action.

A strong political commitment is also present in the eHealth Local Board-governed network. Since the launch of the Apulian eHealth Plan in 2006, many provisions have been produced to formalize the activities of the Apulian eHealth

Board, to regulate the development of regional information systems and particularly of N-SISR, and to address critical issues, such as privacy and data protection.

In contrast, the absence of the regional government among the members of the Consortium Arsenàl.it appears to lead to the absence of its direct involvement in institutional and legal issues. Furthermore, the historical prominence of local health agencies in regional eHealth policy appears to contribute to this lower normative production of Veneto Region in eHealth issues than in the other two regions analyzed in this study. However, the research activities carried out by the Consortium and the recently launched projects suggest that it may also exert a significant influence on these issues in the future.

Finally, the issue of inter-institutional relationships is explicitly addressed in the Region-governed network. The regional government has progressively imposed the integration of private healthcare providers and welfare institutions and providers into the regional healthcare information system. In the eHealth Local Board-governed network, the inter-institutional integration has been planned but not realized, while this issue is not explicitly addressed in the LHA's Consortium-governed network.

Best Practices and Evaluation Tools

The strong pressure exerted at the institutional level—in particular, by the European Community—concerning the identification and promotion of best practices has fostered a strong emphasis on their value and assessment in all three networks. The logic of best practices and "re-use" has especially taken root in the LHA Consortium-governed network, due to its role as the integrator of the projects and activities of the local healthcare agencies; to a lesser degree, best practices and "re-use" have come to play a role in the eHealth Local Board-governed network. These issues are less relevant in the Region-governed network, where a centralized and systematic approach to eHealth development prevails. Regarding the IT evaluation issues, the Consortium Arsenàl.it has explicitly included these issues among its strategic priorities through the launch of a specific project on the subject funded by the European Community. The evaluation of IT projects is one of the activities attributed to the Apulian eHealth Board, while in the Region-governed network this task has been delegated to the technical partner Lombardia Informatica. In both cases, attention is focused primarily on ensuring the consistency of the projects developed by network members with regional eHealth projects.

6 Discussion

This analysis of the three eHealth policy networks demonstrates that the three different modes of network governance produced substantially different decisions affecting the degree of technological innovation in healthcare processes and the degree of innovation diffusion across a territorial area.

In particular, the Region-governed network is notable for its adoption of a systematic approach and the speed with which all the regional healthcare services have been digitized. In the eHealth Local Board—governed network the Board has also provided a significant stimulus for the development of complex initiatives at the regional level over a short time (e.g., the N-SISR project).

All three networks are composed of large numbers of actors competing for the acquisition of the same limited resources and with conflicting objectives. At first glance, a reduction of the decision-making group or the identification of a lead organization could simplify the decision-making process, leading at least to more immediate solutions.

The LHA Consortium-governed network exhibits a higher level of trust among its members than the other two networks. This is the only network that was not imposed at the institutional level but was spontaneously developed by organizations that share a common goal. This fact, along with its relatively small number of members (limited to the 23 local health agencies), suggest that this network may be the best suited for achieving effective network-level outcomes. In addition, the Consortium's strong commitment to the development of specific eHealth competencies and sharing those competencies with its members is highly valuable when tasks that must be developed at the network level require significant interdependence among members along with task-specific competencies. However, the case study results show that the Consortium does not address all the strategic issues and that this network is less effective in extending its approach to eHealth at the regional level.

To better understand the differences among the three models and the apparently lower efficiency of the LHA Consortium-governed network with respect to the dimensions analyzed here, we focus on how the three models respond to three basic tensions inherent in network governance: efficiency versus inclusiveness, internal versus external legitimacy, and flexibility versus stability.

Efficiency versus inclusiveness

The case study shows that in the LHA Consortium-governed network, strategic decisions are made at the Associated General Meeting, a body that is representative of all the consortium members of the Consortium Arsenàl.it. Its operations are managed by a staff that has developed expertise in technological issues and fundraising. This tension between efficiency and inclusiveness is also taken into account and managed in the other two networks analyzed here. The eHealth Local Board-governed network was initially more oriented toward inclusiveness, but it has quickly adopted an approach aimed to reduce the burden of direct involvement in the decision-making process. While the Apulian eHealth Board was originally established to include all the stakeholders of the regional healthcare system, the set of norms detailing its organizational structure only include members representing the regional government and the technical partner. The involvement of the network as a whole is, therefore, limited only to the phases of system development and IT adoption. This choice appears to be essentially oriented to the creation of consensus with respect to IT applications in an effort to increase the likelihood of actual use.

In the Region-governed network, efficiency has traditionally prevailed over inclusiveness. In 2009, the direct involvement of these network' members in eHealth decision-making widened through the establishment of the Strategic Committee composed of a selection of General Managers of local health agencies and representatives of the regional government. This approach, in contrast with the "normal" network evolution (according to Provan and Kenis [43], the evolution of a brokered form to shared governance is quite unlikely) could be due to the increasing complexity of the regional eHealth project (the CRS-SISS project) and to the cultural influence of the emerging participatory governance approach on the regional government.

Internal versus external legitimacy

The LHA Consortium-governed network tends to balance the two forms of legitimacy. As the central network administrator, the Consortium Arsenàl.it can represent the network externally, while the need for interaction between members, which is instrumental to the development of internal legitimacy, can be addressed through the representative structure, i.e., the Associated General Meeting. The other two networks have also developed mechanisms that balance their needs for internal and external legitimacy. In the case of the eHealth Local Board-governed network, internal legitimacy is clearly ensured by a strong participatory focus, but external legitimacy also appears to be established by the institutionalization of the network at the regional level. In the case of Region-governed networks, the use of working groups aiming to involve all members of the network creates an opportunity for internal legitimacy that complements the strong legitimacy reflected by the Lombardy Region onto the network.

Flexibility versus stability

The case study demonstrates that the Region-governed network is particularly stable and that the eHealth Local Board-governed network is stable because it was created by the regional government. In contrast, the Consortium Arsenàl.it relies on fundraising and might, therefore, be considered the least stable. Nevertheless, it is characterized by its members' strong commitment, and it receives legitimacy from the institutional system. Moreover, the Consortium Arsenàl.it has established mechanisms for managing different activities and short-term-oriented tasks, demonstrating its great flexibility.

In conclusion, the analysis performed here shows that the networks' governance structures influence strategic decisions related to eHealth diffusion, along with the ways in which some internal tensions are managed. However, other factors require further investigation, such as the composition of each network and the role of each player in decision making.

To understand the relationships between the governance arrangements of the policy networks and eHealth policy choices more deeply, it appears insufficient to focus narrowly on the degree of centralization of decision making and, hence, on the level of participation of network members. Instead, it is important to investigate the characteristics of the players involved in the decision-making process and how their values and goals may influence the choices being made and the success of eHealth strategies.

The three networks analyzed here are characterized by their different models of network governance, but they also involve different participants. In particular, both the Region-governed network and the eHealth Local Board-governed network feature a strong commitment from the regional government, albeit with different levels of involvement. In contrast, the Consortium Arsenàl.it consists only of local health agencies. The diversity in the choice of strategic priorities, which is oriented more toward interventions in clinical processes in the case of the Consortium and toward interventions in administrative processes in the other two cases, could be due to the prevalence of different goals and values in the different networks. The Consortium represents the goals and values of the professional group, while the other two networks represent the goals and values of institutional management. Moreover, this study emphasizes that while this LHA Consortium excels in the development of new knowledge and technical innovations, it suffers from a lack of commitment at the institutional level, primarily from the regional government, which plays a key role in healthcare IT development strategies in the other two cases.

7 Conclusions

This paper investigates how different eHealth local policy networks operate and the effect of different modes of network governance on the political arrangements related to eHealth diffusion. Using a case study, three Italian health policy networks that exemplify the three types of governance network provided by Provan and Kenis [43] (Region-governed network, eHealth Local Board-governed network and LHA Consortium-governed network) have been analyzed. Moreover the levels of efficacy of each model have been compared, focusing on their ability to face five main eHealth challenges defined by scholars and policy makers: financial challenges; IT challenges; change management challenges; institutional challenges and sharing best practices and evaluation tools. The study found that in the complex issue of eHealth adoption, which features a wide and heterogeneous policy network, the model of the Region-governed network, characterized by a strong institutional commitment, appears to ensure rapid and systemic eHealth adoption. Its success is also due to the capability of the regional government to effectively manage the tensions described by Provan and Kenis [43] that develop inside the network: efficiency versus inclusiveness, internal versus external legitimacy, and flexibility versus stability.

Moreover, the results highlight the need to investigate other factors besides the mechanisms of network coordination and control, such as the network composition and each player's role in the decision-making process, to more deeply understand the relationship between the governance structure of the policy network in which the eHealth policies are defined and the success of these policies.

At a theoretical level, this paper contributes to the debate over the obstacles to the process of eHealth diffusion, emphasizing that this is influenced by both technological maturity and the dynamics developing within the network of actors involved in decision making about eHealth strategies.

Understanding these dynamics also has important practical implications, as it provides insights for healthcare policymakers about how to define a system of governance suitable to speed up the process of innovation in the healthcare system.

Acknowledgments The paper is part of the research project "Technology adoption and innovation in public services" (TAIPS). The project is carried out by the Department of Economics, Society and Politics (DESP), University of Urbino, Italy, and funded by Eiburs–EIB University Research Sponsorship Programme.

References

1. Simon, H. (1982). *The sciences of the artificial* (2nd ed.). Cambridge: MIT Press.
2. Masino, G., & Zamarian, M. (2003). Information technology artefacts as structuring devices in organizations: design, appropriation and use issues. *Interacting with Computers, 15*, 693–707.
3. Grandori, A. (1991). Negotiating efficient organization forms. *Journal of Economic Behavior & Organization, 16*, 319–340.
4. March, J. (1962). The business firm as a political coalition. *Journal of Politics, 24*, 662–678.
5. Hill, C. W. L. (1990). Cooperation opportunism and the invisible hand: Implications for transaction cost theory. *Academic of Management Review, 15*(3), 500–513.
6. Marsh, D. (1998). The development of the policy network approach. In D. Marsh (Ed.), *Comparing policy networks*. Buckingham: Open University Press.
7. Rhodes, R. A. W., & Marsh, D. (1990). Policy networks: a British perspective. *Journal of Theoretical Politics, 2*(3), 293–317.
8. Daguerre, A. (2000) Policy networks in England and France: the case of child care policy 1980–1989. *Journal of European Public Policy, 7*(2), 244–260.
9. Hoeijmakers, M., De Leeuw, E., Kenis, P., & De Vries, N. K. (2007). Local health policy development processes in the Netherlands: An expanded toolbox for health promotion. *Health Promotion International, 22*(2), 112–121.
10. Acevedo, B., & Common, R. (2006). Governance and the management of networks in the public sector. *Public Management Review, 8*(3), 395–414.
11. Rhodes, R. A. W. (1997). *Understanding governance: policy networks, governance, reflexivity and accountability*. Buckingham: Open University Press.
12. Gerber, T. (2009). Health information technology: dispatches from the revolution. *Health Affairs, 28*(2), 390–391.
13. Friedman, C. P., Iakovidis, I., Debenedetti, L., & Lorenzi, N. M. (2009). Across the Atlantic cooperation to address international challenges in eHealth and health IT: Managing toward a common goal. *International Journal of Medical Informatics, 78*, 778–784.
14. Stroetmann, K. A., Artmann, J., & Stroetmann, V. (2011). Developing national eHealth infrastructures—results and lessons from Europe. *AMIA Annual Symposium Proceeding, 2011*, 1347–1354.

15. Eysenbach, G. (2001). What is e-health? *Journal of Medical Internet Research, 3*(2), E20.
16. European Commission (2004). *eHealth—making healthcare better for European citizens: An action plan for a European eHealth Area*. Brussels.
17. Commission, European. (2010). *245 final*. Brussels: A Digital Agenda for Europe.
18. Fleurant, M., Kell, R., Love, J., Jenter, C., Volk, L. A., Zhang, F., et al. (2011). Massachusetts E-Health project increased physicians' ability to use registries, and signals progress toward better care. *Health Affairs, 30*(7), 1256–1264.
19. Jamal, A., McKenzie, K., & Clark, M. (2009). The impact of health information technology on the quality of medical and health care: A systematic review. *Health Information Management Journal* 38:26–3.
20. Stroetmann, K. A., Jones, T., Dobrev, A., & Veli, N. O. (2006). *eHealth is worth it: the economic benefits of implemented eHealth solutions at ten European sites*. Luxembourg: Office for Official Publications of the European Communities, European Commission.
21. Angst, C., & Agarwal, R. (2009). Adoption of electronic health records in the presence of privacy concerns: the elaboration likelihood model and individual persuasion. *MIS Quarterly, 33*(2), 339–370.
22. Bates, D. W. (2005). Physicians and ambulatory electronic health records. *Health Affairs, 24*(5), 1180–1189.
23. Simon, S. R., Kaushal, R., Cleary, P. D., Jenter, C. A., Volk, L. A., & Poon, E. G. (2007). Correlates of electronic health record adoption in office practices: A statewide survey. *Journal of the American Medical Informatics Association, 14*(1), 110–117.
24. ERA Project (2007a). *eHealth priorities and strategies in European countries*. Retrieved from. http://www.ehealth-era.org/publications/publications.htm.
25. Anderson, J. G. (2007). Social, ethical and legal barriers to E-health. *International Journal of Medical Informatics, 76*(5), 480–483.
26. Dixon B. E. (2007) A roadmap for the adoption of e-Health, *e-Service Journal, 5*(3), 3–13.
27. Löfgren, K. (2007). The governance of eGovernment: A governance perspective on the Swedish eGovernment strategy. *Public Policy and Administration, 22*, 335.
28. Ellingsen, G., & Munkovold, G. (2007). Infrastructural arrangements for integrated care: Implementing an electronic nursing plan in a psychogeriatric ward. *International Journal of Integrated Care, 7*, 1–11.
29. Øvretveit, J. (1998). *Integrated care: models and issues*. Goteborg, Sweden: A Nordic school of Public Health Briefing paper.
30. Kodner, D. I., & Spreeuwengerg, C. (2002). Integrated care: meaning, logic, applications, and implications—a discussion paper. *International Journal of Integrated Care, 14*, 2.
31. Gittell, J. H. (2002). Relationships between service providers and their impact on customers. *Journal of Service Research, 4*(4), 299–311.
32. Gittell, J. H., Fairfield, K., Bierbaum, B., Head, W., Jackson, R., Kelly, M., et al. (2000). Impact of relational coordination on the quality of care, post-operative pain and functioning, and the length of stay: A nine-hospital study of surgical patients. *Medical Care, 38*(8), 807–819.
33. Shortel, S., Gillies, R., & Aanderson, D. (1994). The new world of managed care: Creating organized delivery systems. *Health Affairs, 13*, 46–64.
34. Shortell, S., Gillies, R., & Devers, K. (1995). Reinventing the American hospital. *The Milbank Quarterly, 73*(2), 131–160.
35. Lega, F. (1998). Scelte strategiche e definizione dei confini dell'ospedale. *Dalla struttura focalizzata alla struttura a rete, Organizzazione Sanitaria, 1*, 43–66.
36. Larzigoitia, I., & Starfield, B. (1997). Reform of primary health care: The case of Spain. *Health Policy, 41*, 121–137.
37. Fennell, M. L., & Warnecke, R. B. (1988). *Diffusion of medical innovations: An applied network analysis*. New York: Plenum.
38. Starkweather, D. B. (1990). Competition, integration, and diversification: Seven hospitals of Growthville, U.S.A. *Journal of Health Administration Education, 8*(4), 519–570.

39. Meijboom, B. (2004). Networks for integrated care provision: An economic approach based on opportunism and trust. *Health Policy, 69*(1), 33.
40. Phillips, W. (2006). Investigating innovation in complex health care supply networks: an initial conceptual framework. *Health Services Management Research, 19*(3), 197.
41. Gill, L. (2011). Qualitative triadic study of the relational factors influencing the formation of quality in a community-based aged health care service network. *Health Marketing Quarterly, 28*(2), 155.
42. Lewis, J. M. (2005). *Health policy and politics: networks, ideas and power.* Melbourne: IP Communications.
43. Provan, K., & Kenis, P. (2007). Modes of network governance: Structure, management, and effectiveness. *Journal of Public Administration Research and Theory, 18*(2), 229–252.
44. Mount, C. D., Kelman, C. W., Smith, L. R., & Douglas, R. M. (2000). An integrated electronic health record and information system for Australia? *Medical Journal of Australia, 172*, 25–27.
45. Bernstein, K., Bruun-Rasmussen, M., Vingtoft, S., Andersen, S., & Nøhr, C. (2005). Modelling and implementing electronic health records in Denmark. *International Journal of Medical Informatics, 74*(2), 213–220.
46. Stead, W. W., Kelly, B. J., & Kolodner, R. M. (2005). Achievable steps toward building a national health information infrastructure in the United States. *Journal of the American Medical Informatics Association, 12*(2), 113–120.
47. Kevin, C.W. (2010). Accelerating innovation in information and communication technology for health. *Health Affairs, 29*(2), 2789–283.
48. Gil-Garcìa, J. R., & Pardo, T. A. (2005). E-government success factors: Mapping practical tools to theoretical foundations. *Government Information Quarterly, 22*, 187–216.
49. Coiera, E. (1999). The impact of culture on technology… how do we create a clinical culture of innovation. *Medical Journal of Australia, 171*, 508–509.
50. Berg, M. (1999). Patient care information systems and health care work: A sociotechnical approach. *International Journal of Medical Informatics, 55*(2), 87–101.
51. FederSanità ANCI (2010). *Ricerca sui Livelli di Innovazione Tecnologica in Sanità (LITIS).*
52. ERA Project (2007b). *eHealth strategy and implementation activities in Italy,* Retrieved from. http://www.ehealth-era.org/publications/publications.htm.
53. Commission, European. (2007). *eHealth taskforce report 2007-accelerating the development of the eHealth market in Europe*. Luxembourg: Office for Official Publications of the European Communities.

MIX
Papier aus verantwortungsvollen Quellen
Paper from responsible sources
FSC® C105338

If you have any concerns about our products,
you can contact us on
ProductSafety@springernature.com

In case Publisher is established outside the EU,
the EU authorized representative is:
Springer Nature Customer Service Center GmbH
Europaplatz 3, 69115 Heidelberg, Germany

Printed by Libri Plureos GmbH
in Hamburg, Germany